Japan

A Cultural, Social, and Political History

ANNE WALTHALL

University of California–Irvine

HOUGHTON MIFFLIN COMPANY
Boston   New York

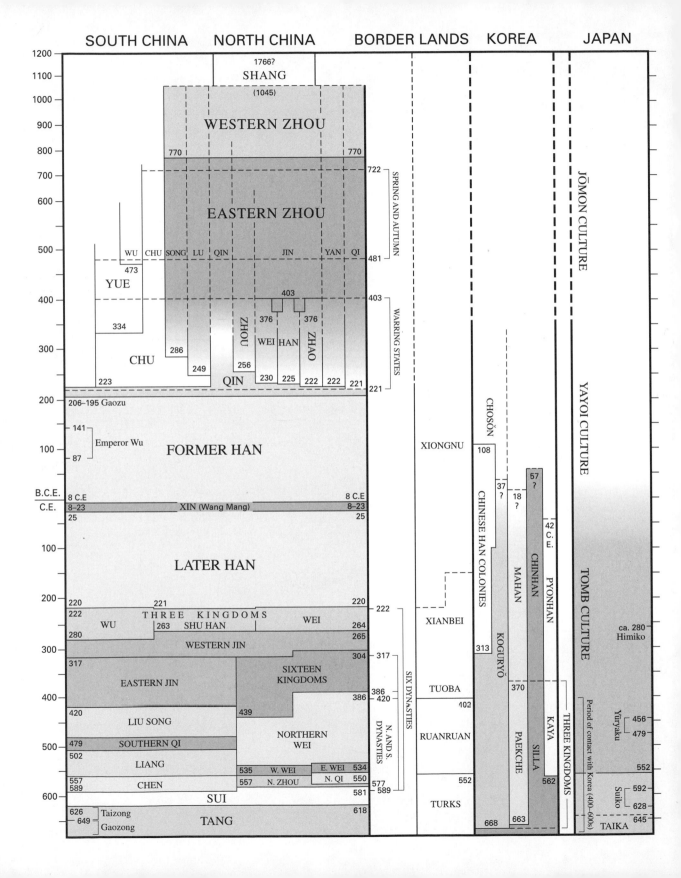

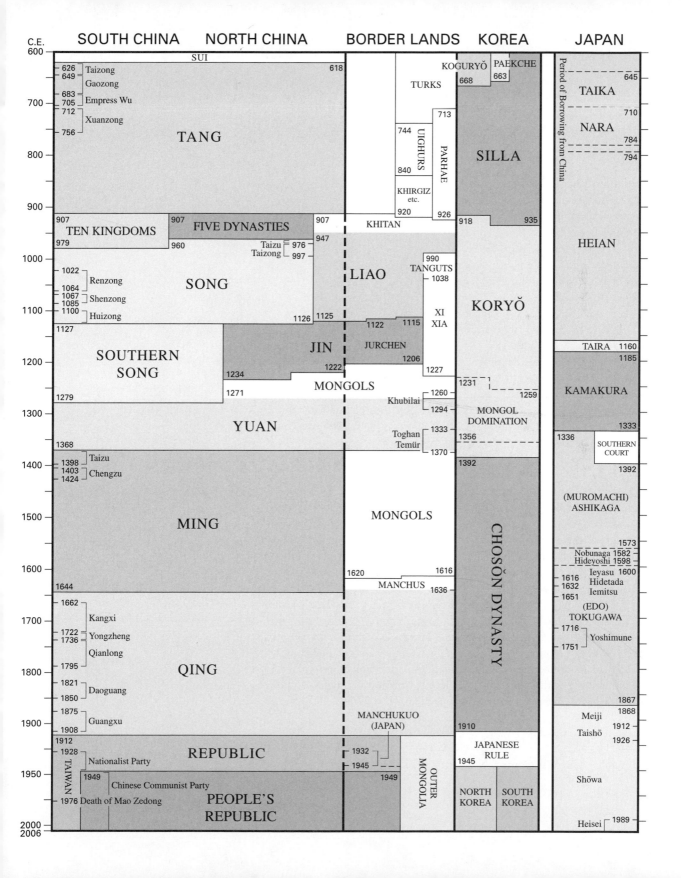

Publisher: Charles Hartford
Senior Sponsoring Editor: Nancy Blaine
Senior Development Editor: Julie Swasey
Senior Project Editor: Jane Lee
Editorial Assistant: Kristen Truncellito
Senior Art and Design Coordinator: Jill Haber
Senior Photo Editor: Jennifer Meyer Dare
Composition Buyer/Manufacturing Coordinator: Chuck Dutton
Senior Marketing Manager: Sandra McGuire
Marketing Assistant: Molly Parke

Cover Image: Caption: Momokawa Choki, Japanese, flourished late 18th–early 19th century. *The Geisha Tamino of Sumiyoshiya and her Attendant Nui,* Japan, Edo Period, ca. 1795. Woodblock print; ink, color and mica on paper. Museum of Fine Arts, Boston. William S. and John T. Spaulding Collection (21.4781). Photograph © 2003 Museum of Fine Arts, Boston.

Text credits appear on page 214.

Printed in the U.S.A.

Library of Congress Control Number: 2001133246

ISBN: 0-618-13388-7

123456789-MP-09 08 07 06 05

CONTENTS

MAPS AND FIGURES

PREFACE

THERE ARE MANY REASONS TO LEARN about Japan. Despite its small size, it has one of the world's largest economies that for many years was second only to the United States. It is one of our staunchest allies and a growing presence in our lives. Globalization means that not only are Japanese and Americans crossing the Pacific in ever increasing numbers, but also that American popular culture draws from many sources, including Japanese anime and manga.

But why approach Japan through its history, rather than, say, its economy or contemporary culture? As an historian, I naturally see many advantages to starting with Japan's past. We cannot gain an adequate understanding of modern phenomena without knowing the stages and processes that led up to them. Moreover, like their neighbors in East Asia, many Japanese people are strongly historically minded. To a much greater extent than in the United States, they know and identify with people and events of five hundred or more years ago. Whether or not they have actually read *The Tale of Genji,* a novel written in the eleventh century, they know who Genji was, and they take pride in Japan's having produced what is often called the world's first novel. Historical consciousness also underlies the strong sense of Japan's separate identity and its conflicts with its neighbors regarding its role in World War II. Yet another reason to learn about Japan's history is its comparative value. As a region that developed nearly independently of the West, Japan sheds light on other ways human beings have found meaning, formed communities, and governed themselves, expanding our understanding of the human condition.

This particular history of Japan owes its inception to an invitation by Nancy Blaine, the editor for Houghton Mifflin's world history textbooks, to join Patricia Ebrey and James Palais in writing a history of East Asia. The idea was to develop a more global perspective on East Asia and to incorporate various features developed for world history texts that would make the book more student and teacher friendly.

When we were students in the 1960s and 1970s, the fullest and most up-to-date textbook on East Asia was the two-volume set published in 1960 and 1965 by Houghton Mifflin, *East Asia: The Great Tradition* and *East Asia: The Modern Transformation,* written by Edwin O. Reischauer, John K. Fairbank, and Albert M. Craig. We learned the basic political chronology from these books, and they introduced us to such central issues as the dynastic cycle, the values of Confucianism, the ways Japan adapted features of the Chinese model, the challenge posed by the West in the nineteenth century, and modern responses to it including war and economic development. When it came time for us to develop our own research agendas, these books still cast a shadow as we pursued questions that they did not pose or delved more deeply into topics that they covered only superficially. For our own book, we wanted to take into account the wealth of scholarship published in the forty-odd years since the original *East Asia* books and yet produce the leaner, more visual book preferred by students and teachers today. The result is an attempt to balance different fields of history and make generous use of features. The basic plan developed for the *East Asia* book is retained in this Japan volume.

BALANCED CULTURAL, SOCIAL, AND POLITICAL HISTORY

Even though the volume of scholarship on East Asia has increased many-fold since the original *East Asia* set was written, we decided to honor its example of striving for balanced coverage of the different strands of history. A basic political narrative is essential to give students a firm sense of chronology and to let them think about issues of change. Moreover, there is no denying that the creation of state structures has much to do with how people lived their lives. Even the fact that people think of themselves as "Japanese" is largely a by-product of political history.

We also believed that students should gain an understanding of the philosophies, intellectual tradition, and religions of East Asia. Confucianism and Buddhism have both been of great importance in Japan, but in diverse ways depending on changes in the historical context. Other elements of high culture also deserve coverage, such as the art of poetry.

Yet we did not want to neglect topics in social, cultural, and economic history, where much of our own work has been concentrated. Even if the state is important to understanding how people lived, so are families, villages, and religious sects. We also wanted to include the results of scholarship on those who had been marginalized in the traditional histories, from laborers and minorities to women at all social levels.

SEEING THE LARGER CONTEXT: *CONNECTIONS* CHAPTERS

To keep in mind that Japan never evolved in isolation, this book periodically zooms out to look at the wider region from a global or world-historical perspective. Thus, every few chapters there is a mini-chapter on developments that link Japan both to China and Korea and to the larger global context. These mini-chapters are called "Connections" because they put their emphasis on the many ways Japan is connected to what went on outside it. For instance, the story of the origins and spread of Buddhism connects Japan with the rest of Asia. Similarly, World War II in East Asia involves much more than just the conflict between Japan and the United States. By stepping back and writing about it from a more global perspective, we can help students see the larger picture.

MAKING HISTORY CONCRETE: BIOGRAPHIES, DOCUMENTS, AND MATERIAL CULTURE

The danger of trying to cover so much in a limited space is that we would have to stay at a high level of generalization. To keep our readers engaged and bring our story down to earth, we decided to devote three or four pages per chapter to closer looks at specific people, documents, and material objects.

Biography

Many chapters have a one-page biography, usually about people who would not normally be mentioned in a history book but whose lives show something of the diverse responses to changing circumstances and the world in which they lived. The people sketched range from the most accomplished (such as the scholar-poet-angry spirit Sugawara no Michizane) to remarkably ordinary people such as a noblewoman who watched her husband killed before her eyes and a local notable whose efforts on behalf of family and community brought him nothing but obscurity. Also included is an iconoclastic critic of the social order, an entrepreneur, the founder of a religious sect, and even a winning volleyball coach.

Documents

Nothing is better than primary sources for giving students the opportunity to view life from the perspective of peoples from the past. For each chapter I chose a document long enough for them to get a sense of different genres, various points of view, and the remarkable wealth of materials available for historical study. One boxed text is excerpted from a famous polemic by Fukuzawa Yukichi. Another is from a well-known piece of literature, the poetry collection *Man'yōshū*. Others will be less familiar to teachers and students alike. I selected legal documents for what they reveal of ordinary people's problems and a religious text for insights into popular beliefs in action. Diaries meant to be read by others show individuals grappling with destitution and death. Some authors are utterly serious, complaining bitterly of war or sexual discrimination, for instance; others have a well-developed sense of humor. All have the potential to prompt critical interpretation as they get readers to listen to the concerns of people of the past.

Material Culture

Texts are not our only sources for reconstructing the past; there is much to be discovered from material remains of many sorts. To give focus to this dimension of history, for each chapter I have selected one element of material culture to describe in some detail. These range from the most mundane—food, night soil, houses, and means of transportation—to art objects, including clay sculptures, scrolls, and the performing arts. Most of the features for the late nineteenth or twentieth century bring out ways material culture has changed along with so much else in modern times—from changes in the food people eat to manga and transistors.

THINKING LIKE A HISTORIAN

The *Documents* and *Material Culture* features challenge students to draw inferences from primary materials much the way historians do. Another way I have tried to help students learn

to think like historians is to present history as a set of questions more than a set of answers. What historians are able to say about a period or topic depends not only on the sources available, but also the questions asked. To help students see this, the introduction to each chapter concludes with the sort of questions that might motivate contemporary historians to do research on the time period. Most of these questions have no easy answers—these are not questions students will be able to answer simply by reading the chapter. Rather they are real questions, ones interesting enough to motivate historians to sift through recalcitrant evidence in their efforts to find answers. The chapter on the Kamakura period, for instance, asks where samurai came from. The chapter on the early nineteenth century points out that historians have studied the period for clues to the causes of the Meiji Restoration, wanting to know the relative weight to assign to foreign pressure and domestic unrest. I hope that posing these questions at the beginning of each chapter will help readers see the significance of the topics and issues presented in it.

ACKNOWLEDGMENTS

Many people have contributed to the shaping of this book. I have been teaching about Japan for over two decades, and the ways I now approach its history owe much to questions from students, conversations with colleagues, and my reading in the outpouring of scholarship in the field. My collaborators on the *East Asia* book had many useful ideas, and I learned a lot from working with them. In addition, Patricia Ebrey deserves thanks for the original formulation of this project as well as for letting me use parts of the preface and conventions and the three *Connections* that she wrote (on Prehistory, Buddhism, and The Mongols). Reviewers also made important contributions. Their reports prompted me to rethink some generalizations and saved me from a number of embarrassing errors. I appreciate the time and attention the following reviewers gave to helping me produce a better book:

James Anderson, University of North Carolina at Greensboro; R. David Arkush, University of Iowa; Anthony DeBlasi, University of Albany; Karl Friday, University of Georgia; Karl Gerth, University of South Carolina; Andrew Goble, University of Oregon; John B. Henderson, Louisiana State University; Jeff Hornibrook, SUNY Plattsburgh; William Johnston, Wesleyan University; Huaiyin Li, University of Missouri-Columbia; Angelene Naw, Judson College; Steve Phillips, Towson University; Jonathan Porter, University of New Mexico; Wesley Sasaki-Uemura, University of Utah; S. A. Thornton, Arizona State University; LU Yan, University of New Hampshire.

I am also grateful for all the work put into this book by the editorial staff at Houghton Mifflin: Nancy Blaine originally convinced me to take on this job; Julie Swasey went through all of the drafts, arranged the reviews, and made numerous suggestions; Linda Sykes secured the photos; Penny Peters handled the art; and Jane Lee managed the production details.

CONVENTIONS

Throughout this book names are given in Japanese order, with family name preceding personal name. Thus, Ashikaga Takauji was from the Ashikaga family, and Tadano Makuzu married into the Tadano family.

Japanese has two phonetic scripts that represent syllables and also makes extensive use of Chinese characters. It is transcribed into our alphabet using the Hepburn system.

The basic vowels, *a, e, i, o,* and *u* in Japanese are pronounced as in Italian and Spanish.

a as in f*a*ther

e as *e*nd

i as the first *e* in *e*ve

o as in *o*ld (shorter in length and with less of the *ou* sound of English)

u as in r*u*de (shorter in length than English)

When one vowel follows another, each is pronounced as a separate syllable.

The macron over the ō or ū indicates that the vowel is "long," taking twice as long to say, as though it were doubled. Macrons have been omitted from common place names well known without them, such as Tokyo and Kyoto.

Consonants for Japanese romanization are close enough to English to give readers little difficulty, although for a native speaker, *shi* does not sound like "she."

Prehistory

THINKING ABOUT THE WHOLE OF EAST Asia before the invention of writing helps to remind us that East Asia has always been a part of Eurasia and did not develop in isolation. During the Pleistocene geological era (the last great Ice Age), plants and animals spread across Eurasia as far as Japan, then connected to the mainland. In later times, peoples, crops, and inventions traveled in many directions.

Early human beings *(Homo erectus)* appeared in East Asia over 1 million years ago, having gradually spread from Africa and West Asia during the Pleistocene. Peking Man, discovered in the 1920s, is one of the best-documented examples of *H. erectus*, with skeletal remains of some forty individuals found in a single cave complex. Peking Man could stand erect, hunt, make fire, and use chipped stones as tools. In recent decades, even earlier examples of *H. erectus* have been found in south China.

Modern human beings *(Homo sapiens)* appeared in East Asia around 100,000 years ago. The dominant theory in the West, supported by studies of the mitochondrial DNA of modern people, is that *H. sapiens* also spread out of Africa and displaced *H. erectus,* which became extinct. Chinese archaeologists have given more credence to the theory that *H. erectus* evolved into *H. sapiens* independently in many parts of the world, making Peking Man the ancestor of modern Chinese. They can point to similarities between Peking Man and modern Chinese, such as the shape of certain teeth.

During the period from 100,000 to 10,000 B.C.E., East Asia was home to numerous groups of Paleolithic hunters, gatherers, and fishermen. Many of these people were on the move, following the wild animals they hunted or searching for new environments to exploit. This was the period that saw the movement of people from northeast Asia to the Americas and also from south China and Southeast Asia to the Pacific and Australia.

During this long period, humans began to speak, and so the affinities of modern languages offer a rough clue to the spread of peoples in early times. In East Asia, three large language families can be identified. Korean and Japanese are related to each other and more distantly to other North Asian languages such as Turkic and Mongolian (the Ural-Altaic languages). Chinese has distant ties to Tibetan and Burman (the Sino-Tibetan-Burman languages). Many of the languages spoken by minorities in south China belong to a large group found widely in mainland and insular Southeast Asia (the Austro-Asiatic languages). Language affinities suggest at least three migratory routes through East Asia: from North Asia into Mongolia, Manchuria, Korea, and Japan; from China into Tibet and Southeast Asia; and from south China to both Southeast Asia and the islands of the Philippines and Indonesia. Other evidence suggests additional routes, for instance, from Southeast Asia and Micronesia to Japan.

All through Eurasia, much greater advance came after the end of the last Ice Age around 10,000 B.C.E. (see Map C1.1). Soon after this date, people in Japan began making pottery, some of the earliest in the world. Pottery is of great value for holding water and storing food. In China and Korea, the earliest pottery finds are somewhat later, but pottery was apparently in use by 6000 B.C.E. Throughout East Asia,

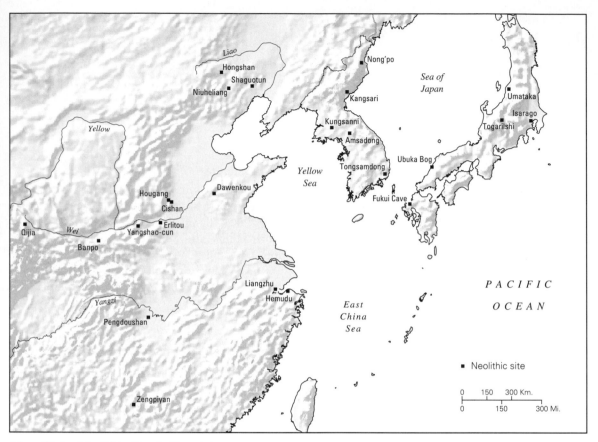

Map C1.1   Neolithic Sites in East Asia

early pottery was commonly imprinted on its surface to give it texture. In Japan this period is referred to as Jōmon and dated from about 10,000 to 300 B.C.E. The comparable period in Korea is called Chulmun and dated from about 8000 to 700 B.C.E. These cultures share many features. From shell mounds found in many places in both Korea and Japan, it is evident that sites were occupied for long periods, that shellfish were collected onshore, and that fish were caught from both rivers and the ocean. Other food sources were animals such as deer and wild boar, which were hunted. Dogs seem to have been domesticated, perhaps used as hunting animals.

China in the millennia after the last Ice Age followed more closely the pattern seen in western Eurasia involving crop agriculture, domesti-

cation of animals for food and work, pottery, textiles, and villages. Agriculture is a crucial change because cultivating crops allows denser and more permanent settlements. Because tending crops, weaving, and fashioning pots require different sorts of technical and social skills than hunting and gathering, it is likely that skilled elders began to vie with hunters and warriors for leadership.

The dozen or more distinct Neolithic cultures that have been identified in China can be roughly divided by latitude into the southern rice zone and the northern millet zone and by longitude into the eastern jade zone and the western painted pottery zone. Dogs and pigs were found in both areas as early as 5000 B.C.E. By 3000 B.C.E. sheep and cattle had become important in the north, water buffalo and cattle in the south.

Whether rice was independently domesticated in China or spread there from Southeast Asia is not yet certain. The earliest finds in China date to about 8000 B.C.E. At Hemudu, a site south of Shanghai and dating to about 5000 B.C.E., Neolithic villagers grew rice in wet fields and supplemented their diet with fish and water plants such as lotus and water chestnut. Hemudu villagers built wooden houses on piles, wove baskets, and made hoes, spears, mallets, paddles, and other tools of wood. They decorated their pottery and lacquered bowls with incised geometrical designs or pictures of birds, fish, or trees.

Millet, a crop domesticated in China, became the foundation of agriculture in north China. Nanzhuangtou, the earliest site found so far, is in southern Hebei and dates to about 8000 B.C.E. At Cishan, a site in Hebei dating to about 5500 B.C.E., millet was cut with stone sickles and stored in cord-marked pottery bowls, jars, and tripods (three-legged pots). Besides growing millet, the local people hunted deer and collected clams, snails, and turtles.

The east-west divide among Chinese Neolithic cultures in terms of expressive culture may well have had connections to less tangible elements of culture such as language and religion. In the west (Shaanxi and Gansu provinces especially), pottery decorated with painted geometrical designs was commonly produced from about 5000 to 3000 B.C.E. In the fully developed Yangshao style, grain jars were exuberantly painted in red and black with spirals, diamonds, and other geometrical patterns.

In the east, from Liaodong near Korea in the north to near Shanghai in the south, early pottery was rarely painted, but more elaborate forms appeared very early, with the finest wares formed on potters' wheels. Some had exceptionally thin walls polished to an almost metallic appearance. Many forms were constructed by adding parts, such as legs, spouts, handles, or lids. The many ewers and goblets found in eastern sites were probably used for rituals of feasting or sacrifice. Eastern cultures were also marked by progressively more elaborate burials.

Jade Plaque. This small plaque (6.2 by 8.3 cm, or 2.5 by 3.25 in) is incised to depict a human figure who merges into a monster mask. The lower part could be interpreted as his arms and legs, but at the same time resembles a monster mask with bulging eyes, prominent nostrils, and a large mouth. *(Zhejiang Provincial Institute of Archaeology/Cultural Relics Publishing House)*

At Dawenkou in Shandong (ca. 5000–2500 B.C.E.), not only were wooden coffins used, but even wooden burial chambers were occasionally constructed. The richest burials had over a hundred objects placed in them, including jade, stone, or pottery necklaces and bracelets. Some of those buried there had their upper lateral incisors extracted, a practice Chinese authors in much later times considered "barbarian," and which is also seen in some Japanese sites.

Even more distinctive of the eastern Neolithic cultures is the use of jade. Because jade does not crack, shaping it requires slow grinding with abrasive sand. The most spectacular discoveries of Neolithic jades have been made in Liaodong near Korea (Hongshan culture, ca. 3500 B.C.E.) and south of Shanghai (Liangzhu culture, ca. 2500 B.C.E.)—areas that literate Chinese in ca. 500 B.C.E. considered barbarian. In the Hongshan culture area, jade was made into small sculptures of turtles, birds, and strange coiled "pig dragons." In the Liangzhu area, jade was fashioned into objects with no obvious utilitarian purpose and which are therefore considered ritual objects. Most common are disks and notched columns.

In China, the late Neolithic period (ca. 3000–2000 B.C.E.) was a time of increased contact and cultural borrowing between these regional cultures. Cooking tripods, for instance, spread west, while painted pottery spread east. This period must also have been one of increased conflict between communities, since people began building defensive walls around settlements out of rammed earth, sometimes as large as 20 feet high and 30 feet thick. Enclosing a settlement with such a wall required chiefs able to command men and resources on a large scale. Another sign of the increasing power of religious or military elites is human sacrifice, probably of captives. The earliest examples, dating to about 2000 B.C.E., involved human remains placed under the foundations of buildings. At about the same time, metal began to be used on a small scale for weapons. These trends in Neolithic sites on the north China plain link it closely to the early stages of the Bronze Age civilization there.

For China, prehistory conventionally stops soon after 2000 B.C.E. It is true that in the Chinese subcontinent outside the core of Shang territories, subsistence technology continued in the Neolithic pattern for many more centuries. In Korea and Japan, the period before writing lasted longer, but during the first millennium B.C.E., technologies from China began to have an impact.

To understand the links between early China and its East Asian neighbors, we must briefly consider the wider Eurasian context, especially the northern steppe region. In terms of contemporary countries, the steppe extends from southern Russia past the Caspian and Aral seas, through the Central Asian republics, into Mongolia and farther east. Horses were domesticated on the southern Russian steppe by about 4000 B.C.E. but spread only slowly to other regions. Chariots spread first, then riding on horseback. A fourteenth-century B.C.E. Hittite text on horsemanship discusses the training of chariot horses; within a century or so, chariots appeared in Shang China. The Scythians appeared as mounted archers in the tenth or ninth century B.C.E. East of them, the Karasuk, with a similar culture, dominated the region from western Mongolia into south Siberia. The Scythians and the Karasuk lived in felt tents, traveled in covered carts, and had bronze technology, including the bronze bit that made possible horseback riding. By the seventh century B.C.E. in the Altai region of Mongolia, there were two distinct groups of nomadic pastoralists: those who buried the dead under mounds and those who buried the dead in stone boxes. Their bronze implements, however, were much the same.

South of these groups on the steppe, but in contact with them, were pastoral-agricultural cultures in China's Northern Zone, stretching in terms of modern provinces from Gansu through northern Shaanxi, northern Shanxi, and northern Hebei, into Liaoning (southern Manchuria). During the late second millennium B.C.E., this zone was settled by a variety of cultures with distinct pottery and burial customs but bronze knives much like those of the steppe to the north. In the early first millennium B.C.E., warrior elites emerged in many of these cultures, and animal raising became more central to their economy, perhaps in response to a climate that was becoming colder and drier. From 600 to 300 B.C.E., evidence of horses becomes more and more common, as does riding astride. Some of these cultures adopted nomadic pastoralism, moving with their herds to new pastures. These cultures also adopted the art styles common on the steppe, such as bronze and gold animal plaques. They made increasing use of iron, which may have spread to them from the Central Asian steppe rather than from China, which was also beginning to use iron in this period. These Northern Zone cultures were in contact with the Chinese states, however, and early Chinese coins have been found at some sites.

The eastern end of this Northern Zone was directly north of Korea. Archaeologists have

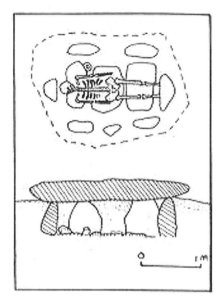
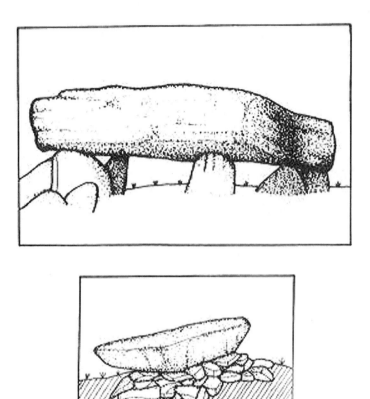

Figure C1.1   **Dolmens.** Burial structures capped with large stones, called dolmens, have been found in both the Korean peninsula and nearby parts of Japan. The two shown on the left were found in northern and southern Korea, respectively. The one on the right, which also shows the arrangement of the bones beneath the capstone, was found in Kyushu, across the Korean Strait.

identified a culture there that lasted eight centuries, from the eleventh to the fourth centuries B.C.E., called Upper Xiajiadian culture. Finds include an ancient mine, along with distinctive bronze knives, helmets, mirrors, and horse fittings. The faces of the dead were covered with a cloth decorated with bronze buttons. During the next phase there was such a radical change in burial practices that archaeologists suspect that a different, and militarily superior, horse-riding group entered the area. This new group used both wooden and stone-cist coffins. A cist burial is one with a burial chamber built of stones to form a box, with a flagstone or similar large, flat stone to cover it. By the third century B.C.E., the cultures of the Northern Zone became

increasingly homogeneous in material culture and rituals, with similar warrior elites and ornamental art.

These societies came into contact with people settled farther south in the Korean peninsula. As mentioned previously, after the end of the last Ice Age, the Korean peninsula was home to the fishing and foraging Chulmun peoples. By the middle of the first millennium B.C.E., a new culture, called Mumun (from the name of its pottery), became established. Mumun sites, in contrast to the earlier Chulmun seaside ones, were on hillsides or hilltops. Grain production became more important, and metalworking was adopted. Bronze began to be used in Korea about 700 B.C.E. and iron by about 400 B.C.E. Mumun farmers grew barley, millet, sorghum, and short-grained rice, a similar mix of crops to north China. Another distinctive feature of this culture, the use of stone cist burials, links it to the Northern Zone. A fifth-century B.C.E. site in west-central Korea has a stone cist burial, twenty-one pit buildings, red burnished pottery, a pottery kiln, a stone mold for casting bronze implements, whetstones for sharpening blades, bronze daggers and swords, and a bronze dagger of the type found farther north in the Northern Zone. Soon, however, Korea was producing its own distinctive metalwork, such as finely decorated mirrors. A new burial form also emerged: large above-ground stone vaults called dolmens.

The shift from Chulmun to Mumun probably reflects the same movement of people seen in southern Manchuria. Without textual evidence, however, it is impossible to decide whether the local Chulmun quickly adopted the superior technology of the Mumun people or whether the Mumun moved into the area in large numbers, gradually pushing out those who were already there. Some scholars speculate that the newcomers were the speakers of languages that were the ancestors of the Korean and Japanese languages.

Another important technology that made its way to Korea and Japan before writing was rice cultivation. Studies based on stone reaping knives suggest that rice spread north along the China seaboard, reaching Korea and Japan by about 300 B.C.E. In the case of Japan, rice seems to have been grown by the end of the Jōmon period, but is more strongly associated with the next stage, called the Yayoi period. The Yayoi period is marked by distinctive pottery, found earliest in Kyushu, then spreading east through Honshu, though farther north more of the Jōmon style is retained in Yayoi pieces. Rice cultivation too was more thoroughly adopted in western Japan, with the marine-based way of life retaining more of its hold in northern Japan.

Iron tools such as hoes and shovels also spread through Japan in this period, as did silk and associated spinning and weaving technology.

It is likely that the shift to Yayoi-style pottery and associated technologies was the result of an influx of people from Korea. Archaeologists have identified two distinct skeleton types in Yayoi period sites in western Japan, which they interpret as the indigenous Jōmon people and the new immigrants from Korea. The Jōmon type were shorter and more round-faced. The influx of the immigrants seems to have been greatest in Kyushu and western Honshu. Some scholars speculate that the Ainu, who survived into modern times only on the northern island of Hokkaido, are of relatively pure Jōmon stock.

Another sign that the influx of Yayoi people was not so great in eastern Japan is that bronze implements did not become important in the east, nor did easterners adopt the western Yayoi style of burying the whole body in a jar, a coffin, or a pit. Rather, in the east, reburial of the bones in a jar predominated. Because contact between southern Korea and western Japan continued through this period and because new technologies entered through this route, western Japan in this period was relatively more advanced than eastern Japan.

As we can see from this review of prehistory, contact among the societies of East Asia did not lead to identical developmental sequences. In China a millennium passed between the introduction of bronze technology and that of iron, in Korea only three centuries, and in Japan they were acquired together. Geography has much to do with the fact that Korea's direct neighbors frequently were not Chinese but nomadic pastoralists with distinctive cultures. Geography also dictates that passage from Korea to Japan was shorter and easier than crossing from China, giving Korea more direct influence on Japan than China had.

SUGGESTED READING

The best book for the archaeology of East Asia as a whole is G. Barnes, *China, Korea, and Japan: The Rise of Civilization in East Asia* (1993). For early China, see also K. C. Chang, *The Archaeology of Ancient China*, 4th ed. (1986), and D. Keightley, ed., *The Origins of Chinese Civilization* (1983). On the Northern Zone, see N. di Cosmo, *Ancient China and Its Enemies: The Rise of Nomadic Power in East Asian History* (2002), and V. Mair, ed., *The Bronze Age and Early Iron Age Peoples of Eastern Central Asia* (1998). On Korea, see S. Nelson, *The Archaeology of Korea* (1993), and for Japan, see R. Pearson, *Ancient Japan* (1992) and K. Imamura, *Prehistoric Japan: New Perspective on Insular East Asia* (1996).

CHAPTER ONE

Early State and Society (to 794)

The Geography of the Japanese Archipelago

Early Kingship

The Formation of a Centered Polity

Material Culture: *Haniwa*

Documents: Poems from *Nihon shoki* and *Man'yōshū*

The earliest human inhabitants of the seven thousand islands now known as Japan probably arrived from Micronesia or Southeast Asia over twenty thousand years ago. They would have moved up the Ryukyu island chain in the East China Sea to subtropical Kyushu and then to the more temperate zones of Shikoku and Honshu. In shallow bays, they collected shellfish and seaweed. Only a few hunters penetrated the volcanic mountains covered with forests that comprise over 80 percent of Japan's landmass in search of monkeys, deer, birds, and wild boar. The severe winters in northern Honshu and Hokkaido limited access to bear and otter hunters and salmon fishers. Archaeologists estimate the population at between 120,000 and 350,000. They have labeled the decorated clay pots that appeared around 10,000 B.C.E. and the culture that produced them Jōmon. (See **Connections: The Prehistory of East Asia.**) Starting around 500 B.C.E., the Jōmon hunter-gatherers had to compete with new arrivals from northeast Asia who introduced rice growing and metallurgy in river basins. Jōmon people disappeared from western Honshu around 200 B.C.E., replaced by the agriculturally based Yayoi culture that maintained prolonged contact with the continent. By the end of the Yayoi era in approximately 300 C.E., the population had risen to between 1.5 and 4.5 million. Agriculture demanded complex social organization and generated a surplus that could be used to differentiate soldiers, rulers, artisans, and priests from full-time cultivators. Role specialization led to hereditary social classes and inequality.

Archaeologists and historians debate the stages in the process of state formation. What role did connections from the continent play? Where were the early states located, what kind of leadership did they have, and how did they expand and coalesce? What kind of impact did Chinese civilization have on elite life, and how did the introduction of Buddhism change religious beliefs and practices?

THE GEOGRAPHY OF THE JAPANESE ARCHIPELAGO

Geographic features shaped the development of Japanese civilization. The earliest centers of human habitation arose on the fertile plains of southwestern Japan bordering on the relatively placid Inland Sea that later facilitated communications and trade. Protected by a spine of mountains, the Inland Sea basin usually enjoys mild winters, monsoon rains at the height of the growing season, and hot, dry days before the harvests. Later in the fall, typhoons provide moisture for winter crops. Occasionally the monsoon does not arrive, or typhoons come too early and devastate nearly ripe crops.

Other regions suffer more extreme conditions. Winter winds from Siberia blow across the Japan Sea, depositing snow six feet or deeper on plains and mountains. Melted snow cascades down short, fast-flowing streams. Although alluvial deltas acquired the fine soil necessary for agriculture, floods carry rocks and other debris tumbling down the mountains to damage fields. Rapids make navigating rivers treacherous, and only a few could support rafts and small boats for any distance. River mouths and innumerable small bays provide harbor for coastal vessels manned by fishers, smugglers, or pirates. Even whalers tended to stick close to shore.

The islands of what is now called Japan lost their land bridge to the Asian continent some fifteen thousand years ago, but the sea continued to permit access. Although visitors from across the vast Pacific had to wait until the sixteenth century, contact with Asia came via the Tsushima Strait, across the Japan Sea, and down the Kamchatka Peninsula, the Kuril islands and Sakhalin to Hokkaido. Each route had its own character. The northern route brought pelts and marine products; the Tsushima Straits provided a bridge for agriculture and civilization. (See Map 1.1.)

EARLY KINGSHIP

The earliest written records of rule are found in Chinese sources. The Han court received emissaries from small kingdoms, probably in Kyushu, in 57 and 107 C.E. In 239, a queen called Himiko sent a tribute mission to the kingdom of Wei. She dominated an alliance of thirty chieftains and lived in a palace fortified by walls with watchtowers and guardhouses. She rarely appeared in public; instead her brother, the only person to see her except for servants, conveyed her commands and prophesies to the people outside the gates. Her subjects trembled before her because they believed she had the power to communicate directly with the gods. When she died, over one hundred attendants of both sexes were buried with her in a giant tomb. Archaeologists debate whether her kingdom of Yamatai existed in Kyushu or in western Japan near present-day Kyoto. Equally problematic is the relationship between brother and sister. Should Himiko be seen not as a queen but as a priestess or shaman whose brother did the work of rule?

During this time, rulers frequently came in male-female pairs. As on the Korean peninsula, kinship was reckoned bilaterally. Important men had four or five wives. Children stayed with their mothers for an indefinite period before moving in with their father, and they relied on both their mothers' and fathers' kin for aid and support. Husbands and wives maintained their own establishments, held property separately, and decided how to divide it among their heirs independently. Sibling rivalry made succession disputes inevitable.

Chinese sources note that warfare was endemic. We can suppose that Himiko sent her tribute mission to China to acquire advanced military technology and the prestige of validation by the Wei court. After her death, the chieftains

Map 1.1   **Islands of Japan**

who had supported her refused to accept a male as their ruler and fought among themselves until they agreed on a young girl to become queen. The remains of fortified hamlets perched high above agricultural plains and the discovery of a formidable array of weaponry indicate that the struggle for paramountcy was more military than political. There must have been several confederacies of chieftains, of whom the Chinese knew but one.

Pseudo-kinship relations structured hamlet life. Each had a chieftain in charge of communication with the gods and relations with the out-

side world. Members of his extended family all claimed descent from a common ancestor, no matter how distant. Their economic foundation rested on dependents who performed the work of cultivation, weaving, pottery, and fishing. When one hamlet fought another, warriors seized goods and turned the vanquished into slaves. Slaves could be traded between houses as a form of currency; tribute missions sometimes carried slaves to China.

The first Japanese historians writing five centuries later struggled to fit early Japanese rulers such as Himiko into a single patrilineage. They claimed that Japan had but one ruling family descended from the sun goddess, Amaterasu, who decreed that her descendant Jimmu was to rule over the land. Aided by his divine ancestress, Jimmu led an expedition eastward to Yamato on the Kinai plain. The histories incorporate a number of myth cycles, suggesting that in addition to the Yamato line that claimed the sun goddess as its tutelary deity, other lineages had deities who at one time had rivaled Amaterasu in importance. Historians today have identified at least four breaks in the Yamato line. When the current emperor recently acknowledged a special feeling of closeness with the Korean people because the mother of his ancestor Kanmu (736–806) was Korean, he alluded to a connection with the Korean peninsula that modern historians have only recently appreciated.

The Korea Connection

Twentieth-century Japanese nationalists preferred to stress the sinitic origins of the cultural artifacts from agriculture to written language that came from the Asian continent, rather than the role by people on the Korean peninsula who modified and transmitted them. Chinese military expansion pushed refugees into the peninsula now known as Korea. Conflicts between polities there, some of which allied with polities in Japan, sent migrants across the Tsushima Strait in three waves that began in the early fifth century and ended in the seventh. Seafarers plied the coasts of Korea and Japan, sometimes launching pirate raids into the interior. The immigrants first settled along the western coast of Honshu and the northern end of Kyushu, then accepted the Yamato ruler's invitation to colonize the Kinai heartland. Historians debate whether the immigrants became assimilated into the indigenous population or whether they took over.

The immigrants brought an Altaic language from northeast Asia that is the ancestor of modern Japanese. In addition to rice, they brought bronze bells, swords, and halberds for rituals as well as wheel-thrown, kiln-fired pottery and stoves. The crossbow and iron used for swords, armor, helmets, and plows originated on the Korean peninsula. The Jōmon people had used horses as beasts of burden; the immigrants had bridles, saddles, and stirrups for warriors to ride them into battle. Immigrants irrigated their fields and brought stone-fitting technology used to build walls and burial chambers in tombs. Goldsmiths crafted crowns and jewelry for rulers; metal casters worked bronze. The first scribes and accountants came from the peninsula before 400. The Hata lineage settled west of what is now Kyoto. It introduced sericulture and silk weaving; it founded a number of temples, among them Kōryūji, which still treasures a sixth-century statue of Maitreya, the Buddha of the future. Items that originated in China but were imported through the peninsula included bronze mirrors, ornaments, and coins.

The immigrants brought techniques of rule that contributed to the process of state building in the Japanese islands. The first system of court titles bore a striking similarity to the Silla bone-rank system. Chieftains acquired surnames that they could then use to denote aristocratic status. Territorial divisions from the district (Korean in origin) to the province (Chinese in origin) achieved an administrative cast. Peninsular burial mounds probably provided the model for the giant tumuli that characterized the fifth to seventh centuries. The peninsular experience with Chinese-style civil and criminal law codes foreshadowed the Japanese adoption in the seventh century. Buddhism as taught in Paekche and Silla had a lasting impact on Japanese society and politics.

Ancient Religion

In Himiko's time, religious beliefs held society together. One of her tasks was to perform rituals that propitiated the deities, leading to the argument that politics and religion in ancient Japan were one and the same. When chieftains had to make decisions, they baked deer bones in a fire and examined the cracks to determine what the future might bring. They supervised the agricultural calendar, performed fertility rites, and prayed for victory in war. Female shamans warded off misfortune and communicated with the deities. Because rituals had to be performed by men and women together, priestesses were idealized as sisters helped by brothers. Women and men held secular and sacred authority.

Early Japanese believed that important people became gods, and the gods ordered the conditions for their existence. Gods had created the natural world; gods vitalized mountains and rocks; gods constituted the energy that made rice grow. Human reproduction recapitulated and stimulated the deeds of the creator deities that brought life to the world. This kind of belief system is called animism because it assumes that spiritual forces animate even inanimate objects. The gods abhorred pollution, especially the pollution of death. The death of a chieftain required the destruction of his residence. By the late fourth century C.E., large tombs filled with ritual objects pacified an otherwise threatening departed spirit; moats and clay figurines (*haniwa*) marked the periphery. (See **Material Culture: Haniwa.**) Sacred texts from the seventh and eighth centuries connected gods and mortals, celebrated sex and procreation, and venerated the natural world. Myths propagated by the Yamato court personified the spiritual forces, giving them names, associating them with local lineages, and ranking them in a hierarchy of kinship with the sun goddess at the top. This system of beliefs is now called Shinto, a term created out of Chinese characters, that means the way of the gods.

Excavations of hamlet burial grounds and giant tumuli show that the early Japanese honored the dead by burying them with items that they had used in life. Clothing, cosmetics, and pottery can be found with pots holding human bones. Equal numbers of men and women were buried one to a tomb that contained armor, swords, and arrowheads, considered valuable because they came from Korea. Since the heavy iron swords forged in Japan with ore from abroad were used less for fighting than for ceremony, they suggest a stratified society in which funeral practices reflected disparities in ranks. Between 425 and 500, the number of iron items buried in tombs multiplied, and the objects themselves became more standardized as political authority became increasingly centered in the Kinai region.

THE FORMATION OF A CENTERED POLITY

Beginning about 350 C.E., rulers in the Yamato basin of the Kinai region began to consolidate their power. By the fifth century, they had organized the manufacture of iron implements and taken control of their distribution. Warriors on horseback improved the speed at which armies could travel and the distances they could cover. Five kings sent tribute missions to China to gain Chinese confirmation of their hegemony and acquire the accouterments of kingship with which to entice the chieftains of other lineages into alliance. They provided military support to their ally Paekche against Koguryŏ. When Paekche fell, many of its best-educated and highly skilled supporters fled to Yamato. They brought with them political and administrative talents that the local rulers put to good use.

Yūryaku (late fifth century), the most notable of these early monarchs, placed immigrant and indigenous chieftains into a ranking system. Each chieftain was deemed a lineage head and received lavish gifts such as mirrors from China and permission to build grand tombs. The lineage received a hereditary title derived from Korean nomenclature that defined its position in a new court hierarchy. The chieftains claimed descent from a lineage deity or from a person who had a special relationship with the lineage deity. They acknowledged Yūryaku's suzerainty with tribute and family members sent to serve at his court in return for the right to administer and tax the territories he allotted them, often those they already controlled. Occupational groups that took responsibility for goods and

MATERIAL CULTURE

Haniwa

Clay figurines from the fifth to seventh centuries illustrate how people lived in ancient Japan. Shamanesses wear swirling headdresses; shamans hold mirrors; a falconer lifts his hawk; warriors ride horses with elaborate saddle trappings and carry bows and arrows; one musician plucks a zither and another strikes a drum; a cultivator carries a hoe. Women balance jugs on their heads with babies on their backs. A bowler-type hat with a broad brim and side curls signifies court rank. Sheep, deer, birds, monkeys, dogs, and rabbits abound. Trading ships carry goods between Japan and the continent. Figurines provide evidence that chieftains sat on chairs and slept in beds, customs that later died out.

Clay figurines and cylinders are called *haniwa*, literally clay rings, because the vast majority are hollow tubes standing 3 to 5 feet high. They are found outside the giant tumuli that dot the Japanese landscape from Kyushu to northern Japan, with most clustered in the Kinai region near Osaka and Nara. Why *haniwa* were placed outside rather than inside the tomb is a matter for speculation. According to *Nihon shoki,* they substituted for the chieftain's attendants. Archaeologists debate whether they served to demarcate the sacred space of the tomb and to protect the deceased, much like the stone sculptures of the twelve animal signs that encircled Silla Dynasty burial mounds, or whether they guarded the living against the dangerously powerful spirit of a deceased chieftain.

Haniwa. Haniwa stand 3 to 5 feet tall. The photo on the right shows a warrior with helmet, side curls and armor. The horse in the photo on the left is likewise equipped for war with studded chest band, saddle, and bridle. *(Christie's/Corbis)*

services were also organized into lineages. One provided weapons and the men to use them; another supplied Yūryaku's kitchens; others performed the ritual work that earlier rulers such as Himiko had done themselves. As Yūryaku expanded his dominion, he balanced the territories bestowed on titled lineages with those reserved for the crown. Men appointed to administer crown lands did not have the hereditary powers of the lineage chieftains; they were dependent on the court.

Yūryaku also used marital alliances to bolster his legitimacy and extend his power. His senior consort came from the lineage of an earlier king. Chieftains contributed other consorts to gain status as royal relatives and to exert influence at court. Combined with the court ranking system and gift giving, these connections placed the king above his mightiest supporters in a hierarchy of wealth and privilege that served to distinguish them from untitled, unconnected commoners.

Yūryaku's successors built on and fought over the state he had created in southwestern Honshu and northern Kyushu. Within twenty-five years of his death, his line had been replaced following power struggles between royal relatives aided and abetted by disgruntled chieftains. Rulers in the sixth century defined the royal regalia as mirror, sword, and jewel and selected a princess to serve the royal family's tutelary deity at the sun goddess's shrine at Ise. By the middle of the 500s, the immigrant Soga lineage had entrenched itself as principal consort givers. In 592 a Soga niece named Suiko became head of the Yamato house on the death of her husband, her half-brother, and ruled until 628, the longest reign for the next twelve centuries. Her capital at Asuka is famous for Japan's first flowering of Buddhist art.

The China Connection

Between 592 and 756, the Yamato kings, male and female, transformed themselves from chieftains of confederacies into Chinese-style monarchs. The efforts to expand the functions and reach of the state arose in part in reaction to the

Prince Shōtoku is the subject of innumerable posthumous portraits. Painted in the eighteenth century, the one shown here features him dressed in the courtly attire of eighth century China. *(Private Collection, Paris/Dagli Orti/The Art Archive)*

resurgence of the Chinese empire under the Sui and Tang Dynasties. Kings also saw the need to overcome the violent factional and succession disputes that had weakened ties between center and periphery and led to regicide and the assassination of chief ministers. Suiko and Prince Shōtoku (574–622), her nephew and adviser, opened relations with the Sui Dynasty in China, paving the way for later study missions and the immersion of elite Japanese men in Chinese culture. They promoted Buddhism as much for its magical efficacy as for its religious teachings. They reorganized the court by instituting a ladder of twelve official ranks bestowed on individuals to correspond to Sui rather than Silla practice.

In the Seventeen Injunctions promulgated in 604, Prince Shōtoku announced a new ideology of rule based on Confucian and Buddhist thought. He put a new distance between the ruling Yamato line and all other lineages by proclaiming, "The Lord is Heaven, the vassal is earth." This relationship was to be expressed in ritual and governed by propriety: "Harmony is to be valued and an avoidance of wanton opposition to be honored." Ministers were to put public duties, their duty to the throne, above the private interests of lineage and self. Only the ruler was to levy taxes because, "in a country there are not two lords; the people have not two masters."[1] Suiko and Shōtoku's successors continued these efforts to distinguish the monarch from his ministers and the court from commoners by drawing on the rituals and regulations of Chinese kingship.

The reform of 645, later heralded as marking the start of monarchical rule, incorporated continental culture in the midst of conflict. It followed a bloody coup in which Nakatomi no Kamatari, founder of the Fujiwara lineage, brought down the Soga. The court appointed provincial governors and abolished private land ownership. It instituted a population census, a centralized tax system, a legal code, and a civil service examination. It tried to curtail the ability of local magnates to harass the people and protected the right of women to remarry. It provided a municipal government for the capital. It inaugurated the use of Chinese-style era names, and as in China at the time, the names worked magic. Just as people changed their names to change their luck, so did era names change when they had lost their potency to ward off disaster. The Great Reform era called *Taika* (645–650) did so little to mitigate bloody factional strife that it was changed to *Hakuchi* (White Pheasant, a lucky omen; 650–654). Monarchs had to rely on powerful lineages in implementing these reforms. The Fujiwara consolidated their position by giving their daughters to rulers,

a tradition they had some success in maintaining down to 1924.

The Fujiwara supported monarchs in promoting Chinese models for administration. Following a large-scale and bloody factional dispute called the Jinshin incident (671–672), Tenmu and his wife, Jitō, daughter of the previous monarch, eliminated collateral claimants to the throne in order to preserve it for their descendants. Tenmu reorganized the bureaucracy and filled it with men he had appointed rather than the former chieftains, now titled aristocrats. In 685 he prohibited the private possession of weapons. Through the creation of a conscript army based on Chinese models, the state was to have a monopoly on the use of force. Tenmu tried to abolish the aristocrats' private economic basis by experimenting with the state allocation of land. He enticed the new aristocrats to court to participate in grand ceremonies of state that drew on Buddhist and Chinese models; he also sent envoys to coordinate worship at the regional shrines for lineage tutelary deities. Jitō claimed the sun goddess as Tenmu's ancestor, thereby projecting his dynasty into the mythic past. When she became ruler, she was styled *tennō*, a combination of two Chinese characters meaning "heaven" and "monarch." This title fell into abeyance in the tenth century as monarchical power declined relative to that of ministers. Rulers were called "lord" (*shujō*) in life and "temple" (*in*) in death. Revived in 1841, the official English translation of *tennō* became "emperor" in 1868.

Jitō and her successors oversaw notable advances in state formation. Tenmu started construction on a Chinese-style palace and capital city at Fujiwara, which Jitō occupied in 694. It marked a decision to use architecture in bolstering the ruler's authority. No longer would palaces be destroyed on the death of a monarch or would the ruler's consorts enjoy separate residences. Three generations of rulers lived at Fujiwara before the capital moved to the more central location of Nara in 710, where it remained until 794. (See Map 1.2.) The eighth

---

1. W. G. Aston, trans., *Nihongi: Chronicles of Japan from the Earliest Times to A.D. 697* (London: Kegan, Paul, Trench, Trübner, 1896), 2:129–133.

century is now called the Nara period. Modeled on the Tang capital at Chang'an, Fujiwara and Nara were laid out on a grid with the palace centered at the north and facing south, because in Chinese cosmology, the ruler's place was fixed like the pole star. By dominating his capital, he brought heaven to earth. The central boulevard divided the city into symmetrical halves just as the Chinese-style bureaucratic structure balanced the minister of the left with the minister of the right lest either one monopolize power that rightfully belonged to the ruler. The physical layout mirrored social relations. Ministers in the Chinese-style bureaucracy took up residence in the capital on assigned building lots in accordance with their rank. Aristocrats and rulers vied in building Buddhist temples. District officials were encouraged to use coins for traveling expenses and land sales. In line with Chinese models and to learn about the realm in order to control it, monarchs had provincial gazetteers compiled that described local customs, places and their deities, specialties, and resources.

During Jitō's reign, officials started to compile official histories and create a set of written administrative statutes and law codes. Modified and expanded during successive reigns, this system became known as the regime of codes. The penal code set out punishments for rebels and robbers as well as for breaching the taboos that conferred sacral status on the king. The administrative code specified relations between the ruler and aristocrats in an effort to freeze the status quo and brought the ruler's jurisdiction down to the level of district magnates. It established political and religious hierarchies of public offices, temples, and shrines that reached from the center to the provinces. Just as district offices fell under the jurisdiction of administrators at the capital, so too were provincial temples subordinated to temple headquarters. The Yamato line's shrines at Ise and Nara ranked above lineage shrines in the provinces. Chief priests appointed by the ruler supervised the conduct of monks and nuns and coordinated ritual while ministers of state ran the bureaucracy.

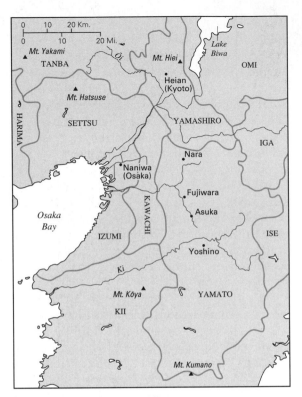

Map 1.2   **Kinai Area of Japan**

The codes also dealt extensively with land rights. All land belonged to the ruler, for him to allot to cultivators, except in the case of new fields. Opening them to cultivation was such an expensive undertaking that the person responsible, whether an individual or a temple, received permanent ownership.

The promulgation of these codes had long-lasting effects. Even chieftains resident in the provinces competed for official appointments and titles as local magnates. County, district, and provincial offices and temples spread across the landscape. Each of the sixty-five provinces had a headquarters supervised by a governor. His official mission was to promote agriculture and register the population. In fact, he concentrated on adjudicating land disputes and collecting taxes in kind—cloth, rice, iron, and other goods produced locally and needed by the court. Officials appointed by the court and local magnates worked in tandem on the governor's staff, which numbered in the hundreds. Despite these achievements, the polity remained more centered than centralized, with each segment of the population—aristocrat, bureaucrat, cleric, cultivator—claiming different rights and privileges relative to the throne.

During the reign of Shōmu from 724 to 756 (he officially retired in 749 but did not relinquish power), the ancient system of Japanese kingship reached its zenith. Over seven thousand men staffed the central bureaucracy. Shōmu rebuilt the palace at Nara to include halls for ceremonies, offices for officials, and private quarters for his family. He lavishly supported the Buddhist establishment with the construction of Tōdaiji as the Yamato lineage temple. It contained the world's largest bronze Buddhist statue. Monks came from China and Champa (Vietnam) for the inauguration ceremony. Shōmu sent armies to expand his sway across the Japanese islands and used diplomatic ritual to assert Japan's precedence over Korea.

Shōmu's successors had to deal with the consequences of his success. As power became more centered at the court, struggles for status and influence intensified. Except for a few families that enjoyed adequate access to economic resources, most aristocrats lived precariously close to poverty. Restive local magnates disobeyed directives and rebelled against the center, as did cultivators unhappy at tax collection efforts. Officials at the county and district levels jealously preserved their autonomy while accepting court rank and office. Despite a history of female monarchs, the spread of Confucian philosophy justified the aristocrats' resentment at being ruled by a woman: Shōmu's daughter who reigned twice, first as Kōken (r. 749–758) and then as Shōtoku (r. 764–770). Deposed in a palace coup, Shōtoku was the last female monarch until 1630. Conflict between the ruler and the aristocratic bureaucracy was repeated in the 780s when two retired monarchs sponsored factional intrigue. Buddhist priests, collateral lines of Fujiwara, and other lineages competed for influence, while disgruntled members of the ruling family plotted against their

chief. A decrease in tax revenues forced rulers to scale back building projects and reduce the size of ceremonies. In 794, frustrated at the endless demands for favor that bedeviled him in Nara, the ruler Kanmu moved the capital to Heian-kyō. There it was to remain until 1868.

The Conquest of Emishi and Hayato

In the early eighth century, aristocrats developed a sense of a Japanese ethnic identity that excluded peoples on the islands beyond the court's control. Many inhabitants in the northeast still practiced late Jōmon-style slash-and-burn agriculture. Since being Japanese was associated with rice-based settled communities, they were deemed barbarians (*Emishi*). The court encouraged the spread of settlements ever farther north, sent emissaries to set up district offices and collect taxes, and dispatched military expeditions to remove or enslave the *Emishi*. By 725, the first year of Shōmu's reign, these expeditions had pacified the region up to today's Sendai. Subsequent waves of soldiers and settlers spread agricultural settlements as far as Morioka.

Shōmu also expanded Yamato rule in Kyushu. In 740 the exiled Fujiwara Hirotsugu raised an army of ten thousand conscript troops against the throne. He gained the support of some district chiefs and members of the Hayato minority from southern Kyushu who, like the *Emishi*, resisted the civilization offered by the Yamato rulers. He even made overtures to Silla in search of allies. According to the official history, *Nihon shoki*, Shōmu dispatched an army of seventeen thousand, the largest royal army raised in the eighth century. Within two months, it had scattered the rebel army and executed Hirotsugu. The Hayato had no choice but to submit. The immigration of people from the Korean peninsula and the development of a stratified state in the Kinai basin divided the Japanese islands into three cultural and ethnic zones. By the end of Shōmu's reign, the central zone centered on Nara had squeezed the southern zone onto the Ryukyu island chain, while the northern zone, which extended up through Hokkaido, was shrinking on Honshu.

The Introduction of Buddhism

Buddhism played a major role in the development of the early Japanese state. First sponsored by the Soga and other immigrants from Paekche, it had to overcome opposition by Shinto ritualists before receiving official government support in 587. Enhanced by scribes, metallurgists, painters, and other artisans, it became the faith of rulers in a symbiotic relationship that strengthened both. Buddhism had a rich textual tradition; its monks paraded in majestic processions and held thunderous sutra recitations. From Paekche rulers the Japanese learned that worshipping the Buddha would bring their realm the protection of the Four Guardian Kings of the Buddhist law. In the Seventeen Injunctions, Prince Shōtoku urged the court to revere the Buddha, Buddhist law, and the monastic order. Tenmu and Jitō recognized the value of Buddhism in providing faith in a universal deity at the same time that they sent offerings to the Ise shrine of the sun goddess and regional shrines and read omens to divine heaven's will. By asserting their leadership in all dimensions of the religious realm, they sought to bolster their authority in secular affairs.

Tenmu and Jitō took advantage of Buddhism's appeal to spread their rule across Japan. They built temples in the capital and provinces and used them as storehouses for population and tax records. They oversaw the copying of sutras, held Buddhist ceremonies, and habitually performed Buddhist purificatory rituals. By restricting hunting, fishing, and the eating of meat, they promoted Buddhist beliefs that valued the lives of all sentient beings. The number of monks and nuns increased, their behavior minutely regulated. During Tenmu and Jitō's reigns, Buddhism became a core component of courtly life and practice.

Shōmu did even more to promote Buddhism and harness its power to the court. In line with the ideology of his day that deemed the natural

order a reflection of the social order, he saw in natural disasters and rebellion his own lack of virtue. To compensate, he ordered sutra readings at temples, austerities such as cold water baths at Shinto shrines, and the construction of religious structures. Following the Hayato rebellion in 741, he ordered each province to build a seven-storied pagoda, a guardian temple, and a nunnery and to provide adequate rice land to support the monks and nuns. In a thanksgiving service for his victory, he presented brocade, prayers, and Buddhist sutra readings to the shrine for Hachiman, the god of war. The giant Buddhist statue at Tōdaiji was cast in the image of Vairocana, the cosmic Buddha who encompasses the thousands of Buddhas and millions of enlightened beings just as Shōmu saw himself as ruling over all aristocrats and commoners. It was enshrined in a hall larger than the royal palace. The temple complex contained Japan's first ordination platform as well as libraries and schools. There, monks translated texts and sutras for the so-called Six Sects. Rather than go to Tang China or Silla Korea, Japanese monks could now study and receive licenses at Tōdaiji under kingly sponsorship and supervision. After Shōmu passed the throne to his daughter, he established the precedent for abdicated rulers to enter the Buddhist priesthood.

Shōmu saw Buddhism primarily as a state religion, leaving it to monks and nuns such as Gyōki to proselytize among the populace. Through his sermons, Gyōki, the descendant of an immigrant Confucian scholar, propagated the Buddhist notions of causality and retribution and the humanistic promise that following the way of the universal Buddha can bring enlightenment to any person at any time or place. His followers built irrigation works, roads, bridges, and inns for commoners delivering tax payments to the capital, a material demonstration that the Buddhist law can benefit everyone, not just kings and aristocrats. In 717 the government accused Gyōki of violating the regulations that restricted nuns and monks to monasteries, collecting an inordinate amount in alms, and confusing the masses by claiming the power to heal, cast spells, and tell fortunes. Gyōki ignored the accusations, and other monks and nuns followed his example of good works and public preaching. The government then tried to co-opt his appeal. In 741 Gyōki received an official appointment to supervise the building of a bridge near the capital. In this way, the government acknowledged that he was indeed the bodhisattva his followers claimed him to be and brought belief in the saving power of the Buddha into line with official policy.

By the eighth century, Buddhism had become so naturalized in Japan that it had started to blend with native beliefs. Mountain ascetics joined the ancient belief in the sacrality of mountains with esoteric forms of Buddhism that emphasized occult practices. They promised to heal the sick and performed rituals to eliminate pollution and evil. The Mahayana Buddhism that entered Japan offered numerous paths to salvation through the pantheon of Buddhas and bodhisattvas (see **Connections: Buddhism in India and Its Spread Along the Silk Road**). Because the Buddha appeared in so many guises, perhaps he had also appeared as local deities. In what would later be known as Ryōbu Shintō, the deities received Buddhist names. Although an edict from 764 placed Buddhism above Shinto, the reverse was as often the case. In the countryside, the style of worshipping the Buddha reflected beliefs associated with Shinto regarding the importance of fertility and worldly benefits rather than eliminating worldly attachments to achieve enlightenment. In place of large tombs surrounded by *haniwa*, provincial chieftains built Buddhist temples to hold memorial services for the dead and replicate the benefits they hoped to acquire when propitiating the deities: good harvests, health, prosperity, and progeny. People learned that deities and Buddhas supported each other, and both needed festivals and ceremonies. Important Shinto shrines acquired Buddhist temples so that the deities might hear sutra recitations, and deities protected Buddhist temples. In this way particular deities (*kami*) and the universal Buddha entered into an enduring symbiotic relationship.

Elite Culture

The Yamato court attracted followers with its access to Chinese elite culture including a written language, Daoism, Confucianism, the literary arts, sculpture (particularly Buddhist icons), painting, and music. The Chinese writing system arrived in Japan at the end of the Yayoi period, in the late fourth century, brought by immigrants from the Korean peninsula who served as a closed occupational group of scribes for the Yamato court. They left traces of their work in sword inscriptions. Not until the unification of China under the Sui and the introduction of Buddhism did Japanese rulers realize the importance of literacy. Pilgrims to China brought back quantities of Buddhist sutras and Chinese books. In addition to his Seventeen Injunctions of 604, Prince Shōtoku sponsored the writing of a history of Japan based on Chinese models. It later disappeared. The earliest examples of Japanese writing Chinese come from over 150,000 wooden tablets, the vast majority dating from the seventh and eighth centuries. Inscribed on the tablets were official documents, including directives to and reports by local officials, summons, transit passes, and labels attached to tax goods. They prove that women joined men as conscripts on public works projects.

After the wooden tablets came Japan's earliest extant histories. The *Kojiki* (Record of Ancient Matters) of 712 and *Nihon shoki* (Chronicles of Japan) completed in 720 relate histories of Japan from the creation of the cosmos to the establishment of the centered state in the seventh century. *Kojiki,* which details the age of the gods, can be read as an attempt by the Yamato court to justify its preeminence over other lineages. *Nihon shoki* opens with a passage that draws on Chinese yin-yang theory and cosmology. It narrates the history of the Yamato rulers in a straight line of descent from the sun goddess. Both histories exaggerate the antiquity of the early Japanese state and its control over local political arrangements.

Poetry had magical properties in the eyes of ancient Japanese. It both summoned and soothed

DOCUMENTS

Poems from *Nihon shoki* and *Man'yōshū*

Compiled in the early eighth century, these documents include poems first composed centuries before. Here we see depicted fifth- to seventh-century rulers in the process of consolidating power by performing rituals to take possession of the land through viewing and naming, building magnificent palaces, and making excursions. In these circumstances, even poems expressing personal feelings had a public dimension because the poet's relationship with the ruler explains the poem's creation.

6th year [462 C.E.], Spring, 2nd month, 4th day. The ruler [Yūryaku] made an excursion to the small moor of Hatsuse. There, viewing the aspect of the hills and moors, in an outburst of feeling, he made a song, saying:

> The mountain of Hatsuse
> Of the hidden country
> Is a mountain
> Standing beautifully,
> Is a mountain
> Projecting beautifully
> The mountain of Hatsuse
> Of the hidden country
> Is truly lovely,
> Is truly lovely.

Thereupon he gave a name to the small moor, and called it Michi no Ono.

Poems by Kakinomoto Hitomaro at the time of the procession [by the divine monarch Jitō] to the palace at Yoshino.

> Many are the lands under heaven
> And the sway of our Lord,
> Sovereign of the earth's eight corners,
> But among them her heart
> Finds Yoshino good
> For its crystal riverland
> Among the mountains,
> And on the blossom-strewn
> Fields of Akitsu
> She drives the firm pillars of her palace

> And so the courtiers of the great palace,
> Its ramparts thick with stone,
> Line their boats
> To cross the morning river,
> Race their boats
> Across the evening river.
> Like this river
> Never ending,
> Like these mountains
> Commanding ever greater heights,
> The palace by the surging rapids—
> Though I gaze on it, I do not tire.

> Envoy
> Like the eternal moss
> Slick by the Yoshino river
> On which I do not tire to gaze,
> May I never cease to return
> And gaze on it again.

> Our lord
> Who rules in peace,
> A very god,
> Manifests her divine will
> And raises towering halls
> Above the Yoshino riverland
> Where waters surge,
> And climbs to the top
> To view the land.
> On the mountains
> Folding upward around her
> Like a sheer hedge of green
> The mountain gods present their
>   offerings.

They bring her blossoms in springtime
To decorate her hair
And, when autumn comes,
They garland her with yellow leaves
And the gods of the river
That runs alongside the mountains
Make offerings for her royal feast.

They send cormorants forth
Over the upper shoals,
They cast dipper nets
Across the lower shoals,
Mountain and river
Draw together to serve her—
A god's reign indeed!

A very god
Whom mountain and river
Draw together to serve,
She sets her boat to sail
Over pools where waters surge.

Poem by Kakinomoto Hitomaro when he parted from his wife in the land of Iwami and came up to the capital.

At Cape Kara
On the sea of Iwami,
Where the vines
Crawl on the rocks,
Rockweed of the deep
Grows on the reefs
And sleek seaweed
Grows on the desolate shore.
As deeply do I
Think of my wife
Who swayed toward me in sleep
Like the lithe seaweed.
Yet few were the nights
We had slept together
Before we parted
Like crawling vines uncurled.
And so I look back,
Still thinking of her
With painful heart,

This clench of inner flesh,
But in the storm
Of fallen scarlet leaves
On Mount Watari,
Crossed as on
A great ship,
I cannot make out the sleeves
She waves in farewell.
For she, alas,
Is slowly hidden
Like the moon
In its crossing
Between the clouds
Over Yagami Mountain
Just as the evening sun
Coursing through the heavens
Has begun to glow,
And even I
Who thought I was a brave man
Find the sleeves of my well-worn robe
Drenched with tears.

Poem upon the death of the Sovereign by one of his concubines (her name is yet unclear).

As the living are unfit
For commune with the gods
So I am separated from you
Lord whom I grieve for in the morning,
So I am kept from you,
Lord whom I long for.
If you were a jewel,
I would wrap you around my wrist.
If you were a robe,
I would never take you off.
Lord whom I long for,
Last night I saw you
In a dream.

Source: Gary L. Ebersole, *Ritual Poetry and the Politics of Death in Early Japan* (Princeton, N.J.: Princeton University Press, 1989), pp. 27, 30–32, 50–52, 175, modified.

the gods, and the words had spirits of their own. The earliest extant poetry collection, the *Kaifūsō* (Fond Recollections of Poetry) compiled in 751, contains the biographies of Japanese poets who wrote in Chinese. It is overshadowed by the *Man'yōshū* (Collection of Ten Thousand Leaves) compiled in 759, the first anthology of Japanese verse. (See **Documents: Poems from *Nihon shoki* and *Man'yōshū***). Its poems had the public function of attesting to the process of state building. They expressed the emotions of courtiers and frontier guards who forsook family and homeland to serve their monarch. They lamented the death of wives and lovers as well as rulers and other powerful personages.

Etiquette, ceremony, dance, and music introduced from China transformed provincial chieftains into court aristocrats. Played on flutes and stringed instruments punctuated by gongs and drums, continental music is said to have entered Japan when the king of Silla sent eighty musicians to attend funeral services for King Ingyō in 453. Stately dance performed by men wearing masks came from Silla in 612. The Court Music Bureau established in 702 and staffed chiefly by immigrants had charge of performing a repertoire of Chinese and Korean music and dance called elegant music (*gagaku*) at court ceremonies. Gagaku incorporated indigenous songs that retold tales of victory in battle, accompanied offerings from remote and hence quaint outposts, pleaded for aid from the gods, and celebrated the sexual union of men and women in fertility rites. The court thus appropriated elements of popular culture into an elite culture characterized by massive infusions from the continent. Viewing and participating in music and dance and learning the correct codes for conduct in ceremonies set ever higher standards for civilized behavior.

A Stagnant Agrarian Base

The spread of rice cultivation in the Yayoi period that had transformed western agricultural regions from slash and burn to settled farming soon reached its ecological limit. In contrast to the intensive agriculture that boosted yields in later centuries, cultivators during the eighth century continued to use extensive methods. They cleared fields and planted crops for a few years, and then repeated the process when a lack of proper irrigation and fertilizer depleted the soil in continuous cycles of cultivation and abandonment. Although an edict from 723 noted that a recent increase in population had led to rural overcrowding, the eighth-century regime of codes made much more elaborate provision for returning fallow fields to cultivation than it did for opening new fields. Fragments of census surveys suggest that a population of from 3 to 5.5 million in 700 had changed little by 800. Population gains at the turn of the century were wiped out by an epidemic of smallpox or some similar disease in 733–737 that killed approximately 25 to 35 percent of the population. It was followed by repeated famines and epidemics later in the century. The state's demand for revenue to fund building projects and ceremonies was not matched by an increase in population or an enlarged economic base.

Rural villages tended to be large in area but small in population. Because depleted fields had to lie fallow for years before they could be returned to production, the earlier pattern of fortified hilltop hamlets gave way to dispersed dwellings, each containing a large household of extended family members along with servants and slaves. Each cultivator received an official allotment of land in return for paying taxes, but it did not suffice for survival. To make up the difference, cultivators planted fields hidden from the tax collector, worked as tenants, or foraged for supplies. To the dismay of officials, cultivators felt little connection to their land. Many simply absconded when times were bad, swelling the population of vagrants and weakening the tax base. Infant mortality was so high that a plan to give each child an allotment of land at birth had to be changed to allotments at age five, raised to age twelve in the case of a slave. The average life expectancy at birth was twenty-eight to thirty-three years, approximately the same as in Europe at that time.

Quarrelling Worker. Scribbled on the margin of a record regarding sutra copying in 740, this sketch of a quarrelling worker provides a glimpse of the garb worn by commoners of the time. *(Shosoin Treasure House/DNPArchives.com)*

In addition to paying taxes for the use of state land, cultivators had to meet service requirements and participate in the state's military adventures. In 713, for example, "For the first time Yamashiro-no-kuni was ordered to establish fifty households in charge of milking cows."[2] In this type of corvée (required labor) system, the culti-

vators' obligation to provide services did not mean they would be paid for them. The corvée built the enormous tombs demanded by fifth-century rulers; it built the capitals, palaces, and temples of the later centuries. The court fielded conscript armies and marched them from Kyushu to Tohoku. Many men caught in this system could expect to be ill treated, malnourished, and abandoned once the project for which they had been pressed into service was completed. Although the centered monarchical structure created through the regime of codes provided relief from marauders and bandits as well as some security of landholding, its benefits for cultivators were decidedly mixed.

SUMMARY

By the end of the eighth century, interactions with the continent had radically modified agriculture, material culture, and religion on the Japanese islands. A centered state spread over Shikoku, Kyushu, and most of Honshu, gradually becoming attenuated as it reached the frontiers. Although historians disagree on the extent to which it enforced its decrees, it became a model for kingly rule for centuries to come.

SUGGESTED READING

For an excellent overview of Japan's place in northeast Asia, see B. L. Batten, *To the Ends of Japan: Premodern Frontiers, Boundaries, and Interactions* (2003). W. H. Coldrake, *Architecture and Authority in Japan* (1996) begins with grand shrines and Nara buildings. J. W. Hall et al., general eds., *The Cambridge History of Japan*, 6 vols. (1988–1999), covers the entire history.

For more specific studies, see M. J. Hudson, *Ruins of Identity: Ethnogenesis in the Japanese Islands* (1999); G. Barnes, *Protohistoric Yamato: Archaeology of the First Japanese State* (1988); K. Imamura, *Prehistoric Japan: New Perspectives on Insular East Asia* (1996); J. R. Piggott, *The Emergence of Japanese Kingship* (1997); W. W. Farris, *Sacred Texts and Buried Treasures: Issues in the Historical Archaeology of Ancient Japan* (1998); and W. W. Farris, *Population, Disease, and Land in Early Japan, 645–900* (1985).

2. Robert Karl Reischauer, *Early Japanese History (c. 40 B.C.–A.D. 1167)* (Gloucester, Mass.: Peter Smith, 1967), p. 173.

Buddhism

EAST ASIAN CIVILIZATION WAS NEVER completely isolated from the rest of Eurasia. Wheat and the chariot arrived in China from west Asia in Shang times. Animal art spread across the steppe in late Zhou times. Nevertheless, ancient China had less contact with other early centers of civilization such as Mesopotamia, India, Egypt, and Greece than they had with each other. India was geographically the closest of those civilizations and therefore it is not surprising that it was the first to have a major impact on East Asia. The vehicle of its impact was one of its religions, Buddhism.

Early India differed from early China in a great many ways. Much farther south, most areas of the Indian subcontinent were warm all year. In the region of the Indus River there had been an ancient literate civilization that was already in decline by 1800 B.C.E. The Aryans, in India by 1000 B.C.E. if not earlier, were Indo-European speaking people who became the dominant group in north India. The culture of the early Aryans is known from the *Rigveda,* a collection of hymns, ritual texts, and philosophical texts composed between 1500 and 500 B.C.E., but transmitted orally for centuries. The *Rigveda* portrays the Aryans as warrior tribes who glorified military skill and heroism; loved to drink, hunt, race, and dance; and counted their wealth in cattle. It presents the struggle between the Aryans and indigenous peoples in religious terms: their chiefs were godlike heroes, their opponents irreligious savages.

Early Aryan society had distinguished between the warrior elite, the priests, ordinary tribesmen, and conquered subjects. These distinctions gradually evolved into the caste system. Society was conceived in terms of four hierarchical strata that did not eat with each other or marry each other: priests (Brahman), warriors or officials (Kshatriya), merchants and landowners (Vaishya), and workers (Shudra). The gods of the Aryans shared some features of the gods of other early Indo-European societies such as the Persians and the Greeks. The *Upanishads,* composed between 750 and 500 B.C.E., record speculations about the mystical meaning of sacrificial rites and about cosmological questions of man's relationship to the universe. They document a gradual shift from the mythical world-view of the early Vedic age to a deeply philosophical one. Associated with this shift was a movement toward asceticism. In search of a richer and more mystical faith, some men retreated to the forests.

Ancient Indian cosmology imagined endlessly repeating cycles. Central concepts were *samsara,* the transmigration of souls by a continual process of rebirth, and *karma,* the tally of good and bad deeds that determined the status of an individual's next life. Good deeds lead to better future lives, evil deeds to worse future lives—even to reincarnation as an animal. The wheel of life included human beings, animals, and even gods. Reward and punishment worked automatically; there was no all-knowing god who judged people and could be petitioned to forgive a sin, and each individual was responsible for his or her own destiny in a just and impartial world. The optimistic interpretation of samsara was that people could improve their lot in the next life by living righteously. The pessimistic view was that life is a treadmill, a relentless cycle of birth and death. Brahmanic mystics sought release from the wheel of life through realization that life in the world was actually an illusion.

The founder of Buddhism was Siddhartha Gautama (fl. ca. 500 B.C.E.), also called Shakyamuni ("sage of the Shakya tribe"), but best known as the Buddha ("enlightened one"). Our knowledge of his life is filtered through later Buddhist texts, which tell us that he was born the son of a ruler of one of the chiefdoms in the Himalayan foothills in what is now Nepal. Within the Indian caste system he was in the warrior, not the priest (Brahman) caste. At age twenty-nine, unsatisfied with his life of comfort and troubled by the suffering he saw around him, he left home to become a wandering ascetic. He traveled south to the kingdom of Magadha, where he studied with yoga masters. Later he took up extreme asceticism. According to tradition, he reached enlightenment while meditating under a bo tree at Bodh Gaya. After several weeks of meditation, he preached his first sermon, urging a "middle way" between asceticism and worldly life. For the next forty-five years, the Buddha traveled through the Ganges Valley, propounding his ideas, refuting his adversaries, making converts, and attracting followers.

In his first sermon, the Buddha outlined his main message, summed up in the Four Noble Truths and the Eightfold Path. The truths are as follows: (1) pain and suffering, frustration and anxiety, are ugly but inescapable parts of human life; (2) suffering and anxiety are caused by human desires and attachments; (3) people can understand these weaknesses and triumph over them; and (4) this triumph is made possible by following a simple code of conduct, the Eightfold Path. The basic insight of Buddhism is thus psychological. The deepest human longings can never be satisfied, and even those things that seem to give pleasure cause anxiety because we are afraid of losing them. Attachment to people and things leads to sorrow at their loss.

The Buddha offered an optimistic message, however, because people can all set out on the Eightfold Path toward liberation. All they have to do is take steps such as recognizing the universal-ity of suffering, deciding to free themselves from it, and choosing "right conduct," "right speech," "right livelihood," and "right endeavor." For instance, they should abstain from taking life and thus follow a vegetarian diet. The seventh step is "right awareness," constant contemplation of one's deeds and words, giving full thought to their importance and whether they lead to enlightenment. "Right contemplation," the last step, entails meditation on the impermanence of everything in the world. Those who achieve liberation are freed from the cycle of birth and death and enter the blissful state called *nirvana*.

Although he accepted the Indian idea of reincarnation, the Buddha denied the integrity of the individual self or soul. He saw human beings as a collection of parts, physical and mental. As long as the parts remain combined, that combination can be called "I." When that combination changes, as at death, the various parts remain in existence, ready to become the building blocks of different combinations. According to Buddhist teaching, life is passed from person to person as a flame is passed from candle to candle.

The success of Buddhism was aided by the Buddha's teaching that everyone, noble and peasant, educated and ignorant, male and female, could follow the Eightfold Path. Within India this marked a challenge to the caste system, central to early Brahmanism and later Hinduism. Moreover, the Buddha was extraordinarily undogmatic. Convinced that each person must achieve enlightenment on his or her own, he emphasized that the path was important only because it led the traveler to enlightenment, not for its own sake. He compared religious practices to a raft, needed to get across a river but useless once on the far shore. Thus, there was no harm in honoring local gods or observing traditional ceremonies, as long as one kept in mind the ultimate goal of enlightenment.

In his lifetime the Buddha formed a circle of disciples, primarily men but including some women as well. The Buddha's followers transmitted his teachings orally for several centuries until they were written down in the second or first century B.C.E. The form of monasticism that developed among the Buddhists was less strict than that of some other contemporary groups in India, such as the Jains. Buddhist monks moved about for eight months of the year (staying inside only during the rainy season) and consumed only one meal a day obtained by begging. Within a few centuries, Buddhist monks began to overlook the rule that they should travel. They set up permanent monasteries, generally on land donated by kings or other patrons. Orders of nuns also appeared, giving women the opportunity to seek truth in ways men had traditionally done. The main ritual that monks and nuns performed in their monastic establishments was the communal recitation of the sutras. Lay Buddhists could aid the spread of the Buddhist teachings by providing food for monks and support for their monasteries, and could pursue their own spiritual progress by adopting practices such as abstaining from meat and alcohol.

Within India the spread of Buddhism was greatly aided in the third century B.C.E. by King Ashoka. As a young prince, Ashoka served as governor of two prosperous provinces where Buddhism flourished. At the death of his father about 274 B.C.E., Ashoka rebelled against his older brother, the rightful king, and after four years of fighting succeeded in his bloody bid for the throne. In 261 B.C.E., early in his reign, Ashoka conquered Kalinga, on the east coast of India. Instead of exulting like a conqueror, however, Ashoka was consumed with remorse for all the deaths inflicted. In this mood, he embraced Buddhism.

Ashoka used the machinery of his empire to spread Buddhist teachings throughout India. He banned animal sacrifices and in place of hunting expeditions, he took pilgrimages. Two years after his conversion, he undertook a 256-day pilgrimage to all the holy sites of Buddhism and on his return he began sending missionaries to all known countries. Buddhist tradition also credits him with erecting throughout India 84,000 stupas (Buddhist reliquary mounds), among which the ashes of the Buddha were distributed, beginning the association of Buddhism

Gate at the Great Stupa at Sanchi. King Ashoka began the stupa at Sanchi in central India as a site for the preservation of the ashes of the Buddha. Each of its four gates, dating from the first century C.E., is decorated with Buddhist imagery. Note the depiction of a stupa on the horizontal support. *(Borromeo/Art Resource, NY)*

with monumental art and architecture. Also according to Buddhist tradition, Ashoka convened a great council of Buddhist monks at which the earliest canon of Buddhist texts was codified.

Under Ashoka, Buddhism began to spread to Central Asia. This continued under the Kushan empire (ca. 50–250 C.E.), especially under their greatest king, Kanishka I (ca. 100 C.E.). In this region, where the influence of Greek art was strong, artists began to depict the Buddha in human form. By this period Buddhist communities were developing divergent traditions and came to stress different sutras. One of the most important of these, associated with the monkphilosopher Nagarjuna (ca. 150–250), is called Mahayana, or "Great Vehicle," because it is a

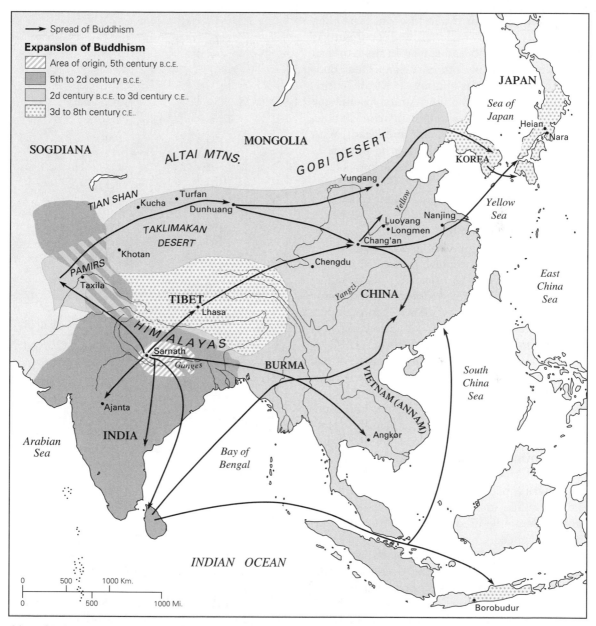

Map C2.1   Expansion of Buddhism from 500 B.C.E. to 800 C.E.

more inclusive form of the religion. It drew on a set of discourses allegedly preached by the Buddha and kept hidden by his followers for centuries. One branch of Mahayana taught that reality is "empty" (that is, nothing exists independently of itself). Emptiness was seen as an absolute, underlying all phenomena, which are themselves transient and illusory. Another branch held that ultimate reality is consciousness, that everything is produced by the mind.

Just as important as the metaphysical literature of Mahayana Buddhism was its devotional side, influenced by the Iranian religions then prevalent in Central Asia. The Buddha became deified and placed at the head of an expanding pantheon of other Buddhas and bodhisattvas (Buddhas-to-be who had stayed in the world to help others on the path to salvation). These Buddhas and bodhisattvas became objects of veneration, especially the Buddha Amitabha and the bodhisattva Avalokitesvara (Guanyin in Chinese, Kannon in Japanese, Kwanŭm in Korean). With the growth of Mahayana, Buddhism became as much a religion for laypeople as for monks and nuns.

Buddhism remained an important religion in India until about 1200 C.E., but thereafter it declined, and the number of Buddhists in India today is small. Long before it declined in India, however, it spread too much of the rest of Asia. One route was east to Sri Lanka and most of Southeast Asia, including Indonesia. Another was northeast to Nepal and Tibet. More important for the history of East Asia, however, was the route northwest through Central Asia. During the first few centuries C.E., most of the city-states of Central Asia became centers of Buddhism, from Bamiyan, northwest of Kabul, to Kucha, Khotan, Loulan, Turfan, and Dunhuang. The first translators of Buddhist texts into Chinese were not Indians but Parthians, Sogdians, and Kushans from Central Asia.

Central Asia in the centuries in which Buddhism was spreading east was ethnically diverse, though Indian and Persian languages were the most commonly used for administrative purposes. The economy of these city-states was dependent on the East-West trade. In Han times, the Chinese had become the overlords in the area, wanting both access to the fabled horses of Ferghana and to keep the area out of the hands of its foes, such as the Xiongnu. After the fall of the Han, most of these cities became independent and trade continued unabated. Buddhism thus reached China first as a religion of foreign merchants. Missionaries soon followed, however, and the hugely complex process of translating Buddhist sutras from Sanskrit or other Indian languages into classical Chinese was accomplished through the collaboration of Central Asian and Chinese monks.

Monk Contemplating a Skull. The painting is from the wall of a cave temple in Kizil, along the Silk Road in Central Asia, and dates from about 500 C.E. *(Museum of Indian Art, Berlin/Art Resource, NY)*

Kumarajiva (350–413 C.E.) was one of the most important of these translators. His father, from a high-ranking family in India, had moved to the Silk Road oasis city of Kucha, attracted by the quality of the Buddhist scholarship there, and he married the younger sister of the king of Kucha. At this time, Kucha reportedly had a population of 100,000, of whom 10,000 were monks. Already in this period spectacular cave temples were being constructed in the nearby small town of Kizil. At home Kumarajiva spoke Tokharian, an Indo-European language. He may also have learned some Chinese from merchants who came regularly to Kucha. From age seven he studied Buddhist texts in Sanskrit as part of his Buddhist training. By age twenty he had established himself as a brilliant Buddhist scholar, and the ruler of a small state in the modern Chinese province of Gansu sent a general to abduct him. He stayed in Gansu seventeen years, becoming fluent in Chinese. In 401 he was able to move to Chang'an where another ruler gave financial support to his plan to translate Buddhist sutras into Chinese. Kumarajiva recruited a large group of learned monks and set up a systematic procedure for checking draft translations. Rather than borrowing terms from Daoism, which often proved misleading, Sanskrit terms were retained, represented by Chinese words borrowed for their sound. About thirty-five sutras were translated, including some of the most famous and popular, such as the *Lotus Sutra* and the *Vimalakirti Sutra*. An exponent of Mahayana, Kumarajiva also translated treatises by Nagarjuna and lectured on their content.

Translating Buddhist texts into Chinese helped Buddhism spread throughout East Asia. Not only did these texts come to circulate throughout China, but they also became the basis for Korean and Japanese schools of Buddhism. The Buddhism that reached Japan, for instance, was filtered through Central Asian, Chinese, and Korean lenses.

SUGGESTED READING

On early India, see L. Basham, *The Wonder that Was India* (1954) or R. Thapar, *History of India* (1966). A. Embree, ed., *Sources of Indian Tradition,* 2nd ed. (1988) has translations of central texts of all Indian religions. On Indian Buddhism, see A. Hirakawa, *A History of Indian Buddhism* (1990) and D. Lopez, *The Story of the Buddha* (2001).

Heian Japan
(794–ca. 1180)

When Kanmu moved the court to Heian-kyō ("capital of peace and stability," now called Kyoto) in 794, he modeled his city on the Chinese imperial layout just as the Nara rulers had. For the next century, the regime of codes continued to provide the basic framework for a bureaucratic-style government. The period from approximately 900 to 1050 marks the apogee of classical refinement during the golden age of the Fujiwara. Rebellions in the provinces suggest that its benefits did not accrue to all. During both periods, political life at the capital remained largely free from violence. The final phase, from 1050 to 1180, saw retired monarchs wrest political power from the Fujiwara while trying to take advantage of the private landholding system. Beginning in the 900s, an outpouring of literary texts ranged in writing styles from royally commissioned poetry anthologies to diaries, memoirs, and the novel *Tale of Genji*. Buddhist thought pervaded the way aristocrats saw the world; Buddhist institutions became a powerful political and economic force.

Scholars debate issues concerning the degree of central control, the naturalization of Chinese civilization, and gender. What changed in relations between state, periphery, and the continent? Why do we see this age as so important for poetry and fiction by women? What kind of impact did the state have on commoners' lives?

THE AGE OF KINGLY RULE

Kanmu continued the bureaucratic and ceremonial practices that had been instituted while the court was at Nara. Men qualified by birth and talent climbed administrative ladders. Commanders of imperial guards rose to generals leading armies against the Emishi in the northeast. Kanmu relied on officials on the Board of Divination to interpret heavenly portents and omens in line with Daoist teachings. Following a factional dispute after his enthronement in 781, he ordered the era name changed to *Enryaku* (prolonged succession) to ensure a long and prosperous reign. Despite assassinations, pestilence, and famine, it remained until his death. Codifying the annual round of celebrations and ceremonies conducted by the Board of Divination began in 823, but the procedures had been in place for over a century.

Despite continuing the fascination with Chinese culture that had characterized the Nara period, Kanmu intended moving the capital to be a break with the past. Perhaps he wanted to free his administration from political interference by Buddhist clergy whose temples encircled Nara. Although he forbade Nara clergy to follow him to Heian-kyō, the court continued to support them financially and send representatives to ceremonies. Kanmu tried to control what was to become the great temple complex of Enryakuji that had opened on Mount Hiei northeast of Heian-kyō in 785 by appointing its abbots and restricting monks to monasteries. Another reason for the move may have been political. Taking advantage of a momentary decline in Fujiwara influence, Kanmu abandoned what had become their stronghold. Finally there was the question of prognostics. Violent factional and succession disputes had tainted Nara. If Kanmu was to launch a new initiative in righteous governance, he needed a fresh venue, one that the diviners promised would be auspicious.

Kanmu retained the formal structure of government defined in the regime of codes, but he also bypassed it in the interest of bureaucratic efficiency. Rather than rely on the large and unwieldy Council of State, he chose a small group of court councilors to advise him. As a necessary retrenchment measure given the limits to government revenues, he and his successors eliminated offices and reduced the number of officials. The Fujiwara having made a comeback, this left fewer positions for other lineages. In 792, Kanmu ended the Chinese-style system of conscripting commoners for the provincial militia. Cultivators made ineffective fighting men, militia commanders had abused their power by ordering conscripts to labor on private projects, and depopulation caused by repeated famines and epidemics threatened the manpower and tax base. Instead of conscripts, the court relied on hired warriors to resist piracy and push back the frontier. To guard the palace and prosecute crimes in the capital, the Office of Police assumed military and juridical responsibilities. In 894 the court ceased formal relations with China, although private trade and religious traffic continued.

The court gradually relinquished direct supervision over the countryside. It set tax quotas by province and appointed inspectors to audit provincial accounts and prevent provincial governors from returning to the capital until all taxes had been paid. Appointed to four-year terms, the governors selected their own assistants, but they delegated tax collection and ongoing administrative responsibilities to registered lineages of local magnates who staffed the district and county offices. The governors essentially became tax farmers because they kept any revenues collected beyond their quotas. Below the officials were the cultivators, hardly an undifferentiated mass. The "rich and powerful" (*fugō*) acted as middlemen in collecting taxes. They too overcollected so as to keep a share for themselves. They owned livestock and slaves whom they employed on large plots of land. Most cultivators barely scraped by on what they could squeeze from marginal plots and work for others. When harvests failed and provincial governors became too rapacious, they abandoned their fields to try their luck in another location.

Commoners in the countryside managed their own affairs. At most the Office of Police might attack an army of bandits that terrorized a community near Heian-kyō. To handle ordinary thieves, the cultivators defined crimes and meted out punishments. In their eyes, the most heinous crime was theft of their food supply. Anyone caught stealing it was killed. In eastern Japan, people supplemented agriculture with hunting and fishing, woodcutting and charcoal burning, and horse breeding. They too punished theft of their livelihood with death. Cultivators also devised trials to determine if a suspect was telling the truth, placing the suspect's hand in boiling water being a typical ploy. Whereas the Heian court exiled criminals in line with Buddhist teachings forbidding the taking of life, cultivators had no such scruples.

The rebellion by Taira no Masakado from 935 to 940 in the Kanto region of eastern Japan dramatizes the connection between court politics and local issues. Under the regime of codes, the ruler's descendants not in the direct line to rule received family names and gradually fell in rank for six generations. Losing royal status allowed them to fill civilian or military positions in the state bureaucracy closed to members of the royal family. Some chose the clerical route and became temple abbots. Since branches of the Fujiwara lineage monopolized the highest central offices, most royal scions went to the provinces where their exalted lineage gave them prestige unobtainable in Heian-kyō. Kanmu's descendants took the name Taira. By the early tenth century, they and cadet branches of powerful aristocratic lineages dominated provincial headquarters staffs as clients of the governors.

Masakado's rebellion began as a family quarrel with his uncle that expanded into an attack on provincial headquarters. The court also had to contend with another revolt closer to Heian-kyō when Fujiwara no Sumitomo (?–941), an erstwhile official in Iyo province on Shikoku and the leader of a pirate band, began attacking granaries and administrative offices. By deputizing rivals of these rebels to fight in its name, the court managed to have both suppressed. Following his death, Masakado became a hero to the cultivators in the Kanto because he had sided with them against the provincial governor's staff. (His uncle had been vice governor.) They erected a shrine to his spirit that still receives offerings in Tokyo today.

Masakado's attack on his uncle and other relatives exemplifies the rivalry that divided kin and undermined the state adapted from Tang models. Because relatives had the same progenitor, they vied for the same slots in the social and administrative hierarchy. Rival branches challenged the titled chieftain's authority to control the lineage's temples and shrines, educational institutions for the lineage's youth, and appointments for lineage members at court. Like the Fujiwara, the Taira became too unwieldy to function as an effective power bloc. Instead the heads of houses (*ie*) based on residence locations competed among themselves for court honors and position regardless of whomever happened to be the chieftain. In eastern Japan the connection between the *ie* and location was especially strong. There, family compounds (*yashiki*) tended to be dispersed. Each contained many members because in the frontier setting, there was a chronic labor shortage. According to the convention of the time, when Masakado married his uncle's daughter, he should have gone to live in his uncle's compound and worked for him. When Masakado refused, he challenged his uncle's dominance in the lineage and threatened his economic base. This type of kin-based struggle over hierarchy and dominance far removed from the court and the treachery, arson, and pitched battles that ensued mark the beginning of a new stage in Japan's history of violence.

Early Heian Culture

Both luxury and privation characterized the Heian court. Aristocrats wore layer upon layer of beautifully dyed silks and Chinese brocades, especially in winter because they lacked any but primitive heating systems. They hosted elaborate banquets with drinking, dancing, and musical entertainment but kept to a meager diet. Their mansions overlooked landscaped gardens and contained almost nothing by way of furniture except for free-standing armrests, bedding, and screens.

Aristocrats refined their understanding of classical Chinese and took the literary arts in new directions. The monarchy sponsored three anthologies of Chinese poetry. The monk Kūkai, who had studied in China, and Sugawara no Michizane, the preeminent scholar of Chinese learning until the seventeenth century, penned some of the best Chinese poetry ever produced by Japanese. For centuries to come, intellectuals in Japan would employ Chinese categories of thought in the Chinese language. By the end of the ninth century, Japanese scribes had sufficiently modified Chinese characters that they had developed a syllabary (*kana*) in which to write Japanese poetry and prose. Such was the prestige of Chinese that men continued to use it for official documents and personal reflections. Being native to Japan and hence of less cultural value, the syllabary was largely though not entirely relegated to women.

Transformations in Religious Practice

In the early 800s two monks, Kūkai and Saichō, returned from China with texts and practices that transformed the teachings of the earlier Nara sects and entrenched Buddhism ever more firmly in Japan's political, economic, and spiritual life. Kūkai's visit to China from 804 to 806 led him to esoteric rites, symbols, and scriptures. Challenging what he saw as an overdependence on Confucianism in political ideology, he developed rituals and wrote texts based on a philosophy of ideal leadership derived from the great cosmic Buddha Mahavairocana that was to be transmitted to the ruler through an esoteric initiation rite during enthronement ceremonies. In Kūkai's vision of the world, the ruler ranked below priests and nuns in the political hierarchy. He built a retreat for the Shingon (True Word) School on Mount Kōya far from Heian-kyō, where he and his disciples prayed for protection of the state and prosperity for the people in rites that invoked the mystical power of prayer. His headquarters at Tōji in Heian-kyō put art to the service of religion. Rather than spend years studying sutras, aristocrats might find enlightenment in viewing the mandala (a stylized representation of Buddhist teachings) and achieve Buddhahood in their own body, without having to die first.

Saichō is often contrasted with Kūkai, but they shared an interest in esoteric teachings and practice. Saichō performed the first officially sanctioned esoteric initiation rite in Japan because he believed it to be the fastest route to attain Buddhahood. He founded the eclectic Tendai school of Buddhism in Japan and made the temple complex of Enryakuji on Mount Hiei its headquarters. From 804 to 805 he studied four schools of Buddhism in China, including Zen (Chan in Chinese), and brought them back to Japan along with the Tendai sect's central text, the *Lotus Sutra*. One of the most important Buddhist sutras, it contains a rich repository of stories and parables for explaining Buddhism to the uninitiated. It teaches that all Buddhist texts have merit because many are the ways that lead to enlightenment, and it promises that under extraordinary circumstances even women may attain Buddhahood.

The court's fascination with new Buddhist sects neither displaced the native deities nor eroded their assimilation to Buddhas. Daughters and sisters of rulers continued to serve as high priestesses at the family's Ise shrine. Geographic, not doctrinal, boundaries differentiated institutions and beliefs. Buddhist and Shinto deities brought prosperity; they also brought misfortune. In the ninth century, the belief was widespread that powerful spirits caused disease and epidemics. *Goryō*, either a cosmic force or the spirit of an aristocrat who had died unjustly, required cults to be appeased. The most famous cult originated at the Gion temple-shrine complex in 876. It climaxed in a midsummer festival performed when epidemics ran rampant. Angry spirits (*onryō*) resulted from an excess of strong emotion, usually after a well-born person had died unhappy. The conjunction of such a death with epidemics, earthquakes, and drought led the living to believe that the dead person's passion prevented his rebirth by trapping him in limbo. Pacifying his spirit required exorcism performed by mountain ascetics, whose knowledge of the realms of the dead and experiences of hell gave them powers unavailable to ordinary monks. The prayers of ritualists and ordinary people also proved efficacious in transforming angry spirits into guardian deities.

Gion Festival. By 1013 the Gion festival procession featured dancers, mounted musicians, and decorated floats pulled by oxen or carried by men. *(Private collection [Tanaka family]. Photo: Chuokoron-Shinsha, Inc./DNP Archives.com)*

Onryō cults culminated with Sugawara no Michizane in 947. (See **Biography: Sugawara no Michizane.**)

THE FUJIWARA ERA

The heyday for the Fujiwara lineage came between approximately 900 and 1050, idealized retrospectively as a peaceful, golden age of court culture. During these years, a small number of aristocratic women and men produced what are universally deemed to be literary classics. They accomplished this feat despite a lack of growth in either the population or the economy. A population of perhaps 5 million in 700 grew by only 500,000 by 900, and it took another three centuries for it to reach at most 7 million in 1200. The lack of economic growth meant competition for scarce resources between ruler, aristocrats, and temples and a miserable existence for commoners.

The Fujiwara helped hollow out the institutions created by the regime of codes. Approximately twenty thousand men and women constituted the aristocracy, and by 900 they formed three distinct groups in a nine-rank system. The highest three ranks had great wealth derived from office lands and private estates, the prestige of the Fujiwara lineage, and the power to set policy. Approximately twenty houses qualified. Ranks four and five consisted of provincial governors and junior officials, who with the right background might advance to higher ranks. The people who filled ranks six through nine possessed specialized skills in scholarship, astronomy, medicine, and law. They had no hope of advancement and suffered under their inferior status. In 1030, for example, they were forbidden to roof their dwellings with cedar-bark shingles or surround them with earthen walls. As the functions of the court came to center increasingly on performing a yearly round of ceremonial observances, the

BIOGRAPHY Sugawara no Michizane

Scholar and bureaucrat, Sugawara no Michizane (845–903) rose unseemly high for a man of his modest birth, but he owes his fame to deeds done after he died.

A child prodigy, Michizane wrote his first poem in Chinese at age ten. In 867 he began his career at the junior sixth rank. He assisted in the reception of emissaries from the Manchurian kingdom of Parhae. When offered the post of ambassador to China, he recommended that missions to the Tang court be halted. He served a term as a provincial governor. He helped compile two histories of Japan and taught at the family school and the court university.

Michizane's reputation for scholarship and astute advice brought him to the attention of the monarch Uda, who ascended the throne in 887. Through Uda's patronage, he rose far beyond the rank normally permitted a man from a scholarly family. In 893 he became a court councilor. In 895 his daughter became one of Uda's consorts. Two years later, when Uda decided to abdicate and rule through his son Daigo, he had Michizane and the head of the Fujiwara lineage, Tokihira, share the highest positions in government. When Uda's son Tokiyo came of age in 898, he married yet another of Michizane's daughters, giving Michizane the intimate marital relations with the royal family customarily enjoyed by the Fujiwara. In 899 Michizane became Minister of the Right. Promotion to junior second rank soon followed. These promotions marked him as the retired monarch's favorite, whom everyone else despised. In 901 Tokihira found a man to accuse Michizane of plotting with Uda to force Daigo to abdicate and place Prince Tokiyo on the throne. Daigo promptly exiled Michizane and made Tokiyo a monk. Michizane died in exile, of grief, it was said, at having to leave his beloved plum trees, the urban amenities, and his cultivated friends for the wilds of Kyushu.

When men who had plotted Michizane's fall died in following years, people whispered that his angry spirit was responsible. Tokihira died mysteriously in 909. In 923 the crown prince, Tokihira's nephew, died. In an act of propitiation, the charges against Michizane were burned, the decree of exile was revoked, and he was restored to his previous court rank. In 930 a lightning bolt killed the man who had accused him of treason. Fearing that heaven had turned against him, Daigo died. Speaking through shamans, Michizane demanded that a shrine be built to transform him from a vengeful spirit to the protector of the nation. In 947 he and his literary works were enshrined at the Kitano shrine-temple complex north of Heian-kyō. Forty years later he officially became a god when the reigning monarch bestowed on him the title of Tenjin (heavenly deity). Over the centuries he became identified as the god of literature. Today children pray to him for help in passing their school entrance examinations.

Source: Based on Robert Borgen, *Sugawara no Michizane and the Early Heian Court* (Cambridge, Mass.: Harvard University Press, 1985).

---

task of everyday administration devolved to household officials.

High-ranked houses required large staffs to manage their economic, social, and legal affairs. Staff members served the house as private officials. They received appointments from the ruler at the behest of the house they served that came with court rank for which they were qualified by birth, normally the fourth through the sixth ranks. Even royal scions who had become military men in the provinces or former provincial governors of the fourth or fifth rank might take service in a Fujiwara household, and they too requested appointments for their servants. Reciprocal relations rather than office in a bureaucratic hierarchy mediated the bond between the head of a house and his court-ranked attendant. Household personnel granted fictive kin ties participated in important family ceremonies along with family members. They accompanied their patrons on outings to the family temples and shrines, to the palace, and on visits to other aristocrats. They served as messengers, prepared documents, and supervised the procurement of supplies. Reward came as protection in disputes and advancement in the court bureaucracy at the recommendation of their patron.

The state soon lost control over the extensive networks of patron-client relationships. Each aristocratic house had numerous helpers, military men as well as personal servants, all of whom were clients in that they worked for the house in the expectation that they would receive a benefit from the state. Even admission to an aristocratic house as a toilet cleaner freed a man and his family from conscript labor demanded by the state. Clientage tended to become hereditary and continue for generations.

Marriage and Politics

Marriage bonds reinforced patron-client relations and integrated different levels of society. Because men could use familial ties to advance, they continued the ancient pattern of visiting a wife in her father's household when the father was of higher rank and could serve as their patron. Since no one outranked the ruler, his women lived with him at court. They returned to their natal family to give birth. Aristocratic women could inherit property from their parents. Not bearing an heir did not constitute grounds for divorce. A man might have additional wives of nondescript background who lived with him and managed his household. A man and woman might also consider themselves to be husband and wife even if she lived alone and he visited her only on occasion. A fourth less common practice was for the wife to move into her husband's parental household.

The Fujiwara dominated political life through their mastery of marriage politics. During the peak of their influence, between 967 and 1068, eight rulers occupied the throne for average reigns of thirteen years. Politically, each functioned primarily as a spouse for Fujiwara women. As soon as a Fujiwara consort with a powerful father or brother bore a son to the ruler, the child was appointed crown prince. When he attained puberty, he received Fujiwara women as consorts. Once he had proven capable of siring sons, his father would be encouraged to abdicate, shave his head, and seek enlightenment. The average ruler ascended the throne at age eighteen and abdicated at age thirty-one. Some took the throne as toddlers and abdicated as teenagers. An under-age ruler needed a regent to advise him, and who better than his maternal grandfather in whose house he had been born and raised? Even adult rulers needed regents to make policy decisions; they too were either Fujiwara grandfathers or fathers-in-law. Fujiwara no Michinaga made himself grandfather to two rulers and father-in-law to three. His son served as regent for three monarchs. The original Fujiwara lineage had already split into four branch houses when the court moved to Heian-kyō. In Michinaga's day, all but his house, the northern branch, disappeared in power struggles. By the middle of the eleventh century, Michinaga's descendants monopolized the positions of regent. They later split into five sublineages that competed for political power and forced the few remaining non-Fujiwara houses from the court.

Even during their days of greatest glory, the Fujiwara always had to contend with the possibility that a non-Fujiwara woman would bear the ruler a son. Women too received court rank, and the ruler's officially designated wife enjoyed a status far above that of concubines. Fujiwara women in the houses of high-ranking Fujiwara men started with significant advantages, but to maintain their position over the generations required a finely honed consciousness of status exclusivity. For the monarch, only a wife of the Fujiwara or royal lineage would do; for the Fujiwara, only a wife from another Fujiwara branch or the ruling family sufficed. Monarchs and Fujiwara men married aunts, nieces, and first cousins. They continued to father children with concubines and serving women lest their official wife prove barren.

The Heyday of Aristocratic Culture

The florescence of female literary triumphs during the Fujiwara era is inseparable from political intrigue. When Fujiwara no Michinaga made his daughter Shōshi the monarch Ichijō's wife in 999, he selected a bevy of educated and engaging women to help her compete for Ichijō's attention. Guaranteeing her success in this regard was crucial because his rival and elder brother had a daughter who was already Ichijō's official wife. In Teishi's retinue was Sei Shonagon, famous for her brilliant wit. She is the author of *The Pillow Book*, a collection of essays on taste. "A preacher ought to be good-looking. For, if we are properly to understand his worthy sentiments, we must keep our eyes on him while he speaks." "A good lover will behave as elegantly at dawn as at any other time."[1] A consummate snob, Sei Shonagon hardly considered commoners to be the same species as herself. "Good people," by contrast, had impeccable lineage, taste, and spiritual virtue. Her contemporary and rival Murasaki Shikibu, who served in Shōshi's retinue, chided Sei Shonagon: "She thought herself so clever, and littered her writings with Chinese characters, but if you examined them closely, they left a great deal to be desired."[2] In addition to poetry and a diary, Murasaki Shikibu wrote *Tale of Genji*, a novel of court intrigue, life, and manners about a royal scion who exemplifies masculine perfection in physical appearance and behavior.

The tenth and eleventh centuries marked the pinnacle of classical women's literature. In the 970s a woman known to us only as the mother of Fujiwara no Michitsuna wrote *Kagerō nikki*, a poetic memoir of her unhappy twenty-year marriage to a high-ranking court official who seldom visited her. *Izumi Shikibu Diary* is another memoir that recounts the life of a low-ranking court woman (also in Shōshi's service) who married a man of her own station, had affairs with two princes, and wrote poetry famous for its passion. A *Tale of Flowering Fortunes*, composed during the 1030s by Akazome Emon, Japan's first vernacular historian, begins in 887 and concludes with a triumphal biography of Michinaga. A daughter of Sugawara no Takasue wrote *Hamamatsu Chūnagon monogatari* (A Tale of Hamamatsu Chūnagon) around 1070, which sets a love story in the travels of the eponymous hero who goes to China and returns. She also wrote *Sarashina nikki*, an autobiography notable for her recollections of her childhood with her father who left eastern Japan to try his luck at court. Steeped in the aesthetic sensibility of their day, these women wrote in the Japanese syllabary. (See **Material Culture: Writing Japanese.**) Encapsulated in the phrase *mono no aware* (beauty, evanescence, and pathos), this sensibility derived from the Buddhist view that the material world is transitory.

Men too wrote in Japanese. The poet and aspiring bureaucrat Ki no Tsurayuki edited the first of the royally commissioned Japanese poetry collections, the *Kokinshū* (Collection of the Past and Present), in 905. Female and male poets contributed approximately eleven hundred poems to this anthology, famous for its polished, elegant, intellectual tone. "The seeds of Japanese poetry lie in the human heart," Tsurayuki claimed, and poetry "moves heaven and earth."[3] He also wrote *Tosa nikki*, an account of a two-month trip to the capital across the Inland Sea by the provincial governor and his retinue. In his Preface he pretended to be a woman so as to justify his use of the syllabary

---

1. Ivan Morris, trans., *The Pillow Book of Sei Shonagon* (New York: Columbia University Press, 1967), 1:29, 33.

2. Robert Bowring, trans. and ed., *Murasaki Shikibu: Her Diary and Poetic Memoirs* (Princeton, N.J.: Princeton University Press, 1982), p. 131.

3. Laurel Rasplica Rodd with Mary Catherine Henkenius, trans., *Kokinshū: A Collection of Poems Ancient and Modern* (Princeton, N.J.: Princeton University Press, 1984), p. 35.

MATERIAL CULTURE

Writing Japanese

When the Japanese first learned to read and write, they did so in Chinese, the only writing system available to them. Chinese is a tonal, monosyllabic language. Japanese is polysyllabic with a dissimilar grammatical structure. Fortunately for the Japanese, the Chinese had already created a system for reproducing the sound of foreign words, primarily Buddhist terms, by using characters for their phonetic value alone. The author of *Kojiki* adopted this method for the names of places, gods, and people. The editor of the *Man'yōshū* also used characters for their phonetic value—twenty-nine of them for the sound *shi* alone. Thanks to the regularity of the poetic meter, it is usually clear when the editor expected characters to be sounded using their Japanese pronunciation—*uma* (horse) instead of *ma* for 馬, for example.

The introduction of calligraphy spurred the development of the Japanese syllabary. The so-called grass style brought from China by Kūkai became a favorite of poets. By the second half of the ninth century, it led writers to streamline commonly used characters, and by the eleventh century these streamlined characters were being used for their sound alone, although each syllable could be written in a number of ways. Called *kana* (borrowed names), the syllables continue to be used for grammatical markers and to soften the appearance of a text by writing out what might also be expressed in visually dense Chinese characters.

Two forms of the syllabary appeared. *Katakana,* angular *kana,* developed from pieces of characters. It was used to transcribe prayers and indicate the Japanese reading of Chinese texts. *Hiragana* has a smooth, round look. Known also as the woman's hand, it was

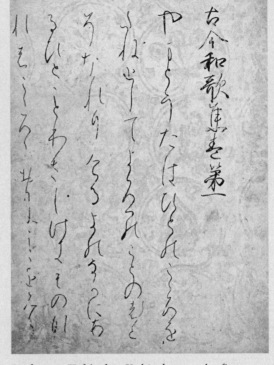

Preface to Kokinshū. *Kokinshū* was the first poetry anthology commissioned by the monarch in 905. Except for the title, the text is written in the cursive syllabary with calligraphy by Ki no Tsurayuki. *(Tokyo National Museum/ DNPArchives.com)*

used for poetry, essays, novels, and diaries. To show off the elegance of their hand, men and women linked individual *kana* in a cursive style that flowed down the page. The aim was to combine calligraphy, text, and paper into a harmonious and attractive whole.

and enhance the pathos of having lost a child while away. Other men wrote anonymously in Japanese, compiling a history, *Ōkagami* (Great Mirror), to supplement and correct Akazome's portrait of Michinaga; the first military tales; a poetic tale titled *Tale of Ise;* and miscellanies of anecdotes and observations. Along with women, they also produced folding screens, wall panels, and handscrolls in what is known as *Yamato-e,* Japanese art. (See Color Plate 1.)

Men such as Ki no Tsurayuki wrote in both Japanese and Chinese, but until recently, modern scholars of Japan's national literature have slighted Chinese works and the activities they portrayed. *Tale of Genji* shows men with women or performing music, dance, and kickball at which women were spectators. But courtiers had another life apart from women. They practiced the martial arts of archery, hawking, and horseback riding. They compiled anthologies of Chinese poetry, copied examinations held in Chinese, made vows to the Buddha in Chinese, and wrote edicts, wills, petitions, and litigation settlements in Chinese. Michinaga's diary records his activities to serve as precedents for his descendants. Like other male officials, he spent three-fourths of his time performing the annual cycle of ceremonial observances designed to arouse respect in subordinates and commoners while influencing supernatural powers to work on the court's behalf. He also fulfilled the duties associated with his position in the bureaucracy. Both ceremony and administration required knowledge of Chinese, from which women were excluded by virtue of their sex. In contrast to prehistoric rites and rituals in which men and women participated together, the Heian court differentiated between a man's world and a woman's. Because men could cross back and forth whereas women could not, gender asymmetry characterized social relations and language.

For women from the middle to lower ranks of the aristocracy, an education in the arts and letters helped them advance at court without ensuring their future. Despite having written great works of literature, Sei Shonagon, Murasaki Shikibu, and Akazome Emon ended their lives in obscurity and probable poverty. Female attendants thronged the court and the mansions of the Fujiwara. When their patron died, they might, if they were lucky, be given a small stipend and paid to recite Buddhist prayers for their master or mistress's salvation. Otherwise, lacking bequests from parents, they might join a group of mendicant nuns.

In the tenth century, female entertainers called players (*asobi*), who lived outside the court but made themselves available for casual relationships, posed a new threat to court women's monopoly over the male courtiers' attentions. They specialized in amusing travelers at river ports and provided song and dance entertainment at banquets. A few *asobi* came from declining aristocratic families and possessed as much education and refinement as any court lady. Some became the consorts of courtiers or even monarchs. The gifts of rice and cloth they received for sexual favors differed only in scale from those received by women who enjoyed longer liaisons with a man, suggesting a continuum of male-female relationships from lifelong to a single evening. In the eleventh century, *asobi* who marketed their skills as entertainers and sex partners had become well established. By the twelfth, *asobi* had been joined by *shirabyōshi* (Masters of the White Clappers) who sang popular songs, danced in male clothing, and brandished swords. They too attracted the patronage of high officials and a retired monarch.

Buddhism and the Fujiwara

During the degenerate last days of the Buddhist law (*mappō*) said to begin in 1052, people had fallen so far from the true teachings of the Buddha that only reliance on the power of the Other could save them from hell. According to the Mahayana tradition, the merciful and compassionate Amida had vowed to take every person who believed in him to the Pure Land of the Western Paradise at death. There they would become buddhas and continue to enjoy their accustomed luxuries in a spiritual realm. Michinaga built an Amida Hall in 1020. He died clutching a silk cord attached to nine statues of Amida who were to pull him to the Pure Land. In 1053 the Fujiwara regent built a graceful building called the *Hōōdō* (Phoenix Hall) at his retirement villa of Byōdōin for the worship of Amida. At this and the other ninety-five Amida halls built before 1192, monks dressed as the Buddha and wearing golden masks cere-moniously welcomed high-ranking patrons to Amida's paradise.

The Amida cult spread widely in the tenth to eleventh centuries. Scriptures describing the Pure Land in the Western Paradise had entered Japan during the Nara period, and monks on Mount Hiei had introduced the practice of chanting Amida's name in the ninth century. By 970, monks who had once spent twelve years studying the entire corpus of Tendai teachings spent ninety days in meditation during which they concentrated their thoughts on Amida, invoked his name, and circumambulated his statue. Holy men (*hijiri*) who shunned monas-teries brought the promise of salvation through faith in Amida to the common people along with simple esoteric rites and devotion to the *Lotus Sutra* in one eclectic package. Kūya (903–972) spent his youth in the mountains, where he practiced spiritual exercises to eradi-cate bodily desires. He ordained himself and then walked all over Japan chanting the name of Amida with sutras and holy images carried on his back. He reached out to people through good works—building roads, burying corpses, and digging wells—because he believed that Buddhism had to be made available to everyone in terms they could understand. His message and that of other *hijiri* appealed to people who had to break the Buddhist precepts against the taking of life, in particular warriors, farmers, hunters, and fishermen.

Buddhist eclecticism coexisted with other teachings and beliefs. Aristocrats chanted Bud-dha's name, invoked the gods, and followed Daoist teachings regarding auspicious days, directions, and omens. Brushing teeth, washing hands, combing hair, and cutting fingernails and toenails had a ritual dimension that tied them to the worship of gods and Buddhas and protected the doer from malignant forces. Some doctrines preached that deity and Buddha existed as one body, others that deities manifested the essence of the Buddha. In the tenth century, a doctrine developed that whereas the Buddhas truly existed, deities did not; what appeared to be a

deity was in reality the manifestation of a Bud-dha in deity form. This combination of Bud-dhism and native belief infused the edifying and didactic tales told to commoners, who learned that personal responsibility for their actions had to take into account the desires of the gods and the compassion of the Buddha. The search for salvation and help in coping with the tribula-tions of disease and famine demanded pilgrim-ages to numerous temples and shrines in the hope that one might prove efficacious.

Men enjoyed a more diverse range of religious practices than did women. The Enryakuji monastery and the rituals it performed on behalf of the court were closed to women. Monks ordained men; they also ordained women and supervised the nunneries to ensure that nuns obeyed the precepts. Being prone to sin and to arousing sinful thoughts in men, women suffered greater obstacles and hin-drances to achieving Buddhahood. In *The Three Jewels* compiled in 984 for the edification of Princess Sonshi (?–985), the scholar-bureaucrat who was its author set forth the teachings that promised to help her overcome these obstacles and described services held on Mount Hiei that she would never be allowed to see. (See **Docu-ments:** *Sanbōe* (**The Three Jewels**).)

RULE BY RETIRED MONARCHS

The last days of the Buddhist law coincided with political turmoil. In 1068 political and marital miscalculations on the part of the Fujiwara regent led to the enthronement of a ruler, Go-Sanjō, whose mother was not Fujiwara and who was already a mature adult. His chief advisers came from the Murakami Genji (the character for Gen can also be read as Minamoto) line of royal scions, and his youngest sons were born to Minamoto mothers. His son, Shirakawa, also exercised considerable authority by manipulat-ing personnel practices in the bureaucracy to promote his supporters. Officials entrusted with provincial administration and tax collection on behalf of provincial governors paid Shirakawa

Heiji War. In the Heiji War of 1159, mounted warriors armed with bows and arrows attacked the retired monarch's residence and set it on fire. *(Museum of Fine Arts, Boston. Fenollosa-Weld Collection, 11.4000)*

enormous kickbacks. Boys in their teens received appointment in provincial offices, and three or four members of one family served simultaneously. None actually ventured to the provinces; they too deputized tax collection. In 1086 Shirakawa abdicated in favor of his son and became the dominant power at court. This initiated the rule by retired monarchs that added another institutional layer to the system already developed under the regime of codes and manipulated by the Fujiwara.

The retired monarchs had even more trouble than the Fujiwara in dealing with lawlessness. For years the local magnate Taira no Tadatsune refused to pay taxes and attacked provincial offices in eastern Japan. When the court delegated a cousin and rival to subdue him, both sides engaged in scorched-earth tactics that left less than 1 percent of the arable land in Tadatsune's home province under cultivation. His revolt of 1031 preceded three major conflicts between 1051 and 1135: two wars in the northeast and piracy on the Inland Sea. In 1051, the

court appointed Minamoto no Yoriyoshi to tackle the Abe family of Mutsu, tax evaders and chiefs of the Emishi. It took Yoriyoshi twelve years to subdue the Abe. The next war, from 1083 to 1087, erupted when Yoriyoshi's son got drawn into an inheritance dispute involving his erstwhile allies, the Kiyowara family of Mutsu; also Emishi. Closer to Heian-kyō on the Inland Sea, provincial soldiers sent after pirates were often pirates themselves. In 1129 and again in 1135, the court dispatched Taira no Tadamori to suppress them. Royal scions figured prominently in all of these incidents, designated either law breakers or court-appointed commanders, and sometimes both. The court also had to deal with obstreperous monks who wielded sacred symbols to gain political demands. Warrior monks from Tōdaiji launched the first violent confrontation when they marched on Heian-kyō in 949. The Fujiwara temple of Kōfukuji repeatedly terrorized the Fujiwara by dispatching monks armed with branches from the sacred sakaki tree prepared by the Kasuga shrine under

DOCUMENTS

Sanbōe (The Three Jewels)

Sponsored by Princess Sonshi and written by Minamoto Tamenori, this was the first Buddhist instruction book to be written in Japan. The first volume explains the essential nature of the Buddha, the second contains biographies of Buddhist monks, and the third describes the monthly round of Buddhist services. The selection here illustrates the wondrous power of the Buddha and Buddhist teachings through stories about ordinary people.

Preface to the Second Volume: The Teachings

Behold, the Buddha's teachings have spread to the east and have come to rest here in our land where they now flourish! Many sages have appeared here and left their marks, and our sovereigns have continuously fostered the spread of Buddhism. . . . The sound of the Law is as efficacious as a "poison drum": even if you hear it just once, your enemy—ignorance—will be destroyed immediately. The names of the sutras are just like medicinal trees: you have only to utter them for the illness—the cycle of birth, death, and rebirth—to be cured. If, in one day, three times as many people as all the sand in the Ganges were to sacrifice themselves, they would not even begin to repay our debt for a single verse in the Buddha's teachings.

A Woman of Yamato Province

There was a woman who lived in the village of Yamamura in Sōkami District in Yamato Province. Her name is unknown. This woman had a daughter who married and had two children. Her husband was appointed governor of another province. He took his wife and children with him and had been living in that province for two years when his wife's mother, back home in their native village, had an inauspicious dream about her daughter. When she awoke, she was full of dread and grief. She wanted to sponsor readings of the sutras, but she was poor and had no property. She took off her own clothes and washed and purified them and gave them as a fee for the readings.

Her daughter lived in the governor's mansion with her husband. Her two children, who had been playing out in the courtyard, called inside to her: "There are seven monks on our roof, chanting sutras! Come out quickly and see!" Indeed, when she listened for sounds from the roof, she could hear voices chanting, just like a crowd of droning bees. Incredulous, she went out into the yard to have a look. In the next instant, the house collapsed. Just as suddenly, the seven monks had disappeared. In fright and alarm, she thought to herself, "Heaven has come to my aid and kept me from being crushed to death beneath the falling house!"

Later her mother sent a courier who reported the inauspicious dream and how she had sponsored the sutra readings. Hearing this, her daughter's reverence for the Three Jewels [the Buddha, his teachings, and the clergy] was many times increased.

its control. The monks from Mount Hiei expressed grievances by carrying portable shrines through the streets of Heian-kyō. It was popularly believed that any damage done to the shrines or to the monks who carried them would incur the wrath of the gods. An ongoing dispute between rival Tendai sects at Enryakuji and nearby Onjōji that began in 980 erupted into violence in 1039 when, furious at an ecclesiastical appointment that favored Onjōji, the

Thus it was known: the power generated by the chanting of the sutras brought her the protection of the Three Jewels.

A Miner of Mimasaka Province

In Agata District in Mimasaka Province there was a mine from which the government took ore. In the reign of Empress Kōken [749–758] the governor of the province ordered ten men to go up to the mine and bring out some of the ore. While they were inside, the entrance suddenly crumbled and collapsed. The men were frightened, and they scrambled out. Nine of them managed to escape, but just as the tenth and last man was about to come out, the entrance caved in and was completely closed.

The governor of the province was terribly upset, and the man's wife and children grieved. Images of the Buddha were painted, sutras were copied, and a forty-nine-day period of memorial rites was observed.

The man inside the mine made a vow: "Long ago I planned to offer a copy of the *Lotus Sutra,* but I have not copied or presented it. If am saved, I swear that I will complete the project without delay."

Just then a crack about as wide as his finger opened between the rocks, and a tiny beam of sunlight shone through. A monk appeared and passed through the crack, gave him some food and said, "This was given to me by your wife and children. I have come to you because you are suffering." Then he disappeared through the crack.

Scarcely a moment after his departure, a crack opened immediately over the miner's head, through which he could see the sky. This opening was more than three feet wide and about five feet long.

Just then, thirty villagers had come to the mountain to cut vines. They happened to pass close to this opening. The man inside heard them draw near and shouted "Help!" The villagers heard him, though his voice seemed no louder than a mosquito's buzz. But the sound made them curious, so they tied a vine to a rock and lowered the end down through the opening, and the man inside pulled on it. Then they knew there was a man inside, so they tied vines together and made a basket, and they twisted more vines together to make a rope and lowered them through the opening. The man inside got into the basket, and the men above pulled him out.

They took him to his parents' house, and when his family saw him, there was no limit to their joy. The governor of the province was amazed, and when he made inquiry, the miner told him all about it. The miner, full of respect and awe, gathered together all the faithful of the province, and following his lead, they all contributed to the preparation of a copy of the *Lotus Sutra* and a grand offertory service.

He survived that which is difficult to survive: This was made possible through the power of his faith in the *Lotus Sutra.*

Source: Edward Kamens, *The Three Jewels: A Study and Translation of Minamoto Tamenori's Sanbōe* (Ann Arbor: Center for Japanese Studies, University of Michigan, 1988), pp. 166–167, 220, 232–233, modified.

Enryakuji monks set the regent's residence on fire. In 1075 they fought Onjōji's request for an ordination platform. In 1081 they burned the Onjōji temple complex, an act repeated in 1121, 1140, and 1163. These incidents and many others marked the militarization of the clergy. While abbots and their disciples continued to accept the precepts that forbade monks to carry weapons or take life, they allowed low-ranking and minimally educated monks to fight for them and summoned soldiers from temple estates to attack their enemies.

THE ESTATE SYSTEM

A backdrop to the wars and political turmoil of the eleventh century was a set of decrees by the monarch Go-Sanjō to regulate tax-exempt estates (*shōen*). Starting in 743 the court had decreed that temples and aristocrats who sponsored land reclamation projects would be allowed to hold the land in perpetuity, albeit subject to taxation. All other land belonged to the state. In this agrarian society, officials and holders of court rank received salaries in the form of land assignments that generated income. The same was provided for temple upkeep. In theory these assignments changed when rank or office changed, but as offices became hereditary, land assignments tended to be seen not as the temporary and revocable grant of state land but as constituting a type of ownership. The labor force came largely from cultivators working state lands who rented the land grants on an annual basis. Occasionally influential aristocrats and temples were able to get tax immunities for their land assignments that turned them into estates. What changed with Go-Sanjō's decree of 1068 and an earlier decree in 1045 was the recognition of a distinction between tax-exempt estates and government land (*kokugaryō*, literally, provincial land) that resulted in making the ownership hierarchy of estates more complicated and estates more permanent. Go-Sanjō tried to restrict the growth of estates by voiding estates created after an earlier decree of 1045 and threatening to confiscate those created before if they were improperly documented. The bureau he set up for this purpose certified each proprietor's claims to income and gave him or her de facto legitimacy. Confiscated estates became not government land but monarchical land, its revenues destined for use by Go-Sanjō and his family. Go-Sanjō took this step because in the late tenth and early eleventh centuries, drought, armed conflict, and epidemics of killer diseases left too few cultivators to work the land and pay taxes. To bring land back into production, he gave institutions and individuals with political power incentive to sponsor land reclamation projects by permitting them to receive a guaranteed income from tax-exempt estates.

Although tax-exempt estates placed limits on the state's ability to tax and control landholdings, they did not replace government lands. Approximately 50 to 60 percent of the land remained subject to taxation by the state. This state land included ports, transportation routes on land and sea, and agricultural plots. Provincial governors or their deputies collected taxes on it, kept a portion for themselves and their staffs, and sent the rest to Heian-kyō.

Tax-exempt estates had political, social, and economic functions. In place of a unified bureaucratic framework, multiple quasi-independent centers of power—temples, high-ranking aristocrats, the retired monarchs, and the monarch—had the authority to levy taxes, conduct censuses, and police the inhabitants on their estates. Local magnates who had amassed extensive taxed holdings through clearance, purchase, or extortion in the tenth century petitioned the court for tax immunity through an aristocratic sponsor, who became the formal proprietor and received a share of the produce. That aristocrat in turn sought protection from temples or higher-ranking families. The local magnate remained in charge of the estate as its manager. The process of commendation from lower to higher levels increased the number and size of estates and complicated the levels of proprietorship without increasing the amount of land under cultivation. Each estate encompassed a broad, though not necessarily contiguous, territory divided into a welter of smallholdings of cultivated wet and dry fields, fallow fields, mountains, forests, swamps, huts for the cultivators, and a residence-office block for the manager. The offices (*shiki*) for everyone from titled cultivators to resident manager and his guards to the urban-based legal proprietor and protector all came with rights to income in recompense for fulfilling their documented responsibilities toward the estate. This income included food, clothing, and items of daily use. By the late Heian period, *shiki* became less associated with the duties of office than with income from and authority over estate residents.

SUMMARY

The last hundred years of the Heian period closely resemble the century that followed. Warrior monks, pirates, and confrontations in the northeast were the harbingers of military conflict that would bring warriors to new prominence. Political and factional strife at court took an increasingly militarized hue as aristocrats, monarchs, and retired monarchs called on warriors in the provinces to come to their aid or saw court nobles take to the profession of arms. The leaders of warrior bands, some of whom were royal scions, competed for the domination, not the elimination, of the court. Infected by the esoteric teachings that Kūkai and Saichō had brought back from China, the court performed ever more elaborate rituals that suffocated the monarch as a political player while individuals both high and low sought salvation in the teachings of the *Lotus Sutra* or faith in Amida. The dual system of estate and provincial lands accommodated military, ecclesiastical, and aristocratic demands for income and power. These three power blocs were to dominate Japanese history for centuries to come.

SUGGESTED READING

The general readings listed at the end of Chapter 1 also apply to this period. Two collections of essays that span the years up to the twentieth century are H. Tonomura, A. Walthall, and H. Wakita, eds., *Women and Class in Japanese History* (1999), and B. Ruch, *Engendering Faith: Women and Buddhism in Premodern Japan* (2002).

Few English-language monographs deal with the Heian period. See I. Morris, *The World of the Shining Prince* (1964); G. C. Hurst, III, *Insei: Abdicated Sovereigns in the Politics of Late Heian Japan, 1086–1185* (1976); and K. Friday, *Hired Swords: The Rise of Private Warrior Power in Early Japan* (1992). See also C. J. Kiley, "Estate and Property in the Late Heian Period," in *Medieval Japan: Essays in Institutional History,* ed. J. W. Hall and J. P. Mass (1974).

For Buddhism, see R. Abe, *The Weaving of Mantra: Kūkai and the Construction of Esoteric Buddhist Discourse* (1999). For entertainers, see J. R. Goodwin, "Shadows of Transgression: Heian and Kamakura Constructions of Prostitution," *Monumenta Nipponica* 55, no. 3 (2000). For literature, see works mentioned in the text and footnotes. A good recent book on art is M. H. Yiengpruksawan, *Hiraizumi: Buddhist Art and Regional Politics in Twelfth-Century Japan* (1998).

Kamakura Japan (1180–1333)

The Kamakura period takes its name from the military government established in the seacoast town by that name. (See Map 3.1.) Located a week's journey northeast of Kyoto and tucked into the mountains of the Miura Peninsula, Kamakura exhibited none of the spacious grandeur of the capital. Instead it provided housing, offices, and places of worship for a military regime. The task of awing visitors was delegated to the colossal statue of Amida and the Tsurugaoka Hachiman shrine to the god of war, tutelary deity of the Minamoto. The Kamakura regime sought not to displace Kyoto but to keep the peace and dispense justice while the royal court continued to perform essential rituals and ceremonies.

During the Kamakura period, new forms of literature and religion began to supplement the courtly tradition. By the middle of the thirteenth century, improved agricultural technologies had overcome the stagnation of the previous centuries. Economic growth made the practice of partible inheritance feasible until the defense against the Mongol invasions of 1274 and 1281 exposed fault lines in warrior society. When they fissured some fifty years later, they brought down the regime.

Where did samurai come from and what was the nature of the relationship between the Kyoto court and the military regime? What kind of roles did women play in samurai families and how did Buddhism enhance its appeal?

RISE OF THE WARRIOR

The samurai plays such a central role in Japanese history from the twelfth to the nineteenth centuries that he appears almost timeless. Where he came from is a matter of debate. His connections with

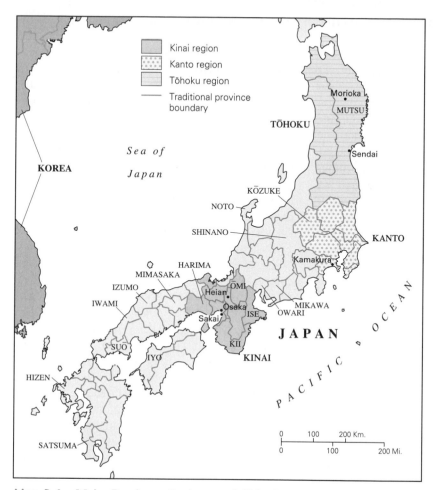

Map 3.1   Major Provinces, Regions, and Cities in Japan

monarchy and court, and what it meant to be a samurai, changed over time. Historians once thought that the aristocracy reneged its responsibility for maintaining peace early in the Heian period when it stopped executing criminals, allowed the conscript army to deteriorate, and permitted provincial governors to hire deputies rather than forsake the capital. By the tenth century, the countryside had fallen into disorder. Men in the provinces active in land reclamation projects armed themselves in local disputes and turned to warfare to protect their interests. A substantial warrior class arose, and in the twelfth century it turned on an effete and ineffectual monarchy.

A number of historians today argue that the monarchy was a dynamic success, functional at least to the beginning of the fourteenth century and capable of manipulating the samurai for its own ends. According to one interpretation, the monarchy deliberately encouraged new forms of military organization after the killer epidemic of smallpox or a similar disease in 733–737. Rather than support a large, ill-trained army, it hired professional mercenaries for police work and military protection.[1] Another interpretation

1. See Karl F. Friday, *Hired Swords: The Rise of Private Warrior Power in Early Japan* (Stanford, Calif.: Stanford University Press, 1992).

is more evolutionary: it claims that conscript armies never completely replaced Yayoi period fighters (300 B.C.E.–300 C.E.) and military men of later times were descendants of these professional warriors. Under the regime of codes, they found a niche in offices at provincial headquarters.[2] By retaining the right to sanction military force, even when it could not control how or when it would be used, the monarchy continued to play a crucial role in legitimizing its use down to the end of World War II. The monarchy also retained the privilege of granting rank and office.

A third argument emphasizes the distinction in culture and values between aristocrats and warriors. Warriors originated as hunters in eastern Japan and seamen along the Inland Sea whose occupations and values contrasted with cultivators, who abhorred killing. Rather than initiate land reclamation, they appropriated fields opened by others through forged documentation or force. Instead of releasing captured animals in Buddhist rites that sought merit through freeing sentient beings, they hunted them for the meat, for recreation, and to test their martial skills. In eastern Japan they raised horses and practiced shamanism. They dressed in iron armor and animal skins rather than silk, and many were illiterate. In the eyes of the Kyoto aristocrats, they were rustic boors, hardly more civilized than the Emishi they were called to fight.[3]

The verb *samurau* means to serve; the first samurai were warriors who held the sixth court rank along with scholars, scribes, and artisans. Other terms for fighting men did not carry the connotation of service to the court. By acquiring court rank and offices, such as guard at the left gate, samurai distinguished themselves from commoners. Warriors either sought rank themselves or accepted the leadership of someone who did. When royal scions or Fujiwara descendants moved to the provinces in search of careers that eluded them at court, their qualifications for rank based on their distinguished lineage helped them attract followers. In political terms, the need to have success at arms legitimized by court approbation, rank, and title always limited warrior autonomy.

Samurai fought with bow and arrows on horseback. Their preferred tactic was to catch the enemy off guard, often in night attacks. They violated promises and truces if that would gain them an advantage. Honor lay in winning. Being of lowly rank, samurai felt none of the compassion a superior exhibits toward inferiors. They did not hesitate to burn villages and kill the inhabitants. The fighting season lasted from the fall harvest to the spring planting, and men stayed with the army only so long as they received rewards. They fought for personal glory and social advancement. There was no point in engaging the enemy if the commander was not watching or in risking one's life against a lowly opponent. Samurai sanctioned by the court engaged not in conquest but in police actions. The goal was to eliminate rivals, not seize territory.

PRELUDE TO KAMAKURA RULE

Competition between and within the Taira and Minamoto lineages epitomized political conflicts of the twelfth century. Royal scions with followers in provincial governors' offices used their military credentials to gain access to power holders at the center. The Minamoto became the retired monarch's clients by serving as the leader of his personal bodyguard, but rival claimants to this position fought each other so viciously in 1106 that they left an opening for Taira no Tadamori, victor against Inland Sea pirates, to replace them. Access to the throne enabled Tadamori to obtain lucrative positions in the

---

2. See Wayne W. Farris, *Heavenly Warriors: The Evolution of Japan's Military, 500–1300* (Cambridge, Mass.: Harvard University Press, 1992).

3. See Eiko Ikegami, *The Taming of the Samurai: Honorific Individualism and the Making of Modern Japan* (Cambridge, Mass.: Harvard University Press, 1995).

provincial governors' offices in western Japan and to promote Taira interests at court. His son Kiyomori was to take the Taira to such preeminence that he rivaled the Fujiwara.

In the middle of the twelfth century, factional disputes in the Heian court merged with warfare, pitting family members against each other in the countryside. The death of the retired monarch in 1156 turned his sons against each other. The retired head of the Fujiwara house wanted his second son to succeed him as chieftain and regent, to the dismay of his first son, who already held these positions. The Minamoto too were divided between father and son. Only Taira no Kiyomori led a unified house. When rival claimants to the throne and the Fujiwara headship called on samurai to aid their cause, Kiyomori and the Minamoto obliged in the Hōgen Incident of 1156. Marked by patricide and fratricide, it brought warfare to the streets of Kyoto for the first time. Kiyomori won and received the fourth rank under the new ruler, Go-Shirakawa. In the 1159 Heiji Incident provoked by renewed conflict within the Fujiwara house, Kiyomori eliminated his chief Minamoto rivals.

Kiyomori's rise from obscure branch of the Taira family to grandfather of ruler followed by the Taira's rapid collapse after his death is the stuff of legend. Kiyomori intended to use his dominance in military affairs to replace the Fujiwara as the monarch's controller. In 1167 he became prime minister and the proud possessor of the first rank, an unprecedented achievement for a samurai. One daughter bore the monarch Antoku. The others married Fujiwara. Kiyomori's kinsmen monopolized the bureaucracy, holding governorships for over thirty provinces, managing over five hundred tax-exempt estates, and amassing a fortune in trade with Koryŏ Korea and Song China. Even before Kiyomori's death, resentment at his usurpation of aristocratic privilege had brought his henchmen under attack.

In 1180, one of Go-Shirakawa's sons issued a proclamation ordering the samurai to punish Kiyomori. Although the hapless prince was immediately forced to commit suicide, this edict provided the justification for samurai, and the warrior-monks of Kōfukuji, to initiate a five-year struggle celebrated in legend as the Genpei War (1180–1185). Minamoto no Yoritomo amassed an army in the Kanto region of eastern Japan and proclaimed himself Minamoto chieftain at a shrine to Hachiman. Other aspiring Minamoto chieftains also revolted against the Taira. Following Kiyomori's death in 1181, the Taira still held the Kinai region around Kyoto and western Japan, but Minamoto forces dominated the Japan Sea coast and the east. Yoritomo's cousin and rival chased the Taira out of Kyoto and installed himself as what the court saw as the boorish leader of a band of hooligans. Go-Shirakawa appealed to Yoritomo for help. Yoritomo dispatched his brothers Noriyori and Yoshitsune to fight under Go-Shirakawa's banner while he stayed in the Kanto to consolidate his control.

Decisive battles in the Genpei War were few; most conflict erupted between close kin in skirmishes that degenerated into endemic lawlessness. Weakened by years of drought in western Japan, the Taira forces melted away. When the first Minamoto forces ventured too far west and remained too long, they too ran out of supplies. Yoshitsune, by contrast, proved to be a brilliant tactician. He quickly defeated rival Minamoto troops and immediately marched west against the Taira who had reassembled around the child monarch Antoku. Yoshitsune's string of naval and land victories against the Taira climaxed at Dannoura at the lower end of the Inland Sea in 1185. The Taira chieftains were annihilated, and Antoku's nurse threw herself into the sea with the child clasped in her arms.

MILITARY GOVERNMENT AT KAMAKURA

While Yoshitsune was fighting battles, Yoritomo was putting together a power base in the east. In

Minamoto Yoritomo. This wooden sculpture of Minamoto Yoritomo depicts the warrior in the robes and hat of a court noble. Realistic portraits and sculptures of Buddhist deities characterize art of the Kamakura Age. *(Tokyo National Museum/DNPArchives.com)*

1180 he summoned housemen and supporters to his residence to witness his claim to jurisdiction over the east as lord of Kamakura by virtue of his distinguished lineage and the call to arms he had received from the now-deceased prince. Each then signed his name to an oath of allegiance under the scrutiny of the head of Yoritomo's Bureau of Samurai. In return, Yoritomo promised to protect each claim to land and office. This oath began the process of differentiating the samurai as a self-conscious class. The estates and offices confiscated from men who might be expected to oppose Yoritomo, in particular the provincial governors' deputies and Taira supporters, were used to reward achievements on Yoritomo's behalf. Although Yoritomo usurped the monarchy's authority to confirm landholdings and office, he did so only

in terms of military personnel. Court officials and temples that had not sided with the Taira retained the rights to income they already enjoyed.

Yoritomo's nascent regime gained new legitimacy in the autumn of 1183. Years of poor harvests, a virtual blockade between eastern and western Japan, and countless refusals to fulfill financial obligations had reduced the revenue owed the government, aristocrats, and temples by provincial headquarters and private estates. After negotiation, Go-Shirakawa bestowed the fifth court rank on Yoritomo, and Yoritomo guaranteed the flow of income from eastern Japan. This official recognition of Yoritomo's de facto jurisdiction in the east proved the springboard for him to assert it across the country, but always as a delegate of the monarchy.

Once Yoritomo received formal recognition of his control over eastern Japan, he exercised it in ways that amassed power to himself while benefiting Go-Shirakawa and the aristocracy. He intervened in land disputes, suppressed outlawry, and issued orders for payments to be made to Kyoto all across Japan, not just in the east. Several weeks after Yoshitsune's first major victory against the Taira in 1184, Yoritomo informed Go-Shirakawa that he was now the emergency protector for the entire country. He claimed the sole right to raise armies, giving him a hold over the entire warrior class. He forbade the monarchy to reward any Minamoto man without his approval. He urged it to restore virtuous rule and to be judicious in its appointments of provincial governors. To assist the operations of provincial headquarters, Yoritomo appointed military governors (*shugo*) who had the power to arrest bandits and pirates, punish traitors, and summon Minamoto housemen to serve their lord. While exercising his authority vis-à-vis the monarchy, he dispatched deputies to western Japan to identify and recruit military men to accept his rule in return for confirmation of their holdings and rewards for defeating his enemies. The monarchy retained its prestige; Yoritomo ended up with a military regime.

Once the Taira had been defeated, Yoritomo found new ways to perpetuate his claim to govern Japan. The defeat had not brought an end to disorder; across Japan, local warriors raided tax-exempt estates and interfered with the collection of taxes by provincial headquarters. To rein in lawlessness and reward his followers, Yoritomo began to appoint estate stewards (*jitō*) to replace Taira supporters on estates with the responsibility to keep the peace and continue to forward the income owed Kyoto. Just as estate personnel remained administratively distinct from provincial governors, so did *jitō* remain independent of military governors. Each *jitō* received his own rights to income (*shiki*), and these *shiki* guaranteed by Kamakura, not by Kyoto, became the means by which Yoritomo

rewarded his followers and demonstrated the necessity for his rule. In 1189 he defeated a family calling itself Fujiwara that had ruled a semi-autonomous state in northern Honshu for a century. This victory enabled him to reward a substantial number of followers with the position of estate steward and its attendant rights to income and to infiltrate his men into the provincial government. Although aristocrats and temples continued to be the protectors and proprietors of estates, the monarchy's sovereignty had been compromised. Yoritomo had taken over the policing of the entire country, and he had created a new office, the *jitō*, that under his control became the backbone for his military.

Family Politics

After the Taira defeat at Dannoura, Yoritomo's kin became his chief adversaries. By executing Yoritomo's elder brothers along with their father, Kiyomori had rid Yoritomo of some rival claimants to the Minamoto chieftaincy. As architect of the Taira's military defeat, Yoshitsune lacked only birth to qualify to head the Minamoto lineage; Yoritomo's mother was the daughter of a shrine official, whereas Yoshitsune's was a menial. When Go-Shirakawa offered Yoshitsune the position of provincial governor and Yoshitsune accepted without waiting for Yoritomo's approval, Yoritomo hounded his brother to his death. Yoritomo dispatched his uncle and his uncle's children in 1186. He had his youngest brother, Noriyori, killed despite the latter's protestations of loyalty. Having eliminated his kinsmen, nothing should have prevented his sons from succeeding him.

In the competition not to overthrow social superiors but to displace kin, a man's staunchest ally became his in-laws. Following his father's execution, Yoritomo had been placed as a hostage in the Hōjō family, followers of the Taira in eastern Japan. There he married his host's daughter, Masako. While Yoritomo was consolidating his power base, the Hōjō proved loyal supporters. His father-in-law even went to

Kyoto in 1184 to get the court's permission for Yoritomo to appoint estate stewards.

As Yoritomo's wife, Masako exercised authority in his name, but she also promoted Hōjō interests. She drove away Yoritomo's mistresses, lest their relatives replace hers. After Yoritomo died, Masako held together the coalition of housemen and allies who had pledged loyalty to him. Their first son, Yoriie, succeeded Yoritomo. In less than five years, Yoriie so preferred his wife's family that Masako and her father killed them all and forced Yoriie to abdicate. He died a few months later. The second son, Sanetomo, then became lord of Kamakura with Masako's father as regent. In 1205 Masako had her father arrested because he favored the children born of his second wife over Masako's full brother. Masako and her brother made the Hōjō not only the dominant power in Kamakura, but also the wealthiest of the Minamoto supporters. When Yoriie's son killed Sanetomo in 1219 and was then summarily executed, Yoritomo's line became extinct. Only Masako provided continuity. As her husband's representative, she adopted a courtier infant to become titular head of the Kamakura regime. When the retired monarch Go-Toba declared Masako's brother an outlaw in 1221, Masako rallied Yoritomo's supporters by presenting herself as the incarnation of his ideals. Despite occasional attempts at coups d'état by the disgruntled descendants of Yoritomo's supporters, successive generations of Hōjō regents governed the samurai through children summoned from Kyoto. Although Masako preserved her husband's legacy, she did so in ways that enriched the Hōjō.

Masako's dual roles as wife and daughter suggest that women played a crucial role in military households. Marriage remained a private matter between a man and a woman, often marked with scant or no ceremony. The Kamakura regime never insisted that marriages be registered nor did it try to prevent marriages across classes. Sanetomo married not a warrior woman but a princess. The property women received or inherited from their mothers and fathers remained theirs and continued to link them to their natal families; it went with them in marriage, left with them at divorce, and was theirs to bestow on their children. Like their brothers, daughters competed for shares in the family estate and frowned when the sibling set grew uncomfortably large. Given the ubiquity of sibling rivalry, people without heirs turned to adoption rather than enrich a brother or sister. Adoption needed no ratification by the state. When a husband died without heirs, his wife, not his siblings, arranged for his successor.

Kamakura Shogunate

The office of *sei-i-tai shōgun* meant little to Yoritomo because it designated a general with only temporary powers to raise troops and suppress barbarians. Yoritomo used it for three years following his investiture in 1192; thereafter, he preferred a title that instantiated higher court rank. Yoriie succeeded his father as lord of Kamakura in 1199; he became shogun in 1202 when his relatives discovered the advantage of an office that could be inherited and thus controlled by one of them. The Hōjō used the title of shogun for the series of figureheads for whom they acted as regents and applied it retroactively to Yoritomo to legitimize their stratagem. Historians often use the term *bakufu* to designate the military dynasties between 1180 and 1867, but it is a nineteenth-century anachronism that elides the substantial differences between regimes.

In 1221 the retired monarch Go-Toba misjudged samurai support for the Hōjō and tried to rally military men in western Japan to crush the Kamakura regime. Following his defeat and exile, the Hōjō extended their reach into western Japan. They confiscated estates belonging to Go-Toba's supporters and apportioned them to estate stewards who fought for Kamakura. They stationed two members of their family in Kyoto to oversee relations with the court and ensure that no future monarch followed Go-Toba's example. They followed the precedent set by Yoritomo in guaranteeing local land rights. All over Japan, estate managers proclaimed themselves loyal followers of Kamakura. They used this stratagem to attack proprietor land rights and appropriate the office of estate steward. As the leaders of the samurai, the Hōjō wanted to have samurai declare themselves for Kamakura. They also had to prevent the fighting that their new followers provoked to gain income. Although the Hōjō and their chief supporters became provincial governors, neither they nor the estate stewards tried to seize territory. Final authority over land rested with the monarchy, and the provincial headquarters continued to administer large portions of it. The hierarchical estate structure remained dominated by Kyoto and defended by Kamakura in a system of dual governance.

Neither Yoritomo nor the Hōjō instituted what would be considered a fully fledged government today. Yoritomo ruled through a chancellery similar to the administrative offices in provincial headquarters, aristocratic households, and temple complexes. In 1225 Masako's nephew Yasutoki established a thirteen-member council composed of the senior Hōjō and the heads of allied families. It made policy decisions and appointments and served as a court of last appeal. There was no public treasury. The thirteen councilors had their own sources of income as the stewards for numerous estates and as Kyoto-appointed officials holding court rank and office. Litigants paid court costs for the judicial system, the residents of Kamakura paid fees for city administration, Minamoto housemen provided the upkeep for the Tsurugaoka Hachiman shrine, and compensation for Yoritomo's followers came out of the revenues generated by the tax-exempt estates.

Legal disputes over land generated the most paperwork (see **Documents: The Estate Stewards in Legal Documents**). Conflict between siblings was common, and women as well as men brought suit. Newly appointed estate stewards wanted clarity in the extent of their authority over the cultivators, their relations with the staff already in place, and the collection of rents. When a steward appropriated too much income

for himself or interfered in the activities of the estate staff, the injured party in Kyoto appealed to Kamakura to restore its rights. For over 150 years, judges in Kamakura made a serious effort to maintain the status quo by adjudicating these cases more or less fairly.

The Hōjō soon realized that disciplining the stewards required clear guidelines. In 1232, Yasutoki published a new code, the *Goseibai shikimoku* (a list of rules for making judgments), the first step in the evolution of juridical procedures passed on contemporary norms. Steeped in the Chinese classics, Yasutoki believed that government had to be just in order to be legitimate. Stewards had to be held accountable for unlawful acts. A steward convicted of starting a brawl, for example, would lose his estates. Adultery and rape were to be punished by exiling the man and woman involved and confiscating their estates. Unlike previous codes based on Chinese models, this code was based on precedent: the decisions made by Yoritomo and Masako cited in the text. When no precedent fit a particular situation, the judges were to rely on reason. In its provisions dealing with inheritance rights, the code made legal what had been customary, including women's legal prerogatives. Women had the right to inherit property and the office that went with it. A woman could become the family head, and a widow could become a steward. The code protected the rights of the monarchy to its income and added legal protection to the land grants made to stewards. The steward in effect owned his or her land rights and could do what he or she liked with them: buy, sell, or divide them among his or her heirs.

Toward Intensive Agriculture and Economic Growth

As an unintended consequence of the tax-exempt estate system, farmers who held permanent title to cultivation rights as *myōshu* had an incentive to cultivate land more intensively. In Kyushu and western Japan they tried growing two crops a

DOCUMENTS

The Estate Stewards in Legal Documents

Underpinning the rise of the samurai was the office of estate steward (jitō shiki), a position central to understanding the nature of Kamakura rule. With it came rights to income that supported a martial lifestyle in return for loyal service. The documents below enumerate the estate steward's responsibilities, adjudicate disputes, recognize women's rights to hold office and receive income, and promote land reclamation. Several are the results of lawsuits over what this office entailed for the steward, his descendants, and previous estate personnel.

Ordered to Shiota Estate, Shinano Province concerning appointment to a *jitō shiki* of Koremune Tadahisa:

The aforesaid person, as *jitō* is to administer estate affairs. Regarding the annual tax and other levies, he shall perform those duties in accordance with precedent. It is commanded thus [by Yoritomo]. Wherefore, this order.

1186, 1st month, 8th day.

Ordered to the residents of paddy and upland areas in Ryūzōji village, Ozu-Higashi Gō, Hizen Province that Fujiwara Sueie shall henceforth be *jitō*.

Concerning the aforesaid place, and owing to Fujiwara Sueie's hereditary claim, an order by the government-general for the island of Kyushu authorizing him to administer it was granted. However, a local chief of Kanzaki district, Shigezane, has reportedly been obstructive. Sueie did not join the Heike rebellion and served loyally, honoring imperial authority. Shigezane plotted rebellion as a Heike partisan, in itself a great crime. Worst of all, his failure to submit formally before the Kamakura lord is evidence of a continuing sympathy for the Heike

rebels. The import of this is outrageous. Accordingly, Shigezane's disturbances are to cease permanently, and Sueie is to hold the *jitō shiki*. Regarding the stipulated taxes and annual rice levy, the orders of the proprietor are to be obeyed and duty discharged in accordance with precedence. It is commanded thus. Wherefore, this order.

1186, 8th month, 9th day.

The chancellery of the shogun's house orders to the residents of three districts—Iwamatsu, Shimo Imai, Tanaka—within Nitta estate, Kōzuke Province that in accord with the last will of the husband, Yoshikane, his widow shall forthwith be *jitō*.

The aforesaid person, in accordance with the will, is appointed to this *shiki*. As to the fixed annual tax and other services, these shall be paid in accordance with precedent. It is commanded thus. Wherefore, this order.

1215, 3rd month, 22nd day.

Concerning the estate manager *shiki* of Tarumi estate, Settsu province:

Regarding the above, the former estate manager Shigetsune had his lands confis-

year, one of rice and one of a lesser grain such as barley. Toward the end of the twelfth century, a hardier rice variety arrived from China that could be grown on previously marginal fields and proved resistant to drought and cold weather.

Cultivators expanded their acreage by using upland areas for dry fields and orchards, and they stopped allowing fields to lie fallow. To keep land in continuous production, they spread processed fertilizer—ashes, mulch, and manure. The dis-

cated because of his Heike affiliation [and bestowed on a *jitō*]. However, the palace woman Izumo-no-tsubone has stated: This estate is a land first opened by my ancestors with a estate managership that is hereditary. Given this original-holder status, we request that the *shiki* be reconferred. Since it is difficult to ignore a suit lodged by a court person, the reappointment will be made to this *shiki*. By command of the Kamakura lord it is decreed thus.
1204, 9th month, 6th day.

Ordered to the *jitō* headquarters of Fukunaga Myō in Matsuura estate in Hizen province that forthwith undeveloped areas shall be opened and taxes paid from them.

Regarding this, a petition from the *jitō* and others states: "this estate is populous, but has too few paddy and upland fields. Accordingly, new fields should be opened and taxes produced." In essence, the restoration of smoke from every house will mean prosperity for the village, and will also ensure the peace. You may open new land, as requested. During the first year of development, taxes will be waived. For the next year the rate will be one-half bushel per .294 acre of whatever the commodity being grown, with an increase of one-half bushel the following year, and ultimately a rate of one and one-half bushels. As regards the miscellaneous obligations, a similar exemption will be in force. Should the newly opened fields become a pretext for the desolation of established ones, payment quotas will conform to those of the old fields, even in newly cultivated areas. As for the stipulated regular taxes, these will be paid, without fail, into the estate warehouse. Also, the

number of workers engaged in developing the new land is to be reported each year when the proprietor's agents conduct their annual survey. In response to the petition, it is so decreed.
1229, 2nd month, 21st day.

Concerning a dispute of Ōeda village, a holding of Kashima shrine, between the Kashima priest Tomochika and Nomoto Shirō Gyōshin.

Although both plaintiff and defense have submitted many details regarding the above, it is evident that the land of this village was divided in 1237 by mutual agreement. Nevertheless, Gyōshin now argues that because the 1237 compromise was effected through negotiations with an uninformed deputy *jitō*, the land should be totally controlled by the *jitō*, with rents paid to the shrine. Relative to the original compromise document, the statute of limitations has passed, with dual possession dating from 1237; it is thus very difficult to attempt to disrupt things now. Therefore, authority will be exercised in accordance with the 1237 document. By command of the Kamakura lord, it is so decreed.
1298, 2nd month, 3rd day.

———
Source: Jeffrey P. Mass, *The Kamakura Bakufu: A Study in Documents* (Stanford, Calif.: Stanford University Press, 1976), pp. 38–39, 41, 48, 55, 101, 151 (modified).

semination and improvement in iron smelting technology to make armor and weapons also produced better plows and harrows. Pulled by draft animals, these tools allowed laborers to till more fields more thoroughly. Irrigation canals regulated the flow of water to paddy fields, and human-powered water wheels lifted water from streams to canals. The result was higher agricultural productivity that more than compensated for population growth.

Intensive agricultural practices did not spread uniformly. In the east, only the northern lowlands of the Kanto plain grew wet rice. Mulberry leaves raised on dry fields provided the fodder for silkworms. Alluvial terraces supplied pasturage for horses. The central Kanto plain sheltered deer, boars, and bandits. Areas separated by mountains from the core agricultural regions such as southern Shikoku, southwestern Kyushu, and the regions along the Japan Sea had lower populations and fewer cultivators.

Cultivators included *myōshu*, responsible for paying taxes to the state and rents to proprietors, and the *myōshu's* dependents. Although squeezed by estate managers and stewards, the *myōshu's* cultivation rights made them wealthy. The dependents ranged from slaves to serfs to small holders. The Kamakura shogunate issued bans on trade in human beings several times in the thirteenth century, but professional slave traders continued to kidnap women and children or people voluntarily sold themselves when they were destitute. A type of serf called *shojū* (those who obey) had their own parcels of land and huts for their families. They were not free in that their masters disposed of them as though they were property in wills and legal testaments. Small holders leased fields from the *myōshu* and tilled dry field plots that they had cleared from marginal land. Since these were less likely to be taxed than rice-bearing paddies, they gave their cultivator a measure of independence and a tiny income.

Although regional crop failures owing to drought or unseasonal cold continued to cause famines, demographic crises had been relegated to the past. Major contagious diseases had become endemic, mostly killing children rather than adult workers. After 1189 warfare ceased to be a problem. A population of perhaps 7 million at the beginning of the Kamakura period had grown to roughly 8.2 million by its end, more densely concentrated in western Japan than in other regions. The roads built by the state in the seventh and eighth centuries still centered on Kyoto.

Shinran. The illustrated scroll of Shinran's life portrays him expounding on his teachings as he traveled around Japan. *(Bukkoji, Kyoto/DNPArchives.com)*

In addition to aristocrats, clerics, warriors, and cultivators, there was a large unsettled population. It included entertainers, itinerant artisans and traders, traveling proselytizers, prostitutes, fishermen, pirates, hunters, bandits, and an amorphous category of outcasts deemed polluted or unclean for reasons of disease, work with dead animals, or ill fortune. Fishermen and people of the forest enjoyed longstanding ties to the court expressed in tribute of fish, game, seaweed, and wild vegetables. Between the eleventh and thirteenth centuries, they received privileges from aristocrats, temples, shrines, and retired monarchs that enabled them to travel freely and avoid taxes. Artisans who traveled in search of the raw materials and markets for their products also sought the court's protection. Female entertainers and prostitutes received licenses to travel and organized themselves into fictive kin groups under the control of influential female chiefs. Buddhist monks castigated entertainers for leading men astray and practiced same-sex relations to satisfy their sexual needs. Some didactic tales told of prostitutes who became nuns; in others they were depicted as bodhisattvas who led men to salvation. Most outcastes enjoyed the protection of religious establishments or the court. They performed police work for warriors. They ran inns where they offered hot baths to travelers. Even beggars performed a useful function because they enabled the wealthy to perform acts of charity.

Buddhism

The six Nara sects as well as the Tendai and Shingon sects dominated mainstream Buddhism and religious life during the Kamakura period, and they attracted some of the greatest minds of the age. A cult grew up around Prince Shōtoku for having propagated Buddhism. Zenkōji in the mountains of central Japan had what was reputed to be a living icon that attracted pilgrims from all walks of life, as did the bronze statue of Amida at Kamakura completed in 1252. Simplified practices and doctrines plus hope for salvation in the latter days of the Buddhist law contributed to Buddhism's mass appeal. In 1245 a group of aristocratic nuns received the precepts for novices at the Hokkeji nunnery in Nara, reviving an order that had died out in the ninth century. Mendicant nuns raised money for the shrine-temple complex at Kumano. Ceremonies that pointed to the mysteries of esoteric Buddhism spread to provincial temples; their audience contained commoners as well as nobles. Aristocrats drew on esoteric initiation rites in formulating secret traditions for the transmission of poetic styles and explained the hidden meaning of poetry collections in terms of Tantric Buddhism. Samurai modeled themselves on aristocrats in patronizing and building shrines and temples. In the history titled *Gukanshō* (*Humble Interpretations*), the Tendai priest Jien explained the court's lack of virtue and the warrior's rise to power in the context of the latter days of the Buddhist law. Temple-shrine complexes constituted one of the three power blocs, along with the Kyoto court and Kamakura regime. The relations between them were never stable and the distinctions between aristocrats, warriors, and clerics easily blurred.

Outside the mainstream appeared teacher-monks who reformulated doctrines taught at the Tendai headquarters on Mount Hiei and instituted new practices. They criticized the established temples for their superficial ceremonies and monastic decadence. They reached out to new constituents, including women, and addressed female concerns, especially the issue of whether women could be reborn after death in the Buddhist paradise called the Pure Land.

Faith in Amida was already prevalent when Hōnen and Shinran started preaching. Hōnen told crowds of listeners that Buddhism was available to all through absolute faith in the saving power of Amida. The best way to achieve faith was not through pious deeds or religious study but by reciting "praise to Amida Buddha." In 1207 Hōnen was exiled when some of his disciples overstepped the bounds of propriety in taking his message to the ladies-in-waiting at Go-Toba's court. Following his death in 1212, his disciples created the Jōdo (Pure Land) sect. Shinran took Hōnen's teachings to low-ranking warriors, the poor, and criminals. He preached that Amida had vowed to save everyone, sinners, murderers, thieves, the humble, and evil alike, even people who did not know he would save them. All that was required was faith. "At the moment that faith is established, birth in the Pure Land is also established."[4] He rejected monasticism because cutting oneself off

---

4. Quoted in Endō Hajime, "The Original Bōmori: Husband and Wife Congregations in Early Shin Buddhism," in *Engendering Faith: Women and Buddhism in Premodern Japan*, ed. B. Ruch (Ann Arbor: Center for Japanese Studies, University of Michigan, 2002), p. 513.

from the world in order to study and pray was meaningless. He married, begot children, and encouraged his disciples to do the same. He had not planned to start a new sect, but after his death in 1262, his children and disciples founded *Jōdo shinshū* (True Pure Land sect).

Hōnen and Shinran taught people to rely on Amida for salvation; Zen taught reliance on the self. Its teachers had such close ties with China and knowledge of the Chinese language that the shogunate used them as envoys to the Yuan court. Following his training on Mount Hiei, Eisai went twice to China and then settled in Kamakura, where he founded the Rinzai school that uses riddles (*kōan*) to concentrate the mind during meditation. By exposing the limits to rational thought, riddles helped achieve enlightenment. Eisai became the shogunate's master of religious ceremonies when he developed close ties with Hōjō Masako that brought the Rinzai school wealth and power. Dōgen went to China for five years, where he studied Zen in what is now popular in Japan as the Sōtō school. Upon his return, he taught that the essence of Buddha is in everyone, but it is concealed under layers of desire. To remove these layers, the practitioner has to achieve an inner awakening through sitting meditation (*zazen*). Chanting sutras, reciting the Buddha's name, were secondary. During his lifetime, Dōgen's austere search for absolute truth attracted few disciples.

Nichiren opposed all forms of Buddhism that did not center on the *Lotus Sutra*. Only it offered a sure way to salvation. He taught his followers to beat drums and chant, "Praise to the glorious teachings of the *Lotus Sutra*," because the sutra's title contained the essence of the sutra and the sutra contained the summation of Buddhist teaching. Performing the chant enabled the achievement of buddhahood in this very body or at least access to the Pure Land. Salvation came through faith, not doctrinal study or meditation. Calling on the *Lotus Sutra* could bring wealth and good luck for individuals and protection for the state. At the end of his life, when he had been exiled to Sado for having

provoked religious dissension with his intolerant views, Nichiren taught that he was the reincarnation of the bodhisattva to whom the original Buddha Sakyamuni had entrusted the *Lotus Sutra*. Buddhism had arisen in India, but it reached its ultimate moment of truth in Japan. In the name he chose for himself, the character for *nichi* represents the sun and alludes to the Japanese word for Japan, Nihon, the origin of the sun. *Ren* means lotus.

Literature and Popular Arts

Buddhist beliefs permeated Kamakura period literature and the visual arts. A section in the seventh royally commissioned poetry anthology, the *Shinkokinshū* (*New Collection of Ancient and Modern Poems*), completed in 1206, was devoted to Buddhist poetry. The court-poet-turned-priest Kamo no Chōmei wrote an account of his life as a recluse in *Hōjōki* (*An Account of My Hut*) that explored the tension between his pleasure in artistic pursuits and his desire to renounce the world to seek salvation. The realism of portrait sculptures took on meaning only in the context of Buddhist images that served as a focus for religious devotion. Picture scrolls (*emakimono*) depicted the battles that ushered in the Kamakura period and the Mongol invasions; they also brought to life the torments that await the unbeliever in hell. (See **Material Culture: The Mongol Scroll and Mongol Combat.**) The classic war tale, *Tale of the Heike*, began with an evocation of the transience of existence expressed in the tolling of a temple bell. Didactic tales recounted miraculous stories of the Buddha's power. Even the chronicle *Azuma kagami* (*Mirror of the East*), a major source of information on the day-to-day affairs of the Kamakura regime, dwells on Yoritomo's and his successors' pilgrimages to and support for temples.

War tales recounted the course of major conflicts. *Tale of Masakado* (*Shōmonki*) contained imaginative reconstructions of battles and traced Taira no Masakado's defeat in 940 to

MATERIAL CULTURE

The Mongol Scroll and Mongol Combat

In 1293 or thereabouts, the samurai Takezaki Suenaga commissioned scrolls of the Mongol invasions to commemorate his achievements. He had just succeeded in getting the Kamakura shogunate to recognize his merit in having been the first to engage the enemy in 1274. His aim in acquiring the scrolls may have been to provide a pictorial record for his descendants or to present them as an offering to the shrine of his tutelary deity in gratitude for having survived the conflict.

With a troop of five mounted men, Suenaga galloped into battle. The Mongols let fly a withering hail of arrows. Suenaga's standard-bearer fell when his horse was hit. Suenaga was hit in the left chest and left knee.

His horse too was wounded, and a Mongol arrow made a direct hit on his helmet. At this critical juncture, a troop of mounted samurai arrived to rescue him.

The Mongols sent masses of cavalry into battle. They received orders via gongs that launched attacks and drums that signaled retreats. The Mongol infantry followed the cavalry lined up behind tall shields. They used crossbows that fired heavy arrows capable of piercing armor, and the arrows were tipped with poison. Their catapults hurled cannonballs filled with gunpowder that exploded with a roar and gushed fire. Samurai picked off Mongol soldiers with their longbows.

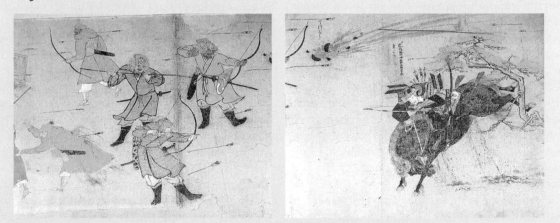

Mongol Scroll. Commissioned by Takezaki Suenaga, the Mongol Scroll shows him in the vanguard of the attack, his horse frightened by an exploding shell. On the left stand the Mongols in long coats, their faces covered with whiskers. *(Laurie Platt Winfrey, Inc.)*

arrogance. It reproduced historical documents supplemented by stories created decades after the event. Yoshitsune was a particular favorite of storytellers, from his youth in Kyoto where he challenged the Herculean warrior monk Benkei to his death in the mountains of northern Japan. Accounts of the Genpei War portrayed it as an epic struggle between the Taira and the Minamoto for control of Japan. Political intrigue and fierce battles filled these tales, as they did *Tale of the Heike.*

Tale of the Heike began as stories recited by blind storytellers to assuage the souls of the Taira who had fallen in battle. Accompanied by the lute, storytellers traveled across Japan to bring people to an understanding of the Buddha by crafting miraculous and edifying tales. Each generation of storytellers enriched the story, adding embellishments and anecdotes before it was written down in the fourteenth century. Their accounts featured Kiyomori, entertainers, guards, widows, and a host of warriors. By speaking their names, storytellers summoned the departed. By recounting their exploits, storytellers pacified the spirits of the dead and sought to save them from hell. *Heike* is permeated with examples of the relationship between humankind and unseen forces and the importance of karma in deciding one's fate.

Another category of tale is *setsuwa* (popular tales). The most famous, *Tales of Times Now Past,* compiled in the early twelfth century, contains more than a thousand short stories set in India, China, and Japan. The Japanese corpus encompasses Buddhist tales, stories about aristocratic and warrior families, and anecdotes, many humorous, about ordinary people such as artisans, criminals, unhappy wives, and abducted ladies, as well as animals and the supernatural. A later collection contains stories that trace the appearance of the supernatural in everyday life. *Kokonchomonjū* (*Stories Heard from Writers Old and New*), compiled in 1254, contains folk stories, stories about the gods, and stories illustrating the Buddha's teachings. There, Yoritomo's pilgrimage to the mountain temple of Zenkōji reveals that its central icon was alive.

War tales and popular tales brought new classes of people into literature, but they did not displace the aristocrats who continued to compile poetry collections, keep diaries, and write essays in the manner of their Heian forebears. Fujiwara no Teika set high standards for poetic diction and kept a diary of distinction. His niece wrote *Mumyōzōshi* (*Anonymous Writing*), which critiqued the classical literary tradition. In 1307 Lady Nijō wrote an autobiography that illustrates how the court continued to model its ceremonies on the past, albeit with considerable

attention to drinking and fornication. The Hōjō and their supporters at Kamakura avidly sought training in the civilizing arts. They hired teachers from Kyoto, studied poetry, and immersed themselves in Buddhist texts.

THE MONGOL INVASIONS

Under threat of Mongol invasion, Kamakura summoned the samurai to defend Japan starting in 1271 after the fall of Korea. (See **Connections: The Mongols.**) Fierce fighting in 1274 proved that the Japanese enjoyed near military parity and numerical superiority. Unable to prevail, the Mongols retreated. The samurai strengthened their fortifications before the second onslaught in 1281. Stone walls on the landing beaches hedged in the Mongol troops and ships harassed their fleet. Fighting raged for almost a month before an epidemic ravaged the tightly packed attacking forces and a typhoon sank Mongol ships. The samurai then killed the thirty thousand troops left stranded. In later centuries, the shrine-temple complexes that had prayed for supernatural intervention claimed that a divine wind (*kamikaze*) had destroyed the Mongols.

The invasions extended Kamakura's reach into Kyushu and made the shogunate a truly national government. It came at a cost. Preparations for the second invasion curtailed food production. The Hōjō made promises of rewards they could not keep and pressured temples for money. They appointed new provincial governors in the west, all of them from the Hōjō family or its allies. Many of the warriors from Kyushu who fought against the Mongols had not previously been subject to Kamakura rule. Their only recompense was confirmation of their rights to the income from estates they already held. For warriors from western Japan who joined the battle, Kamakura announced debt amnesties, a tactic it also used to placate the shrines and temples that had prayed for victory. Since warriors fought not for glory or love of country but for reward, these returns were paltry indeed.

FALL OF THE KAMAKURA REGIME

The growing sophistication of the Hōjō underscored the gulf developing between them and the majority of provincial warriors. Every aristocratic or royal child brought to Kamakura to serve as the figurehead shogun had a retinue of highly cultivated female and male attendants. Yoritomo had emphasized austerity and simplicity; his successors led lives of luxury. They were also growing more despotic. In 1293 the Hōjō regent abolished the councilor form of government. He and his successors exiled opponents, seized governorships, and had their housemen fill positions in the shogunate. In 1297 the regent announced an "edict for virtuous government" aimed at restoring land to impoverished samurai, especially the stewards who had been forced to sell or mortgage their land over the preceding twenty years. It was based on the notion that the sale of land did not mean the original owner lost all claim to it; rather, a family that had worked land for generations possessed it by inalienable right. Under this ruling, former owners retrieved ancestral land. Any satisfaction they obtained was only temporary, because it did not alleviate their poverty and made it more difficult to sell their land in the future. The former buyers were naturally disgruntled. The result of the edict was to lose friends for the regime and narrow its support base.

Partible inheritance was a major cause of the stewards' impoverishment. When every child received a portion of the patrimony, the result was an expansion in the size of the warrior class without a concomitant growth in the income at its disposal. Bequeathed an inadequate inheritance, stewards easily fell into debt and had to mortgage their rights to income. Although the patrimony could be divided, the obligation to fulfill the duties of military service to Kamakura was not divisible. Even women had to field a warrior on horseback should the need arise.

Generations had passed since Yoritomo had rewarded loyal followers by making them estate stewards. Diffused by time and space, the stewards' descendants stayed on their land save when a lawsuit called them to Kamakura. In 1285, the Hōjō regent decided that the shogunate would no longer intervene in disputes between its retainers and Kyoto aristocrats. Instead litigants had to seek redress from Kyoto, a move that heightened conflict between supporters of the two centers. This decision estranged Kamakura from its followers in the provinces. With Kamakura now reluctant to guarantee land rights, loyalty attenuated.

Challenges to the shogunate multiplied in the early fourteenth century. Stone-throwing brawls had long erupted in Kyoto on festival days, but in Kamakura in the early 1300s, they turned into deadly gang warfare. Bands of mounted bandits ravaged the provinces of central Japan, sometimes in league with estate stewards who refused to send income to protectors and proprietors. Pirates ranged as far as Korea, attacking coastal settlements, carrying off goods, and enslaving the inhabitants. The swell of disorder suggested to people both high and low that they could act with impunity.

SUMMARY

Changes during the Kamakura period heralded trends that would continue for centuries. Samurai attained new prominence in governance with the establishment of a military regime. New sects brought new practices to Buddhism. Increases in agricultural production laid the foundation for an increase in trade and manufacturing. One practice that did not carry forward was the division of family assets among all children and female economic autonomy.

SUGGESTED READING

No study of this period would be complete without the works by J. P. Mass, *Antiquity and Anachronism in Japanese History* (1992), *Lordship and Inheritance in Early Medieval Japan* (1989), *Yoritomo and the Founding of the first Bakufu: The Origins of Dual Government in Japan* (1999), and many others.

For a social and economic history of the first military regimes, see P. F. Souyri, *The World Turned Upside Down: Medieval Japanese Society* (2001). For the Mongol invasions, see T. Conlon, *In Little Need of Divine Intervention: Takezaki Suenaga's Scrolls of the Mongol Invasions of Japan* (2001).

A sampling of books on Kamakura Buddhism includes R. K. Payne, *Re-Visioning Kamakura Buddhism* (1998); B. D. Ruppert, *Jewel in the Ashes: Buddha Relics and Power in Early Medieval Japan* (2000); and J. C. Dobbins, *Jōdō Shinshu: Shin Buddhism in Medieval Japan* (1989). For the connection between literature, theater, and religion, see S. B. Klein, *Allegories of Desire: Esoteric Literary Commentaries of Medieval Japan* (2002).

The Mongols

BY THE THIRTEENTH CENTURY, CHINA and Korea had had many centuries of experience with northern nomadic pastoralists who from time to time formed wide-ranging confederations that threatened and occasionally conquered parts of their territory. To China and Korea, these neighbors may have seemed a local problem, but in fact settled societies across Eurasia had to cope with horse-riding herders skilled at warfare and raiding.

The grasslands that supported nomadic pastoralists stretched from eastern Europe to Mongolia and Manchuria. Twice before, confederations that rose in the East led to vast movement of peoples and armies across the grasslands. The rise of the Xiongnu in the East beginning in the third century B.C.E. caused rival groups to move west, indirectly precipitating the arrival of the Shakas and Kushans in Afghanistan and northern India and later the Huns in Europe. The Turks, after their heyday as a power in the East in the seventh century C.E., broke up into several rival groups, some of whom moved west into Persia and India. By the twelfth century, separate groups of Turks controlled much of Central Asia and the adjoining lands from Syria to northern India and into Chinese Turkestan, then occupied by Uighur Turks. It was not until the Mongols, however, that the military power of pastoralists created a unified empire linking most of Asia.

In Mongolia in the twelfth century, ambitious Mongols aspired not to match nomads who had migrated west but those who had stayed in the East and mastered ways to extract resources from China. In the tenth and eleventh centuries, the Khitans had accomplished this; in the twelfth century, the Jurchens had overthrown the Khitans and extended their reach even deeper into China. Both the Khitans and the Jurchens formed hybrid nomadic-urban states, with northern sections where tribesmen continued to live in the traditional way and southern sections politically controlled by the non-Chinese rulers but populated largely by Chinese. Both the Khitans and Jurchens had scripts created to record their languages, and both adopted many Chinese governing practices. They built cities in pastoral areas as centers of consumption and trade. In both cases, their elite became culturally dual, adept in Chinese ways as well as their own traditions.

Chinese, Persian, and European observers have all left descriptions of the daily life of the Mongols in the thirteenth century, which they found strikingly different from their own. Before their great conquests, the Mongols did not have cities, towns, or villages. Rather, they moved with their animals between winter and summer pastures. To make them portable, their belongings had to be kept to a minimum. Mongols lived in tents (called yurts), about 12 to 15 feet in diameter, constructed of light wooden frames covered by layers of wool felt, greased to make them waterproof. A group of families traveling together would set up their yurts in a circle open to the south and draw up their wagons in a circle around the yurts for protection. The Mongols' herds provided both meat and milk, with the milk used to make butter, cheese, and fermented alcoholic drinks. Wood was scarce, so the common fuel for the cook fires was dried animal dung or grasses. Without granaries to store food for years of famine, the Mongols' survival was threatened whenever weather or diseases of their animals endangered their food supply.

Because of the intense cold of the grasslands in the winter, Mongols needed warm clothing. Both men and women usually wore undergarments made of silk obtained from China. Over them they wore robes of fur, for the very coldest times of the year, in two layers: an inner layer with the hair on the inside and an outer layer with the hair on the outside. Hats were of felt or fur, boots of felt or leather.

Mongol women had to be able to care for the animals when the men were away hunting or fighting. They normally drove the carts and set up and dismantled the yurts. They were also the ones who milked the sheep, goats, and cows and made the butter and cheese. In addition, they made the felt, prepared the skins, and sewed the clothes. Because water was scarce, clothes were not washed with water, nor were dishes. Women, like men, had to be expert riders, and many also learned to shoot. Women participated actively in family decisions, especially as wives and mothers. *The Secret History of the Mongols,* a book written in Mongolian a few decades after Chinggis's death, portrayed his mother and wife as actively involved in family affairs and frequently making impassioned speeches on the importance of family loyalty.

Mongol men made the carts and wagons and the frames for the yurts. They also made the harnesses for the horses and oxen, the leather saddles, and the equipment needed for hunting and war, such as bows and arrows. Men also had charge of the horses, and they, rather than the women, milked the mares. Young horses were allowed to run wild until it was time to break them. Catching them took great skill in the use of a long springy pole with a noose at the end. One specialty occupation among the nomads was the blacksmith, who made stirrups, knives, and other metal tools. Another common specialist was the shaman, a religious expert able to communicate with the gods. Some groups of Mongols, especially those closer to settled communities, converted to Buddhism, Nestorian Christianity, or Manichaeism.

Kinship underlay most social relationships among the Mongols. Normally each family occupied a yurt, and groups of families camping together were usually related along the male line (brothers, uncles and nephews, and so on). More distant patrilineal relatives were recognized as members of the same clan and could call on each other for aid. People from the same clan could not marry each other, so clans had to cooperate to provide brides for each other. A woman whose husband had died would be inherited by another male in the family, such as her husband's younger brother or his son by another woman.

Tribes were groups of clans, often distantly related. Both clans and tribes had recognized chiefs who would make decisions on where to graze and when to retaliate against another tribe that had stolen animals or people. Women were sometimes abducted for brides. When tribes stole men from each other, they normally made them into slaves, and slaves were forced to do much of the heavy work. They would not necessarily remain slaves their entire life, however, as their original tribe might be able to recapture them, make an exchange for them, or their masters might free them.

Although population was sparse in the regions where the Mongols lived, conflict over resources was endemic, and each camp had to be on the alert for attacks. Defending against attack and retaliating against raids was as much a part of the Mongols' daily life as caring for their herds and trading with nearby settlements.

In the mid-twelfth century, the Mongols were just one of many tribes in the eastern grasslands, neither particularly numerous nor especially advanced. Their rise had much to do with the leadership of a single individual, the brilliant but utterly ruthless Temujin (ca. 1162–1227), later called Chinggis. Chinggis's early career was recounted in *The Secret History of the Mongols.* When Chinggis was young, the Mongol tribes were in competition with the Tatar tribes. Chinggis's father had built up a modest following and had arranged for Chinggis's future marriage to the daughter of a more powerful

Nomads' Portable Housing. This painting by a Chinese artist illustrates an event that took place in Han times, but it reflects the conditions on the grassland in Song times, when it was painted. *(The Metropolitan Museum of Art, Gift of the Dillon Fund, 1973 [1973.120.3])*

Mongol leader. When Chinggis's father was poisoned by a rival, his followers, not ready to follow a boy of twelve, drifted away, leaving Chinggis and his mother and brothers in a vulnerable position. In 1182 Chinggis himself was captured and carried to the camp of a rival in a cage. After a daring midnight escape, he led his followers to join a stronger chieftain who had once been aided by his father. With his help, Chinggis began avenging the insults he had received.

As he subdued the Tatars, Kereyids, Naimans, Merkids, and other Mongol and Turkic tribes, Chinggis built up an army of loyal followers. He mastered the art of winning allies through displays of personal courage in battle and generosity to his followers. He also proved willing to turn against former allies who proved troublesome. To those who opposed him, he could be merciless. He once asserted that nothing surpassed massacring one's enemies, seizing their horses and cattle, and ravishing their women. Sometimes Chinggis would kill all the men in a

defeated tribe to prevent any later vendettas. At other times he would take them on as soldiers in his own armies. Courage impressed him. One of his leading generals, Jebe, had first attracted his attention when he held his ground against overwhelming opposition and shot Chinggis's horse out from under him.

In 1206 at a great gathering of tribal leaders Chinggis was proclaimed the Great Khan. Chinggis decreed that Mongol, until then an unwritten language, be written down in a script used by the Uighur Turks. With this script, a record was made of Mongol laws and customs, ranging from the rules for the annual hunt to punishments of death for robbery and adultery. Another measure adopted at this assembly was a postal relay system to send messages rapidly by mounted courier.

With the tribes of Mongolia united, the energies previously devoted to infighting and vendetta were redirected to exacting tribute from the settled populations nearby, starting with the Jurchen state that extended into north China

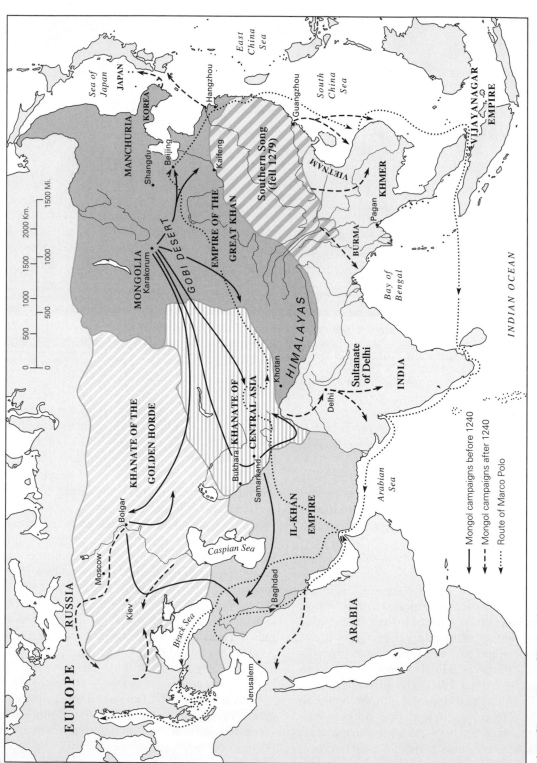

Map C3.1   **Map of Mongol Conquests**

(the Jin Dynasty). After Chinggis subjugated a city, he sent envoys to cities farther out to demand submission and threaten destruction. Those who opened their city gates and submitted without fighting could become allies and retain local power, but those who resisted faced the prospect of mass slaughter. Chinggis despised city dwellers and sometimes used them as living shields in the next battle. After the Mongol armies swept across north China in 1212–1213, ninety-odd cities lay in rubble. Beijing, captured in 1215, burned for more than a month. Not surprisingly many governors of cities and rulers of small states hastened to offer submission when the Mongol armies approached.

Chinggis preferred conquest to administration and left ruling north China to subordinates while he turned his own attention westward to Afghanistan and Persia, then in the hands of Turks (see Map C3.1). In 1218 Chinggis proposed to the Khwarazm shah of Persia that he accept Mongol overlordship and establish trade relations. The shah, to show his determination to resist, ordered the envoy and the merchants who had accompanied him killed. The next year Chinggis led an army of one hundred thousand soldiers west to retaliate. Mongol forces not only destroyed the shah's army, but pursued the shah to an island in the Caspian Sea, where he died. To complete the conquest, Chinggis sacked one Persian city after another, demolishing buildings and massacring hundreds of thousands of people. The irrigation systems that were needed for agriculture in this dry region were destroyed.

On his return from Central Asia in 1226, Chinggis turned his attention to the Tanguts who ruled the Xia state in northwest China. They had earlier accepted vassal status, but Chinggis thought they had not lived up to their agreements. During the siege of their capital, Chinggis died of illness.

Before he died, Chinggis instructed his sons not to fall out among themselves but to divide the spoils. Although Mongol tribal leaders traditionally had had to win their positions, after Chinggis died the empire was divided into four

khanates, with one of the lines of his descendants taking charge of each. Chinggis's third son, Ögödei, became great khan, and he directed the next round of invasions.

In 1237 representatives of all four lines led 150,000 Mongol, Turkic, and Persian troops into Europe. During the next five years, they gained control of Moscow and Kievan Russia and looted cities in Poland and Hungary. They were poised to attack deeper into Europe when they learned of the death of Ögödei in 1241. In order to participate in the election of a new khan, the army returned to the Mongols' newly built capital city, Karakorum.

Once Ögödei's son was certified as his successor, the Mongols turned their attention to Persia and the Middle East. When the Abbasid capital of Baghdad fell in 1258, the last Abbasid caliph was murdered and much of the population was put to the sword.

Under Chinggis's grandson Khubilai (r. 1260–1294), the Mongols completed their conquest of Korea and China. Not all campaigns succeeded, however. Perhaps because after the fall of the Song surrendered Chinese soldiers and sailors came to make up a large share of the invasion forces, the attempts to conquer Japan, Vietnam, and Java in the 1270s–1290s all failed.

Chinggis and His Descendants

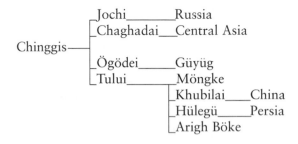

Why were the Mongols so successful against so many different types of enemies? Although their population was tiny compared to that of the large agricultural societies they conquered, their tactics, weapons, and organization all gave them advantages. Like nomadic herdsmen before them, they were superb horsemen and excellent archers. Their horses were short and stocky, almost like ponies, and able to endure long journeys and bitter cold. Even in the winter they survived by grazing, foraging beneath the snow. Their horses were extremely nimble, able to turn direction quickly, enabling the Mongols to maneuver easily and ride through infantry forces armed with swords, lances, and javelins. On military campaigns Mongol soldiers had to be able to ride for days without stopping to cook food; they would carry a supply of dried milk curd and cured meat, which could be supplemented by blood let from the neck of their horses. When time permitted, the soldiers would pause to hunt, adding to their food dogs, wolves, foxes, mice, and rats.

Marco Polo left a vivid description of the Mongol soldiers' endurance and military skill:

> They are brave in battle, almost to desperation, setting little value upon their lives, and exposing themselves without hesitation to all manner of danger. Their disposition is cruel. They are capable of supporting every kind of privation, and when there is a necessity for it, can live for a month on the milk of their mares, and upon such wild animals as they may chance to catch. The men are habituated to remain on horseback during two days and two nights, without dismounting, sleeping in that situation whilst their horses graze. No people on earth can surpass them in fortitude under difficulties, nor show greater patience under wants of every kind.[1]

The Mongols were also open to new military technologies and did not insist on fighting in their traditional ways. To attack walled cities, they learned how to make use of catapults and other engines of war. At first they used Chinese catapults, but when they learned that those used by the Turks in Afghanistan were more powerful, they quickly adopted the better model. The Mongols made use of exploding arrows and gunpowder projectiles developed by the Chi-

nese. Mongols made good use of intelligence and tried to exploit internal divisions in the countries they attacked. Thus, when attacking the Jurchens in north China, they reminded the Khitans of their bitter defeat by the Jurchens a century earlier. In Syria, they exploited the resentment of Christians against their Muslim rulers.

Because of his early experiences with intertribal feuding, Chinggis mistrusted traditional Mongol tribal loyalties, and as he fashioned a new army, he gave it a nontribal structure. Chinggis also created an elite bodyguard of ten thousand sons and brothers of commanders, which served directly under him. Chinggis allowed commanders to pass their posts to their sons, but he could remove them at will.

Since, in Mongol eyes, the purpose of warfare was to gain riches, they regularly looted the settlements they conquered, taking whatever they wanted, including the residents. Land would be granted to military commanders, nobles, and army units, to be governed and exploited as the recipients wished. Those who had worked on the land would be distributed as serfs. To bring Karakorum up to the level of the cities the Mongols conquered, they transported skilled workers there. For instance, after Bukhara and Samarkand were captured, some thirty thousand artisans were seized and transported to Mongolia. Sometimes these slaves gradually improved their status. A French goldsmith working in Budapest named Guillame Boucher was captured by the Mongols in 1242 and taken to Karakorum, where he lived for at least the next fifteen years. He gradually won favor and was put in charge of fifty workers making gold and silver vessels for the Mongol court.

In Central Asia, Persia, and Russia, the Mongols tended to merge with the Turkish nomads already there and converted to Islam. Russia in the thirteenth century was not a strongly centralized state, and the Mongols were satisfied to see Russian princes and lords continue to rule their territories as long as they paid adequate tribute. The city of Moscow became the center

---

1. *The Travels of Marco Polo, the Venetian*, ed. Manuel Komroff (New York: Boni and Liveright, 1926), p. 93.

of Mongol tribute collection and grew in importance at the expense of Kiev. In the Middle East, the Mongol Ilkhans were more active as rulers, continuing the traditions of the caliphate.

Mongol control in each of the khanates lasted about a century. In the mid-fourteenth century, the Mongol dynasty in China deteriorated into civil war, and in the 1360s the Mongols withdrew back to Mongolia. There was a similar loss of Mongol power in Persia and Central Asia. Only on the south Russian steppe was the Golden Horde able to maintain its hold for another century.

The Mongol empire did more to encourage the movement of people and goods across Eurasia than any earlier political entity. The Mongols had never looked down on merchants as the elites of many traditional states did, and they welcomed the arrival of merchants from distant lands. Even when different groups of Mongols were fighting among themselves, they usually allowed caravans to pass unharassed.

Once they had conquered a territory, the Mongols were willing to incorporate those they had conquered into their armies and governments. Chinese helped breach the walls of Baghdad in the 1250s, and Muslims operated the catapults that helped reduce Chinese cities in the 1270s. Chinese, Persians, and Arabs in the service of the Mongols were often sent far from home. Especially prominent were the Uighur Turks of Chinese Central Asia, whose familiarity with Chinese civilization and fluency in Turkish were extremely valuable in facilitating communication. Literate Uighurs provided many of the clerks and administrators running the Mongol administration.

One of the most interesting of those who served the Mongols was Rashid al-Din (ca. 1247–1318). A Jew from Persia, the son of an apothecary, Rashid al-Din converted to Islam at the age of thirty and entered the service of the Mongol khan of Persia as a physician. He rose in government service, traveling widely, and eventually became prime minister. Rashid al-Din became friends with the ambassador from

China, and together they arranged for translations of Chinese works on medicine, agronomy, and statecraft. He had ideas on economic management that he communicated to Mongol officials in Central Asia and China. Aware of the great differences between cultures, he believed that the Mongols should try to rule in accord with the moral principles of the majority in each land. On that basis, he convinced the Mongol khan of Persia to convert to Islam. Rashid al-Din undertook to explain the great variety of cultures by writing a history of the world that was much more comprehensive than any previously written. The parts on Europe were based on information he obtained from European monks. The sections on China were based on Chinese informants and perhaps Chinese Buddhist narratives. This book was richly illustrated, with depictions of Europeans based on European paintings and depictions of Chinese based on Chinese paintings, leading to the spread of artistic styles as well. (See Color Plate 2.)

The Mongols were remarkably open to religious experts from all the lands they encountered. Khubilai, for instance, welcomed Buddhist, Daoist, Islamic, and Christian clergymen to his court and gave tax exemptions to clerics of all religions. More Europeans made their way as far as Mongolia and China in the Mongol period than ever before. This was the age of the Crusades, and European popes and kings sent envoys to the Mongol court in the hope of enlisting the Mongols on their side in their long-standing conflict with the Muslim forces over the Holy Land. These and other European visitors were especially interested in finding Christians who had been cut off from the West by the spread of Islam, and in fact there were considerable numbers of Nestorian Christians in Central Asia. Those who left written records of their trips often mention meeting other Europeans in China or Mongolia. There were enough Europeans in Beijing to build a cathedral and appoint a bishop.

The most famous European visitor to the Mongol lands was Marco Polo, who was enormously impressed with Khubilai and awed by the wealth and splendor of Chinese cities. There have always been skeptics who do not believe Marco Polo's tale, and some scholars think that he may have learned about China from Persian merchants he met in the Middle East. But most of what he wrote about China tallies well with Chinese sources. The great popularity of his book in Europe contributed greatly to familiarizing Europeans with the notion of Asia as a land of riches.

The more rapid transfer of people and goods across Central Asia in the thirteenth century spread more than ideas and inventions: it also spread diseases, the most deadly of which was a plague called the Black Death in Europe (long thought to be the modern bubonic plague, though some recent scholars have argued that it more closely resembles Ebola-like viral diseases). Europe had not had an outbreak of the plague since about 700 and the Middle East since 1200. There was a pocket of active plague in the southwestern mountains of modern Yunnan province in China, the area that had been the relatively isolated Nanzhao kingdom of Thai speakers. Once the Mongols established a garrison there, plague was carried to central China, then northwestern China, and from there to Central Asia and beyond. By the time the Mongols were assaulting the city of Kaffa in the Crimea in 1346, they themselves were infected by the plague and had to withdraw. But the disease did not retreat and was spread throughout the Mediterranean by ship. The Black Death of Europe thus was initiated through breaching the isolation of a remote region in southwestern China. The confusion of the mid-fourteenth century that led to the loss of Mongol power in China, Iran, and Central Asia probably owes something to the effect of the spread of this plague and other diseases.

Traditionally, the historians of each of the countries conquered by the Mongols portrayed them as a scourge. Russian historians, for instance, saw this as a period of bondage that set Russia back and cut it off from Western Europe. Today it is more common to celebrate the genius of the Mongol military machine and treat the spread of ideas and inventions as an obvious good, probably because we see global communication as a good in our own world. There is no reason to assume, however, that every person or every society benefited equally from the improved communications and the new political institutions of the Mongol era. Merchants involved in long-distance trade prospered, but those enslaved and transported hundreds or thousands of miles from home would have seen themselves as the most pitiable of victims, not the beneficiaries of opportunities to encounter cultures different from their own.

In terms of the spread of technological and scientific ideas, Europe seems to have been by far the main beneficiary of increased communication, largely because in 1200 it lagged far behind the other areas. Chinese inventions such as printing, gunpowder, and the compass and Persian expertise in astronomy and mathematics spread widely. In terms of the spread of religions, Islam probably gained the most. It spread into Chinese Central Asia, which had previously been Buddhist, and into Anatolia as Turks pushed out by the Mongols moved west, putting pressure on the Byzantine Empire.

Perhaps because it was not invaded itself, Europe also seems to have been energized by the Pax Mongolica in ways that the other major civilizations were not. The goods from the East brought to Europe whetted the appetites of Europeans for increased contact with the East, and the demand for Asian goods eventually culminated in the great age of European exploration and expansion. By comparison, in areas the Mongols had conquered, protecting their own civilization became a higher priority for elites than drawing from the outside to enrich or enlarge it.

SUGGESTED READING

On Inner Asia in world history, see D. Simon, ed., *The Cambridge History of Early Inner Asia* (1990); S. Adshead, *Central Asia in World History* (1993); and J. L. Abu-Lughod, *Before European Hegemony: The World System A.D. 1250–1350* (1989). On the Mongols more specifically, see E. D. Phillips, *The Mongols* (1969). The Mongol conquest is treated in H. D. Martin, *The Rise of Chinghis Khan and His Conquest of North China* (1950); P. Ratchnevsky, *Genghis Khan: His Life and Legacy* (1992); J. Saunders, *The History of the Mongol Conquests* (2001); and T. Allsen, *Culture and Conquest in Mongol Eurasia* (2001). P. Kahn, trans., *The Secret History of the Mongols* (1984), is a readable translation of the best source for Mongol values and way of life.

For Marco Polo, see L. Olschki, *Marco Polo's Asia* (1960), and F. Wood, *Did Marco Polo Go to China?* (1995), which assembles the evidence against believing that Marco Polo saw everything he said he did, and J. Larner, *Marco Polo and the Discovery of the World* (1999), which takes the opposite stance. Many translations of Marco Polo are available; the most authoritative is A. Moule and P. Pelliot, *Marco Polo: The Description of the World* (1938). On other East–West travelers during the period of Mongol domination, see I. de Rachewiltz, *Papal Envoys to the Great Khans* (1971). On the links between the Mongols' conquest and the spread of bubonic plague, see W. McNeill, *Plagues and Peoples* (1976). Juivaini's Persian account of the Mongols has been translated by J. A. Boyle, *The History of the World Conqueror* (1958).

CHAPTER FOUR

Japan's Middle Ages (1330–1600)

New Political Alignments

Biography: Hino Meishi

Material Culture: Nō

Civil War

Documents: *The Journal of Sōchō*

Historians today see the fourteenth century as marking a decisive break between ancient Japan and its middle ages. Political power became increasingly fragmented among contending military configurations, the court, ecclesiastical establishments, urban residents, and cultivator leagues. Trade networks expanded, carrying a greater variety of goods over longer distances than ever before, while urban markets supplied the needs of social and political elites as well as ordinary residents. Women exchanged economic autonomy for domestic authority. Samurai became moralists and poets. The fourteenth century began with conflict between samurai and the court. The fifteenth and sixteenth centuries saw civil war. Europeans brought new weapons and a new religion in the middle of the sixteenth century. At its end, the world turned upside down: a commoner ruled Japan and sent his armies to invade Korea.

Historians disagree over who were significant political actors, the losers such as Go-Daigo, the religious establishment, and commoner leagues, or the winners among the samurai. Much of the dynamism in this period came from its unsettled margins. What impact did they have on the center? How did men and women protect their interests? How did the arts manage to flourish in the midst of unrest?

NEW POLITICAL ALIGNMENTS

The monarch Go-Daigo's plan to restore power to the monarchy provided the catalyst for the Kamakura shogunate's fall. In 1321 Go-Daigo got his father to agree to renounce the political power held by the retired monarch. Go-Daigo revived the monarchical records office and attracted able administrators who reasserted the royal prerogative of adjudicating lawsuits. Three years later the shogunate learned of his plots against it and arrested his accomplices. Go-Daigo continued to insist on monarchical privilege. When the shogunate tried to force him to abdicate in favor of his cousin's line in 1331, he called on loyalists across Japan to revolt.

Although the shogunate exiled Go-Daigo to the remote island of Oki, men all over Japan rallied to the monarchical cause. Some believed in it; others saw an opportunity to gain wealth and power. Ashikaga Takauji first led Kamakura's legions against Kyoto and then switched sides. In 1333 his forces set fire to Kamakura. The Hōjō family and its retainers, over eight hundred men, women, and children, committed suicide. Takauji brought Go-Daigo back from exile, only to turn on him when forced to share spoils of war with members of the aristocracy. Having overcome a string of reversals, Takauji drove Go-Daigo out of Kyoto and placed his cousin on the throne. Takauji built his headquarters in the Muromachi section of Kyoto where he could supervise the new monarch and oversee his followers. Claiming descent from Minamoto Yoritomo to legitimize his rule, he had himself named shogun in 1338. Despite this title, the administrative structure that he and his successors put together over the next sixty years owed nothing to the Kamakura regime and everything to the exigencies of the moment.

Takauji's victories over Go-Daigo did not bring peace to an increasingly militarized Japan. Go-Daigo's sons established a rival southern court in the mountains of Yoshino that held out until 1392. The coexistence of two courts, northern and southern, allowed men to fight in the name of rival claimants to the throne, depending on which suited their interests. Takauji's grandson Yoshimitsu brought an end to the rival courts by promising to alternate rule between their descendants. He later broke this promise. He brought recalcitrant fighters in Kyushu under his control, but he had less success with military leaders under a rival Ashikaga branch in eastern Japan. In 1402 he received the title "king of Japan" from the Ming emperor (a title not heretofore used in Japan although analogous to the Yi Dynasty's ruler being titled "king of Korea") and appeared poised to

replace the monarchy with his son. His reign marked the high point of Ashikaga power. It declined thereafter, although the shogunate remained in Ashikaga hands to 1578.

The Ashikaga shoguns tried to rule Japan through a combination of family ties and marriage politics. As a gesture at institutional continuity with the Kamakura shogunate, they used the title of *shugo* (military governor). The *shugo* appropriated the administrative functions of the provincial governors appointed by the court. By the end of the fourteenth century, they had also taken over the responsibilities and the income of the estate stewards (*jitō*). Fourteen *shugo* were branches of the Ashikaga family; the remaining seven, such as the Shimazu of Satsuma in Kyushu, lived far from Kyoto and supported the Ashikaga in return for a free hand at home. *Shugo* served as high officials, military governors, and the Ashikaga's chief retainers. Takauji and his heirs exchanged women with *shugo* to maintain their allegiance and solidify alliances. Each ruled large, unwieldy territories defined in patents of appointment made by the shogun. The Ashikaga shoguns were the chief of the *shugo* and derived some of their income from being *shugo* of two provinces. They also controlled some sixty estates scattered across Japan.

The most important office under the shogun was the deputy shogun (*kanrei*), normally filled by the Shiba, Hatakeyama, or Hosokawa. They had prestige as the shogun's close relatives, governing Japan's richest provinces as *shugo* made them wealthy, and their office gave them authority. By combining these three constituents of power, they formed an inner bastion of support for the shogun. When they acted together on his behalf, they made it possible for him to dominate the other *shugo* and his retainers. When they quarreled, they tore the country apart.

The *shugo* normally supported the shogun because they also had weaknesses. Although they had jurisdictional authority over entire provinces, they did not control land. Even when a military man had managed to expropriate the aristocrats' claims to income from estates, he still had to contend with temples, other *shugo,* or even the shogun. Not all military families within a *shugo*'s province were his direct retainers. With increasing frequency, rustic warriors (*kokujin*) accepted no one as their overlord. The longer the *shugo* resided in Kyoto with the shogun, the more they relied on deputies to manage provincial administration. To intimidate their underlings, they needed the prestige bestowed by the shogun. The crucial problem left unsolved by both the Kamakura and Ashikaga regimes was how to maintain the connection between center and periphery. Unlike China, where a bureaucracy marinated in a common ideology was first gathered to the center, then dispatched to the provinces, Japan remained in danger of fragmentation.

Apologists for the Ashikaga wrote the history of the Kamakura regime in such a way as to provide precedents for the new relationship between the Ashikaga shoguns, the *shugo,* and the monarch. The *shugo* had much broader power than any single office at Kamakura. The monarchy had lost so much of its income and autonomy that one ruler had to put off his enthronement ceremony for twenty years because the shogun refused to fund it. The Kamakura regime had subsisted on a relatively small income generated from land. The Ashikaga shoguns cast their net more broadly, collecting fees to license both foreign and domestic trade, demanding kickbacks from temples, dunning the populace in the name of the monarch, and erecting toll barriers to tax commerce. Whereas during Kamakura times, monarch and shogun had ruled Japan together, if not to the same ends, during the Muromachi period, neither can be said to have exercised effective governance.

Changes in Roles for Women

Nothing better marks the break between ancient and medieval Japan than the changes that took place in the relationships between men and women, especially at the higher reaches of society. Even before the Mongol invasions, it had become clear that dividing property among all children, men and women alike, seriously weakened a family's viability. At the same time, the fluidity in marriage arrangements that had characterized the Heian period largely disappeared. Women increasingly moved to their husband's residence. If they took property with them, less was left for their brothers. Loath to bestow property on daughters or too many sons, powerful families selected a single heir. With women and their husbands out of the picture, brothers and cousins competed to inherit the family estate. Property rights in cultivator households evolved differently. Increases in agricultural productivity plus new commercial opportunities left more income in cultivator hands. Women as well as men traded in land and other goods. Women continued to manage their own property even when they moved into their husband's household.

Marriages became more durable and of greater consequence. When seen as a way to ally two families, the exchange of betrothal gifts and the bride's entry into her husband's residence became ceremonies. Once ensconced in her new home, the bride served her parents-in-law as well as her husband. Her trousseau supplied her with what she needed for daily life, but she lost the autonomy that had come from owning real property. She became her husband's property. No legal distinction was made between adultery and rape because both constituted crimes against the husband. On the other hand, the woman's position as wife became much more secure. The elaboration of the marriage ceremony and its public character meant that only compelling political reasons justified divorce. If a man fathered children on a concubine, his wife became their official mother. A wife became the person primarily responsible for domestic affairs. When her husband was off at war, she managed the household economy and dispatched his supplies. A mark of her responsibilities was her title: *midaidokoro* (the lady of the kitchen).

Women at the Kyoto court had always participated in public ceremonies; during the medieval period, they assumed administrative functions

BIOGRAPHY Hino Meishi

Aristocrat, official, mother, and writer, Hino Meishi (?–1358) lived through a time of high political intrigue and learned what it meant to be a wife while the family structure was in transition.

Meishi was the daughter of Hino Sukena who served the monarch Kōgon (r. 1331–1333). When she was about ten years old, she became a maid to Kōgon's mother, Kōgimonin. Meishi developed an expertise in court ceremonies at Kōgon's coming-of-age ceremony. When he was enthroned by the Kamakura shogunate as a replacement for Go-Daigo, she stood directly behind the new monarch.

While Meishi was fulfilling official public functions, sometime before 1331 she started a romance with Kōgimonin's nephew, Kinmune, from the powerful Saionji branch of the Fujiwara lineage. They continued to see each other while Kyoto was thrown into turmoil by Go-Daigo's return, Kōgon's dethronement, and her father's involuntary decision to shave his head and become a monk. For a while they met at hideaways far from the eyes of their parents or their employers. In 1333 Meishi became Kinmune's recognized consort when he wrote her a poem pledging his fidelity. He then visited her publicly at her father's home and stayed the night. A few months later, the Saionji family summoned Meishi to its main residence at Kitayama as Kinmune's official wife, in a move that united two aristocratic opponents to Go-Daigo's rule.

In 1335 Kinmune and Sukena were both arrested for having plotted against Go-Daigo. The night before Kinmune was to be exiled to Izumo, Meishi visited him at the mansion where he had been confined. They exchanged a tearful farewell, and Kinmune handed over several mementos. Before Meishi left, a messenger arrived with the news that Kinmune was to be transferred to another residence. As he was bending down to enter a palanquin, the messenger cut off his head. The pregnant Meishi fled to the Saionji mansion, where she gave birth to her son, Sanetoshi. A messenger from Go-Daigo's court arrived with an offer to find a wet nurse for the child. Kinmune's mother told him that Meishi had miscarried to protect her grandson from his enemies. When the northern court was restored in 1337, Meishi used her connection with the now retired monarch Kōgen to promote her son and restore the Saionji family to its former glory.

Meishi wrote a two-volume memoir. The first volume covers the period of her romance with Kinmune from 1329 to 1333; the second takes up the restoration of the northern court in 1337 and the revival of the Saionji family fortunes. She thus omitted the years of turmoil that exposed the political calculations behind her marriage.

_____

Source: Based on Hitomi Tonomura, "Re-Envisioning Women in the Post Kamakura Age," in *The Origins of Japan's Medieval World: Courtiers, Clerics, Warriors, and Peasants in the Fourteenth Century*, ed. Jeffrey P. Mass (Stanford, Calif.: Stanford University Press, 1997).

as the circle around the monarch shrank. (See **Biography: Hino Meishi.**) Only the highest-ranking aristocrats managed to survive the turmoil of the age; others rusticated to keep close to their sources of income. Women replaced them in running the monarch's household, a transformation in female function seen especially in their writing. Earlier women's diaries and memoirs had been subjective and recorded their lives and thoughts. Those from the fourteenth century and later recorded men's deeds. Women also served as secretaries, writing letters and transmitting orders on behalf of monarch, regent, and shogun.

Trade in Town and Country

The fourteenth century saw a series of transformations in rural Japan. The conversion of dry fields to paddy, the growing of two crops per year, and the extensive use of irrigation made possible by water wheels brought increased yields, population growth, and commercial expansion. Estates split into corporate villages. On estates, each cultivator manager (*myōshu*) had his own distinct legal relationship with multiple overlords. In villages, former *myōshu*, who might also be warriors, plus smallholders dealt with overlords as a unit. They presented petitions for reductions in taxes and corvée labor, and they asserted corporate control over common land and irrigation systems. This process was hastened by the development of self-governing organizations encouraged by overlords as a way to replace the Kamakura-sanctioned estate stewards. Land rights became transferable commodities rather than being associated with office and status. During times of endemic social disorder when overlords were far away, cultivators banded together in nucleated villages, constructed walls and moats, and defended themselves. They met in committee to handle village administration—irrigation procedures and tax payments, for example—and deal with judicial issues. In central Japan these village assemblies took the form of shrine associations that discriminated between members according to status and gender. Many of today's hamlets trace their names back to this century, suggesting the creation of a village identity that excluded outsiders and regulated the behavior of insiders.

Trade had spread in Kamakura times, but the early fourteenth century saw new developments. First was the monetization of commerce by relying on coins imported from Ming China. Although cultivators continued to present taxes in kind and bartering never disappeared, large and small transactions came to be denominated in cash. Second, commercial centers evolved out of places where people congregated: at toll barriers, river crossings, harbors, post houses, and the entrances to shrines and temples. Men and women from nearby villages brought their wares for sale, primarily vegetables, but also processed food such as bricks of tofu. As in earlier ages, proselytizers followed the crowds; some used pictures to teach faith in Amida or to warn of the torments of hell. Nuns solicited donations for the Kumano temple complex. The authorities tried to keep people tied to a specific place and required that travelers carry a passport. Markets received a dispensation from such regulation, making them a zone where people could mingle and exchange goods and information.

The third development centered on the spread of guilds (*za*). They first appeared in the twelfth century and reached their peak in the fourteenth to fifteenth centuries. The idea behind a guild was that the traders or artisans dealing in a specific product would pay a fee to a patron (court noble, religious establishment, shogun) and receive two privileges in exchange: a monopoly on the sale or production of their product and the right to travel in pursuit of trade. Comb makers, sesame oil producers, metal casters, and potters all joined guilds. Many of them lived in the countryside, where they were listed in land records as *hyakushō* (the hundred names). Although this term came to specify cultivators in the seventeenth century, in the fourteenth century it simply meant anyone who was not an aristocrat or warrior. It thus included fishermen, salt makers, and other people who did not grow crops. Horse traders from central Japan relied for centuries on a monarchical decree that gave them exclusive rights to trade in horses. They expanded their monopoly to everything carried by horses from the Pacific to the Japan Sea. Not until modern times did researchers discover that the decree was a forgery.

Kyoto functioned as both the political and economic center of Japan. The court, shogunate, and religious establishments competed as well as cooperated to control and tax commoners in cross-cutting systems of overlord authority that made for interdependence, exploitation, and tax evasion. During the Kamakura period, low-ranking monks from Enryakuji on Mount Hiei had begun to brew and sell sake and lend

Female Moneylender. This segment from a twelfth-thirteenth century scroll of diseases (*yamai no sōshi*) depicts a female moneylender so suffering from obesity brought on by her wealth that she needs help to walk. *(Fukuoka Art Museum)*

money. By the fourteenth century, wealthy moneylenders provided cash loans to aristocrats, warriors, townspeople, and cultivators at annual interest rates of up to 300 percent. Enryakuji issued business licenses and ran a protection racket, fending off attempts by other overlords to tax the moneylenders and helping to collect debts. As lobbyist for its clients, Enryakuji paid stipends to shogunal officials to protect their interests, and moneylenders bribed them to grant tax exemptions. The shoguns made prominent moneylenders their storehouse keepers and later their tax agents in return for 10 percent of the take and the prestige of an official appointment, although the relationship was more ad hoc than bureaucratic. The shogunate's income shrank while individual officials grew rich.

The shogunate strove mightily to control and profit from the maritime trade that flourished regardless of political boundaries. Seafarers of mixed ethnicities pursued trade and piracy with equal aplomb, ravaging the Korean, Japanese, and Chinese coasts. Communities of foreign traders thrived in all the port cities of East Asia, including Japan. The Ming Dynasty closed China to foreign commerce after 1368, with the only exception being official trade carried on between states under the rubric of tribute. In 1402, the Chinese emperor agreed to provide two ships a year with the official seal that allowed them to trade in China. By 1465, two *shugo* had taken over the trade, although the shogunate continued to assess a fee of 10 percent on private merchandise. Late-fourteenth-century state formation in the Ryukyu Islands led three principalities to merge into one under King Sho Hashi in 1429. The Ryukyuans sent tribute missions to China and received official permission to pursue trade. As a maritime nation, they sailed their ships from Southeast Asia to Japan and Korea. Through their delegations to the shogunate, piracy, and legitimate trade, Japan participated in economic networks stretching across the East Asia seas and established a community in Vietnam's Hoi An. In the sixteenth century, these networks brought Europeans in search of trade and Christian converts. (See **Connections: Europe Enters the Scene.**)

Life on the Margins

Trade did not alleviate the disruptions caused by crop failures. Famines forced desperate people to sell themselves into bondage, a form of slavery that could last for generations. Disease was another scourge. Leprosy terrorized people in Japan as it did in Europe. The afflicted suffered increasing disfigurement as their flesh rotted away. How could it be other than a punishment for evil committed in a previous life? Lest they contaminate the healthy with their pollution, lepers had to leave their families and join groups of paupers, the infirm, and entertainers, referred to as the people of the riverbank (*kawaramono*).

The *kawaramono* were outcasts. They included people whose occupations brought them into contact with things deemed to be polluting, death in particular. Tanners, butchers, policemen, and undertakers were excluded from ordinary society. For them, the only fit habitation was on untaxed land that nobody wanted. Occasionally riverbank people were hired to cleanse a shrine after it had been desecrated by fire or the loss of life in a fight. Purifying the shrine involved the dirty work of removing dead bodies. Such rites performed by outcasts suggest a social imagination in which two negatives become a positive and the power to purify lies with the impure.

Other people used marginal spaces carved out of ordinary life as temporary refuges. Markets, river crossings, the entrances to temples and shrines, and graveyards offered sanctuary to unfree people fleeing bondage. Mountains provided shelter for entire villages that absconded to protest unjust taxes or forced labor. Another form of protest was for groups of warriors or cultivators to dress in the persimmon-colored robes reserved for lepers. It was a desperate measure because it cut them off from normal human interaction. It worked because spaces set apart from ordinary life were under the inviolable protection of the deities and Buddhas.

Changes in Religious Practice

An important characteristic of Japan's Middle Ages was the power of the Buddhist establishment. Although Ashikaga shoguns dominated the court, they had to conciliate the temples that largely controlled the urban economy and had their own police force as well as deep roots in the lives of Japanese people. The major temples that had received support from the Heian court continued to flourish; the popular sects that originated in the Kamakura period attracted sometimes vehement converts. Zen Buddhism made major contributions to Japanese aesthetics and played an important political role.

Rather than patronize the temples already entrenched in the Kyoto court, Ashikaga shoguns preferred the Rinzai Zen sect. At the suggestion of a Zen monk, Takauji and his son set up official temples named Ankokuji (temples for national peace) in each province to console Go-Daigo's spirit and raise the shogun's pres-

tige. They also had pagodas built in the precincts of temples belonging to other sects for the same purpose. Later shoguns promoted and ranked Zen temples in Kyoto and Kamakura in loose accord with the system already developed for Zen (Chan) temples in China. Priests jockeying for position and shogunal preference meant that the ranking shifted considerably. By 1410, ten temples enjoyed the top rank of "five mountains" (*gozan*), and all the Kyoto temples ranked above their Kamakura counterparts. Next in importance were the sixty-odd "ten temples" (*jissetsu*). At the bottom were the "multitude of temples," patronized by powerful provincial families. Many had originally been temples of other sects that changed their affiliation to Zen to become part of this ranking system that bestowed prestige and connections to the center on its afffiliates.

The Ashikaga established a hierarchy of priests that aligned the Rinzai sect even more closely with its fortunes. When Yoshimitsu built Shōkokuji next to his palace on Muromachi Street in 1382, he had the chief Rinzai priest reside there. This priest decided appointments to the heads of the Rinzai temples, recommended promotions, and determined ceremonial procedures. Owing to his prowess in the Chinese language, he prepared documents related to maritime trade and foreign affairs. In the fifteenth century, the shogunate appointed men from aristocratic families to this position, with the result that the chief priest often had little interest in routine administration or religious observances.

As the Rinzai school became increasingly associated with the dominant power structure, its teachings and practice moved further from what is conventionally associated with Zen. Instead of seeking the path to enlightenment through meditation, Rinzai became syncretic. It absorbed secret teachings and incantations from esoteric Buddhism that had proved popular with the aristocracy. Even in provincial temples, question-and-answer sessions between master and disciple took a fixed form based on oral tradition handed down in secret. In Kyoto the chief priests participated with the military and civilian aristocracy in literary and artistic pursuits.

Yoshida Shinto (also called Yuiitsu Shinto—"one and only") opposed Zen Buddhism and Buddhist-Shinto syncretism by insisting on the worship of deities only as deities rather than as bodhisattvas. Based on his claim to a tradition stretching back to the creation of Japan through his Urabe lineage of court diviners, Yoshida Kanetono (1435–1511) invented Shinto rituals that spread across Japan. Some had an open, exoteric dimension accessible to ordinary worshipers. Secret esoteric rituals for initiates surprisingly similar to Buddhist rites drew on Buddhist hand gestures called *mudras* and used quotations from *Nihon shoki* in place of mantras. Yoshida Shinto dogma and practice reasserted the centrality of the monarch in indigenous terms and rescued Shinto from complete submersion in Buddhism.

Muromachi Culture

The cult of sensibility (*aware*) from the Heian period and the Kamakura aesthetic characterized by austerity were combined in the fifteenth century into a notion of beauty and elegance modified by stern simplicity. The key term was *yūgen*, used to describe the profound, the remote, the mysterious—a term taken from Nō, the quintessential dramatic form of the day. (See **Material Culture: Nō.**) In Nō every gesture must be refined, the dance graceful, and the language elevated. The most meaningful moments are those when the actor's unspoken, unmoving spiritual presence allows the audience a glimpse of the inexpressible. The same search for the presence behind the form can be seen in monochrome ink brush painting wherein the spaces left blank give shape to the composition, flower arranging based on the asymmetrical placement of a blossom or two, and the tea ceremony.

Zen permeated the arts and architecture of the time. Natural settings depicted in ink brush paintings became allegories to doctrinal points just as did the late-fifteenth-century rock garden at Ryōanji. Raked white sand surrounds fifteen rocks, only fourteen of which are visible from any one perspective. It takes the experience of enlightenment to grasp all fifteen at once. Partly inspired by Song Dynasty architecture, the Golden Pavilion (Kinkakuji) and its pond built in 1398 were designed to model paradise. Ashikaga Yoshimasa built the Silver Pavilion (Ginkakuji), a more modestly refined building, seventy-five years later. A truncated cone of white sand designed to reflect moonlight on the pavilion dominates its Zen garden.

Literary arts also reflected Buddhist influence. Between 1310 and 1331, the poet and recluse Yoshida Kenkō wrote *Essays in Idleness*, a collection of reflections on his time, didactic statements, and meditations, all suffused with longing for the past. In the late fourteenth century, stories about the conflict between the northern and southern courts coalesced in *Taiheiki* (*Records of Great Pacification*). Castigating Ashikaga Takauji as a traitor and emphasizing the legitimacy of the southern court, this late military history became a favorite of storytellers. Ghost stories, didactic tales, folktales, testimonials to the saving power of the Buddha, and sermons were sold in booklets later called *otogi zōshi* (chapbooks).

The tea ceremony, from which women were excluded, assimilated warriors and priests to aristocratic standards of taste. In the first century of Ashikaga rule, imbibing bitter green tea provided the occasion for parties at which the host displayed his finest art treasures in a beautifully appointed sitting room overlooking a garden. With the coming of warfare in the late fifteenth century, this florid style gave way to a simpler, more ritualized and disciplined ceremony performed in a modest hut. Instead of richly decorated Chinese vessels, the emphasis shifted to plain, often misshapen pots because the aesthetic of the time expressed in the combination of *wabi* and *sabi* (elegant simplicity) celebrated the beauty of imperfect objects. The practitioners included provincial samurai and merchants from Kyoto and Sakai who found the tea ceremony an excellent excuse to mingle with

MATERIAL CULTURE

Nō

Combining music, dance, and story, Nō drew on rural dances that appealed to the gods for good harvests, comical skits, popular songs, and tales told by jongleurs. The early spectacles were vulgar and exuberant, attracting crowds of people from all walks of life. At a performance in 1349, monks solicited donations, princes and the Fujiwara regent were among the spectators, and thieves tried to steal the actors' costumes.

Protégé and lover of Ashikaga Yoshimitsu, Zeami transformed Nō into art. In some plays he took themes from *The Tale of Genji,* and in others he used the elevated diction of the court to recast *The Tale of the Heike.* He crafted stories about ghosts, condemned by jealous passion or murderous deed to wander the netherworld between death and salva-

tion. Not content to remain spectators, the shoguns and daimyo performed Nō and made it a state ceremony.

The accouterments of Nō are simple yet elegant. The wooden stage is bare, with a pine tree painted across the backdrop. The musicians and chorus perform on drums and flute for one or two performers. Men in black arrange costumes and provide the occasional prop. One performer wears a mask denoting men and women of various ages, gods, the possessed, and demons. Subtle movements of the head combined with skillful carving lend these masks great expressive power. In contrast to the stern simplicity of the set, the robes are of brilliant brocade, their glitter designed to catch the light from the torches that light the stage.

Nō Performance. One detail on a folding screen showing scenes in and around Kyoto depicts a Nō performance in the early sixteenth century. *(National Museum of Japanese History/DNPArchives.com)*

Color Plate 1
The Tale of Genji. This picture scroll contains text interspersed
with illustrations. Both men and women blackened their teeth
and painted eyebrows high on their foreheads. Men wore hats,
women let their hair trail down their backs.
(Goshima Art Museum in Tokyo/Corbis)

Color Plate 2
Persian View of the Mongols. This fourteenth-century illustration of Rashid
ad-Din's *History of the World* shows the Mongols attacking Chengdu. Chinese
sources report that the entire population of the city was slaughtered, something
one would never guess from the Persian depiction.

(Bibliotheque Nationale, Paris/The Art Archive)

**Color Plate 3
Rice Planting.** This sixteenth-century painting of *Rice Planting* depicts it as a fertility festival with men providing the music while women work.

(Tokyo National Museum/ DNP Archives.com)

**Color Plate 4
Arrival of the Portuguese.** This six-panel folding screen depicts the *Arrival of the Portuguese*—soldiers in short pants, merchants in balloon pants, and priests in black robes accompanied by African servants.

(Musee des Arts Asiatiques-Guimet, Paris, France/RMN/Art Resource, NY)

**Color Plate 5
Dry Goods Store in
Surugacho.** In this
painting entitled *Dry
Goods Store in
Surugacho, Edo,*
customers take off their
shoes to enter the shop.
Male clerks serve female
customers while others
gather around the
manager. The owner is
at the back of the store.

(Corbis)

**Color Plate 6
The Foreign Quarter in
Guangzhou.** Before the
Opium War, foreign traders in
Guangzhou were not to leave
the small strip of land outside
the city where their "factories"
were located. They could live
there only while arranging
shipments and had to return
to Macao once their ships
were loaded.

(Winterthur Museum)

aristocrats. Linked verse (*renga*), a collaborative form of poetry writing, provided a venue for the talented but lowborn to attract attention. Traveling priests such as Sōchō carried the practices of poetry and tea to provincial strongmen across Japan. (See **Documents:** *The Journal of Sōchō*.)

In contrast to the Zen-influenced arts of earlier times, exuberant color characterized the Momoyama period at the end of the sixteenth century. Epitomized in Toyotomi Hideyoshi's golden tearoom, parvenu extravagance marked lacquer boxes dusted with gold, and wall paintings with gold leaf background. Vividly painted screens depicted European traders and missionaries and celebrated local customs. (See Color Plate 3.) Artistic triumphs based on technological innovation led to elaborate textile designs and towering castle keeps.

CIVIL WAR

The hundred years of civil war that began with the Ōnin conflict of 1467–1477 diffused elite cultural practices across the country. The breakdown of unified public authority spurred innovations from military organization to village life. Estates vanished. Buddhist temples lost power and income when they were not simply destroyed. Without their protection, the Kyoto moneylenders and other guild organizations disappeared. Territorial units of domains and villages replaced the former patchwork of competing jurisdictions.

Succession disputes provided the pretext for retainers and overlords to push their own interests. In the Hatakeyama case, the aging *shugo* first appointed a nephew to be his heir, but when a son was born to his concubine, he tried to have his decision reversed. In the 1450s, powerful retainers and the shogunal deputy backed the nephew and got the shogun to censure the son. Son and nephew fought on the political front, each being censured three times and forgiven three times, and on the military front where their retainers demanded rewards after each battle. This conflict foreshadowed the dispute in the Ashikaga house when Yoshimasa appointed his younger brother his successor, only to be forced to change his mind when his wife, Hino Tomiko, gave birth to Yoshihisa in 1465. Her dedication to her son's future shows how family loyalties had changed from Hōjō Masako's day. Already at odds over the Hatakeyama dispute, the two chief *shugo* each picked a rival claimant.

The *shugo* fought their first battles in and around Kyoto in 1467. Their chief weapon was arson, used to punish and exorcise enemies. Temples, aristocratic mansions, and the treasures of the ages burned. Commanders marched armies through the streets to intimidate their opponents. When they fought, they did so during the day, and seldom did they pursue a fleeing adversary. In the early years, a defeated opponent might be sent into exile or allowed to retire to a monastery. Later, a demand for retribution led to the slaughter of hostages and prisoners, the mutilation of corpses, the lacquering of an enemy's skull for use as a drinking cup. By the end of the Ōnin war, Kyoto's palaces had become fields, the *shugo* had become pawns of their erstwhile retainers when they had not disappeared, and Yoshihisa had inherited an empty office. He died in 1489 while trying to subdue a recalcitrant retainer who had organized rustic warriors in Ōmi to expropriate estates that paid tithes to nobles and temples.

The shogunate became irrelevant to power struggles that rent Japan. *Shugo* families split in fratricidal disputes over titles and the power to control land holdings that they conferred. Retainers embroiled themselves in factional disputes or betrayed one lord for another. Believing their honor to be at stake in every encounter, they fought bloody duels over imagined slights. Fortunately for the residents of Kyoto, even before the Ōnin war drew to an inconclusive close in 1477, battlefields had shifted to the provinces, closer to the spoils of war.

Local Leagues

The power vacuum at the top provided an opportunity for locally based leagues (*ikki*—literally,

DOCUMENTS

The Journal of Sōchō

Written by Saiokuken Sōchō, an acclaimed master of linked verse and a Zen monk, these entries show how the poet received commissions to write poetry from a high shogunal official amid the ravages of civil war. During his travels around central Japan in search of patrons and poetic inspiration, Sōchō turned a critical eye on his society in describing people on the margins, merchants, sake brewers, impoverished samurai, and lazy priests.

1522: We crossed to Ōminato harbor in Ise and proceeded to Yamada, where we visited Ise shrine. The matter had been raised earlier of a thousand-verse sequence to be presented to the shrine, and I had invited the priest Sōseki down for that purpose. He arrived near the end of the seventh month, and we began composing the sequence soon thereafter, on the fourth of the eighth month. Two hundred verses a day for five days. The work was commissioned as a votive sequence by the present shogunal deputy, Hosokawa Takakuni, when he returned to the capital from Ōmi. His opening verse (*hokku*) for the first hundred verses was sent from Kyoto:

> Everywhere aglow
> in the morning sunlight—
> the haze!
> > Takakuni
> Plum trees blossom,
> willows bend, and even
> the wind abates!
> > Sōchō

Sōseki then left for Owari. Knowing it was likely to snow before long, I decided to set out for the north on the sixteenth. There has been fighting in this province beyond Kumozu river and Anonotsu, making it difficult to get from place to place.

Anonotsu has been desolate for more than ten years, and nothing but ruins remains of its four or five thousand villages and temples. Stands of reeds and mugwort, no chickens or dogs, rare even to hear the cawing of a crow.

1525: Asahina Tokishige came to visit. We had a pleasant conversation by the hearth about frustrations at year's end, the repayment of loans, the allotment of rice stipends, and the lack of enough of anything, during the course of which I rambled on in my dotage as follows:

Item. There is nothing like going into business for profit. People who do so never speak of gods or Buddhas, give no thought to the world's prosperity or decline, know nothing of the elegant pursuits of snow, moon, and blossoms, grow distant from friends, reject appeals from their near and dear, and spend every waking moment thinking of making money. But that is how to get on in the world. Note, though, that those with even nominal lands, and monks with temple properties, should not take an interest in business. But note too that the sake dealers in the capital, Sakai, the Southern Capital, Sakamoto, and also in this part of the country do very well.

Item. Consider the low-ranking samurai, starving with no land to call his own. There is no help for him. He obviously cannot part from his wife and children. Their food runs

union of minds) to escape from the vertical hierarchies that had tied them to aristocratic, ecclesiastical, and military patrons. In 1487 rustic warriors in Yamashiro united province-wide to resist the incursions of overlords. Theirs was a horizontal alliance of self-reliant men of no particular pedigree. They developed tactics of mass demonstrations organized village by village. On

out, and the woman must draw water and the man must gather brushwood. Their children are taken away before their eyes to slave for others. Their bowing and scraping is pitiful. Driven to that pass, those with self-respect may even do away with themselves. Someone said that to such unfortunates one should give a little something. That is the essence of charity. Of course one must give as well to those who beg by the roadside and wait by houses and gates.

Item. Lion dancers, monkey trainers, bell ringers, bowl beaters, and the like have something they can do for a living. People somehow provide for them, though their need is no greater than that of those I have just mentioned. It is the latter, for whom there is no help at all, who are the world's true unfortunates, even more than lepers and beggars. They are truly wretched.

Item. People who pursue the study of Zen are embarked on a difficult and estimable course. But those who are perfunctory in their Zen practice, even highly placed samurai in the capital and provinces, easily fall into error.

Item. Where today can one find an inspirational teacher of the doctrines of "separate transmission outside the teachings" and "nonverbalization"? Some call today's Zen practitioners a pack of devils, of the lowest guttersnipe sort. Abbots, monks, and novices these days consort with the high and mighty, curry donations from provincial gentry, pursue their austerities only when it suits them, run hither and yon all day, and dally with other practitioners. But who are the masters they practice with themselves? Some say it is far better to repeat the Holy Name [of Amida]. I am more attracted to those who follow a simple and ignorant practice, as I do.

Item. Acquiring bows, horses, and armor and maintaining good retainers—that is the way of the samurai. But there is no need to run out and buy things for which one has no specific purpose. Constant spending and extravagance must be avoided, I am told.

1526, fourth month: We crossed the Mountain of Meeting and entered the capital at Awataguchi without meeting a soul. This route used to be filled with horses and palanquins, everyone bumping shoulders and tilting hats to squeeze by. As I looked out over the city, I saw not one in ten of the houses that had been there formerly, either rich or poor. The sight of tilled fields around farmhouses, with the Imperial Palace in the midst of summer barley, was too much for words.

1527: On the fourth of the third month I left Yashima. A village called Minakuchi [Water's mouth] in Kōga continued for about ten chō, and I recalled the old palace built here once for an imperial pilgrimage to Ise. There are many toll gates in these parts, and as we went along people would shout "Stop! Toll!" at every one, whereupon I composed the following:

> I must have appeared
> at the water's mouth,
> for at every gate
> "Stop! Toll!" is what
> they cry together.

Source: H. Mack Horton, trans. and anno., *The Journal of Sōchō* (Stanford, Calif.: Stanford University Press, 2002), pp. 15–16, 84–86, 104, 143.

occasion they looted, burned, and killed. Between 1428 and 1526, twenty-four *ikki* demanding debt amnesty from moneylenders erupted in Kyoto and its environs. Many were at least partially suc- cessful; indeed they ceased to be a threat only when moneylenders mobilized Kyoto townspeople to go on the offensive in 1536. They took the lead in consolidating the cityscape into two

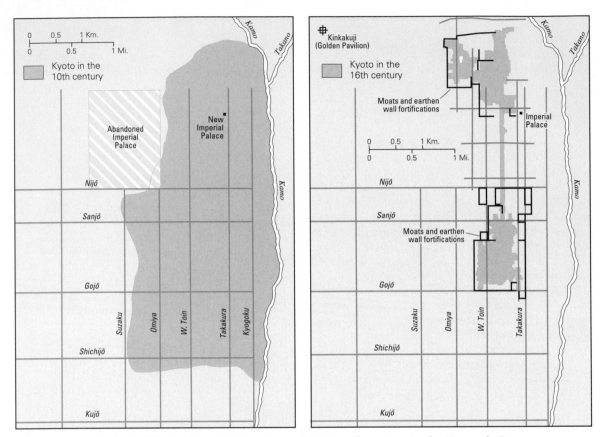

Map 4.1   **Kyoto in the Tenth–Eleventh Centuries and Its Transformation in the Sixteenth Century**

sectors—for defense and in building fortifications. (See Map 4.1.) They had already organized neighborhood associations for crime prevention, mutual protection, and firefighting. When the shogun proved unable to defend the city, the associations hired mercenaries. Many moneylenders helped build the temple fortresses belonging to the Lotus sect that dominated the commoners' religious life.

The Lotus League (*hokke ikki*) attracted adherents in urban areas with its exclusive faith in the saving power of the *Lotus Sutra*. In teaching that this world can be the Buddhist paradise, it encouraged worldly success. It provided institutional support independent of traditional elites, thus making it feasible for moneylenders to end their subordination to Enryakuji. It supported a paramilitary organization useful in times of disorder. With the shogun on the run

after 1521, believers in the *Lotus Sutra* massed in tens of thousands not only to defend the city but to attack military commanders and adherents of different Buddhist sects. They withheld some rents, collected taxes, and settled disputes, in effect setting up a commoner-run city government, though the merchants in Sakai went further in developing the instruments of self-rule. Enryakuji was the first to organize opposition to the league, soon joined by a military commander in Ōmi. In eight days of fighting in 1536, the attackers destroyed all the Lotus temples, burned the entire lower city and one-third of the upper, and slaughtered men, women, and children suspected of being true believers. Kyoto suffered worse damage than it had during the Ōnin war. From a military point of view, suppression had to be brutal because the Hokke teachings placed commoners on the same level as their masters.

The most radical renunciation of allegiance to overlords came in the One-Mind Leagues (*Ikkō ikki*) that flourished in central Japan after the Ōnin war. Adherents to the True Pure Land school of Buddhism believed that Amida offered salvation to all who accepted his gift of faith. Since everyone was equal in Amida's eyes, the One-Mind Leagues rejected both religious and secular hierarchies. Although their adherents lived in largely autonomous communities organized around a lay teacher and temple, they were linked to a nationwide organization through the sect's headquarters situated in the fortified temple complex called Ishiyama Honganji built in Osaka in 1532. The most militant and long lasting of the One-Mind Leagues on the Noto peninsula held out against warlords from 1488 to 1578.

Rise of Warlords

Out of the same crucible of lawlessness and disorder that produced *ikki* appeared military men determined to create a new vertical hierarchy. Unlike the *shugo* who depended on the shogun for patents of rule, the new leaders, called *daimyo,* relied on nothing other than military force. Daimyo constructed domains from the inside out. They ignored provincial boundaries in favor of natural defenses—rivers, mountains, and seas. Their domains were much smaller than those held by the former *shugo,* but they were more secure. To the impoverishment of the Kyoto aristocrats and temples, they tolerated no absentee proprietors. In order to survive, monarch and court sold themselves as arbiters of taste and erected toll barriers to tax goods in transit.

Warlords acquired territory through conquest, alliance, or marriage. Territory came with fighting men, the samurai, and cultivators, often one and the same. Samurai were incorporated into the warlord's retainer band through an oath of loyalty in return for land or perhaps a stipend. Sometimes this meant confirming a samurai's hold over the land he brought with him, though when possible warlords preferred to move retainers to a different area, often with the promise of a raise, in order to break their ties with former supporters. Even village headmen swore allegiance to a warlord in return for protection. They were expected to fight in time of war in addition to cultivating their land, maintaining order, and collecting taxes.

Warlords tried to mold their territories and retainer bands into a cohesive unit. They surveyed land to find out how much it produced and who was responsible for its taxes. They promoted irrigation works to open new land. They forbade cultivators to move away. They relaxed restrictions on commerce. They issued laws to maintain order and tame the samurai. They suppressed private feuds by announcing that in cases of quarrels, both sides would be judged equally guilty and punished accordingly. They wrote house codes that warned against fomenting factions or indulging in luxury. Income and responsibility rewarded dedication to duty, loyalty, and obedience. In this way, warlords created competing power blocs, centered on castle towns, each based on the principle of vertical hierarchy.

The most notable warlords of the sixteenth century were self-made men who rose from obscurity to become mighty conquerors, a process summarized in the term *gekokujō* (the overthrow of those above by those below). Maeda Toshiie of Kaga started his career as a low-ranking retainer. He initiated land surveys and reorganized his retainer band to reduce its autonomy. Takeda Shingen fought nearly constantly from age twenty to his death. Realizing that military force legitimizes nothing, he claimed that his quest for personal gain was done in the name of public authority (*kōgi*). The political experiments tried by Maeda, Takeda, and others laid the groundwork for Japan's unification through military conquest.

The Conquerors

The earliest conqueror was Oda Nobunaga, born to a junior branch of an obscure lineage. His first accomplishment was to wipe out his kin. He brought masterless samurai who had been living by robbery and extortion into his retainer band and demanded that they swear loyalty to him personally. Although Nobunaga commanded fewer troops than his opponents, he used them more effectively. He marched on Kyoto in 1568 on the pretext of installing Ashikaga Yoshiaki as shogun. There he provided sorely needed material assistance to the impoverished court. When Yoshiaki proved recalcitrant, Nobunaga drove him out of Kyoto in 1573, bringing the Ashikaga Dynasty to an ignominious end.

Nobunaga's signal achievement was to destroy the Buddhist temples' military, economic, and political power. He began with Enryakuji, which had allied with his enemies after he seized some of its land. In 1571 he burned three thousand buildings in its temple complex on Mount Hiei and massacred the monks. By threat or force, he expropriated the holdings of several other monasteries and ordered them to reduce their personnel. Between 1570 and 1580 he waged war against the *Ikkō ikki,* showing no mercy to its adherents and slaughtering tens of thousands. To destroy the fortified headquarters at Ishiyama Honganji, he built armored ships outfitted with cannon. As a result of his efforts, the power of the Buddhist establishment, which had characterized Japan's Middle Ages, was permanently eliminated.

As befit a man who aspired to bring the entire realm under one military regime, Nobunaga designed new economic and social policies. He freed merchants from having to seek the protection of guilds in return for monetary contributions called "thank-you money." He eliminated toll barriers within the areas he controlled. He tried to stabilize the exchange rates between different types of coins, and he minted his own, the first time since 958 that a Japanese government had issued currency. He collected tax registers to gauge how much his land was worth and assert his authority over its disposal. In this way, he could argue that his retainers held their ancestral lands only at his pleasure. They had to be willing to move from place to place as he deemed fit; otherwise they would be marked as traitors and

destroyed. Fearing Nobunaga's growing power, one of his generals, Akechi Mitsuhide, launched a surprise attack on Nobunaga in 1562. Nobunaga and his son committed suicide.

Nobunaga's avenger, Toyotomi Hideyoshi, exemplified the social turbulence of the time. He came from little more than cultivator stock, rising through his own efforts to become hegemon of Japan. Although Nobunaga had pacified central Japan, independent warlords still controlled northern Japan and most of the western reaches of Honshu, Kyushu, and Shikoku. Hideyoshi either subdued them or so intimidated them that they acknowledged him as overlord. When he defeated the Shimazu of Satsuma in 1586, he allowed them to keep a portion of their domain, and he did the same for the Mōri of Chōshū. Preferring the security of subordination to the vicissitudes of battle, the northern warlords surrendered without a fight after he defeated the Hōjō (no relation to the Kamakura Hōjō) at Odawara in 1590. For the first time in over 250 years, Japan had a single ruler.

Although Hideyoshi epitomized the self-made man and created a new government structure, he looked to the monarchy to validate his rule. He rebuilt the Kyoto palace and paid for court ceremonies. He took the name Fujiwara and had himself appointed retired regent (*taikō*). He allowed his chief supporters and even his rivals to remain as daimyo of domains, though he carefully interspersed them to prevent collusion. He rewarded his faithful supporter Tokugawa Ieyasu with the eight Kantō provinces after the defeat of the Hōjō in a move that shifted Ieyasu from his homeland in Mikawa to an unfamiliar region swarming with rustic warriors. Hideyoshi commanded enormous resources through the land he controlled and his taxes on commerce in Osaka and Sakai. Rather than spend his own money, he had the daimyo pay for construction projects and provide military service on demand. He created an ideological basis for his rule by claiming descent from the sun god who had entered his mother's womb, a drama he enacted on the Nō stage for the benefit of aristocrats, daimyo, and foreign visitors.

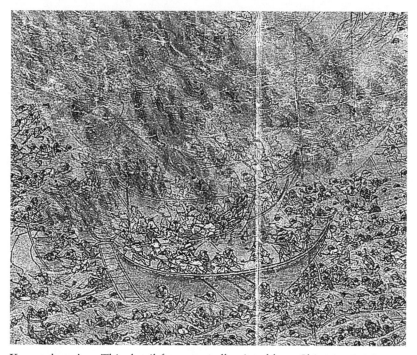

Korean invasion. This detail from a scroll painted by a Chinese participant shows a Japanese ship set on fire by Ming pursuers. Samurai armed with swords leap into the waves. *(Laurie Platt Winfrey, Inc.)*

Desiring order and stability above all, Hideyoshi tried to ensure that no one would be able to rise as he had. Building on the work of his rivals, he instituted a nationwide land survey to determine the extent of arable land and to fix a name to every plot. Hideyoshi's land survey marked the beginning of efforts to quantify landholdings and estimate tax revenues. By eliminating intermediary claims to landed income, the land survey marked the end of the largely defunct estates. He ordered subsidiary castles torn down and destroyed the remaining fortified neighborhoods in Kyoto. In 1588, he also tried to insist on a rigid status distinction between samurai and commoners by forbidding all but samurai from wearing two swords, one long and one short. Thereafter, commoners might own swords, but they could not put them on display. Hideyoshi issued a series of decrees prohibiting samurai from leaving their lord's service to become merchants or cultivators and preventing farmers from deserting their fields to become city folk. Although it proved impossible to make clear distinctions between various statuses and some domains such as Satsuma or Tosa continued to recognize rustic samurai (*gōshi*), Hideyoshi's intent remained the law of the land until 1871.

In 1592, Hideyoshi turned his attention to an invasion of Korea. He mobilized 158,000 samurai supported by 9,200 sailors and kept 100,000 men as a backup force, one indication of how heavily militarized Japanese society had become. In his most grandiloquent pronouncements, Hideyoshi promised to conquer both Korea and China and put the Japanese monarch on the Chinese throne with Hideyoshi's adopted heir as regent. (He later withdrew the adoption when his concubine bore a son.) The first invasion went as far as Pyongyang. It drove the

Korean king from Seoul, decimated the regular Korean army, and devastated the countryside. It was forced to retreat when supplies ran low, the Ming came to Korean aid, and the Korea admiral Yi Sunsin won a major sea battle with armorplated ships and cannon. Hideyoshi tried again in 1597. When he died the next year, the Japanese troops in Korea decamped to participate in the succession dispute to come.

Hideyoshi had hoped to pass his dominion to his son by establishing a balance of power in the five-man advisory council created shortly before his death. Its most powerful member was Tokugawa Ieyasu, who like Nobunaga and Hideyoshi came from an obscure background in central Japan. Ieyasu strengthened his retainers' devotion and loyalty by making them completely dependent on him for their rewards. Rather than kill his kin, he left them with the original Matsudaira name when he took the Tokugawa name in 1566. He honored them as his relatives while he relied on men he had made to be his advisers and generals. Upon moving from central Japan to the Kantō plain, he turned the village of Edo into his castle town and started to build an administrative and personnel system based on the initiatives of his peers. He fought only those battles he knew he could win. By the time the advisory council fell apart in 1600, he had neutralized, compromised, or won over most of his rivals.

The battle of Sekigahara in 1600 brought the civil wars to a close. Although Hideyoshi's son remained ensconced in Osaka castle, his supporters were samurai who had lost their masters (*rōnin*) and other warriors who found that peace left little outlet for their talents. When Ieyasu decided to move against the castle in two campaigns in 1615 and 1616, the resistance was fierce but futile. Another threat to peace was the Shimabara Christian rebellion of 1637 in Kyushu, the last of the religiously based *ikki*. Like its predecessors, it was suppressed with the slaughter of approximately ten thousand men, women, and children. Its end marked the last military conflict Japan was to suffer for over two hundred years.

SUMMARY

The warfare of the middle ages destroyed Japan's estate system and forged new political institutions from the ground up. Although religion continued to be important in people's lives, religious institutions lost economic and political power. Shifting patterns in marriage and inheritance practices affirmed patriarchal authority in the ruling class. The popularity of the tea ceremony among merchants prefigured the spread of popular culture centered on townspeople.

SUGGESTED READING

For political histories, see M. S. Adolphson, *The Gates of Power: Monks, Courtiers, and Warriors in Premodern Japan* (2000), and A. Goble, *Kenmu: Go-Daigo's Revolution* (1996). For the fourteenth-century transformation, see J. P. Mass, ed. *The Origins of Japan's Medieval World: Courtiers, Clerics, Warriors, and Peasants in the Fourteenth Century* (1997). For villages, see H. Tonomura, *Community and Commerce in Late Medieval Japan: The Corporate Villages of Tokuchin-ho* (1992). For an imaginative exploration of the late fifteenth and sixteenth centuries, see M. B. Berry, *The Culture of Civil War in Kyoto* (1994). For trade and commerce, see S. Gay, *The Moneylenders of Late Medieval Kyoto* (2001). For culture, see D. Keene, *Yoshimasa and the Silver Pavilion: The Creation of the Soul of Japan* (2003). An innovative study of the estate system is in T. Keirstead, *The Geography of Power in Medieval Japan* (1992). See also J. W. Hall and T. Toyoda, *Japan in the Muromachi Age* (1977).

Europe Enters the Scene

TRADE ROUTES FLOURISHED BETWEEN Northeast and Southeast Asia long before European merchants and Catholic missionaries entered the South China Sea. Lured by Asian silks, ceramics, and spices, ships under the Portuguese flag were the first to risk the voyage in the early sixteenth century. The Spanish, British, and Dutch followed. In early seventeenth-century Japan, early eighteenth-century China, and early nineteenth-century Korea, rulers put a stop to missionary activities, albeit for different reasons. Trade between Europe and East Asia continued, but it was confined to Guangzhou in China and Nagasaki in Japan.

Hemmed in by Spain, Portugal relied on trade to fill royal coffers. At the beginning of the fifteenth century, Portuguese ships started exploring the west coast of Africa in search of gold. African gold then financed a voyage around the Cape of Good Hope in 1488. From there, the Portuguese established a colony at Goa on the west coast of India and followed Muslim and Indian trade routes to the Spice Islands of Indonesia. Once Queen Isabella and her husband, Ferdinand, captured Grenada, the last Muslim emirate in Spain, in 1492, they funded Christopher Columbus's voyage across the Atlantic in hopes of finding an alternative route to China. In 1494, the pope divided the world beyond Europe between Spain and Portugal. Spain's sphere included most of the western hemisphere except Brazil; Portugal went east.

China's contact with Portugal began in 1511 when Admiral Alfonso de Albuquerque captured the Chinese entrepôt of Malacca near the tip of the Malay Peninsula. With this as a base, the first official Portuguese embassy followed traders to China in 1517. It behaved badly by refusing to conform to Chinese customs. Ship captains acted more like pirates than traders. Few Portuguese were willing to risk the long voyage in tiny ships around the Horn of Africa, across the wide expanse of the Indian Ocean and through the Strait of Malacca to Macao. Most were neither officials dispatched from the Portuguese court nor explorers seeking glory and territory. What they had in limited resources and manpower had to go toward making a profit in an already thriving commercial milieu (see Map C4.1).

Periodic prohibitions on maritime travel by Ming emperors at Beijing did not stop the Portuguese or seafaring people on the south China coast who made little distinction between trade, smuggling, and piracy. In 1521 the Ming tried to ban the Portuguese from China. Two years later an expeditionary force commissioned by the Portuguese king and charged with negotiating a friendship treaty defeated its mission by firing on Chinese warships near Guangzhou. In 1557, without informing Beijing, local Chinese officials decided that the way to regulate trade was to allow the Portuguese to build a trading post on an uninhabited bit of land near the mouth of the Pearl River. This the Portuguese called Macao. It became the first destination for all Europeans going to China until the nineteenth century, and it remained a Portuguese settlement until 1999.

The only significant new products Portuguese traders brought to networks that had already developed in East Asia were firearms and New World crops such as corn, sweet potatoes, and tobacco. They reached Japan by accident in 1543 when a typhoon blew three ships with a mixed crew of Southeast Asians to a small

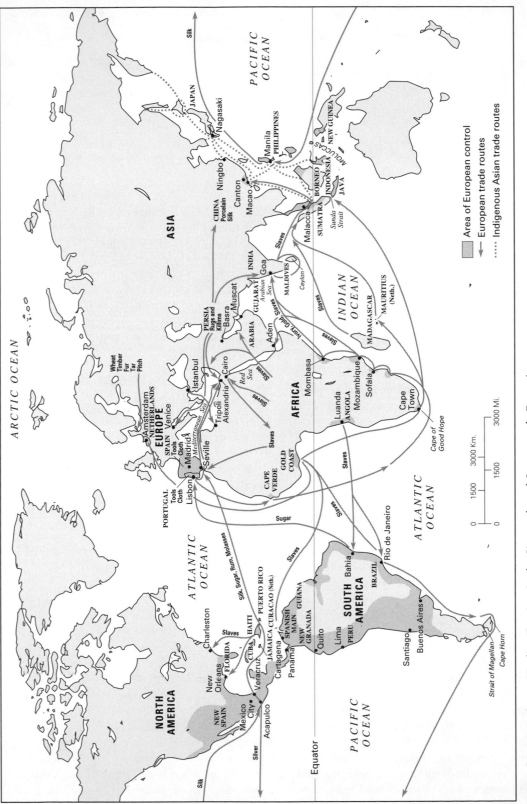

Map C4.1 Seaborne Trading Empires in the Sixteenth and Seventeenth Centuries

island called Tanegashima. The islanders helped repair their ship and bought their cargo. Among the goods exchanged for Japanese silver was the harquebus, a clumsy ancestor of the musket. The island's ruler ordered his retainers to study its operation and manufacture and distributed samples to more powerful mainland warlords. In 1570, Japanese troops deployed the Tanegashima harquebus in battle. In the meantime, Portuguese traders profited from the Ming ban on Japanese ships because they had raided the coast. The Portuguese carried 20 metric tons of Japanese silver a year to China in exchange for silk, sugar, medicine, and dye.

Trade between China and Europe increased in the late sixteenth century through an economic conjuncture that included the Americas. China needed silver because its monetary system depended on it and domestic production had declined after 1430. Chinese merchants bought Japanese silver carried on Portuguese ships. China also absorbed 50 percent of silver mined in Mexico and Bolivia and carried in Spanish ships to Manila, founded in 1571 when Spain made the Philippines a colony. Disruptions in the flow of silver from Japan and the western hemisphere in 1639 contributed to the fall of the Ming. Spanish silver bought manufactured goods—Chinese silk, porcelain, and lacquer—that dominated the luxury trade in Europe and funded Spain's wars against multiple enemies for generations.

Portuguese merchants seeking profits in East Asia faced competition from their government when the Portuguese viceroy at Goa made the Japan trade a royal monopoly in 1550. The Ming approved because their officials also wanted to see trade regularized. Each year a captain major appointed by the crown sent ships to Japan where warlords competed to attract the ships to their ports. (See Color Plate 4.) The governor of Macao forbade the sending of goods to Japan on private ships via third countries, especially the Philippines. His directives were futile; Portuguese and Spanish traders with crews drawn from all over East and Southeast Asia found Manila too convenient to abandon.

Catholic missionaries seeking converts who followed the traders hoped to keep the religious wars that undermined the pope's spiritual hegemony secret from Asia. The first were Jesuits, from the order founded by Ignatius Loyola in 1534 to promote Catholic scholarship and combat the Protestant Reformation initiated by Martin Luther in 1517. Jesuits insisted that Christianizing China and Japan was not to be done with the intent to conquer, as had been the case in the western hemisphere. As individuals, they displayed a rare sensitivity to other cultures. They were willing to find universal principles of belief outside a European context, but they served an institution that refused to compromise with indigenous beliefs and practices. Despite the efforts of charismatic missionaries, the Catholic church never gained the ascendancy in East Asia enjoyed by that other foreign religion, Buddhism.

The Jesuit priest Francis Xavier had worked in India and the Indies before China and Japan attracted his attention. After many misadventures, he landed on Satsuma in 1549. The Satsuma lord hoped that by treating Xavier well, he would attract the official Portuguese trading ships the next year. When the ships went instead to the island of Hirado, the lord expelled Xavier's party. Xavier traveled throughout western Japan as far as Kyoto, proselytizing wherever warlords gave permission. Asked why the Chinese knew nothing of Christianity if it was indeed an ancient and true religion, Xavier decided that Japan would become Christian only if China led the way. His efforts to enter China ended when he died on an uninhabited island off the China coast in December 1552.

Jesuits and Dominicans soon joined the missionaries and converts Xavier left behind in Japan. In 1565 Louis Frois met Oda Nobunaga who befriended the Jesuits to discomfort his Buddhist enemies. In 1580 Jesuits acquired Nagasaki from a warlord interested in promoting trade with Portuguese ships. In 1582, four young Kyushu samurai left Nagasaki for Lisbon and Rome, where they helped Jesuits get a papal bull that put Japan off limits to other orders. It proved to be ineffective, and quarrels between the Catholic orders over how best to present Christianity to East Asia damaged the missionaries' credibility in the eyes of Asian rulers.

Warlords trying to unite Japan under secular authority became increasingly suspicious of Christianity. If an absolute god demanded absolute loyalty, where did that leave the bonds between lord and retainer? Repression began in 1587 and intensified nine years later when the pilot of a ship wrecked on the Japanese coast allegedly pointed out that soldiers had followed Spanish missionaries to the Philippines. In 1614 Tokugawa Ieyasu decided that missionaries undermined the social order and were not essential to foreign trade. He ordered them expelled under threat of execution. He also tortured and killed Christian converts who refused to apostatize. Among the martyrs were Koreans who had been brought to Japan as slaves during Toyotomi Hideyoshi's invasions in the 1590s. The shogunate broke off relations with Catholic countries in 1624. The remaining Christians practiced their religion in secret by crafting statues of the Virgin Mary in the guise of Kannon, the Buddhist goddess of mercy.

Christianity arrived later in China. Not until 1583 did the Jesuit Matteo Ricci receive permission to move farther inland than Macao. Once he had educated himself in the style of Chinese literati, he set himself up in Nanjing. In 1601 he received tacit imperial permission to reside in Beijing. From him the Chinese learned western-style geography, astronomy, and Euclidean mathematics. In the years after Ricci's death in 1611, Jesuits regulated the Chinese lunar calendar. They suffered occasional harassment from xenophobic officials, but they retained their standing with Chinese literati during the turmoil that led to the collapse of the Ming Dynasty and the founding of the Qing in 1644. Catholic mendicant orders allowed into China in 1633 criticized Jesuits for aiming their efforts at the ruling class and trying to fit Christian ideas into the Chinese world-view rather than remaining European in approach and appealing to the masses.

Ricci and his Jesuit successors believed that Confucianism as a philosophy could be assimilated to monotheism. Confucianists and Christians shared similar concerns for morality and virtue. Rites of filial piety performed for the ancestors did not constitute a form of worship,

Matteo Ricci. Matteo Ricci is shown here in a French lithograph holding a map of the world to which he offers the crucified Christ. *(The Granger Collection)*

which made them compatible with Christianity. Mendicant orders disagreed. In 1715, religious and political quarrels in Europe exacerbated by longstanding antagonism to the Jesuits resulted in Ricci's accommodation with Chinese practices being deemed heretical. Angry at this insult, the Kangxi emperor forbade all Christian missionary work in China, although he allowed Jesuits to remain in Beijing to assist with the calendar. A Jesuit portrait painter later proved popular at the courts of his son and grandson. The outcome of the rites controversy over whether converts should be allowed to maintain ancestral altars, exacerbated by accusations that missionaries had meddled in the imperial succession, led the Qing to view all Europeans with suspicion.

China's rulers also tried to limit trade for strategic reasons. Between 1655 and 1675 the Qing banned maritime trade and travel to isolate Ming loyalists on Taiwan. In addition to official trade at the state level, the Qing permitted merchants to trade with foreigners, but only under tight control. After 1759, all maritime trade, whether with Southeast Asia or Europe, was confined to Guangzhou. Merchants put up with burdensome restrictions because in exchange for silver, China provided luxury items and tea, a bulk ware, introduced to Europe in 1607.

The profits to be made in East and Southeast Asia lured traders from Protestant countries following the religious wars of the latter half of the sixteenth century. Determined not to allow their Catholic rivals to dominate the world, Protestant nations sent explorers across the oceans. Britain's defeat of the Spanish Armada in 1588 began Spain's long decline. Early in the seventeenth century, the Dutch started their assault on Portuguese trade and colonies, especially in what is now Indonesia. Both nations established East India Companies in 1600 whose ability to capitalize trade far exceeded that of the merchants of Spain and Portugal.

Like Qing emperors, seventeenth-century Japanese shoguns tried to regulate foreign trade by confining it to specific harbors. In contrast to the sixteenth century, they also tried to prevent the increasingly short supply of precious metals from leaving the country by practicing import substitution for silk and sugar. A Dutch ship carrying a mixed crew of men from Europe and the western hemisphere arrived in 1600. (Of five ships with a crew of 461 men, only one ship and twenty-five men survived to reach Japan.) The next ships that arrived in 1609 received permission to set up quarters on Hirado, as did the British, who arrived in 1613. Both the Dutch and British arrived as representatives of trading companies, not their governments. Disappointed with scant profits, the British soon shut down their quarters. Unhappy with what it deemed smuggling, in 1635 the shogunate

issued a maritime ban that forbade all Japanese from sailing overseas and ordered those who had migrated to Southeast Asia to return home or face permanent exile. The thriving Japanese community at Hoi An in Vietnam disappeared. In a further attempt to control unregulated trade and piracy, the shogunate later banned the building of ocean-going ships. In 1641 it ordered the Dutch to move from Hirado to the artificial island called Dejima in Nagasaki bay originally constructed for the Portuguese. The annual visits by Dutch ships allowed an exchange of information, continued Japan's connections with Southeast Asia, and opened the door to western science and medicine.

Korea proved inhospitable to merchants and missionaries alike. In the early seventeenth century British and Dutch traders made several attempts to insert their goods into the Japanese trade route through the islands of Tsushima, but memories of piracy, fear of unregulated trade that smacked of smuggling, and suspicion of European intentions led the government to refuse entry to their goods. Korean scholars in residence at the Chinese court read the Jesuits' religious, scientific, and mathematical treatises and took them back to Korea, where they attracted a small following for Catholic Christianity. The converts soon became embroiled in the factional infighting that characterized politics in eighteenth century Korea. No European missionary or merchant tried to visit Korea until three French priests landed illegally in 1836–1837. The Korean court had them and their converts executed in 1839 for spreading the "evil teaching" that ran counter to the dictates of filial piety.

SUGGESTED READING

For Southeast Asian networks, see A. Reid, *Southeast Asia in the Age of Commerce: 1450–1680*, vols. 1 and 2 (1988, 1993). For a recent book that compares trade in Europe and Asia, see K. L. Pomeranz, *The Great Divergence: China, Europe, and the Making of the Modern World* (2000). For the Jesuits in China, see J. Spence, *The Memory Palace of Matteo Ricci* (1984). For Japan see M. J. Cooper, *They Came to Japan: An Anthology of European Reports on Japan, 1543–1640* (1965); G. Elison, *Deus Destroyed* (1974); and D. Massarella, *A World Elsewhere: Europe's Encounter with Japan in the Sixteenth and Seventeenth Centuries* (1990).

CHAPTER FIVE

Edo Japan
(1603–1800)

Tokugawa Settlement

Material Culture: Night Soil

Documents: Ihara Saikaku's "Sensible Advice on Domestic Economy"

Biography: Tadano Makuzu

Maturation and Decay

The social and political order imposed under the Tokugawa shoguns consolidated trends long in the making. The demarcation of villages as corporate communities, the separation of samurai from commoners, the creation of bounded domains, and the growth of and restrictions on commerce all had antecedents in the late sixteenth century. The structure of family life, in particular the emphasis on primogeniture and the custom of brides serving their husbands' families, continued practices already apparent in the fourteenth century. Yet peace also made possible economic developments that some historians deem proto-industrialization, unprecedented urbanization, and a flourishing of theater, fiction, poetry, and intellectual life.

What distinguished the Tokugawa shogunate from previous military regimes? What were the consequences of the political settlement for economic and demographic growth? To what extent did shogunal efforts to restrict foreign contact isolate Japan? What did samurai do without battles to fight? How did urban and rural commoners make their presence felt?

TOKUGAWA SETTLEMENT

The cadastral surveys and separation of warriors from the land begun under Hideyoshi and continued in the seventeenth century aimed at ordering society according to unchanging criteria. The Tokugawa brought an end to the conflicts caused by sibling rivalry by insisting on strict primogeniture for the military ruling class and confiscating domains rived by succession disputes. As a result, a ruler's personality and level of competence mattered less than his office, and the retainers' loyalty focused on the position, not the individual. The monarch and his court lived, according to popular parlance, "above the clouds" in Kyoto. Samurai stood at the top of the official status order, followed by commoners in order of their contributions to society. In principle no one was to change residence or status, nor was marriage permitted across status lines. In reality, status boundaries were fluid. Since changing names changed identity, a commoner woman took an aristocratic name when serving a military household. Individual actors and prostitutes became celebrities, and the exclusive right to work with animal skins made some outcasts wealthy.

Tokugawa Social Hierarchy		
Core Social Statuses	Other Social Groups (Between Statuses)	Outcasts
Samurai	Priests	Blind Female Entertainers
Cultivators	Doctors	Beggars
Artisans	Monks	Prostitutes
Merchants		Actors
		Non-Humans (Hinin)
		Polluted Ones (Kawata)

This status order restricted rural communities to cultivators. In the seventeenth century, most villages had at least one dominant family, often descended from a rusticated warrior, which monopolized the position of headman. A council of elders comprising landholding cultivators known as *honbyakushō* provided a sounding board for matters pertaining to village affairs. The *honbyakushō* households included family members, house servants, and fieldworkers. In central and eastern Japan, villages contained complex lineage systems with multiple branches. Across Japan social, economic, and political inequality structured village life. The men who claimed descent from village founders expected to be treated with deference, they claimed the largest and best fields, and they dominated village politics. Their wives shared their prestige; a male of lesser standing had to treat such women with respect.

Villages divided up the countryside. A village contained residential plots, rice paddies, and dry fields, each assigned to households. In some regions the agricultural lands periodically rotated from family to family. These households cooperated in doing the heavy work of leveling rice paddies and building dikes, managing irrigation networks, and transplanting rice seedlings into the paddies. Women performed this last backbreaking task in a carryover of medieval religious beliefs that sanctified it as a fertility ritual. Beyond this basic level, each household was on its own to prosper or to fail. Village boundaries also enclosed wastelands and forests with access to their products carefully regulated by the village council. As a corporate entity embodied by the headman, the village was collectively responsible for paying taxes, both the yearly tribute measured in units of rice (*koku*—1 koku equals 5.1 bushels of rice, the amount needed to feed one man for a year) and various ancillary exactions, for example, fees for the privilege of exploiting forest resources.

Bounded, contiguous villages constituted the building blocks of domains ruled by daimyo that typically were bounded and contiguous. The shogun had the largest domain concentrated chiefly in eastern and central Japan totaling approximately one-fourth of the total agricultural base. Vassal daimyo (*fudai*) were hereditary retainers. They governed domains; they also served as the shogun's chief advisers and his first line of defense against potential foes. According to a decree of 1634, only vassals whose domains contained over 10,000 *koku* enjoyed the status of daimyo. The shogun's retainers with smaller fiefs, often made up of parcels in several villages, were called *hatamoto* ("beneath the banner"). In addition the shogun commanded the services of thousands of housemen who received stipends from the shogun's warehouses. Daimyo who had been shogun Tokugawa Ieyasu's rivals or peers were deemed outside lords (*tozama*). Fewer in number than the vassal daimyo, the mightiest controlled large domains that functioned almost as nations. Some of the shogun's collateral relatives also numbered among the daimyo. They were neither wealthy nor politically powerful, but they enjoyed great prestige. All daimyo, who numbered between two hundred fifty and two hundred eighty, had retainer bands to be supported and employed.

Government

The government pieced together by the Tokugawa shoguns over some forty years developed an elaborate bureaucratic structure (later called a *bakufu*—tent government). The senior councilors—four to five men who rotated on a monthly basis, each of them a vassal daimyo worth at least 30,000 *koku*—took responsibility for policy decisions, personnel matters, and supervising the daimyo. Their assistants, also vassal daimyo, handled matters relating to the shogun's retainers. The *hatamoto* staffed the administrative positions, beginning with the magistrates in charge of finances, cities, and temples and shrines. Finance magistrates supervised the intendants responsible for seeing that the villagers paid their taxes and general agrarian affairs. They also managed the increasingly futile task of balancing expenditures with income. Their staff, and those of the other magistrates, included an array of functionaries, guards, and servants. Although the shogun tried to reduce the size of his army in the seventeenth century, he was never able to provide more than part-time employment to his retainers: 42 percent of *hatamoto* (1,676 in 1829) served in the fatigue regiment, the default category for men without office. Each daimyo likewise had an overly abundant staff of advisers, accountants, liaison officers, attendants, tax collectors, doctors, teachers, guards, servants, and placeholders.

The shogunal and domainal governments developed the most complex, sophisticated, and coherent administrative systems Japan had ever seen. Retainers learned to wield a brush as well as a sword, understand high finance, and accustom themselves to routinized office jobs. Administrative systems also retained distinctly unmodern bureaucratic elements. The shogun bestowed his former family name of Matsudaira on important *fudai* and *tozama* daimyo, both as an honor and as a reminder that rulers were kin. Opportunities for promotion depended on hereditary rank; men born of guards stayed guards. The senior councilors may have been policy experts, but they were also the shogun's vassals. Their duties included watching him perform ancestral rites, lecture on the Chinese classics, and dance in Nō. When he left the castle to go hawking or visit one of their number, they and their subordinates had to attend him. The shogun maintained a large staff of palace women ordered in a female bureaucracy to serve him, his wife, and his mother in the great interior (*ōoku*). Their responsibilities included a yearly round of ceremonies and managing gift exchanges with the Kyoto court and daimyo families.

Although the daimyo ran their domains as they saw fit, the shogunate started to issue decrees to regulate their behavior in 1615. It limited the number of guns allowed per castle and restricted castle repairs. The daimyo could not harbor criminals, collude against the shogun, or marry without the shogun's permission. All daimyo had the responsibility of contributing men and money to the shogun's building projects, and they could be relocated from one region to another at the shogun's pleasure. Most important, the shogunate issued increasingly stringent guidelines governing the daimyo's attendance on the shogun. Known as *sankin kōtai* and formalized in 1635, this system stipulated that each daimyo spend half of his time in his domain and half in the shogun's capital at Edo. Each daimyo's wife and heir had to reside in Edo as hostages. Designed to keep the daimyo both loyal to the shogun and effective in local administration, the system balanced the centrifugal forces that had weakened the Kamakura regime and the centripetal tendencies that had destroyed the Ashikaga. *Sankin kōtai* also had the inadvertent consequence of stimulating trade, encouraging travel, and spreading urban culture to the hinterland.

The shogunate appropriated certain national responsibilities to itself. It refurbished the highway system with post stations and checkpoints to keep guns out of Edo and female hostages in. For its own defense, it forbade the building of bridges over major rivers. It oversaw the development of coastal shipping routes, took over the mines for precious metals, and minted copper, silver, and gold coins. It initiated an official handwriting style for documents. It forbade the practice of Christianity and set up a nationwide system of temple registration to ensure compliance. In 1635 it forbade Japanese to travel overseas and banned foreign books. In 1639 it regulated relations with the West by allowing only the Dutch to trade at Nagasaki. It delegated the oversight of trade and diplomacy with neighboring countries to three domains: Satsuma for the Ryukyus, Tsushima for Korea, and Matsumae for the Ainu and the north. The shogunate supervised trade with China that took place at Nagasaki; it had less control over the Chinese goods that arrived indirectly through the Ryukyus and Hokkaido.

Under the Tokugawa regime, people inhabiting the Ryukyu Islands found themselves forced into much closer proximity to Japan. An independent kingdom with tributary ties to China as well as Japan in the sixteenth century, the Ryukyus suffered invasion by Satsuma in 1609. Although the king survived and trade with China continued, he had to surrender control over his islands' diplomatic and economic affairs, to the detriment of the islanders' well-being. Intellectuals in the Ryukyus tried to craft a new identity by claiming that although they were politically subservient to Japan, they achieved moral parity with both Japan and China by cultivating the way of the Confucian sage.

Relations with the Ainu in Hokkaido evolved differently. There the shogunate had the Matsumae family with longstanding ties to the region establish a domain on the island's southern tip. The Matsumae received the privilege of monopolizing trade with the Ainu in exchange for a pledge of loyalty. In 1669, conflict between Ainu tribes over access to game and fish escalated into a war to rid Hokkaido of the Japan-

Ainu Feeding a Hawk. This mid-nineteenth century drawing of an Ainu feeding a hawk depicts the bird as almost as large as its captor. The Ainu is stereotypically hairy with full beard and heavy eyebrows. *(Brett Walker/Collection for Northern Studies, Hokkaido University Library)*

ese. Following its bloody suppression, the Ainu and the Japanese solidified distinct ethnic identities that incorporated elements of the other—eagle feathers and otter pelts for the Japanese ruling class and ironware, rice, and sake for the Ainu. Between 1590 and 1800, the Ainu became increasingly dependent on trade with the Japanese for their subsistence, while periodic epidemics brought by traders ravaged their population. Many ended up working as contract laborers in fisheries that shipped food and fertilizer to Japan.

The Tokugawa shogunate survived for over 250 years not simply because it dominated Japan militarily but because, like Oda Nobunaga and Toyotomi Hideyoshi, Ieyasu and his heirs recognized the importance of ideology in transforming power into authority. Nobunaga claimed that he acted on behalf of the realm (*tenka*), not his private, selfish interests. Governance of his domain became public administration (*kōgi*). He also built a shrine to himself; Hideyoshi actively promoted a cult to his own divinity.

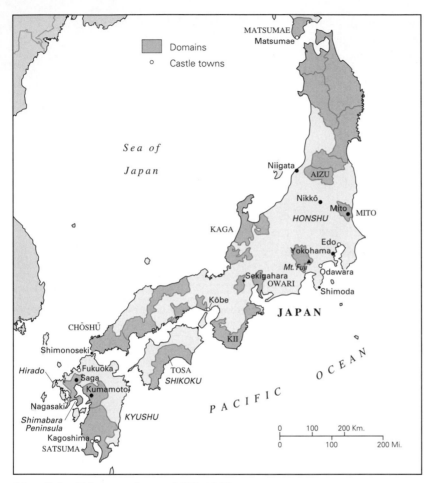

Map 5.1   Tokugawa Japan, 1600–1868

Ieyasu's posthumous title apotheosized him as *Tōshō daigongen*—the Buddha incarnate as the sun god of the east. Enshrined at Nikkō, he protected the shogunate from malignant spirits and worked for the good of all people. (See Map 5.1.) The third shogun Iemitsu claimed that the shogunate manifested a just social order that followed the way of heaven (*tendō*). This way is natural, unchanging, eternal, and hierarchical. The ruler displays the benevolence of the Buddha, the warrior preserves the peace, and the commoners are obedient. The fifth shogun, Tsunayoshi, tried to domesticate the warriors by codifying mourning rituals, lecturing on Confucian classics, and forbidding the killing of ani-

mals, especially dogs (used for target practice). His successor reversed the last stricture, and the eighth shogun Yoshimune sought to revive the martial arts. One aim of later reforms between 1787 and 1793 was to redress the balance between brush and sword, suggesting that for samurai, how to follow the way of heaven was not self-evident.

Agricultural Transformations and the Commercial Revolution

Cultivators, merchants, artisans, and rulers quickly exploited the peace dividend. Large- and small-scale reclamation projects, often funded

Artisans. Cottage industries relied on families. Both the pattern dyers depicted on the screen to the right and the weavers shown on the screen to the left employed men and women, children and grandparents. *(LEFT: Werner Forman/Corbis; RIGHT: Sakamoto Photo Research Laboratory/Corbis)*

by merchants at a daimyo's behest, opened rice paddies and expanded arable land by 45 percent. Rivers were diked and new channels dug to bring irrigation water to fields. Countless building projects, partly to repair the ravages of war in Kyoto but mainly to build the plethora of daimyo mansions, shogunal palaces, and merchant quarters in the new capital at Edo and the castle towns, seriously depleted forests. By the end of the seventeenth century, floods sweeping down denuded mountains threatened hard-won fields. The shogunate led the way in regulating the use of forestry products, but the agricultural base continued to press against ecological limits. (See **Material Culture: Night Soil.**)

The introduction of better seeds and new crops intensified the use of land and labor. The accumulation of small innovations based on observations of soil types and climatic condi-

tions led to the development of rice varieties suited for specific local conditions. Fast-ripening rice spread cultivation into the marginal lands of the northeast. Farther south, it allowed the sowing of a second crop, often wheat, although some paddies in Kyushu supported two rice crops a year. Corn, tobacco, and sweet potato, products of the western hemisphere, became dry field staples along with barley and millet. In a trend that continued throughout the Tokugawa period, seventeenth-century agronomy experts traveled Japan building social networks of like-minded experimenters, seeking the most advanced methods for increasing crop yields, and disseminating their findings in books.

Cultivators also grew cash crops and developed products based on Chinese technology. The spread of cotton growing in western Japan beginning in the sixteenth century reduced the

MATERIAL CULTURE

Night Soil

The Edo city government left waste disposal in the hands of individual landlords. Daimyo and *hatamoto* contracted with nearby villages to bring fresh vegetables to their compounds and remove waste. Communal toilet facilities in each commoner ward also had to be cleaned.

In the eighteenth century, cultivators planted crops where they had once foraged for green fertilizer. The more intensive use of land forced them to look outside their communities for soil amendments. Vegetable farmers near Edo carted away night soil and other organic wastes to supplement the manure they produced themselves. Separated into solids and liquid and cooked in its own heat to kill harmful organisms, night soil became a valuable commodity.

In the late eighteenth century, townspeople expected cultivators to pay for the privilege of collecting night soil. Landlords insisted that tenants use their toilet facilities and tried to sell their product to the highest bidder. Transactions between subcontractors, wholesalers, and middlemen raised costs. Regional alliances of cultivators petitioned the shogunate to keep prices down.

The value placed on night soil reflected status inequality. Landlords segregated toilets by sex because men's excrement was valued more highly than women's. Samurai received more for their waste than did commoners. An eighteenth-century farmhouse had a toilet for samurai made of polished wood. The tenant farmers and family members used an open pit.

Toilets. The photo on the left depicts a toilet for the use of samurai officials next to the formal reception room at a village headman's house. On the opposite side behind the stable is the pit for family and servants to use (right). *(Photos courtesy of Anne Walthall)*

hours women had to spend preparing cloth for their families while revolutionizing clothing and bedding. During the seventeenth century, Japan imported Chinese silk and sugar. By the 1730s for silk and the 1830s for sugar, domestic production provided substitutes. The daimyo competed in developing products for export to fund

their mandated trips to Edo. They hired teachers to show cultivators how to harvest lacquer, make paper, and raise silkworms. They promoted distinctive styles of wooden combs, paper hair ties, and ceramics. Merchants supplied the capital, and cultivators supplied the labor, although a few rural entrepreneurs managed to profit from the distribution of raw materials and the transportation of goods. Lights fueled by rapeseed oil enabled work to continue into the night. Increases in agricultural productivity spurred demand for nonagricultural goods produced by rural households. The growth of cottage industries diversified income sources and led to a virtuous cycle of interaction between agriculture and manufacturing. Neither entrepreneurs nor domains tried to set up large-scale production units. Instead they emphasized quality and variety, trying to beat the competition by producing regional specialties found nowhere else.

The agricultural and commercial revolutions meant higher per capita productivity and a trend toward smaller families. After almost a threefold increase in the seventeenth century, Japan's population remained surprisingly stagnant. In villages the extended families characteristic of earlier times broke down by the end of the seventeenth century into main families and branches or landlords and tenants. Most households cultivated parcels just big enough to support a stem family of grandparents, parents, and children. There was not enough to bestow on more than one heir. Historians have supposed that cultivators practiced abortion and infanticide lest they have more children than they could afford. Even if the heir died, the ease of adoption meant that a family could usually find someone to carry on the family line. Other factors were also at work. Men often left their homes for months at a time to work in towns and cities, especially during the winter. The female age at marriage went up in central Japan because women increasingly worked to gain experience before settling down. Disease mattered: smallpox, for example, can reduce male fertility by 50 percent. Syphilis struck urban populations. Periodic famines hit some regions harder than others. In the early nineteenth century, population decline in the impoverished northeast offset growth in the more commercially developed and prosperous west.

One characteristic of Japan's early modern growth was that while labor remained in the countryside, capital largely concentrated in the cities. Not until the late eighteenth century did rural entrepreneurs amass significant amounts of capital, and they often depended on urban merchants for financial backing. Daimyo traveling on *sankin kōtai* marketed rice they collected in taxes to merchants in Osaka who advanced them currency and letters of credit. These promissory notes, redeemable at the merchant's branch in Edo, served as Japan's first paper money. Domains later printed their own currency, modeled on religious talismans to gain users' trust. Merchants either advanced the money to make specialty products or bought them at a discount to sell to urban consumers. Some merchants acted as purveyors to daimyo and their women, stimulating the desire for high-quality labor-intensive goods. Others catered to the broader market by selling cotton cloth, lamp oil, and soy sauce. At the end of the seventeenth century, a few Osaka and Edo merchants had become extremely wealthy, and a number of daimyo found themselves deeply in debt.

Urban Life and Culture

Edo's spatial layout mirrored the shogun's strategic concerns. Taking advantage of technological advancements in fortifications, the shogun's castle was enclosed behind multiple stone walls surrounded by moats. The shogunate drained the swamp on which the city was built through canals that provided transportation for goods and people. Bridges over the moats were faced with guardhouses, forcing the traveler to make a sharp turn, and no roads led directly to the castle. Vassal daimyo and the shogun's retainers lived in its immediate vicinity, providing another ring of protection. The wealthy *tozama* daimyo had large compounds containing barracks for their retainers, storehouses, mansions, and gardens. None was allowed moats and stone walls, and quarters for the vassal daimyo surrounded them. Each daimyo maintained multiple compounds; the total number was over one thousand. The ruling class took the salubrious highlands for itself, leaving the lowlands directly east and south of the castle for commoners. Scattered throughout the city were shrines and temples. Daimyo castle towns followed a similar pattern of segregating people according to status and occupation.

The seventeenth century saw an unprecedented increase in urban growth, from little more than 1 percent of Japan's population to almost 15 percent after 1700. In addition to the castle towns were three metropolises: Kyoto became a manufacturing center of luxury goods, Osaka served as Japan's chief market, and Edo's swollen population of daimyo and bureaucrats made it a consumption center. Urbanization stimulated the growth of commercial publishing that created and fed a reading public hungry for knowledge and entertainment. It provided space for exhibitions from religious icons to botanical specimens and for private salons where scholars, artists, and writers met patrons. Urban residents paid for services—hairdressing, amusements—that had once been provided by servants. They bought processed food and cloth that their ancestors had made themselves. Labor and leisure were oriented toward the market, and purchasing finished products saved time. This transformation stimulated a consumption revolution—the increased demand for a greater variety of goods from durable luxury items such as elaborately carved transoms to drug foods such as sake and tobacco.

Unprecedented urban prosperity culminated in the Genroku era (1688–1704), the heyday of townsman (*chōnin*) culture, justly celebrated in art and literature. Ihara Saikaku wrote stories about the samurai passion for boys, but most of his works focused on the foibles of the townspeople in books such as *Five Women Who Loved Love* and *The Life of an Amorous Man*. He also wrote books on how to make and keep money. (See **Documents: Ihara Saikaku's "Sensible Advice on Domestic Economy."**) Matsuo Bashō raised the seventeen-syllable verse form known as haiku to a fine art, in the process making poetry accessible to commoners in town and country. Chikamatsu Monzaemon wrote librettos for the puppet theater that explored the complex interplay between social obligations and human feeling, as when a young man in love with a prostitute wants to buy the contract that indentures her to the brothel owner but lacks the resources to do so without causing irreparable harm to his family's business. Caught between love and duty, the couple resolves the dilemma by committing double suicide. Although Chikamatsu wrote for puppets, the literary artistry of his scripts endeared them to amateur performers and raised the quality of theatrical performances.

Two pleasure zones are associated with the Genroku era: the brothel district and the theaters, often located in close proximity to each other on the margins of respectable society. These constituted the "floating world" (*ukiyo*), celebrated in woodblock prints of courtesans and actors along with pornography. In the early seventeenth century, entrepreneurs in the three metropolises petitioned the shogunate to establish districts for prostitution where it could be regulated and controlled. A moat and walls surrounded Edo's Yoshiwara with a main gate where guards noted the men who entered and prevented women from leaving. The earliest customers were daimyo and samurai. Merchants whose lavish spending brought them great renown soon eclipsed them. In this status-conscious society, courtesans too were ranked.

Kabuki began in the early seventeenth century on a riverbank in Kyoto where a prostitute erected a stage on which to sing and dance to attract customers. Fights over her charms led the shogunate to forbid women to appear on stage in 1629. Boys then replaced them as actors and prostitutes. Again the shogunate stepped in to quell disorder, banning all but mature men from performing in public. To make up for what they lacked in sex appeal, actors developed the techniques of acting, singing, and dancing performed on elaborate and frequently changing sets that made kabuki the spectacle known today. It became enormously popular, with the highest acclaim reserved for the men who specialized in playing women. It staged reenactments of the scandals arising in townspeople's society, but it became best known for swashbuckling melodramas set in the past, for the shogunate forbade any discussion of its own affairs or those of contemporary samurai society.

Intellectual Trends

The Edo period saw an explosion in intellectual life. Deprived of the opportunity to gain fame in battle, some samurai turned to scholarship and made serious efforts to understand society. In the seventeenth century, Hayashi Razan formulated the Tokugawa ideology in neo-Confucian terms that saw the social order as a reflection of the visible natural order in that both realized an underlying metaphysical principle. Among his students was Yamaga Sokō, famous for defining a way for samurai to survive during a time of peace: "The business of the samurai consists in reflecting on his own station in life, in discharging loyal service to his master . . . in deepening his fidelity in associations with friends, and . . . in devoting himself to duty above all."[1] Kyoto scholar Itō Jinsai likewise began as a neo-Confucianist, only to reject the notion of metaphysical principle in favor of studying Confucius himself. For him, the purpose of scholarship was to show how to put morality based on benevolence and love into practice, a goal achievable by commoners as well as samurai. Such was the cachet of Chinese philosophy that any man who had pretensions of becoming learned had to employ Chinese categories of thought. Women were not subject to this restriction, but for that reason, they had no formal access to scholarship beyond the study of Japanese poetry. (See **Biography: Tadano Makuzu**.)

Ogyū Sorai gained influence by attacking the neo-Confucian Hayashi school and Itō Jinsai. He argued that only the most ancient Chinese texts, those that predated Confucius, were worthy of study because they contained the teachings of the sage kings, the creators of civilization. The social order did not reflect the unchanging natural order of beasts; instead it was an artificial construct, made in history, and that was a good

thing. Men needed rules lest their passions run away with them. Japan was fortunate that its own sage king Ieyasu had created the shogunate, and his deeds were not for mere mortals to challenge. Sorai's rational bureaucratic view of government called on the samurai to devote themselves to public duty. In 1703 forty-seven retainers from the Akō domain assassinated their dead lord's enemy (an incident dramatized as "The Treasury of Loyal Retainers," *Chūshingura*) because, they claimed, their honor as samurai left them no choice. Sorai applauded the deed but acceded to the official position that since they had broken the law against private vendettas, they had to atone by committing suicide. As long as people obeyed the law, government had no business interfering in their private lives.

The eighteenth century saw a proliferation of schools and thinkers. Dazai Shundai explored the ramifications of political economy. He urged daimyo to supplement the flat revenues derived from an agrarian tax base by promoting the production of goods for export. Kaiho Seiryō took Shundai's ideas a step further by arguing that all social relationships are predicated on the measured exchange of goods and services, a principle understood by merchants but not, unfortunately, by samurai. Andō Shōeki claimed that Sorai's sage kings were thieves and liars who created governments to deceive and cheat the cultivators. In his eyes, the samurai were no better than parasites.

Merchants pondered business ethics. Troubled by the excesses of the Genroku period when some financiers had gone bankrupt through lavish spending and making too many bad loans to the daimyo, Ishida Baigan founded the Shingaku school (literally, study of the heart). He argued that merchants deserved to make a just profit because their profit was equivalent to the samurai's stipend. They should devote themselves to their enterprises with the same devotion a samurai showed to his lord, and like the samurai they should strive for moral perfection. Texts and teachers could guide this quest, but it could be completed only through meditation and the practice of diligence, thrift, and fortitude. Baigan and his

---

1. Ryusaku Tsunoda et al., eds., *Sources of the Japanese Tradition* (New York: Columbia University Press, 1959), 1:390.

DOCUMENTS

Ihara Saikaku's "Sensible Advice on Domestic Economy"

Ihara Saikaku (1642–1693) is often considered Japan's first professional author because he lived by his pen, writing haiku, short stories, novels, and essays that described life in Osaka during the heyday of the townspeople. Here he feeds the merchants' obsession with the making and saving of money by focusing on the details of daily life and the qualities desired in a wife.

"The immutable rule in regard to the division of family property at the time of marriage," said the experienced go-between from Kyoto, "is as follows: Let us suppose that a certain man is worth a thousand *kan*. To the eldest son at his marriage will go four hundred *kan,* together with the family residence. The second son's share will be three hundred *kan,* and he too is entitled to a house of his own. The third son will be adopted into another family, requiring a portion of one hundred *kan*. If there is a daughter, her dowry will be thirty *kan,* in addition to a bridal trousseau worth twenty *kan*. It is advisable to marry her off to the son of a family of lower financial status. Formerly it was not unusual to spend forty *kan* on the trousseau and allot ten *kan* for the dowry, but because people today are more interested in cash, it is now customary to give the daughter silver in the lacquered chest and copper in the extra one. Even if the girl is so ugly that she can't afford to sit near the candle at night, that dowry of thirty *kan* will make her bloom into a very flowery bride!"

"In matchmaking, money is a very important consideration. If thirty *kan* of silver is deposited with a trustworthy merchant at six-tenths percent interest per month, the income will total one hundred and eighty *momme* monthly, which will more than suffice to support four women: the bride, her personal maid, a second maid, and a seamstress. How unselfish must be the disposition of a bride who will not only look after the household faithfully, meantime taking care never to displease her husband's family, but also at the same time will actually pay for the food she eats! If you are looking merely for beauty, then go where women are made up solely to that end, to the licensed quarters. You are free to visit them any time of night you may wish, and thoroughly enjoy it, but next morning you will have to pay out seventy-one *momme*—which is not in the least enjoyable!"

"It is better on the whole to give up dissipation in good time, for a roué is seldom happy in later life. So even if life at home seems dry and tasteless, you'd better have patience with a supper of cold rice, potluck

followers had no political agenda; the idea that merchants might have something to say to samurai was left to the merchant academy in Osaka, the Kaitokudō, founded in 1724. Its teachers denied that merchants caused the ills of famine and indebtedness through their pursuit of profit. Merchants, they argued, played a crucial role in society by facilitating the circulation of goods based on objective and accurate calcu-

lations. When they applied this principle to domain finances, their advice regarding fiscal policy ought to be followed. A number of them gained coveted positions as advisers to daimyo and shogun.

Other thinkers found inspiration in the Japanese past. The greatest of them was Motoori Norinaga, whose prodigious memory enabled him to decipher the patterns of Chinese charac-

bean curd, and dried fish. You may lie down whenever you like, at perfect ease, and have a maid massage you down to the very tips of your toes. If you want tea, you may sip it while your wife holds the cup for you. A man in his own household is the commander supreme, whose authority none will dare to question, and there is none to condemn you. There's no need to seek further for genuine pleasure."

"Then, too, there are certain business advantages to staying home. Your clerks will stop their imprudent visits to the Yasaka quarters and their clandestine meetings at that rendezvous in Oike. And when in the shop, since they can't appear to be completely idle, maybe they'll look over those reports from the Edo branch office, or do some other work that they have been putting off doing—all to the profit of you, the master! The apprentice boys will diligently twist wastepaper into string, and in order to impress you, the master, sitting in the inner room, they will practice penmanship to their profit. Kyushichi, whose habit it is to retire early, will take the straw packing from around the yellowtail and make rope on which to string coins; while Take, in order to make things go more smoothly tomorrow, will prepare the vegetables for breakfast. The seamstress during the time you're at home will take off as many knots of Hino silk as she ordinarily does in a whole day. Even the cat keeps a wary watch in the kitchen and when she hears the least sound in the vicinity of the fish hanger she will mew to scare away the rats. If such unmeasured profit as this results from the master's remaining at home just one night, think how vast will be the benefits that will accrue within the space of a whole year! So even if you are not entirely satisfied with your wife, you have to exercise discretion and realize that in the gay quarters all is but vanity. For a young master to be well aware of this is the secret of the successful running of his household."

Such was the counsel offered by the veteran go-between.

Be that as it may, let me say that the women of today, under the influence of the styles of the gay quarters, dress exactly like professional entertainers. Prominent drapers' wives, who in public are addressed as mesdames, are so attired as to be mistaken for high-class courtesans; while the wives of small shopkeepers, who once served as clerks of the drapers, look exactly like courtesans one grade lower. Again, the kimono worn by wives of tailors and embroiderers who live on the side streets bear a startling resemblance to those of the women employed in teahouses. It is fun to spot them in a crowd dressed in conformity with their respective degrees of fortune.

Source: Saikaku Ihara, *This Scheming World*, trans. Masanori Takatsuka and David C. Stubbs (Rutland, Vt.: Charles E. Tuttle Company, 1965), pp. 54–57 (modified).

ters used to write *Kojiki,* Japan's most ancient history. Through the study of history and literary classics, he affirmed Japan's unique position in the world as the sole country ruled by descendants of the sun goddess, and he celebrated the private world of the individual. Based as they were on the spontaneity of human feeling, Japanese values were superior to those of other peoples. "In foreign countries, they place logic first, even when it comes to revering the gods . . . all this is but shallow human reasoning." The Chinese had introduced rules that while they might be necessary in China where people were naturally inclined toward error, were entirely unsuited to Japan, where people were intrinsically perfect in their possession of the "true

BIOGRAPHY Tadano Makuzu

Male intellectuals focused on morality, politics, and economics; Tadano Makuzu (1763–1825) drew on her observations and experience as a daughter of the samurai to analyze human relations.

Born Kudō Ayako, she grew up in a lively and prosperous family of parents, her father's mother, and seven siblings. At age nine she insisted that her mother teach her classical Japanese poetry. Ayako enjoyed her grandmother's company because she was a cheerful and attractive woman who loved kabuki. To complete her education, at fifteen Ayako became an attendant to the lord of Sendai's daughter, a position she held for ten years.

Ayako's father, Heisuke, had many friends who shared his interests in medicine, botany, foreign trade, and western countries. He hoped to arrange a good marriage for Ayako should his proposal of 1780 for the colonization of Hokkaido and trade with Russia lead to a position with the shogunate. The fall of his patron in 1786 stymied his career and his plans for his daughter.

When Ayako left service, she was too old to make a good match. In 1789 she was married to a man so decrepit that she cried until she was returned to her parents. In 1797 her father found her a husband in a widower with three sons, Tadano Iga Tsurayoshi, a high-ranking Sendai retainer with an income four times that of the Kudō family. Marrying Iga meant that Ayako had to leave the city of her birth for Sendai, a move she likened to "the journey to hell." There she spent the remainder of her life visited only occasionally by her husband, who remained on duty in Edo.

Signed with the pen name Makuzu, "Solitary Thoughts" (*Hitori kangae*) encapsulates Ayako's views on her society distilled during her years of isolation in Sendai. She bemoans her ignorance of Confucianism because her father thought it inappropriate knowledge for a woman. It was of little use even for men, she believed, because it was too clumsy to regulate the niceties of Japanese behavior. Like other intellectuals of her day, she pitied the samurai for not understanding the principle of money. Instead of a well-ordered harmonious society, she saw competition, hatred, and strife: "Each person in our country strives to enrich him or herself alone without thinking of the foreign threat or begrudging the cost to the country." Townspeople despised warriors: "They take secret delight in the warriors' descent into poverty, hating them like sworn enemies." Antagonism governed even relations between the sexes: "When men and women make love, they battle for superiority by rubbing their genitals together."

Source: Janet R. Goodwin, Bettina Gramlich-Oka, Elizabeth A. Leicester, Yuki Terazawa, and Anne Walthall, "Solitary Thoughts: A Translation of Tadano Makuzu's *Hitori Kangae*," *Monumenta Nipponica* 56 (Spring 2001): 21, 25, 36; 56 (Summer 2001): 179.

---

heart" (*magokoro*).[2] Even when he was asked by a daimyo to comment on the conditions of his day, Norinaga took a resolutely apolitical position, claiming that rulers should live in accordance with the way of the gods discernable in the study of history and poetry.

Official interest in western studies began in 1720 when Shogun Yoshimune lifted the ban on western books so long as they did not promote Christianity. Japanese doctors and scientists

2. Sey Nakamura, "The Way of the Gods: Motoori Norinaga's Naobi no Mitama," *Monumenta Nipponica* 46 (Spring 1991): 39.

attracted to what was called "Dutch studies" paid little attention to western philosophy; their enthusiasm was for practical matters, in particular the study of human anatomy, astronomy, geography, and military science. Sugita Genpaku discovered that a Dutch human anatomy book provided names for body parts not found in Chinese medical texts. In 1771 he watched the dissection of a criminal's corpse, a fifty-year-old woman, performed by an outcast. Although this was not the first dissection performed in Japan, the evidence of his own eyes plus the Dutch text led him to invent Japanese terms for pancreas, nerve, and other body parts; these terms were later exported to China. The belief in empirical reason and the efficacy of experiment promoted by the Chinese "practical learning" school already constituted one strand of Japanese intellectual life; the opportunity to engage with western scientific texts developed it further. Sugita spread his ideas through his writing and salons, whose members ranged from merchants to daimyo. Western instruments such as the telescope and microscope fascinated intellectuals. The insights they gained into the natural world percolated into popular culture when Utagawa Kunisada drew pictures of greatly magnified insects to illustrate a story about monsters.

MATURATION AND DECAY

Following the excesses of the Genroku period, shogunal and domainal officials fretted over the state of government finances and their retainers' morale. The miserly Ieyasu had left stores of gold bullion, but his heirs spent them so freely that by the 1690s, the shogunate had to devalue the currency. Creeping inflation eroded the value of tax revenues and samurai stipends, while the growing availability of consumer products stimulated demand. Shogun Yoshimune responded by instituting reforms in the 1720s. To aid the samurai who received their stipends in rice, he supported rice prices even though urban consumers complained. He assessed a "voluntary contribution" from all daimyo of a rice donation in proportion to their domain's size in return for spending less time in Edo on *sankin kōtai*. Instead of basing taxes on each year's harvest, he tried to eliminate fluctuations in revenues by establishing a fixed tax rate. He allowed villages to open new fields in regions previously set aside to provide forage and fertilizer and encouraged the cultivation of cash crops. To reduce expenditures, he issued sumptuary legislation and cut the staff of palace women. He inaugurated a petition box, already tried in some domains, to allow commoners' suggestions and complaints to reach his ear. A famine caused by a plague of locusts in western Japan in 1732 brought the reform period to an end.

Popular Culture

In contrast to the ruling class, urban commoners generally enjoyed the benefits of the consumption revolution. By 1750 Edo's population had reached well over 1 million inhabitants, making it perhaps the largest city in the world at the time. A fish market dominated the hub of the city at Nihonbashi; the surrounding streets were lined with shops selling goods of every sort. Restaurants catered to people for whom dining out had become a pleasure. Innkeepers who specialized in accommodating plaintiffs became proto-lawyers in an increasingly litigious society. The draper Echigoya innovated a fixed price system for cash (see Color Plate 5). The world's first commodity futures market opened in Osaka. Kabuki actors incorporated advertisements into their routines starting in 1715. In 1774 a popular actor affixed his name to cosmetics sold in his store, mentioned his products on stage, and placed them in woodblock prints. Best-selling authors accepted money to praise products such as toothpaste and pipes.

The spread of commerce made education both possible and necessary. In thousands of villages across Japan, priests, village officials, and rural entrepreneurs opened schools to provide the rudiments of reading and mathematics. Coupled with the private academies in castle towns and cities for samurai and merchants, their

School Children and Teacher. In this early nineteenth cartoon by Hokusai, the teacher listens to three boys recite. Another student counts on his toes; rough housing turns into a fight. *(Corbis)*

efforts led to impressive rates of literacy by the mid-nineteenth century: approximately 40 percent for men and between 10 and 15 percent for women. Students studied didactic texts; those for women emphasized docility, modesty, and self-restraint lest the young working woman slip from seamstress to prostitute. Publishers supplied a growing market with one-page almanacs and Buddhist mandalas as well as pamphlets giving advice on agriculture and etiquette. Some students learned to read well enough to enjoy multivolume works of historical fiction, but for many, the aim was more practical: to learn when to plant crops and calculate profit and loss.

The national road system designed to bring daimyo to Edo began to attract increasing numbers of commoners in the eighteenth century. Although the shogunate prohibited travel in the interests of preserving order, it allowed pilgrimages, visits to relatives, and trips to medicinal hot springs. With a passport issued by a local official giving name, physical description, and destination, travelers set off, usually on foot, always in groups, accompanied by neighbors to see them to the community border. Many traveled in confraternities that raised money to send a few members on pilgrimage each year. The most popular destination was Ise, with its outer shrine to the god of agriculture. Since few trav-

elers were likely to repeat the pilgrimage experience, they were determined to see as much as possible. They took enormous detours through temple circuits and stopped in Edo and Osaka for sightseeing and theater. Men traveled in the prime of life; women traveled either before they were married or after they had a daughter-in-law to raise the children and run the household. Rather than suffer the invasive inspection procedures required at checkpoints, women hired guides to show them byways. Men and women bought quantities of souvenirs to ship back home and distribute to those who had given them money before they left. They kept diaries of their trip; some were little more than expense accounts, and others were lengthy descriptions of things seen and heard.

Not every pilgrim was literate or had the permission of his or her local official. Fired, they said, with the imperative to make a pilgrimage to Ise or some other sacred spot, they escaped from parents or employers with nothing but the clothes on their backs. They depended on the charity of strangers who hoped to accrue some of the merit of making the pilgrimage by giving alms. They also fell prey to bandits and procurers. At approximately sixty-year intervals, thousands of people, men and women alike, left towns and villages to make a thanksgiving pilgrimage (*okage mairi*) to the inner shrine of the sun goddess at Ise. Many never returned home. Instead they found their way to cities, where they joined a floating population of day laborers and prostitutes.

Hard Times and Peasant Uprisings

The underside to prosperity, continuing inequities, and injustice gave rise to thousands of incidents of rural protest. The corporate structure of the village meant that protest was organized collectively. When cultivators lodged complaints against unjust officials or pleas that the tax burden be reduced following a crop failure, they petitioned the lord to show compassion to the honorable cultivators because their hardships threatened their survival. As the village's representative, the headman was supposed to take the responsibility for seeking redress from samurai officials dealing with rural affairs. If officials deemed the matter worthy of consideration, they passed it up the chain of command. If at any point an official decided not to trouble his superiors, those below had no legal recourse. According to rural lore, in the seventeenth century a few brave headmen, epitomized by Sakura Sōgorō, made a direct appeal to the daimyo, or, in Sōgorō's case, to the shogun. Sōgorō paid for his audacity by suffering crucifixion along with his wife and saw his sons executed before his eyes. Although historians doubt his existence, he became Japan's most famous peasant martyr.

Few headmen in the eighteenth century were willing to risk their families to help their neighbors. Instead of an individual groveling before his superiors, cultivators marched together to assert their grievances en masse. They called their deeds *ikki,* harking back to the leagues that had bedeviled political authorities in the sixteenth century. In 1764, approximately two hundred thousand cultivators marched toward Edo to protest new demands for forced labor to transport officials and their goods on the national roads. Smaller outbursts roiled domains, peaking at times of economic hardship. Seldom did any district erupt more than once, and protestors wanted redress, not revolution. Yet fear that rural protest would expose such weaknesses in domainal administration that the shogun would transfer the daimyo or simply dispossess him limited efforts to expropriate the products of cultivators' labor.

The 1780s brought hard times to Japan. Mount Asama erupted in 1783, spewing ash that blocked sunlight all summer. Widespread crop failures exacerbated by misguided governmental policies led to famine, a catastrophe repeated in 1787. It is said that the population declined by nine hundred twenty thousand. In the eyes of many sufferers, the cause of their plight was not so much natural disaster as human failing. Unlike earlier rural protests that had demanded tax relief and government aid, the majority of incidents in the 1780s focused on commercial issues and the perfidy of merchants accused of hoarding grain while people starved. Commoners rioted for five days in Edo, punishing merchants by smashing their stores, trampling rice in the mud, and pouring sake in the street.

The famine exposed problems at all levels of society. The shogunate had struggled for years with an inadequate tax base and the increasing competition between daimyo, merchants, and cultivators for access to commercial income. Under the aegis of senior councilor Tanuma Okitsugu, it had proposed schemes to force merchants to buy shares in guilds granted a monopoly over trade in a specified item. The guild then paid regular fees in "thank you" money to the shogun. These monopolies angered those excluded, manufacturers forced to accept lower prices for their products, and daimyo who had their own schemes for profiting from trade. Following the Edo riot, the shogunate launched a second reform led by essayist, novelist, and staunch neo-Confucian Matsudaira Sadanobu to rectify finances and morals. He established new standards for bureaucratic conduct that endured to modern times. His "Edo first" policy ensured that the city remained quiescent for almost eighty years.

Sadanobu's reforms also had a darker side. A floating population of men without families or property worked as day laborers in fields and cities. Sadanobu had those in Edo rounded up and confined to an island in the bay. From there they were transported to the gold mine on Sado in the Japan Sea, where most of them died within two or three years. The harshness of this measure brought universal condemnation, and it was not repeated. Instead governments encouraged urban wards and rural villages to police themselves.

SUMMARY

By the beginning of the nineteenth century, the Japanese people had enjoyed almost two centuries of peace. Most cultivators seldom saw samurai officials. Despite the village and ward notice boards hung with placards admonishing commoners to refrain from luxuries, people let their pocketbooks regulate their behavior. To be sure, cultivators suffered under heavy taxes. Merchants had to accept arbitrary restrictions on commerce and pay ad hoc forced loans to meet the governments' endemic financial crises.

Sankin kōtai kept the daimyo coming to Edo to pay homage to the shogun and scheming to enhance their domain's prosperity. Many samurai could not afford the pleasure districts nor did their offices keep them occupied. Rather than concentrate on the public performance of duty, they retreated to the private world of intellectual stimulation and the pursuit of pleasure.

SUGGESTED READING

For the best overview, see C. Totman, *Early Modern Japan* (1993). The most recent book on relations between the shogunate and domains and domainal institutions is M. Ravina, *Land and Lordship in Early Modern Japan* (1999). For foreign relations, see R. P. Toby, *State and Diplomacy in Early Modern Japan: Asia in the Development of the Tokugawa Bakufu* (1984).

For intellectual history, see H. Ooms, *Tokugawa Ideology: Early Constructs, 1570–1680* (1985); T. Najita, *Visions of Virtue in Tokugawa Japan: The Kaitokudō Merchant Academy of Osaka* (1987); P. Nosco, *Remembering Paradise: Nativism and Nostalgia in Eighteenth Century Japan* (1990); and D. L. Keene, *The Japanese Discovery of Europe: Honda Toshiaki and Other Discoverers, 1720–1798* (1954).

For recent work on proto-industrialization, see D. L. Howell, *Capitalism from Within: Economy, Society, and the State in a Japanese Fishery* (1995); T. Morris-Suzuki, *The Technological Transformation of Japan: From the Seventeenth to the Twenty-First Century* (1994); and K. Wigen, *The Making of a Japanese Periphery, 1750–1920* (1995). For transformations in village life, see H. Ooms, *Tokugawa Village Practice: Class, Status, Power, Law* (1996). An excellent summary of demographic issues is by L. L. Cornell, "Infanticide in Early Modern Japan? Demography, Culture, and Population Growth," *Journal of Asian Studies* 55 (Feb. 1996): 22–50. For disease, see A. Jannetta, *Epidemics and Mortality in Early Modern Japan* (1987). The most recent book on social protest is J. W. White, *Ikki: Social Conflict and Political Protest in Early Modern Japan* (1995).

For popular culture, see S. Hanley, *Everyday Things in Premodern Japan: The Hidden Legacy of Material Culture* (1997); M. Nishiyama, *Edo Culture: Daily Life and Diversion in Urban Japan, 1600–1868* (1997); P. F. Kornicki, *The Book in Japan: A Cultural History from the Beginnings to the Nineteenth Century* (1998); and C. N. Vaporis, *Breaking Barriers: Travel and The State in Early Modern Japan* (1994).

For peripheries, see G. Smits, *Visions of Ryukyu: Identity and Ideology in Early Modern Thought and Politics* (1999), and B. L. Walker, *The Conquest of Ainu Lands: Ecology and Culture in Japanese Expansion, 1590–1800* (2001).

For sexuality, see G. M. Pflugfelder, *Cartographies of Desire: Male-Male Sexuality in Japanese Discourse, 1600–1950* (2000), and C. S. Seigle, *Yoshiwara: The Glittering World of the Japanese Courtesan* (1993).

Western Imperialism (1800–1900)

IN CONTRAST TO THE FRAIL WOODEN-hulled sailing ships that carried Europeans to the Pacific Ocean in the sixteenth century, nineteenth-century vessels were increasingly powered by coal-fueled steam engines. The industrial revolution that rescued Europe from the ecological trap of reliance on agrarian products propelled technological innovations in weaponry and an expansion in the state's ability to command men and resources. Following in the wake of trading companies, government officials began to regulate and tax commerce, then administer territories, and finally recruit natives into tightly disciplined, uniformed battalions capable of projecting force thousands of miles from European homelands. No longer mere participants in maritime trade, Europeans transformed their trading posts from India to Indonesia into colonies.

During the eighteenth century, European states had established trading posts throughout the Indian Ocean and the Pacific, the only colony being Spain's in the Philippines. Under Catherine the Great, Russia extended its reach across Siberia to Alaska and sent teams of explorers down the Kamchatka peninsula, along the coast of Sakhalin, and into Hokkaido. Confrontations with Japanese officials led to sporadic efforts to open diplomatic relations. Having defeated French efforts to challenge its forays into India in the middle of the eighteenth century, the British East India Company spearheaded the battle for markets that brought administrators and troops to protect mercantile interests and made Britain the greatest of the European powers. While France was embroiled in revolution, Britain sent an official mission to China in 1793. Headed by Lord George Macartney, its aim was to eliminate what the British saw as frivolous restrictions on trade that limited the number, destination, and schedules for their ships. Since controlling trade helped stabilize the social order, reduced smuggling, and reaffirmed the Qing emperor's superiority over all other monarchs, the mission failed.

The Napoleonic Wars following the French Revolution remade the map of Europe and contributed to a new sense of nationalism. In Asia Britain took over the Dutch colony at Batavia because Napoleon had tried to make his brother king of the Netherlands. The Dutch never told the Japanese that the only place flying the Dutch flag was Dejima in Nagasaki harbor. The Napoleonic Wars had spilled over into European colonial possessions in Latin America. There, wars of liberation starting in 1809 resulted in the establishment of independent nations in the 1820s. The heightened focus on nationhood required a clear demarcation of sovereignty and a clear delineation of boundaries. No longer would small states such as Vietnam, the Ryukyus, and Korea be permitted to claim quasi-autonomy under China's mantle, and every inch of land had to belong to a nation. Regardless of whether peasants saw themselves as Frenchmen, their rulers and the educated classes imagined communities in which everyone spoke the same language, professed similar beliefs, and despised foreigners. The cosmopolitan Enlightenment admiration for Chinese civilization and Confucian rationality gave way to disdain for godless heathens who failed to appreciate the superiority of western technology.

Timeline: Western Advances in Asia

1793: Earl of Macartney travels to Beijing seeking diplomatic recognition; Russians seek same in Japan.

1797: Broughton, a British captain, surveys east coast of Korea.

1804: Russian advances in Siberia and Sea of Okhotsk culminate in emissary to Japan.

1805–1812: Russia builds forts in Alaska and northern California.

1808: British warship enters Nagasaki harbor.

1811: Britain captures Java from the Dutch; returned in 1816.

1816: Anglo-Nepalese War.

1819: Raffles, a British official, occupies Singapore for Britain.

1820: Vietnam bans Christianity and expels missionaries.

1824–1826: First Anglo-Burmese War.

1837: U.S. ship *Morrison* tries and fails to establish relations with Japan.

1839–1840: Opium War and First Anglo-Afghan War.

1842: Treaty of Nanjing.

1846: U.S. Commodore Biddle seeks trade with Japan; refused.

1852: Second Anglo-Burmese War.

1853–1854: U.S. Commodore Perry forces unequal treaty on Japan.

1856–1857: Arrow War between Britain, France, and China.

1858: Treaties of Tianjin; Japan signs commercial treaty with United States.

1857–1858: Great "Indian Mutiny"; British East India Company abolished.

1860: British and French troops occupy Beijing.

1862: Treaty of Saigon: France occupies three provinces in south Vietnam.

1863: France gains protectorate over Cambodia.

1866: France sends punitive expedition to Korea.

1871: United States sends ships to open Korea to foreign trade by force; repulsed.

1874: France acquires control over all of south Vietnam; Japan sends expeditionary force to Taiwan.

1876: Japan signs unequal treaty with Korea.

1877: Queen Victoria proclaimed empress of India.

1882: Korea signs unequal treaties with United States and other Great Powers.

1884–1885: France makes Vietnam a colony.

1885–1886: Third Anglo-Burmese War.

1893: France gains protectorate over Laos.

1894–1895: Sino-Japanese War.

1898: Scramble for concessions in China by European powers.

1898: United States seizes the Philippines from Spain; annexes Hawai'i.

1900: Boxer Rebellion.

In contrast to older empires that allowed natives the opportunity to participate in running their affairs, new empires discriminated between the white man and everyone else.

By bringing decades of peace to Europe, Napoleon's defeat at Waterloo in 1815 freed nations to concentrate on expanding trade networks while competing for Great Power status. Great Power status required colonies, and competition with other nations spurred imperialism. France reestablished its preeminence in North Africa, contended with Britain for ports in Burma, and tried to force a commercial treaty on Vietnam. In 1816 Britain was at war with Nepal when it dispatched a second mission to the Qing court. Because the envoy refused to participate in the customary rituals that regulated relations between tribute nations and the Son of Heaven, including the kowtow, the emperor refused to see him. Britain had already established ports on the Malay Peninsula; adding Singapore gave it a harbor to protect and provision British ships sailing between India and China. British ships started appearing off the coast of Japan, sometimes threatening the natives in their quest for food and fuel. Britain and France clashed over Burmese ports while Burmese troops threatened Bengal. The first Anglo-Burmese War ended in victory for Britain, a large indemnity extracted from the Burmese, a British diplomat stationed at the Burmese court, and British hegemony over the Bay of Bengal.

Bengal supplied the opium that Britain used to buy tea. By 1750, Britain was importing well over 2 million pounds of tea from China a year, and demand was rising. Having little that the Chinese found of value, the British at first had to pay for tea with silver, thus leading to a negative trade balance. After 1761, the balance began to shift in Britain's favor. The East India Company allowed the illegal export of Bengali opium into China, bought tea for homeland consumption, and used the silver accruing as a result of the trade surplus to finance its operation and the British administration of Bengal. From the British point of view, that drug addicts multiplied as the price went down and the supply went up, that bribes to allow drug trafficking corrupted local officials, simply demonstrated Chinese racial inferiority.

British merchants remained unhappy with trading conditions in China. Textile manufacturers wanted to sell machine-made cloth, and private traders resented the East India Company monopoly. When the monopoly was abolished in 1834, the government named Lord Napier to be superintendent of trade in Guangzhou. He tried to bypass the Cohong, the merchant guild responsible to the Qing court for managing foreign trade, and negotiate directly with the provincial governor-general, who saw no reason to sully his dignity by dealing with barbarians. Diplomatic incident led to a confrontation between British warships and Chinese defenses. Napier was forced to withdraw. Trade continued, albeit with British merchants calling for more warships to enforce their demands for the elimination of the Cohong monopoly over foreign trade and the opening of ports farther north.

The Opium War tested Chinese morality against British technology. In 1839, Imperial Commissioner Lin Zexu arrived in Guangzhou with orders to suppress the drug trade. He moved swiftly against dealers and users and demanded that opium under foreign control be turned over. When the British merchants proved recalcitrant, he stopped trade altogether. He appealed to Queen Victoria to allow him the same right to regulate trade and suppress drugs that administrators enjoyed in Britain. When the traders reluctantly relinquished their stocks, he allowed them to flee to the Portuguese city of Macao and thence to Hong Kong while he washed twenty thousand chests of opium out to sea. Indignant at the expropriation of their property without compensation, the traders appealed to Parliament. A fleet that included four armed steamships carrying Indian troops under British officers refused to contest the defenses Lin had built upstream to protect Guangzhou. Four ships blockaded the river mouth while the rest of the fleet sailed north to harass Chinese shipping along the coast. By the time it reached Tianjin, the closest port to Beijing, the Qing court realized that it had to negotiate. In the first round of negotiations, China agreed to pay an indemnity to compensate British merchants for their destroyed property and allow expanded trade in Guangzhou, direct access to Qing officials, and British possession of Hong Kong. When these terms proved unsatisfactory to the British home government, another round of fighting forced additional concessions.

China's defeat in the Opium War forced it to open to the West and inaugurated a new era in western imperialism. (See Color Plate 6.) It marked the first time a western power had emerged victorious in battle in East Asia, a debacle that sent shock waves through Japan and Korea. The Treaty of Nanjing opened five ports to British residency and trade, abolished the Cohong, and ceded Hong Kong to Britain. A supplementary treaty signed a year later fixed low tariffs on British imports and included the most-favored-nation clause whereby any privilege granted any western power automatically accrued to Britain. In 1844, Americans signed a treaty with China that gave them the right to build churches and hospitals and to protect American nationals from the Chinese judicial system. "Extraterritoriality" meant that with the exception of opium traders, Americans in China were subject to American laws, judges, courts, and prisons. The British automatically participated in this infringement on Chinese sovereignty, as did the other western powers that signed treaties with China. Historian Akira Iriye has termed this "multilateral imperialism."[1] Because China and its subjects did not enjoy the same privileges abroad, most favored nation and extraterritoriality became the hallmarks of the unequal treaty system.

Following in the British wake, American traders, whalers, and missionaries lured their government into engagement across the Pacific. During the 1840s, swift clipper ships with clouds of sail dominated trade routes. In 1846, an American ship shelled what is now Danang in central Vietnam to win the release of an American missionary who had ignored proscriptions on proselytizing. That same year, Commodore James Biddle tried to open negotiations with Japan, only to suffer a humiliating rejection. The United States completed its westward continental expansion in 1848 when it wrested California from Mexico. (It acquired Alaska by purchase from Russia in 1867.) In developing steamer routes across the Pacific to Shanghai, it saw Japan's coal fields as playing an important role. Whalers too needed access to fuel and fresh

water. In 1853, Commodore Matthew Perry sailed four ships, two of them steamers, into Uraga Bay near Edo. He forced shogunal authorities to accept a letter proposing a friendship treaty and promised to return the next year for their response. Despite Japanese efforts to fend him off, Perry obtained the Kanagawa treaty of friendship that opened two small ports to American ships, allowed an American consul to reside on Japanese soil, and provided for most-favored-nation treatment.

The Americans led in imposing modern diplomatic relations on Japan because Britain was busy elsewhere. Angry at what it considered unwarranted obstruction of trade and the exploitation of Burma's magnificent teak forests, Britain launched two more wars against Burma that resulted in Burma's becoming a British colony. Allied with France, Austria, Prussia, and the Ottoman Empire, Britain also fought the Crimean War of 1853–1856 against Russia for control over the mouth of the Danube and the Black Sea. Britain's rule in India suffered a temporary setback with the 1857 revolt, but the result was to strengthen Britain's hand in dealing with the remaining principalities, many of which had to accept British advisers and the protection of British troops.

Determined to open markets, western powers soon imposed fresh demands on China and Japan. After suppressing the 1857 revolt, Britain joined with France to attack Guangzhou and capture its governor-general who had refused to pass their demands on to Beijing. Again the menace of foreign ships at Tianjin compelled the emperor to sign new treaties. Eleven new treaty ports, foreign vessels on the Yangzi, freedom of travel for foreigners in the interior, tolerance for missionaries and their converts, low tariffs, foreign ambassadors resident in Beijing, and the legalization of opium imports accrued to Britain, France, the United States, and Russia. When the Qing court tried to postpone the ambassadors' arrival and had the temerity to fire on British ships from new fortifications at Tianjin, the British and French retaliated by marching twenty thousand troops, many from

1. A. Iriye, "Imperialism in East Asia," in *Modern East Asia: Essays in Interpretation*, ed. J. B. Crowley (New York: Harcourt, Brace & World, 1970), p. 129.

A Factory at Guangzhou. Supervised by a merchant, Chinese workers prepare tea and porcelain for export. *(Bridgeman Art Library)*

India, to Beijing, where they destroyed the summer palace outside the city. In 1858, Townsend Harris, the American consul resident in Japan, pointed to what the European powers had achieved with their gunboats in China to convince the shogun's government to sign a commercial treaty with the United States. In addition to setting low tariffs on American goods, it extended the principle of extraterritoriality to westerners in Japan. Angry at the murder of missionaries, a combined French and Spanish fleet attacked Vietnam in 1858. France went on to acquire most of southern Vietnam, a large indemnity, and a commercial treaty.

Western encroachment on East Asia waxed and waned in consort with conflicts elsewhere. In 1861, Russian sailors occupied Tsushima, an island in the strait between Japan and Korea, for

six months, in part to forestall a similar action by the British, in part to gain a warm water port. Unable to win official backing for this maneuver, they eventually withdrew. During the American Civil War, 1861–1865, the United States managed only one military initiative: support for reopening the straits of Shimonoseki after the Japanese tried to close them. France, by contrast, made considerable gains. In 1863, it forced the Cambodian king to accept its protection. Two years later, it annexed two more provinces in south Vietnam and attacked Korea in retaliation for the execution of Catholic priests who had entered the country illegally. France's defeat in the Franco-Prussian War in 1871 put a temporary halt to its ambitions in Asia. In the meantime, a small American squadron tried to replicate Perry's success in

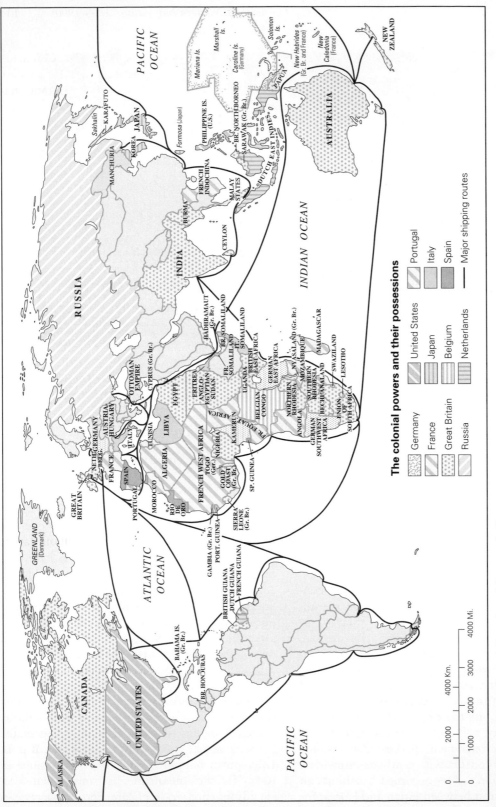

The colonial powers and their possessions

Germany	United States
France	Japan
Great Britain	Belgium
Russia	Netherlands

Portugal	
Italy	
Spain	
— Major shipping routes	

PACIFIC OCEAN

ATLANTIC OCEAN

INDIAN OCEAN

PACIFIC OCEAN

RUSSIA

CANADA

UNITED STATES

ALASKA

GREENLAND (Denmark)

GREAT BRITAIN

PORTUGAL

SPAIN

FRANCE
BELG.
NETH.
GERMANY
AUSTRIA-HUNGARY
ITALY
OTTOMAN EMPIRE
CYPRUS (Gr. Br.)

MOROCCO
RIO DE ORO
TUNISIA
ALGERIA
LIBYA
EGYPT
FRENCH WEST AFRICA
TOGO (Ger.)
GOLD COAST (Gr. Br.)
NIGERIA
KAMERUN
FR. EQUATORIAL AFRICA
SP. GUINEA
SIERRA LEONE (Gr. Br.)
PORT. GUINEA
GAMBIA (Gr. Br.)

ANGLO-EGYPTIAN SUDAN
ERITREA
FR. SOMALILAND
BR. SOMALILAND
IT. SOMALILAND
UGANDA
BRITISH EAST AFRICA
GERMAN EAST AFRICA
BELGIAN CONGO
ANGOLA
NORTHERN RHODESIA
NYASALAND (Gr. Br.)
MOZAMBIQUE
MADAGASCAR
SOUTHERN RHODESIA
GERMAN SOUTHWEST AFRICA
BECHUANALAND
SWAZILAND
LESOTHO
UNION OF SOUTH AFRICA

INDIA
BURMA
CEYLON
HADHRAMAUT (Gr. Br.)

MANCHURIA
KOREA
JAPAN
Sakhalin
KARAFUTO
Formosa (Japan)
FRENCH INDOCHINA
MALAY STATES
PHILIPPINE IS. (U.S.)
BR. NORTH BORNEO
SARAWAK (Gr. Br.)
DUTCH EAST INDIES

Mariana Is.
Marshall Is.
Caroline Is. (Germany)
Solomon Is.
PAPUA
New Hebrides (Gr. Br. and France)
New Caledonia (France)
AUSTRALIA
NEW ZEALAND

BAHAMA IS. (Gr. Br.)
BR. HONDURAS
BRITISH GUIANA
DUTCH GUIANA
FRENCH GUIANA

0	2000	4000 Mi.
0	1000 2000	3000 4000 Km.

Map C5.1 Western Imperialism, Late Nineteenth Century

Korea. When the Koreans refused to negotiate, it raided Korean forts guarding the entrance to Seoul and withdrew.

Western imperialism demanded new counter-measures from China and Japan. Both nations started sending diplomatic missions abroad in the 1860s, in part to try to revise the unequal treaties or at least mitigate their effects, in part to study their opponents. Korea too sent study missions to China, Japan, and the United States in the early 1880s. Trade increased, especially after the completion of the Suez Canal in 1869 halved travel time. The laying of telegraphic cables made communication between East and West practically instantaneous. To the north, China resolved its boundary disputes with Russia. Chinese laborers migrated to Southeast Asia, the United States, Hawai'i, Cuba, and Peru, where they were brutally exploited because their government was perceived as too weak to protect them.

Japan soon began to mimic the western claim that imperialism was necessary to civilize the savages by acquainting them with the material and spiritual benefits of modern technology and mechanisms of social control. In 1871, it proposed an unequal treaty with China, only to be rejected. Three years later, it dispatched a military expedition to Taiwan to retaliate for the murder of Ryukyuan fishermen. After the Qing court agreed to pay an indemnity, Japan withdrew. A similar plan to invade Korea did not materialize only because Japan's leaders did not think they were ready. Instead, Japan imposed a treaty on Korea that gave it the same privileges of most-favored-nation status and extraterritoriality that westerners enjoyed in Japan. It also solidified its northern boundary by agreeing with Russia that while Sakhalin would become part of Russia, the Kuril Islands belonged to Japan.

Rivalries between the Great Powers brought a fresh wave of western imperialism across Asia and Africa. In 1882, the United States became the first western power to sign a commercial treaty with Korea. Thanks to the most-favored-nation clause, the European powers and Japan immediately gained the same privileges. Follow-ing Vietnam's appeals for help from China, its nominal overlord, the French attacked a new naval base in China. China had to grant that Vietnam existed as a separate country and watch it be combined with Cambodia and, later, Laos into a French colony. Sandwiched between British Burma and French Indochina, Thailand remained independent by acquiescing to a series of unequal treaties. Russia and Britain tried to outbid each other for influence in Korea, while one faction at the Korean court sought American intervention to preserve Korean independence. Following decades of European exploratory trips through Africa, King Leopold II of Belgium in 1876 fostered the founding of the International Association for the Exploration and Civilization of Africa while the British and French took over Egyptian finances to manage that country's debt to its European creditors. Britain performed a similar role in China when it undertook to collect customs duties for the Qing court. Belgium, Germany, Italy, Portugal, and Spain joined Britain and France in carving up Africa into protectorates and colonies notable in varying degrees for the exploitation of natural resources and the brutal treatment of natives. (See Map C5.1.)

Imperialism in Asia entered a new phase when China and Japan fought over Korea in 1894–1895. When the Korean king requested help from China in suppressing rebellion, Japan responded first, lest China gain what it saw as unacceptable influence over the Korean court. After Japan sank a British ship transporting Chinese troops, China and Japan declared war on each other. Japan's victories on land and sea enabled it to claim Taiwan, the Pescadores islands, the Liaodong peninsula in Manchuria, forts on the Shandong peninsula, commercial concessions, and the usual bank-breaking indemnity. Russia opposed the Japanese land grab because of its own designs on Manchuria and Korea. Germany had growing commercial interests in China and wanted to divert Russia away from central Europe. France had an alliance with Russia. The three nations launched the Triple Intervention to make Japan restore the Liaodong and Shandong peninsulas to China. In a move that the Japanese public saw as blatant hypocrisy, the French then gained concessions in southern China for railroads and mines, and Russia got an eighty-year lease over the Liaodong peninsula from China that was later expanded to include Port Arthur. When the Germans built forts on portions of the Shandong peninsula, Britain took a naval base across from Port Arthur. Competition between the European powers precluded any of them from making China its colony. Instead they scrambled for concessions by carving out spheres of influence dominated by their officials and traders, primarily along the coast and up the Yangzi River. Uneasy at the prospect of being shut out of the market for Chinese goods and souls, American merchants and missionaries called on their government to act. Secretary of State John Hay urged the European powers and Japan to adopt an "open door" policy that would preclude the spheres of influence from excluding Americans. The other powers agreed, albeit with reservations that protected their interests.

Even beyond the spheres of influence, missionaries brought change to northern and eastern China. They built hospitals, schools, and orphanages where none had existed before. They educated women and tried to prevent foot binding. They taught western science and political philosophy, opening a window on the West used to advantage by Chinese reformers. Their letters to parishes back home heightened awareness of and interest in Chinese affairs. The missionaries also proved disruptive. When they forbade the rituals associated with ancestor worship, they seemingly threatened the fabric of family life. Since converts often came from the lower rungs of society, missionary efforts to protect them against the gentry or to rescue them from district magistrates' courts provoked outrage by entrenched local interests. When the missionary presence provoked violence, the western powers dispatched gunboats and troops to intimidate local officials. Worst of all, Christian teachings subverted the Confucian doctrines that fostered loyalty to the state.

Although attacks on missionaries often roiled relations between the western powers and China, none matched the consequences of the so-called Boxer Rebellion. It began in Shandong in 1898 as an antiforeign movement that combined martial arts with rituals promising invulnerability to weapons, somewhat similar to the Ghost Dance that rallied the Sioux against American encroachment in the Dakotas in the late 1880s. Boxers attacked converts and missionaries, sometimes with the quiet approbation of Qing officials. They routed western troops sent to reinforce the defenses for the diplomatic community in Beijing and tore up railroad tracks between Tianjin and the capital. The court ordered the massacre of all foreigners on Chinese soil and declared war on the foreign powers.

Faced with a common threat, the western powers and Japan united against China. Efforts by Chinese generals in central and south China to suppress antiforeign elements in their areas helped Americans to convince the other powers not to expand the scale of conflict beyond an expeditionary force sent to liberate the diplomatic community besieged in Beijing. When it reached the city in August 1900, the Qing court fled to Xi'an. Japanese soldiers watched with amazement as western troops ran amok for three days in an orgy of looting, rape, and murder. Negotiations over the size of the indemnity to be extracted from China and its distribution among the powers dragged on for a year. The indemnity imposed a crushing financial burden on the Chinese government and absorbed funds needed for economic development. Only rivalry among the powers, and particularly distrust of Russia, precluded proposals for China's dismemberment.

The nineteenth century marked the heyday of western imperialism as practice and ideology. Following the spread of Darwin's revolutionary ideas on evolution and the survival of the fittest, Herbert Spencer and others developed the notion of social Darwinism. They thought that not just species but nations stood in danger of extinction unless they emerged victorious in the ceaseless competition between them. States that did not understand this principle or found themselves too weak to resist modern military technology naturally fell prey to conquerors from afar. Social Darwinism provided new justification for the westerners' sense of racial superiority. Some used this notion to justify brutal exploitation of native populations. Others felt it their duty to bring civilization to the heathens. After the American colonization of the Philippines and annexation of Hawai'i, Rudyard Kipling wrote, "Take up the White Man's burden/Send forth the best ye breed/Go bind your sons to exile/To serve your captives' need; . . . /Your new-caught, sullen peoples,/Half-devil and half-child."[2]

Western imperialism in East Asia took a different form than in the rest of the world. Rather than establish colonies (Hong Kong and Macao

being the exception), the western powers imposed unequal treaties. Although they sought Asian labor for difficult, dangerous jobs such as building the transcontinental railroad, they issued various discriminatory exclusion laws to prevent first Chinese and then Japanese from residing permanently in their countries or becoming citizens. By dint of a vast westernization project that included the enactment of western-style commercial, civil, and criminal legal codes plus the creation of a modern army, Japan managed to gain abolition of most-favored-nation treatment and extraterritoriality in 1899. Its victory in war with Russia to win control of the Liaodong peninsula in 1904–1905 gave hope to people all over Asia that western dominance might pass.

SUGGESTED READING

For the long view of relations between Asia and the rest of the world, see W. I. Cohen, *Asia at the Center: Four Thousand Years of Engagement with the World* (2000). Studies include P. Chatterjee, *Nationalist Thought and the Colonial World: A Derivative Discourse* (1993), and R. Eskildsen, "Of Civilization and Savages: The Mimetic Imperialism of Japan's 1874 Expedition to Taiwan," *American Historical Review* 107 (2002): 388–418.

---

2. R. Kipling, "The White Man's Burden," *McClure's Magazine* 12:4 (February 1899): 0-004.

Japan in Turmoil (1800–1867)

Many commoners in Japan's cities and villages prospered during the first three decades of the nineteenth century, but the same could not be said for the laboring poor, low-status samurai, or daimyo wrestling with shortfalls in domainal finances. Belying prosperity were problems such as vagrancy, gambling, and prostitution that threatened the social order propped up by administrators and wealthy entrepreneurs. Added to these signs of domestic distress was an increasing fear of threats from abroad. The shogunate's ineffectual and inconsistent attempts to deal with these problems weakened it in the eyes of the military ruling class. Its decision to seek approval for foreign treaties from the monarch opened the door for wide-ranging debate that enabled commoners as well as officials to participate in a new political public realm. Beset on all sides, the shogunate collapsed at the end of 1867, ushering in a regime headed by the newly named emperor.

Historians have long searched the early nineteenth century for clues as to what brought about the Meiji Restoration. Those who emphasize domestic factors point to how the social and political order came unglued in the early nineteenth century. But that begs the question of whether the fall of the Tokugawa shogunate should be seen as a coup d'état or a revolution. Was it primarily the effect of domestic changes or a reaction to foreign pressure?

DOMESTIC SECESSIONS

Early nineteenth-century villages had to deal with internal conflict. Outcasts deemed polluted by their association with dead animals protested discrimination and the indignities they had to suffer. Long accustomed to apportioning the village tax assessment, headmen tended to treat expenses for family business and village administration as one and the same. The walls around their houses had gates; the roofs had eaves that marked their superior status. Complaints against headmen perceived to be unjust in dividing the tax burden, efforts to clarify the costs of village administration, and demands that the headman cease to lord it over his neighbors led to lawsuits that sometimes dragged on for decades. A recalcitrant headman might be subjected to ostracism. Sometimes disputes resulted in the village council's being expanded to include a cultivator's representative to verify the tax assessment. In villages where the position of headman had once been hereditary, it might instead rotate among a group of families. Some villages started a system of having the heads of household elect the headman. When a woman was the house head, she too voted.

In eastern Japan, village leaders agonized over fields gone to waste because of population decline. Worse, gamblers and bandits disrupted the social order. Village officials organized regional leagues, inserting a new level of administration between the village and ruling authority. In the region around Osaka, these leagues launched province-wide appeals beginning in the 1780s to eliminate restrictions on commerce and regulate the price of herring meal fertilizer from Hokkaido. In 1827 the shogunate started sending security patrols through the Edo hinterland, where villages might be fragmented among several domains. Some headmen organized militia; others hired unemployed swordsmen, some running protection rackets, to keep the peace. Longer-term solutions came in the teachings of the peasant sage Ninomiya Sontoku. Sontoku revitalized villages, increasing their population and bringing fields back into production by preaching an ethic of diligence, fortitude, and frugality to repay the bounty of the gods while instituting mutual aid associations to give villagers who had fallen into dire straits access to low-interest loans. His emphasis on rational planning to wring the most from land and labor demanded steady work habits instilled in men and women alike.

Hirata Atsutane and his followers offered a vision of a just social order that largely ignored existing political arrangements. Although they acknowledged shogunal authority and the Confucian principles of social inequality, they sought the wellspring of human virtue in Japan's ancient past and looked to the monarch as a manifest god who linked the divine and human worlds. Atsutane claimed to be a disciple of Motoori Norinaga, thus putting him in the mainstream of nativist thought. Unlike his teacher, he did not envision the afterlife as a filthy, polluted realm but rather as an invisible world that parallels the visible world. From that vantage, the deceased watch over and protect their descendants. Atsutane's teachings placed primacy on agricultural practices that brought people into close communion with the gods and each other. Village officials and rural entrepreneurs were his most numerous disciples because they believed his message to contain the secret for revitalizing the village community without threatening their role either socially or economically (see **Biography: Kitahara Inao**).

Domainal Reforms

Faced with challenges from below, rural entrepreneurs sought new ways to bolster their prestige. Rather than marry within the village, they sought marriage partners of similar background a day's walk or more away. They educated themselves; they also educated their daughters to standards beyond what could be achieved by an ordinary cultivator. They studied Chinese philosophy and classical poetry as well as western science and geography. They took up swordsmanship. In the 1830s and 1840s, their quest for ways to enhance their dignity meshed with the ruling authorities' need for funds. In return for loans, wealthy commoners received permission to wear swords on official business and use a surname, privileges supposedly reserved for the samurai.

The willingness of daimyo to sell markers of prestige to commoners was but one sign that their governments verged on bankruptcy. Owing to rural opposition, tax revenues had long since ceased to cover the expenses of carrying redundant personnel on the books, supporting the

BIOGRAPHY Kitahara Inao

In the early nineteenth century, rural entrepreneurs dominated their villages politically, socially, and economically. A representative figure was Kitahara Inao (1825–1881), who had wide-ranging interests and an abiding concern with national affairs.

Based in the mountains of central Japan, Inao's family claimed warrior connections through an ancestor who died in battle in 1575 and through him to the Minamoto lineage. His father received permission to wear swords and use a surname for his work on water control projects; he also served as one of the village's headmen, managed the family's land, and sold the silk produced by Inao's mother. He educated himself, his children, and his neighbors in western geography and Japanese poetry. When his eldest son wished to learn a musical instrument called the *samisen,* he sent him to Kyoto. The boy was murdered en route. Thus did Inao become his father's heir.

The short-tempered Inao had a short career as village headman. In 1852, cultivators from the village's upper elevations complained that they had to pay for flood control that benefited only their wealthier neighbors on the plain. Four years later, they questioned the way costs had been assessed. A meeting with Inao turned into a shouting match. One man called Inao a liar, and Inao slugged him.

The cultivators announced that to strike one was to strike them all. Inao had to resign his office and concentrate his efforts on teaching village boys and girls.

Inao helped found the Hirata school in the Ina valley by hosting study groups, proselytizing, and publishing Atsutane's works. He used his own capital to publish a chronology composed by Atsutane that traced the monarchy back to the creator gods and raised money to publish Atsutane's magnum opus, the multivolume *Koshiden* (Lectures on Ancient History). In 1867 he helped build a shrine to the four great nativist teachers ending with Atsutane. Through these efforts, his valley acquired the largest population of Hirata disciples outside Edo.

Following the Meiji Restoration, Inao organized a development fund to promote new agricultural products and bring mechanized filatures to the Ina valley. Conditions for loans were so strict and interest rates so high that only landlord families could benefit, to the resentment of poor folk who had contributed to it. Despite his promotion of industrialization, Inao continued to castigate westernizers who did not understand the fundamental principle of respecting Japanese ways and despising the foreign. At the end of his life, he wrote a set of precepts for his descendants that emphasized harmony, diligence, and frugality. He urged them to be modest in dress, eat simple food, and marry plain but intelligent women.

daimyo's women and children in the style to which life in Edo had accustomed them, and paying for the trips made by the daimyo and his retinue back and forth to Edo. Daimyo borrowed money from merchants with the promise of repayment out of future tax receipts. In the 1830s, domains across Japan launched administrative and financial reforms. Those that tried to increase exports and restrict imports disrupted markets and created shortages. Some instituted monopolies by strengthening existing controls: Satsuma doubled its profits in sugar. Most domains sought to reduce expenditures by cutting costs. Concerned that luxury-loving commoners both threatened samurai privilege and encouraged samurai extravagance, governments issued sumptuary legislation forbidding socially inferior people to wear silk garments, ornamental hairpins, and other products of the commercial revolution.

The samurai, especially those in the lower ranks, saw themselves beset on all sides. Wealthy commoners in crested kimono carrying swords challenged their sense of status superiority. Educated, capable samurai were frustrated by the system of hereditary ranks that relegated them to dead-end menial tasks. During domainal reforms, low-ranking samurai proposed that men of talent and ability be promoted to decision-making positions. Satsuma heeded this call, allowing Saigō Takamori to rise from rural administrator to the daimyo's adviser in 1854. Efforts to promote men from below often led to factional disputes when upper-status samurai fought to preserve their hereditary privileges. "Borrowing" stipends posed the most ubiquitous threat to samurai welfare. While some domains tried to confine the practice to samurai without regular bureaucratic appointments and pretended that cuts were temporary, others insisted that everyone must make sacrifices. In one case, guards assigned to escort a daimyo to his regular audience with the shogun protested the arrears in their salary by going on strike.

Conditions reached a crisis when poor harvests in the 1830s recalled the famines of the 1780s. Commoners assumed that food shortages owed more to greedy merchants than to crop failures. They turned on village leaders for not offering prompt relief, and they called on the gods of world renewal (*yonaoshi*) for salvation from economic hardship and political ineptitude. Women played an active role, marching with men to protest arbitrary government policies and complaining to rice merchants that hoarding grain threatened the poor with starvation. A retired shogunal policeman named Ōshio Heihachirō decided that government and merchants had become morally bankrupt. Raised in the Confucian tradition that deemed bureaucratic work a service to the people, Ōshio had also studied Wang Yangming, who argued that at time of crisis, a man had to use his intuition, not institutional norms, to guide his behavior. In 1836 Ōshio petitioned the Osaka city magistrate to save the starving. When he refused, Ōshio sold his books to buy food. In a last desperate effort, he issued a manifesto that charged shogunal officials with corruption and led a rural army against the city. A quarter of Osaka burned before shogunal troops caught up with him, and he committed suicide.

Religion and Play

One secessionist response to economic dislocation and political ineptitude came in the form of new religions. In 1838 a long-suffering rural woman named Nakayama Miki was possessed by a spirit who deemed her to be the "shogun of heaven" and the mouthpiece for the true and original god of salvation. She insisted that her family sell its property, the proceeds of which were used to succor the poor. According to the god's divine wisdom (*tenri*), the shogun and daimyo were far too removed from daily life to aid the people; instead, the people should trust in the god of world renewal and work together, offering mutual assistance in time of need. Like other new religions of the time, Tenri-kyō envisioned a world opposed to the hierarchical and socially stratified system of the past and present. In a renewed world saturated with divine goodness, the poor would receive relief, and everyone, men and women, would be equal.

An alternative to the secessionist impulse found in the new religions came in the form of play. Dominated by the theater, urban culture celebrated bodily pleasures. Townspeople employed the possibilities presented by multiple identities—merchant, poet, sword-wearing samurai—to escape from the rigidities of the status system (see **Documents: Kohei's Lawsuit**). By the 1830s, readers of popular literature had alternatives to didactic tracts that bolstered the official status order. They indulged in novels that depicted the immediate world of human feelings such as Jippensha Ikku's travelogues featuring an irreverent pair, Kita and Yaji, who poked fun at self-important samurai, stole when they could, seduced serving maids, and laughed at farts. Woodblock prints and kabuki, in particular ghost stories staged by Tsuruya Namboku and his successors,

DOCUMENTS

Kohei's Lawsuit

In a litigious society, people turned to the shogun's court to decide disputes. The summation of a conflict over inheritance that follows, titled "Action by Kohei of Haruki-chō, Hongō, against Heisuke of Sugamo-chō and Kurōbei of Fujimae-chō, Komagome as to the succession and division of personality of Sawamura Gisaburō, Master Carpenter," exposes a particularly complex set of family relations and the permeability of supposedly strict occupational and status boundaries. Note that the people involved in the suit, including the deceased, took different names depending on the occupation of the moment. Why is the conflict over Gisaburō's personality, not simply his possessions?

5th month, 1849, Inquiry by the city magistrate to the engineering magistrates:

Kohei demanded succession and division of personality of Sawamura Gisaburō, master-carpenter, subject to your lordships' authority, producing for evidence Gisaburō's will written by a person other than the testator; the defendants, on the other hand, deny the validity of the will, and the parties are at issue.

Kohei alleges that his sister's husband Sawamura Gisaburō made a will so that his personality may be divided according to the will, and that Gisaburō's adopted son Kosuke may be made to succeed Gisaburō.

Rubric: This Kosuke was one who, calling himself Utazō, tenanted the land of Ichibei in Yanaka, and was engaged in the management of a public bath-house. Four years ago, in 1845, he was adopted by Gisaburō, and in the 11th month of the same year, his petition to be a master-carpenter on probation was granted. It has been found that he is still living in a separate house on Ichibei's land and is working as a master-carpenter on probation.

What Heisuke alleges is as follows: His adoptive father Sawamura Gisaburō was a master carpenter in service of the shogunate.

Gisaburō was formerly called Heisuke and was engaged in the management of a tavern at Sugamo-chō. About that time this person [Heisuke] was adopted by Gisaburō and in 1835 he succeeded to Gisaburō's family name. Gisaburō served as a master-carpenter from 1810, and from 1812 to 1834 he was also registered in the census book of Sugamo-chō under the name of Heisuke. Therefore it seems that he was entered in two different census registers.

Gisaburō bought two years ago in 1846 a piece of land at the market in front of Yushima Tenjin Shrine, and on this occasion Heisuke advanced part of the purchase money. On the deed of sale, the land was entered as the property of Sei, daughter of Saku, Gisaburō's concubine. Gisaburō had a house on this land repaired for Saku to occupy. Lately he himself moved into this concubine's house, and because of old age, he called in one Kosuke, who is more in the relation of a servant to him, to wait on him, and had this Kosuke, by nominally adopting him, serve as a master carpenter on probation. Besides the above piece of land, some other lots in Gisaburō's possession have been nominally the property of Gisaburō's grandson Chōsuke, for whom Heisuke has acted as guardian. The deeds of sale of these lands were kept by Gisaburō, as they were often used, by agreement of Gisaburō and Heisuke, for financing the business when Gisaburō engaged in various contracts, government and otherwise. When in 1847 Gisaburō married Sei, Saku's daughter [by her former husband] to one Mohachi and had Mohachi inherit the family name of Yoshikawa, palanquin-maker for the Shogunate, Heisuke on Gisaburō's request, advanced 500 *ryō* to Gisaburō to cover the expenses. Since Heisuke had advanced Gisaburō great sums of money for the latter's contract business, government, and otherwise, Heisuke should be given the right to decide on the succession and other matters.

Yasuda Chōsuke is son to Hanzaemon and grandson to Gisaburō and was formerly called Toraichirō. He is registered as a houseowner of Fujimae-chō. He has served, under the guardianship of the defendant Heisuke, as purveyor and contractor of commodities and laborers for the Fukiage Garden [in the shogun's palace] and is living with his father.

Nakamura Hanzaemon is adopted husband to Hisa born to Gisaburō by Gin, his former wife, since divorced. He was formerly called Shōgorō, and while tenant of a shop belonging to Kanbei, Fujimae-chō, Komagome, was engaged in dealing in socks. He is said to have become a guard in service of the Banner Magistrates for the Shogunate.

The defendant Kurōbei is nephew to Sawamura Gisaburō and head of Gisaburō's original family. Because of this relationship, Gisaburō, repairing a house on his land, had Kurōbei and his wife Chiyo, whose other name is Shige, live there. Even now Gisaburō's domicile is registered at the office of the Engineering Department as at this house on Kurōbei's land. So it was rumored

that the boxes containing Gisaburō's papers and books etc. are kept in the above Kurōbei's godown [storehouse], including the instruments pertaining to the various money transactions which Gisaburō mentioned in his will.

The plaintiff says that when, during this autumn, he went to negotiate with Heisuke and Kurōbei, Kurōbei together with the ward officers admitted plainly that he had in his care the papers in question. The plaintiff continues that it seems possible, however, that Heisuke, taking advantage of his having access to the household of the Lord of Kaga through his business in contracting for transport horses, may have here done something tricky; that there is no box containing instruments kept now at Kurōbei's house in Fujimae-chō. It is suspected that it has since been taken to Heisuke's house. Heisuke has for several years past been in the habit of advancing loans to the household of the Lord of Kaga out of money belonging to Sawamura Gisaburō.

Instrument of Settlement to be filed: Both parties have agreed that we should petition for Gisaburō's adopted son Sawamura Kosuke to succeed Gisaburō, and should agree that neither party has grounds on which to dispute further about the deposit instruments said to be entrusted by Gisaburō with Heisuke and Kurōbei and about the money which Heisuke claims to have advanced Gisaburō, since the issue utterly lacks proof. Therefore we have come to a compromise, and will never in future resort to action or dispute.

Source: John Henry Wigmore, ed., *Law and Justice in Tokugawa Japan, Pt. VIII-A: Persons: Legal Precedents* (Tokyo: University of Tokyo Press, 1982), pp. 214–242 (modified).

portrayed bloodshed and gruesome murders. In 1850 the story of Sakura Sōgorō appeared on stage with scenes of his crucifixion and reincarnation as an angry spirit. Although these dramas went to extraordinary lengths to rivet their audience's attention, they remained linked to social mores. Dramas might be set in the daimyo's domestic quarters, but the subjects of action were commoners who acted according to the logic of everyday life.

Japanese commoners played hard. Festivals in town and country became increasingly elaborate, and laborers demanded ever more of them. Kabuki troupes discovered the money to be made in touring the countryside. In prosperous regions, villages built kabuki stages and competed in presenting plays to their neighbors. City folk flocked to entertainment districts. The shops with female clerks, theaters, and variety shows surrounding Asakusa temple in Edo combined appeals to prayer and play. Play constituted one way to appeal to the gods, and the pursuit of pleasure had a spiritual dimension.

Another sign that the practices of everyday life had escaped governmental control can be seen in prostitution. Unlicensed prostitutes, both men and women, plied their trade in informal entertainment districts that had sprung up across Edo and in castle towns. Post stations employed maids to lure customers to inns and teahouses, where singers, dancers, and servants often doubled as prostitutes. The development of a commercial economy contributed to the spread of prostitution in two ways: it put more money in the pockets of potential customers and stimulated the monetization of female labor. When families' expectations that their women supplement the family income by raising silkworms or working for wages went unmet, prostitution became the logical alternative.

As part of a far-reaching reform effort in 1841, the shogunate tried to curtail what it saw as the excesses of urban culture. It clamped down on unlicensed prostitution by closing teahouses and other venues where women sold their bodies. It forbade women to dress men's hair, teach them music, serve as attendants at archery ranges, or perform onstage in public. It even outlawed men and women sharing public baths in an effort to promote public morality. Gambling, lotteries, and full-body tattoos were forbidden. The shogunate tightened censorship over the publishing industry, refusing to permit romantic novels or erotica, including the serial best-seller, *The False Murasaki and the Rustic Genji,* produced by Ryūtei Tanehiko between 1829 and 1842. Theaters and entertainment districts received undesired attention. The shogunate condemned extravagance and ordered commoners not to dress, eat, or house themselves above their station. It tried to enforce these strictures by making an example of egregious violators in hopes of intimidating the rest. These measures had but a temporary effect.

FOREIGN AFFAIRS

The Russians were the first foreigners to encroach on Japan. During the eighteenth century, they started to trade with the Ainu in the Kuril Islands and Kamchatka. In 1793 Adam Laxman, a delegate to Catherine II, tried to open relations between Russia and Japan. He got as far as Nagasaki, only to be rebuffed by Matsudaira Sadanobu, who insisted that respect for his ancestors required that he not initiate new foreign relations. In 1798 the shogunate sent an expedition to Hokkaido to assess the Russian threat. Based on its report, the shogunate decided to annex Hokkaido and Sakhalin. Its reach exceeded its grasp; it did not have the forces to defend either. Russians again asked for permission to trade at Nagasaki in 1804. When that was not forthcoming, officers attacked trading posts on Sakhalin and the Kurils in 1806 and 1807. In 1811 the Japanese captured Vasilii Golovnin, the captain of a Russian surveying crew, and held him at Hakodate for two years before Russia secured his release. His captivity narrative intrigued readers across Europe.

The Closing of Japan

The British posed a more serious threat. In 1808 their warship *Phaeton* barged into Nagasaki bay in search of Dutch ships. Despite orders from the Nagasaki city magistrate to destroy it, the *Phaeton* left with food and supplies. In two separate incidents in 1824, British whaling ships raided villages on the coast north of Edo and southern Kyushu. The first village belonged to the Mito domain, home to one of the shogun's relatives and a leading xenophobe, Tokugawa Nariaki. The second was located in Satsuma, the powerful outside (*tozama*) domain that dominated the Ryukyus. The next year, the shogunate issued new instructions for dealing with westerners. With the exception of the Dutch ships allowed at Nagasaki, all foreign ships, regardless of the circumstances, were to be driven off without hesitation. This order announced that the shogunate was closing the country (*sakoku*) to the West, its first truly isolationist policy.

The decision to close the country came as a result not only of foreign intimidation but also of information gathered by scholars and officials. The head of the shogunate's translation bureau established in 1811 argued that foreigners must be kept away from Japan lest they subvert the credulous masses with Christian teachings. In 1825, an adviser to Tokugawa Nariaki named Aizawa Seishisai wrote his "New Theses" (*Shinron*). Mito scholars believed that loyalty to their lord had to be predicated on his loyalty to the monarch. Although they based their arguments on neo-Confucian principles, their ideas were readily assimilated to the nativist belief that Japan was superior to all other countries, including China, because the monarch was descended from the sun goddess. Aizawa had studied writings about the West, and he interrogated the British sailors who had landed on the Mito coast in 1824. *Shinron* argued that Japan had to beware of foreigners, even if they said they came only to trade. Trade would weaken Japan because Japan would lose precious metals, and the pursuit of novelty and luxury items would erode the people's moral fiber. But traders brought something more pernicious than goods: Christianity. They hoped to beguile the foolish commoners with their religion, turn them against their rightful leaders, and "conquer from within by recruiting the local inhabitants into their ranks." To counter the threat of "barbarian teachings," Aizawa urged his lord to convince the shogunate to launch educational, religious, and military initiatives that would reform the armed forces by allowing daimyo to recruit cultivators as soldiers and educate the masses in Japan's unique spiritual essence (*kokutai*).[1] *Shinron* had a lasting impact on nationalist thought.

Despite domainal penury, the Mito reform movement of the 1830s largely involved strengthening coastal defenses, a policy followed by a handful of other domains. Domains ignored shogunal restrictions on the number of guns permitted each castle. Mito built a reverberatory furnace to cast cannon, and Saga in Kyushu did the same. *Tozama* domains in southwestern Japan—Satsuma, Fukuoka, Kumamoto, and Chōshū—bought mortars, howitzers, and field guns from weapons dealers in Nagasaki and tried to manufacture their own. Fear of foreigners spurred a renewed emphasis on military training. Domains also mobilized militia to man coastal lookout points and serve as a first line of defense. They competed for access to military technology, and they refused to cooperate in developing systems to warn of approaching foreign ships. They saw themselves as defending not an entity known as Japan but rather their own territory. Building coastal fortifications increased their isolation from each other while weakening the shogun's authority in matters of defense.

The shogunate too tried to bolster its military preparedness, spurred by reports of the British victory over China in the Opium War. (See **Connections: Western Imperialism [1800–1900].**) In the 1841–1842 reform, it began to adopt western military technology and trained a small contingent of foot soldiers in the use of guns. It also tried

---

1. Bob Tadashi Wakabayashi, *Anti-Foreignism and Western Learning in Early Modern Japan* (Cambridge, Mass.: Harvard University Press, 1986), p. 211.

to reassert its dominance by ordering an end to domain monopolies that interfered in commerce, seeking to transfer daimyo from one domain to another, and threatening to suppress copper coins and paper money minted in the domains. In 1843 the shogun went to Nikkō to worship at the shrine for his ancestors, escorted by one hundred fifty thousand men provided by the daimyo, who had to serve as his retinue in an affirmation of Tokugawa supremacy. At the same time, the shogunate announced a more conciliatory policy toward foreigners: shipwrecked sailors succored, Japanese castaways allowed to return home, and ships in need to receive supplies before being sent on their way.

Unequal Treaties with the United States

When Commodore Matthew C. Perry sailed four ships into Edo Bay on July 8, 1853, he had been preceded by the 1846 expedition under Commodore James Biddle, and the Dutch had warned of his arrival. Perry treated the shogunate's exclusion order with disdain, and he refused to shift anchorage until he had handed over a letter from President Millard Fillmore addressed to the monarch. He paraded his men, opened his gunports to expose his weaponry, and announced that he would return the next year for a reply. This time he had six ships under his command, having commandeered two more in Hong Kong. Confronted with this display of force, the shogunate reluctantly signed a friendship treaty with the United States. Japan made all the concessions: American ships were to be allowed to call at Shimoda and Hakodate and to obtain coal and other supplies. Shipwrecked sailors were to be treated fairly, and the United States had the right to station a consul at Shimoda.

Perry brought gifts that displayed the wonders of the industrial revolution—a telegraph using Morse code and a quarter-size steam locomotive with carriages and track. Sailors put on a minstrel show in blackface. Men and women flocked to see the strange black ships with their steam stacks and cannon.

Portrait of American Official. This image depicts an American official who landed with Perry at Uraga bay. This woodblock print emphasizes facial features most like those of demons—large nose, red mouth with gaping teeth. *(Peabody Essex Museum, Salem, MA/Bridgeman Art Library)*

The shogunate soon found itself making further concessions. In 1856, Townsend Harris arrived as the first U.S. consul at Shimoda, to the consternation of shogunal officials, who had never expected a barbarian to live on Japan's sacred soil. A failed businessman in the China trade, Harris was determined to sign a commercial treaty with Japan. Realizing Shimoda's isolation, he bullied Japanese officials to allow him to negotiate in Edo. Fearing that delay might bring the same gunboats to Japan that had devastated China's coast, shogunal officials signed the treaty Harris wanted on July 29, 1858. According to its provisions, the two countries were to exchange diplomatic representatives.

Japan was to open six cities—Edo, Osaka, Kanagawa (later Yokohama), Hyōgo (Kōbe), Nagasaki, and Niigata—to foreign residence and trade just as the Chinese treaty ports had earlier been opened. Japan had to accept low tariffs on imported goods, whereas its own exports faced steep tariffs in the United States. Finally, Japan had to allow foreign residents and visitors the privilege of extraterritoriality. Japan soon signed similar treaties with the Netherlands, Britain, France, and Russia.

Debates on the Foreign Threat

Unnerved by the unprecedented responsibility of signing treaties with western powers, the shogunate revoked its two hundred fifty-year-old monopoly over foreign policy. In 1854 it asked leading daimyo for their opinions; in 1858 it asked the monarch Kōmei to endorse the Harris commercial treaty. In neither case was a consensus forthcoming. Worse, Kōmei rejected the treaty, urged the shogun to consult the leading daimyo, and demanded the foreigners' expulsion. When the shogunate signed the treaty against Kōmei's wishes, it was considered treasonous. People from many walks of life began to collect and debate information on political affairs. By ignoring prohibitions on discussion of contemporary events and creating a new public political realm, they helped bring about what hindsight has deemed as the last days of the shogunate.

Some voices supported engagement with the West. Sakuma Shōzan argued for a proactive policy of seeking advanced western military technology in order to strengthen Japan and of fusing western science to Japan's Confucian ethical base. Only by opening Japan to trade could it achieve the knowledge and tools it needed to compete in the emerging world order. His ideas found supporters among advisors to important daimyo such as Yokoi Shōnan, who popularized the slogan *fukoku kyōhei* (rich country, strong army), taken from a line in the Chinese classics. Both Sakuma and Yokoi died at the hands of xenophobic assassins.

The men who opposed signing treaties with the West had a rational basis for their stance. Tokugawa Nariaki believed that allowing trade with the West would weaken Japan both materially, in that Japan would lose precious metals in exchange for fripperies, and spiritually, because it would be infected by Christianity. The only way to revive Japan's martial spirit was to fight, even though it meant certain defeat. Yoshida Shōin had studied military science in Chōshū. In 1854, he opened a small school where he taught public policy under the rubric *sonnō jōi* (revere the monarch and expel the barbarian). By this he meant that the monarch should participate in policy decisions and the foreigners must be driven off. He was furious that by spinelessly signing the treaties, the shogunate had made Japan look weak in the eyes of the world.

The social networks that had previously transmitted information on agricultural innovation and the rice market now disseminated news of current events. Doctors, merchants, and samurai in Edo told friends and relatives in the countryside about Perry's arrival and the shogun's response. Their letters circulated widely, and their recipients copied their contents into diaries to discuss with like-minded neighbors. Proselytizers for the Hirata school and experts in swordsmanship linked people across domainal boundaries. Broadsheets (*kawaraban*) reported gossip on the treaty negotiations. They circulated primarily in urban areas, where they could be easily and anonymously sold, but travelers also took them back to villages. A few commoners presented plans for coastal defense to their daimyo for forwarding to the shogun. They traveled to Edo and Kyoto to see for themselves the changes taking place (see **Material Culture: Foot Traffic**).

POLITICAL TURMOIL

The shogunate found itself stymied by Kōmei's disapproval of the Harris treaty and a dispute over shogunal succession. Prodded by Satsuma,

MATERIAL CULTURE

Foot Traffic

Before the coming of the railroad, feet provided the means of locomotion for most Japanese travelers. Arising at 4:00 A.M. and moving briskly on straw sandals, they generally covered thirty miles a day before seeking an inn for the night. Occasionally a traveler rented a horse for a day's journey, but most horses carried merchandise. Boats plied the Inland Sea and Lake Biwa, carrying travelers as well as goods. Given their reputation for capsizing, many travelers preferred to walk.

The chief alternative to feet was the palanquin. These came in several sizes and styles, depending on their function and the status of the user. Most travelers rode in a wicker basket seated on a cushion, grasping a strap to keep their balance. Rural entrepreneurs transported their brides in enclosed palanquins; in cities these were reserved for the daimyo and high-ranking samurai. Most palanquins were carried by two men, with relays running in front and back.

The rickshaw superseded the palanquin. Invented in 1869 by Izumi Yōsuke, a restaurateur in Tokyo, it substituted human-powered carriages for horse-drawn coaches. Built in various sizes to carry up to four people and various designs depending on whether strength or speed was the object, rickshaws spread from Japan to China and the rest of Asia. They made unmerciful demands on human labor, but they were cheap, simple to make and repair, and nonpolluting. Nothing could beat them for short distances until the taxi arrived in 1912.

Fifty-Three Stations on the Tōkaidō. At Kusatsu, one of the fifty-three stations on the Tōkaidō depicted in woodblock prints by Hiroshige, travelers rest their weary feet. Three types of palanquins are featured in this scene. *(Tokyo National Museum/TNM Image Archives/DNPArchives.com)*

Mito, and other activist daimyo, Kōmei urged shogunal officials to appoint Nariaki's son, Hitotsubashi Yoshinobu, perceived as more capable than the man who had the strongest claim by blood, Tokugawa Iemochi. The senior councilors rejected interference in the decision that was theirs alone to make. They appointed a vassal daimyo, Ii Naosuke, regent for Iemochi and chief senior councilor. Ii purged his daimyo opponents and arrested, exiled, or executed over one hundred men employed as agents by daimyo and court nobles. In 1859, the shogunate executed Yoshida Shōin for plotting to assassinate the shogun's emissary to Kyoto. The daimyo cowed, opponents silenced, Ii asserted that the shogunate had sole responsibility for foreign affairs.

On a snowy morning in the third month of 1860, young samurai from Mito and Satsuma assassinated Ii outside Edo castle. Angry at the execution of men they revered, they believed passionately in the politics of direct action. Their deed galvanized public opinion against Ii by deeming him a traitor for having executed men of high purpose (*shishi*) whose only aim was to serve the monarch. Equally alarming, the assassins had overcome the antipathy that distanced *tozama* domains such as Satsuma from Mito, home to the shogun's relative. The shogunate abandoned its authoritarian stance for a more conciliatory posture. It proposed a union of court and military (*kōbu gattai*) that would give important *tozama* and collateral daimyo advisory positions on foreign affairs and reinstated daimyo purged by Ii. It sealed the deal by having Shogun Iemochi wed Kōmei's younger half-sister, Kazunomiya, in return for a promise to expel the barbarians.

Within this framework of cooperation, a number of self-styled able daimyo called for national reforms to match the military reforms they had carried out at home. They urged the shogunate to employ men of talent and ability, regardless of their domainal affiliation, promote the study of western technology, and strengthen the nation's defenses. To fund these goals, the shogunate agreed to cut its expenses, reduce the daimyo's attendance in Edo to one hundred days every three years, and permit the daimyo to take their families held hostage in Edo to their domains. Women and servants had to abandon the only city they had ever known for life in provincial backwaters.

The *shishi* demanded immediate expulsion of the barbarians in accordance with Kōmei's wishes. Young and reckless, they absconded from their domains to study swordsmanship in Edo and Kyoto and imbibe the ideas of Aizawa Seishisai and Yoshida Shōin. Filled with the Japanese spirit (*Yamato damashii*), they swaggered through the streets, less concerned with personal grooming than with purity of purpose. As soon as Yokohama opened as a treaty port in 1859, they launched a reign of terror against foreign merchants, sailors, and officials. (See Color Plate 7.) Following Kazunomiya's marriage, *shishi* in Kyoto assassinated advisers to the daimyo and nobles they held responsible.

Monarch, shogun, and daimyo feared that the *shishi*'s antics would so weaken the established political order as to invite foreign invasion. Satsuma forced its radicals to return home in disgrace. When *shishi* tried to capture the palace in the eighth month of 1863, planning to place Kōmei at the head of an army to unite western Japan under the slogan of "Restore monarchical rule," Satsuma allied with shogunal forces to drive them from Kyoto. Many fled to Chōshū. The daimyo of Tosa forced *shishi* in his domain to leave or commit suicide. *Shishi*-led uprisings in the foothills of Yamato and at Ikuno near the Japan Sea were brutally suppressed. Conflict between radical expulsionists and conservatives in Mito erupted in civil war. In the seventh month of 1864, Chōshū *shishi* returned to Kyoto with supporters from other domains and rural militia in tow. Once again, the shogunate routed them.

The exploits performed by *shishi* had less impact on policy than on public opinion. They dramatized the monarchy's cause and ruptured the alliance between shogun and court. But how significant was the expansion of a public political sphere based on the discussion and exchange of information given that 60 percent of the population was illiterate? Most commoners remained bystanders because they lacked an organizational structure to mobilize effectively. Historians who claim that commoners remained quiescent during the years leading to the Meiji Restoration and therefore it cannot be deemed a revolution from below overlook a similar inertia in the ruling class. Most daimyo did nothing, either because they sided with the shogun out of loyalty and self-interest, he being the ultimate guarantor of their office, or because opposing factions had gridlocked domainal administration. Most samurai remained embedded in the vertical hierarchy predicated on loyalty and obedience to their lord. They had less to do with the eventual outcome than rural entrepreneurs who provided supplies to traveling *shishi,* enlisted their tenants in rural militia, and supported the monarchical cause or the shogunate with their pocketbooks.

THE FALL OF THE SHOGUNATE

The *shishi's* attacks on foreigners and shogunal forces had unforeseen consequences. The British demanded that the men from Satsuma responsible for killing a British merchant be turned over to them and an indemnity paid. When Satsuma refused, British ships bombarded Kagoshima in the seventh month of 1863. For all its military reforms, Satsuma was still no match for foreign gunboats. In the eleventh month, it signed a peace treaty, acceding to British demands. In compliance with Kōmei's decree that the barbarians be expelled in the fifth month of 1863, Chōshū gunners fired on French and American ships in the straits of Shimonoseki. In the eighth month of 1864, the foreigners retaliated. These salutary lessons were not lost on their victims. Both Satsuma and Chōshū began to rebuild their military along western lines. Just days before foreign ships attacked Chōshū, the shogunate had it branded an enemy of the court for harboring *shishi* and sent a coalition of daimyo troops to its borders. Chōshū backed down. It

apologized for its misdeeds, expelled radical court nobles who had sought refuge there in 1863, and executed three high-ranking officials. The shogunate declared victory and withdrew its forces.

The shogunate had less success controlling the consequences of foreign trade. Beginning in 1859, foreign merchants in the treaty ports at Nagasaki and Yokohama discovered that the silver-to-gold ratio in Japan was one-third what it was in the West, meaning that any man with silver in his pockets could buy gold at ludicrously low prices. The gold rush ended only when the shogunate recoined and devalued gold, silver, and copper. When it granted daimyo permission to mint money, counterfeiters flooded the market, and inflation soared. Foreign merchants bought tea and silk in exchange for weapons, making gunrunning a lucrative enterprise, but also leading to a sudden expansion in cash crops on rice paddies. Weavers lost work because they could not compete with foreigners for silk thread. In the summer of 1866, rising unemployment, crop failures, inflation, and shogunal efforts to tax trade created the conditions for the most widespread riots in Edo history, particularly in the shogun's stronghold of eastern Japan.

The shogunate hoped to use new taxes levied on foreign trade to subsidize its military modernization program. It imported thousands of weapons through Yokohama and drilled its retainer band in rifle companies supplemented by rural recruits. It sent missions abroad. The first in 1860 signed a friendship treaty with the United States; subsequent envoys emphasized the study of foreign technology. In 1861 it opened a naval training school at Hyōgo. In 1865 it started an ironworks at Yokohama and a shipyard at Yokosuka. It also received Kōmei's sanction for signing foreign treaties, and it marginalized the *tozama* daimyo by excluding them from policy making circles.

The shogunate's revitalization campaign destabilized the balance of power with the daimyo. When it announced a second punitive campaign against Chōshū because *shishi* had returned to

Ee ja nai ka. As amulets fall from the sky, men, women, and children, some in costume, dance in thanksgiving, shouting, "ain't it great" (*Ee ja nai ka*). *(National Diet Library, Tokyo, Japan)*

positions of power, it pushed former enemies together. Chōshū and Satsuma formed an alliance in the first month of 1866. Both had launched self-strengthening programs, using emergency funds to buy arms through Nagasaki, sending retainers on fact-finding missions abroad, and organizing western-style armies. Now they argued that the shogunate ought not move against Chōshū when pressing domestic and foreign problems remained to be solved. Few domains responded to the shogun's call, riots in Edo and Osaka tied down garrisons, and the attack on Chōshū ended in ignominious defeat. Iemochi's death at just that juncture provided the shogunate with a face-saving out. But when Kōmei died unexpectedly just five months later, the shogunate lost its strongest supporter at court. Unlike the shogun's opponents who had come to believe that Japan should have but a sin-

gle monarch, Kōmei supported the division of powers that left administrative and foreign affairs in the shogun's hands.

Hitotsubashi Yoshinobu reigned as shogun for less than a year. At first he moved vigorously to reassert shogunal authority and continue military reforms. His efforts stirred up turmoil and strengthened the alliance against him. In the eighth month of 1867, a new popular movement swept the coast from the inland sea to Edo. Claiming that amulets inscribed with the name of the sun goddess that portended a prosperous future had fallen from heaven, men and women danced in the streets chanting, "Ain't it great" (*ee ja nai ka*). When the movement reached eastern Japan, dancers threw stones at foreigners to drive out the barbarian demons and rehearsed a mock funeral for the shogunate. In the tenth month, the court issued a secret decree to Satsuma and Chōshū to overthrow the Tokugawa. Realizing he could no longer fulfill the duties of shogun, Yoshinobu returned his patent of office to the monarch. The restoration of monarchical rule was at hand.

In the name of the Meiji emperor, Kōmei's fifteen-year old son, leaders of the Sat-chō forces abolished the offices of shogun and regent and replaced them with new advisory positions open to daimyo, court nobles, and "men of talent." They declared Yoshinobu a traitor to the emperor, revoked his court rank, and confiscated his family lands. When the shogunate fought back, it was defeated after four days of heavy fighting outside Kyoto in the first days of 1868. The imperial armies moved slowly north, hamstrung for lack of cash, which they tried to ameliorate by demanding loans from wealthy commoners. The long-standing animosity between eastern and western Japan prolonged the fighting until Aizu fell in the ninth month, after suffering heavy casualties of men and women. The last stronghold of shogunal support at Hakodate did not surrender until the middle of 1869, supported to the last by the American envoy. Both official and popular opinion feared that prolonged civil war might give foreign troops an excuse to invade Japan. A better alternative was to unite around the new

emperor. Although many retainers died, Yoshinobu and the daimyo of Aizu survived to take their places in the new imperial peerage and join their efforts to the task of strengthening state and economy to compete in the new world order. Hirata disciples and other imperial loyalists rushed to offer their services to the new government; people in Edo watched warily as their old masters were replaced with new.

SUMMARY

Long before the Meiji Restoration, the social and political order crafted in the seventeenth century had ceased to fit everyday practice. The commercial economy, opportunities for travel, and information networks eroded the status and geographical divisions that kept people in their place. Reforms by shogun and daimyo to shore up their authority and fill government coffers could not rectify the gap between reality and their ideal of the proper relations between rulers and commoners. Debates over how to deal with the foreign threat added further strain to the system. When it collapsed in 1867, it left behind a dynamic economy, a large pool of able administrators, and a population well educated for its time.

SUGGESTED READING

Many books have been written on the fall of the shogunate. The most recent include G. M. Wilson, *Patriots and Redeemers in Japan: Motives in the Meiji Restoration* (1992), and A. Walthall, *The Weak Body of a Useless Woman: Matsuo Taseko and the Meiji Restoration* (1998). For a collection of essays focused on the nineteenth century, see M. B. Jansen, ed., *Cambridge History of Japan*, vol. 5 (1989).

For nativism see H. D. Harootunian, *Things Seen and Unseen: Discourse and Ideology in Tokugawa Nativism* (1988). For popular culture,

see N.-L. Hur, *Prayer and Play in Late Tokugawa Japan: Asakusa Sensōji and Edo Society* (2000). For Mito, see J. Victor Koschmann, *The Mito Ideology: Discourse, Reform and Insurrection in Late Tokugawa Japan, 1790–1864* (1987), and K. Yamakawa, *Women of the Mito Domain: Recollections of Samurai Family Life*, trans. K. W. Nakai (1992). For an entertaining look at samurai life, see K. Katsu, *Musui's Story: The Autobiography of a Tokugawa Samurai*, trans. T. Craig (1988).

Meiji Transformation (1868–1900)

The restoration of the Meiji emperor as head of state marked the beginning of profound changes in Japanese politics, culture, and society. A small group of self-selected men, who had led the drive to overthrow the shogun, implemented programs to abolish status distinctions that had compartmentalized social groups and to centralize government. Fearful of the West, they acknowledged the necessity of importing western military technology, industry, legal norms, constitutional thought, science, dress, and food. (See **Material Culture: New Food for a New Nation.**) They built railroads, shipyards, and schools. They propounded a new ideology to rally the citizens. They colonized the Ryukyu Islands and Hokkaido. They projected Japan's power abroad in Taiwan and Korea and renegotiated treaties. They faced considerable opposition, often from within their own ranks. Farmers rioted against new state policies that threatened their livelihood; samurai rebelled at the loss of their traditional identity. Local notables promoted democracy. Intellectuals, novelists, and essayists hammered out new identities that refused to fit a single pattern. By the end of the century, modernity had arrived.

To what extent did changes in the latter half of the nineteenth century build on what had gone before? Did the Meiji Restoration herald a revolution in politics and society, or simply a transition? Did modernization mean westernization?

THE MEIJI STATE

The oligarchs who created the institutions for a centralized government had little idea of what they hoped to accomplish and disagreed on what

135

MATERIAL CULTURE

New Food for a New Nation

Although rice had been grown in Japan since the third century B.C.E., it did not become a staple of the average Japanese diet until imported from Korea and China starting in 1873. Before that, most people ate wheat, barley, and millet. Between 1869 and 1900, the per capita consumption of rice went from 3.5 bushels a year to 5.0 bushels a year. Rice balls became ubiquitous in lunch boxes, and except for the poor, steamed rice replaced rice gruel for breakfast.

The Meiji government officially promoted the eating of meat because it was thought to produce stronger workers and soldiers. In 1869 it established the Tsukiji beef company. In 1871, a butcher shop in Tokyo's Asakusa district became popular selling beef for sukiyaki, a Meiji period invention, as well as milk, cheese, and butter. In the 1880s, butcher shops started selling horse meat. It was cheaper than beef or pork and redder than chicken.

Vegetables, fruits, and breads had a harder sell. Asparagus, cabbage, cauliflower, and tomatoes did not blend easily into Japanese cuisine. Importing apples, peaches, and grapes stimulated the cultivation and spread of indigenous fruits such as persimmon, Satsuma tangerine, and Asian pear. Bread and cakes became popular only after they were modified to suit Japanese taste.

Aguranabe. This flyer advertising Aguranabe, a butcher show, linked eating beef to "civilization and enlightenment." *(Tokyo Metropolitan Foundation for History and Culture/ DNPArchives.com)*

By selectively adapting western foods, Japanese people developed a much more varied diet than they had had in the past. They ate more, and what they ate was more nutritious. An improved diet made them stronger and healthier. It increased life expectancy and child-bearing rates. A population of approximately 33 million at midcentury had grown to 45 million by the end of the nineteenth century.

---

to do. An amorphous group of samurai from Satsuma and Chōshū, plus a few activist Kyoto aristocrats and imperial loyalists from other domains, they had diverse interests and goals. Their first pronouncement came in the Oath of 1868, offered by the emperor in the company of court nobles and daimyo to the gods of heaven and earth. In it he promised that everyone was to unite in promoting the nation's well-being, government policy was to be decided through public discussion, all would be allowed to fulfill their just aspirations, "the uncivilized customs of former times shall be broken through," and "intellect and learning shall be sought throughout the world in order to establish the foundations of the Empire."[1] The Five Injunctions issued to commoners the next day had a different message. It ordered them to practice the Confucian virtues of

1. Donald L. Keene, *Emperor of Japan: Meiji and His World, 1852–1912* (New York: Columbia University Press, 2002), p. 139.

loyalty, filial piety, chastity, obedience, and harmony; to desist demonstrations and protests; to abjure Christianity; to conform to international public law; and to stay in Japan. Emigration to the United States began almost immediately.

Ambiguities in the oath speak to the lack of agreement on national goals. The nation's well-being could justify a national land tax and universal military conscription; it could require promoting entrepreneurship and compulsory education. None of the men present envisioned public discussion of national affairs to include anyone but themselves. In the context of the past, in which each daimyo had set policy for his domain, it meant that decisions and power were to be centralized. It did not mean parliamentary democracy, although it was later interpreted that way. The third clause implied that hereditary status distinctions would be abolished and held out the promise of social mobility. Abolishing old customs acknowledged the reality of cultural imperialism inherent in international law and unequal treaties. The purpose of gaining knowledge was to serve the state.

At first, the oligarchs looked to eighth-century models for a new government. The Council of State became the highest deliberative body. It was assisted by a board of 106 advisers, the activists in the Meiji Restoration, who made the real decisions. The Council of Shinto Affairs enjoyed a brief existence equal to the Council of State. This structure was reorganized four times in the next four months. Most daimyo remained in control of their domains, leaving the oligarchs who spoke in the emperor's name only the former shogun's lands. Monetary proof of support for the emperor from daimyo, former shogunal retainers, merchants, and rural entrepreneurs staved off fiscal crisis in the short run. The necessity of finding sufficient tax revenues to fund the government forced the oligarchs to take hesitant steps toward centralization.

Centralization required convincing the daimyo to give up their domains. Some daimyo hoped to play a larger role in national affairs; some concentrated their efforts on self-strengthening. Most stayed aloof from the court and isolated from each other. In 1869, the daimyo of Satsuma and Chōshū agreed to make a formal declaration of returning their land and population registers to the emperor, with the understanding that he would then confirm their holdings as governors. The government put all domainal retainers above the level of foot soldiers into one general category called former samurai (*shizoku*). To eliminate the redundancies of two hundred seventy independent domain administrations and centralize tax collection, the oligarchs in 1871 abolished the domains and established prefectures (see Map 7.1). They started the process of consolidating one hundred seventy thousand towns and villages into larger administrative units with a new hierarchy of local officials and inaugurated a household registration system whereby each household head had to establish a place of legal residence and inform the government of births, deaths, marriages, and divorces in his family.

The daimyo accepted the loss of their hereditary lands with equanimity. The most important became prefectural governors. Since the number of prefectures was seventy-two, later reduced to fifty, the area under their control expanded. All daimyo benefited by no longer having responsibility for their domains' debts and being guaranteed a substantial income for their personal use. They did not have to support standing armies of retainers. In place of their former titles, they received court rank. In return for giving up their already circumscribed autonomy, they received wealth and prestige.

Abolishing domains disinherited roughly 2 million *shizoku*. All they received were small stipends later commuted to government bonds. The oligarchs urged them to find another line of work, in agriculture, forestry, business, and the colonization of Hokkaido. Some succeeded; many did not. Former shogunal bureaucrats staffed the new government offices, but most domain samurai remained in castle towns. Political power had become sufficiently bureaucratized over the course of the Edo period that neither samurai nor daimyo became landed gentry.

Having taken the first steps toward a more centralized state, in 1871 one faction of the

Map 7.1   **Modern Japan**

oligarchs left for the United States and Europe. Forty-nine officials and fifty-eight students, including five girls, made up the delegation. Headed by Iwakura Tomomi, a former court noble, their goal was to convince the western powers to revise the unequal treaties that infringed on Japanese sovereignty. Informed by President Ulysses S. Grant that western powers would never consent to treaty revision unless Japan reformed its laws and institutions along western lines, the diplomatic mission became a study mission. Wealth and power that the West had created through industrialization and centralized political institutions came as a shock. Officials inspected prisons, schools, factories, and government agencies. They expected their absence to preclude any initiatives by the leaders left behind; in 1873 when Saigō Takamori proposed to invade Korea for having insulted the emperor in the first diplomatic exchange following the restoration, they rushed home to stop him. They opposed not the use of force but its timing. Domestic reform had to precede military engagements abroad.

Reforms and Opposition

The abolition of domains took place in the context of social reforms that did not suit everyone. For many farmers, the emperor's progress from Kyoto to Edo (renamed Tokyo in 1869) in 1868 symbolized the Meiji Restoration. This, they felt, would usher in new prosperity and social justice. Instead, village officials continued to collect taxes, rents remained the same, and moneylenders charged exorbitant interest. Disappointment fueled the rage with which rural and urban people punished what they saw as wrongdoing. When the new government replaced familiar faces in domain administrations with men from foreign parts, this too led to protest, as did the official end to discrimination against outcasts when status distinctions were erased and the outcasts became "new commoners." The first ten years of the Meiji period saw more protest and more violence than at any time during the Edo period.

Bureaucrats initiated reforms and technological innovations to strengthen the state against its domestic and foreign enemies. They hired western experts to transform government, economy, infrastructure, and education. Drawing on western models, they issued civil and criminal codes that replaced different regulations for different statuses with rule by law that considered only the nature of the crime. They built telegraph lines and railroads to improve communications and foster unity. On January 1, 1873, they replaced the lunar calendar that farmers had used as a guide to planting and harvesting with the western calendar. They outlawed traditional hairstyles for men and suppressed village festivals. They issued these laws and directives without warning or explanation. In defense of time-honored custom, farmers rioted.

Religious practices also provoked controversy. In the third month of 1868, the oligarchs ordered the separation of Shinto and Buddhism and the conversion of what had been shrine-temple complexes into shrines by eliminating Buddhist icons, rituals, and priests. In some regions officials infected with Hirata Atsutane's doctrines destroyed Buddhist temples where the farmers' ancestral tablets were kept. The establishment of Yasukuni shrine to the war dead in 1869 used Shinto to promote national goals. The development of State Shinto in the 1870s consolidated local shrines and brought them into a hierarchy with the Ise shrine to the sun goddess at the top. Rather than shrines containing only deities particular to their region, they had to accept deities of national significance in addition. New religions founded in the Edo period received official recognition as Sect Shinto. Meiji period new religions were viewed with suspicion, if not proscribed outright. (See **Biography: Deguchi Nao.**) Farmers protested the destruction of their familiar temples, and Buddhist priests fought back by associating Buddhism with anti-Christian sentiment, recalling ties to the imperial house, and helping immigrants in Hokkaido.

The directives that had immediate effects and aroused the strongest opposition dealt with education, the military, and taxes. In 1872, the government decreed eight years of compulsory education for all children (shortened to four in 1879 and then increased to six in 1907) to fit them for their responsibilities as productive citizens in a modern nation. Communities had to pay for schools themselves. Enraged at the cost, farmers destroyed or damaged nearly two hundred schools between 1873 and 1877. Pre-Meiji teachers continued their unlicensed schools and dissuaded parents from sending their children to new ones. Needing their child's labor or unable to afford tuition, many parents never enrolled daughters or even sons or allowed them to attend only a few months. Over time, compliance increased until it reached 90 percent in the twentieth century.

The slogan of the day was "Rich Country, Strong Army." In January 1873 the government issued the conscription ordinance that summoned all males over the age of twenty to serve three years on active duty in the armed forces,

BIOGRAPHY Deguchi Nao

Women have played a major role in the founding of Japan's new religions; Deguchi Nao (1836–1918), an illiterate commoner, became a prophet.

Nao was born in a castle town near Kyoto to a family in declining circumstances. Her grandfather had the privilege of wearing a sword and using a surname as an official carpenter. Her father squandered his life on drink; he died when she was nine. Nao went to work for a merchant who provided her with room and board. Her earnings went to her mother. Nao helped with the cooking and cleaning; she spun thread and strung coins, thereby gaining a reputation for diligence and hard work. In her third year of service, the domain awarded her a prize for being a filial daughter.

Nao hoped to marry the man she loved, but her widowed aunt Yuri insisted that she accept an arranged marriage and be adopted into the Deguchi family as Yuri herself had done. Yuri drowned herself after Nao repeatedly rejected her offer. A few days later Nao developed a high fever and lost consciousness. Upon her recovery, she attributed her illness to Yuri's vengeful spirit. To placate it and care for the Deguchi ancestral tablets, Nao agreed to marry the man Yuri had selected for her and continue the Deguchi house.

Nao's husband was no better than her father. By 1872 she had borne five children and was living in a rented house in Ayabe. She opened a small restaurant, and when it failed she sold sweet-bean buns. She continued to have children—eleven in all, three of whom died in infancy. When her husband became paralyzed from a fall off a roof in 1885, Nao collected rags to support her family. His death in 1887 freed her to work in a filature as well.

One winter morning in 1892 as she was out collecting rags, Nao became possessed by a god. The experience transformed her personality and her outlook on the world. Instead of being gentle and deferential, she became dignified, filled with divinely inspired authority. She rejected the social order because it rewarded vice and valued money. Since the oligarchs and the emperor were responsible for these conditions, they exemplified absolute evil. They would soon be destroyed and replaced by a divine order of harmony and equality. Under the spell of her god, this formerly illiterate woman wrote hundreds of texts that spelled out what was wrong with the world and what was to come. She also became a faith healer. In 1899, her adopted son Deguchi Onisaburō organized a sect called Ōmoto-kyō based on her revelations. Under his leadership, the group grew rapidly and suffered repeated government persecutions. Nao quarreled with him over his interpretation of her writings and his refusal to reject all that was modern. She died frustrated that she had not been able to reconstruct the world in accordance with her beliefs.

Source: Based on Emily Groszos Ooms, *Women and Millenarian Protest in Meiji Japan: Deguchi Nao and Ōmoto-kyō* (Ithaca, N.Y.: East Asia Program Cornell University, 1993).

followed by four years in the reserves. In accord with the French system, heads and heirs of family farms and businesses received exemptions, and exemptions could be purchased. Its architect was Yamagata Aritomo from Chōshū, who had spent 1869–1870 in Europe studying French and German conscript armies. The conscription ordinance put Japan's defense on the shoulders of the masses. It provided a way to educate conscripts and their families in the goals of government leaders. By revoking the samurai's monopoly of force, it did more than any other reform to eliminate status distinctions and create equality of opportunity.

Both farmers and *shizoku* opposed conscription. The ordinance used the term "blood tax," meaning that all citizens should willingly sacrifice themselves for their country. Farmers who took it literally assumed that the government wanted their blood. Even those who understood the message believed that farmers could best contribute to the nation by growing crops. Commoners opposed to conscription rose up in sixteen localities in the months after the ordinance's promulgation. Samurai opposition took longer to develop but cost more lives. Conservative oligarchs such as Saigō Takamori had already insisted that the national army be composed of the men bred to military service. When Iwakura and his faction outvoted Saigō on whether to invade Korea, he left the government. In 1876, the government ordered *shizoku* to stop wearing the two swords that distinguished them from the rest of the population. Between 1874 and 1877, over thirty rebellions erupted in defense of samurai privilege. The largest and last, in Satsuma, led by Saigō, required the mobilization of sixty-five thousand troops and took eight months to suppress. Saigō committed suicide. In 1878 samurai counterrevolution ended with the assassination of the oligarch Ōkubo Toshimichi, also from Satsuma, because he had opposed invading Korea and arbitrarily initiated reforms.

The Satsuma rebels had had reason to oppose the 1873 tax law. Applied nationwide to agricultural land, its aim was to provide a steady flow of income for the government by replacing the old hodgepodge of domain taxes on fluctuating harvests with a single, uniform property tax. In most regions of Japan, the land surveys that accompanied the new tax simply confirmed de facto proprietary rights farmers already enjoyed. Satsuma domain had allowed *gōshi* (rustic warriors) to assign land to the cultivators and treat them like tenant farmers. Faced with the loss of income as well as hereditary status and privilege, *gōshi* became the shock troops for the Satsuma rebellion.

Even though the Meiji oligarchs tried to promote industry and demanded loans from merchants, they had an agrarian mind-set. Nearly 80 percent of the government's revenues came from tax on agricultural land through the 1880s. Farmers with market access for their products benefited; those who misjudged the market or suffered a crop failure had to sell their land to pay taxes. In some areas, officials imposed the new tax while requiring farmers to continue to pay ancillary taxes it was supposed

Fiscal Year	Land Tax	Liquor Tax	Customs Duties	Income Tax	Corporation Tax	Business Tax	Sugar Excise	Inheritance Tax	Other
				Composition of Tax Revenues, 1872–1940 (%)					
1872	90.1	1.5	3.3	—	—	—	—	—	5.1
1880	72.3	14.9	4.4	—	—	—	—	—	8.4
1890	58.1	22.9	6.9	1.6	—	—	—	—	10.5
1900	34.6	38.0	10.9	4.3	1.2	3.9	1.3	—	5.8
1910	23.8	26.2	15.3	10.0	2.9	7.0	5.1	0.9	8.8
1920	10.2	22.6	11.1	23.5	11.8	6.6	6.8	1.1	6.3
1930	7.9	26.4	15.1	22.1	6.6	6.2	9.6	3.5	2.6
1940	0.9	8.9	2.9	34.0	11.7	2.6	3.2	1.6	33.9

Source: Based on Minami Ryōshin, *The Economic Development of Japan: A Quantitative Study,* trans. Ralph Thompson and Minami with assistance from David Merriman (New York: St. Martin's Press, 1986), p. 340.

to replace. Farmers petitioned for redress; they killed officials suspected of being corrupt. In 1876 widespread, if uncoordinated, opposition to the tax forced the government to reduce it from 3 percent of assessed value to 2.5 percent.

While dealing with opposition from outside the government, oligarchs also quarreled among themselves. They created and abolished ministries to consolidate their power or deny a rival and disputed what kind of government Japan was to have. In the early 1870s, Kido Takayoshi and Ōkubo advocated some measure of popular representation in government lest arbitrary rule generate unrest. Their proposal contained a veiled attack on Itō Hirobumi and Yamagata. Disgruntled at having been shut out of power, Itagaki Taisuke left the government in 1874, joined with disaffected *shizoku* from his home domain of Tosa to form the Patriotic Party, and petitioned the government to establish an elected national assembly. He disbanded the party when he was invited back into the government in 1875 at the Osaka Conference. There, the oligarchs agreed to establish prefectural assemblies (done in 1878) and plan for a national assembly. Four months later, the emperor announced that he would promulgate a constitution after due deliberation.

Constitution and National Assembly

The publicity attracted by the promise of a national assembly and a constitution stimulated responses that coalesced into the Popular Rights Movement. *Shizoku,* village officials, rural entrepreneurs, journalists, intellectuals, and prefectural assemblymen held lengthy meetings and circulated petitions for an immediate national assembly that collected hundreds of thousands of signatures. Radicals and impoverished farmers rioted and planned attacks on the government in the name of human rights. A woman who held property demanded she be allowed to vote in prefectural elections (she was denied). Kishida Toshiko and Fukuda Hideko gave public lectures at which they demanded rights, liberty, education, and equality for women. Baba Tatsui drew on social Darwinism to argue that since democracy based on an egalitarian society was the most advanced form of government, it should be established forthwith. Local notables drafted model constitutions. Activists criticized the oligarchs for blocking communication between emperor and people. They argued that a representative government would harmonize imperial and popular will by providing a forum for the free expression of popular opinion, thereby strengthening the nation. Drawing on the natural rights theories propounded by French and British philosophers, Ueki Emori propounded a theory of popular sovereignty and right of revolution.

The oligarchs responded to the Popular Rights Movement by issuing increasingly draconian peace preservation laws. Press censorship began in 1875; the 1880 Ordinance on Public Meetings stationed policemen at assemblies to ensure that the speakers did not deviate from texts that had been approved beforehand. Excluded from audiences were soldiers, off-duty police, teachers, and students. Demonstrations in Fukushima opposed to a particularly arbitrary governor in 1882, the Chichibu uprising of 1884 that mobilized tenant farmers in demanding debt relief, and other violent incidents met with mass arrests and executions. Having learned the cost of direct action, local notables turned to organizing political parties in anticipation of the first election for the national assembly promised in 1890.

The Meiji Constitution defined institutions established before its promulgation. In 1878 the military General Staff was made directly responsible to the emperor, bypassing the War Ministry run by bureaucrats. A new peerage destined to fill the upper house of the bicameral national assembly known as the Diet was announced in 1884. It included oligarchs, former daimyo, and Kyoto nobility. Over time it expanded to include entrepreneurs and academics. The lower house was to be elected by commoners. The highest policymaking institution, the cabinet, replaced the Council of State in 1885. It was composed of ministers in charge of education, finance, foreign affairs, and other bureaucracies under the prime minister appointed by the emperor.

Itō Hirobumi drafted the constitution in great secrecy. He traveled to Europe in 1882 where he studied nine months in Berlin under the most respected constitutional theorists of his day. Itō and his brain trust then created a document that defined the emperor in terms of his descent from the gods and employed western notions regarding the rights and obligations of citizens. Once they had finished, a new institution, the Privy Council, headed by Itō, met to discuss it. On February 11, 1889, the date chosen to be the anniversary of Jimmu's accession 2,349 years earlier, the Meiji emperor bestowed the constitution on the prime minister. Three days of festivities announced to people across the nation that they were now citizens of a state founded on principles enshrined in a constitution.

The oligarchs wanted a constitution that secured the governing bodies and protected the imperial house through which they exercised power, and they mistrusted the "ignorant" masses. After its promulgation, they designated themselves *genrō*, elder statesmen, charged with picking cabinet ministers for the emperor. The constitution defined the emperor as sovereign and sacred. The emperor:

- exercises executive power through the cabinet
- exercises legislative power with the consent of the Imperial Diet
- has supreme command of the army and navy
- declares war, makes peace, and concludes treaties
- determines the organization of the government
- convokes the Diet and dissolves the lower house

Subjects had these rights and duties:

- present petitions, provided that they observe the proper form of respect

- within limits not prejudicial to peace and order, and not antagonistic to their duties as subjects, enjoy freedom of religious belief
- enjoy freedom of speech, within the limits set by law[2]

Subjects had to serve in the military, a clause that excluded women from the category of subject.

Japan's first experiment with parliamentary democracy nearly did not work. Although Itō and Yamagata had assumed that party politics had no place in an institution directly responsible to the emperor, they had to deal with opposition parties headed by Itagaki and other men who had been ejected from the oligarch's inner circle. Suffrage was limited to men paying at least 15 yen a year in property taxes, a qualification met by only 1.1 percent of the population, most of them in rural areas. Once elected, members discovered that the Diet had more power than the oligarchs had intended. Diet members could criticize the cabinet in memorials to the emperor; they could make speeches, published in newspapers, that outside the Diet might have landed them in jail. They had the power to approve the budget. If they refused, the previous year's budget remained in effect, but it seldom sufficed for the government's needs. When the Diet stood up to the cabinet, the prime minister dissolved it, forcing members into costly reelection campaigns. Campaign finance scandals and vote buying tarnished the reputations of politicians and oligarchs alike. Twenty-five men died during the 1892 election, most at the hands of the police.

Divided by personality, political preference, and self-interest, the oligarchs had to seek political support outside their narrow circle. In so doing, they enlarged the realm of political actors to include bureaucrats, military officers, and politicians. In 1898 Itō had the quasi-oligarchs, Ōkuma Shigenobu, head of the Progressive Party, and Itagaki Taisuke, leader of the Liberal Party,

---

2. Hugh Borton, *Japan's Modern Century* (New York: Ronald Press Co., 1955), pp. 490–507.

Triptych Showing Inauguration of the First Diet. Members of the upper house dressed in uniform are in the foreground; lower house members sit farther back. The emperor is in the box at upper left. *(Museum of Fine Arts, Boston. Jean S. and Frederic A. Sharf Collection, 2000.535)*

participate in a coalition cabinet as prime minister and home minister, respectively. Aghast at this concession to politicians, Yamagata Aritomo sabotaged their cabinet by having the army minister refuse to accept cuts in the military budget. A few months later, Yamagata became prime minister for the second time. To increase military autonomy, he made it a requirement that all army and navy ministers be active-duty officers. To dilute the power of political parties and their resistance to higher taxes, he expanded the suffrage to 2.2 percent of the population and gave more representation to urban districts. In 1900 Itō responded by forming and becoming president of a new political party, the Friends of Government (*Seiyūkai*). His compromise with politicians dramatized the oligarchs' difficulty in controlling the institutions they had created.

Industrialization

The oligarchs promoted economic reform and industrialization. They appropriated the arms-related industries already established by the domains and the shogunate. Some came under state control to supply the military; others were sold at favorable terms to cronies. Iwasaki Yatarō founded Mitsubishi enterprises on the maritime shipping line he acquired from Tosa and expanded it with low-interest government loans. The oligarchs had foreign experts write banking laws; they set up banks and issued paper currency. Their initial investments were in advanced and expensive technologies, the kind needed to build railroads and shipyards. Although building support industries for the military constituted their first priority, they also worried about the effects of unequal treaties on the balance of payments and unemployment. To maintain social stability and to compete with foreign products, they built cotton spinning and weaving factories to make cloth for domestic consumption and imported French silk spinning technology to produce thread for export. They founded a sugar refinery to help growers market their crop and compete with Chinese sugar. By bringing the state's resources to bear on industry, the oligarchs squeezed out private capital.

Agriculture supported industrial growth. Agricultural development groups, seed exchange

Color Plate 7
People of the Five Nations: A Sunday. This woodblock triptych
published in 1861 showed Japan how westerners dressed and
entertained themselves in the foreign settlement at Yokohama.
(Arthur M. Sackler Gallery, Smithsonian Institution, Washington, DC:
Gift of Ambassador and Mrs. William Leonhart, S1998.96a–c)

Color Plate 8
Gas Lights. Gas lights illuminating the streets of Tokyo became
a favorite subject for modern woodblock print artists.
(Edo Tokyo Museum/Tokyo Metropolitan Foundation for History and Culture Image
Archives/DNP Archives.com)

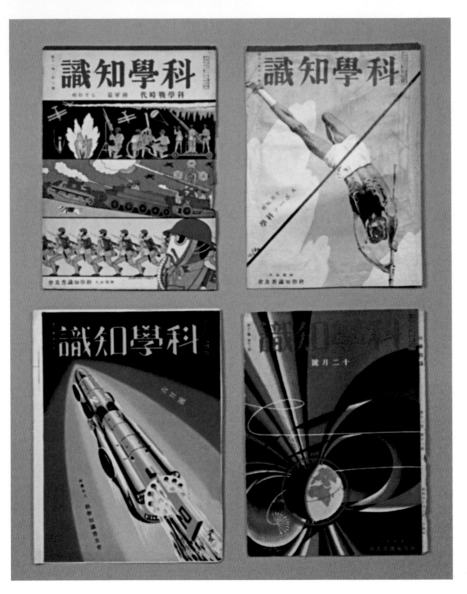

Color Plate 9
Magazine covers for *Kagaku chishiki* (Scientific Knowledge) by
Sugiura Hisui from 1931–1935 illustrated the wonders of science
and technology for young readers.

(The National Museum of Modern Art, Tokyo)

Color Plate 10
Industrial Plants. This photo depicts industrial plants stretching along
Japan's Pacific coast, transforming what had once been scenic views of
mountains and water into a modern landscape.
(Corbis)

Color Plate 11
The Takenoko Zoku (Bamboo Tribe). Young people gather each Sunday on the bridge between trendy Harajuku and the Yoyogi stadiums built for the 1964 Tokyo Olympics to dance and show off.

(Lonely Planet Images)

Steam Engine. The steam engine epitomized the industrial age. Its use on the railroad that paralleled the Tōkaidō eliminated palanquins and most foot traffic. *(Yokohama Archives of History)*

societies, journals, and lecture circuits taught farmers about new seed varieties, commercial fertilizers, and equipment. Without expanding the amount of arable land, annual agricultural productivity rose between 1.5 and 1.7 percent in the late nineteenth century. Since the land tax remained fixed, the increase put more income into the hands of rural entrepreneurs for use in promoting small-scale industry. Farmers were already accustomed to producing handicrafts; the elimination of internal restrictions on trade made it easier for them to market their goods.

Entrepreneurs and artisans developed intermediate technologies that adapted western machines to Japanese circumstances. They modified the manufacture of new daily necessities such as matches to suit the domestic and Asian markets and undersold western brands. The metric system, the new calendar, and western timepieces brought the standardization and regularization modeled by military organization to ordinary work practices. Local clubs tried to preserve handicrafts in the face of foreign imports and sought national and international markets for specialty products. They pooled capital to upgrade indigenous skills, brought in foreign

technology when it fit their needs, and hosted industrial exhibitions to diffuse technological knowledge and stimulate competition. In the mid-1870s, small water-powered filatures spread throughout the mountain valleys of central Japan, close to the silk-producing regions and a work force of young women. By 1900 silk thread accounted for one-third of the value of Japan's commodity exports and textiles totaled over half.

Another model for private enterprise was Shibusawa Eiichi. The son of a rural entrepreneur, he used his connections with oligarchs to become president of the First National Bank. In that capacity he provided capital for the construction of a privately owned shipyard at the mouth of Tokyo Bay. In 1880 he started the Osaka Spinning Mill and went on to found more than one hundred companies. Thanks to investments like his, Japan's imports by the beginning of the twentieth century were of raw materials; it exported manufactured goods. Other entrepreneurs built equipment for railroads, mines, and factories. Many thrived with the government as their biggest customer. They justified their immense wealth by insisting that they worked for the good of the nation.

In 1880 the government faced financial disaster. It had printed money recklessly during the 1870s to finance its projects, and private banks issued their own notes. It spent heavily suppressing *shizoku* rebellions and other police actions; most of the industries it built operated at a loss. Inflation that doubled the price of rice in Tokyo between 1877 and 1880 reduced the value of property tax revenues, and taxes did not cover expenditures. The negative balance of payments sucked gold and silver out of the country. From an economic point of view, Japan faced the most serious crisis of the Meiji period.

After acrimonious debate, the oligarchs decided on a deflationary policy of retrenchment. Finance Minister Matsukata Masayoshi balanced the budget, reduced government expenditures until they fell within revenues, and established a sound currency backed by gold and silver. Except for railroad, telegraph, and military-related industries, he sold at a loss all industries that the government had tried to develop. He recalled students sent abroad on government scholarships, fired foreign experts, enacted sin taxes on tobacco and sake, and increased old taxes. Between 1881 and 1885, he reduced the quantity of currency by 20 percent and stifled commerce. Farmers who saw the price of rice fall 50 percent while taxes remained the same worked longer hours to increase production. Bad loans bankrupted banks started with samurai capital. Small businesses collapsed. The ranks of tenant farmers and factory workers swelled. By 1886 key industries had become concentrated in the hands of a few wealthy capitalists with excellent government connections. The government had rid itself of drains on its income, the budget was balanced, and prices were stable.

By the 1890s Japan had a substantial work force in light and heavy industry. Filatures employed single farm women who worked eighteen-hour days when demand was high. When they contracted tuberculosis, as many did, they were returned to their families. Spreading of the disease made it modern Japan's most severe epidemic. The women who worked twelve-hour shifts in cotton mills were often married. Factory owners assumed that since women did not maintain households independent of fathers or husbands, they had no need to pay a living wage. The first strike in Japan's industrial history occurred at a filature in Kōfu in 1885 where women protested a proposed increase in hours and decrease in pay. Women unable to find factory work turned to prostitution. Poor women from Kyushu were lured to brothels in Southeast Asia. Money remitted to their families helped Japan's balance of payments.

Male factory workers in heavy industry earned up to five times the wages of women. They worked under bosses called *oyakata* who contracted for specific jobs. Because workers ran the factory floor, they were able to retain a measure of autonomy that gave them pride in their work. They moved at will from one factory to another because they possessed skills in high demand. Despite these advantages, wages barely covered the rent for a shack in the slums and a dismal diet of rice and vegetables. In 1898 railroad workers launched the largest strike of the nineteenth century. They demanded respect, higher status, and an increase in overtime pay.

Conditions for miners were worse. The low wages, dangerous work, and prison-like barracks made it so difficult to attract workers that the owner of the Ashio copper mine contracted for convict labor. By the end of the nineteenth century, the mine's demand for timber had stripped surrounding hills, leading to deadly floods. Effluent from the mine had killed the marine life in the Watarase River, devastated farmland, and caused premature deaths. Responses to environmental damage pitted proponents of "Rich Country, Strong Army" against the well-being of ordinary citizens in a conflict that was to play out repeatedly in Japan's modern history.

Civilization and Enlightenment

The local notables who had responded enthusiastically to the Popular Rights Movement wanted to bring a cultural revolution to their villages. In place of the hidebound customs of the past, they wanted "Civilization and Enlightenment," a slogan promoted by urban intellectuals and by oligarchs bent on modernizing communications, hairstyles, and education. The Meiji 6 Society founded in Tokyo in 1873 published a journal in which the members debated representative government, foreign affairs, modernizing the Japanese language, ethics and religion, and roles for women. That same year, local notable Ida Bunzō bought a copy of Samuel Smiles's *Self Help.* In a local magazine, he explained the virtues of perseverance and frugality, competition and progress, moral responsibility and the national interest. Other local notables used informal discussion groups to promote better hygiene and social improvement through hospitals, new foods, better roads, and technological innovation based on western models. They tried to overcome their neighbors' antipathy to the government-mandated schools that they saw as the best hope for improving conditions for rural people and for raising Japan's standing in the world.

The man who coined the phrase "Civilization and Enlightenment" was Fukuzawa Yukichi, a leading member of the Meiji 6 Society. In 1868 he founded Keiō University for the study of western science and business. His multivolume *Seiyō jijō* (*Western Matters*) described modern institutions—schools, hospitals, newspapers, libraries, and museums and western ideas regarding the importance of entrepreneurship and achievement. In the best-seller *Encouragement of Learning,* he indicted Japan for its backwardness and urged citizens to seek learning for its practical value in the modern world. He also served as adviser to Mitsubishi and Mitsui, destined to become the largest conglomerates in Japan. Although he advocated equality, freedom, and education for women, he kept his daughters ignorant and arranged their marriages.

Civilization and enlightenment also pertained to personal appearance. To use western technology, it was more efficient to wear western-style clothes. Replacing distinctive styles of samurai armor with standardized military uniforms submerged the individual in the ranks. Uniforms distinguished policemen from civilians. Changing appearances might help Japan gain the respect of foreigners who flaunted their cultural superiority. The government issued directives to men to stop shaving their pates and to women to stop blackening their teeth and shaving their eyebrows. Emperor and empress led the way. At his first public performance, the Meiji emperor had dressed in the court robes of his ancestors. He wore cosmetics and powder and had false eyebrows smudged on his forehead. Within two years he had changed to western-style uniforms, cut his hair, and grown a beard. The empress too appeared in western-style clothing and hairstyles.

The new nobility and educated elite followed the imperial family's example. In 1883 the foreign minister built a modern two-story brick building called *Rokumeikan* (Deer-Cry Pavilion) that contained a restaurant, billiard room, and ballroom. Invitations to garden parties, charity balls, and receptions included Japanese and foreigners, husbands and wives, a startling innovation because samurai women had not previously socialized with their husbands. Western-style dance by couples was de rigueur, even at parties far from Tokyo sponsored by prefectural governments. The late 1880s government became known as the "dancing cabinet."

Newspapers, journals, and other mass media exemplified and promoted civilization and enlightenment. Woodblock prints used chemical dyes to depict the marvels of westernization. Prints of horse-drawn carriages, steam locomotives, imposing new schools, and red brick buildings illuminated by gaslight in Tokyo's downtown Ginza district inspired progressive youths to seek modernity. (See Color Plate 8.) Magazines for women urged them to become educated in modern modes of thought to help them fulfill their roles as "good wives and wise mothers" (*ryōsai kenbo*). Fukuchi Gen'ichirō epitomized the professional journalist. He covered Saigō's rebellion in 1877 and later became chief editor of the influential *Tōkyō nichinichi shinbun* (Tokyo Daily Newspaper). It was a so-called big paper written in a style only the highly educated could read, with a focus on politics and serious editorials. Founded in 1874, the *Yomiuri Newspaper* aimed at the barely literate. Like other "small papers," it covered scandals and titillating stories of sex and murder. Hawked on street corners, it exploited the growing market for information and entertainment.

Modern newspapers serialized modern novels. In 1885 the aficionado of kabuki and student of English literature Tsubouchi Shōyō wrote *Essence of the Novel,* which tried to define a new realistic literature. Japan's first modern novel is deemed *Floating Clouds* (1887–1889) by Futabatei Shimei, because it tried to get inside the protagonist's head and used language close to the colloquial. Perhaps the most subtle and gifted writer was Higuchi Ichiyō, who garnered recognition in the male world of letters only at the end of her short life. Dominated at the end of the century by the medical doctor Mori Ōgai who had studied in Germany, and Natsume Sōseki who had studied in Britain, this world embraced modernity while questioning the superiority of western civilization.

CONSERVATIVE RESURGENCE

By the middle of the 1880s, many people thought that aping western customs had gone too far. They tried to retain traditional values while accepting the need for western rationalism in scientific inquiry and western technology. In 1882 Kanō Jigorō began the transformation of martial arts into judo and other forms through the scientific selection of techniques from earlier jujitsu schools. He emphasized that judo built character in a way that complemented developments in the study of ethics by religious figures and western-trained philosophers. By establishing an absolute standard for "the good," they sought to promote community suppression of socially disruptive thought. The head of the Hygiene Bureau, Gotō Shimpei, claimed that the only way to get people to respond to public health initiatives was to work through established community structures and appeal to community values. Bureaucrats argued the need for the state to promote social welfare and a collectivist ethic through factory laws, tenancy laws, and agricultural cooperatives lest a social revolution undo their efforts to build a strong state. In 1890 the revised Police Security Regulations forbade women to participate in politics. The intent was to eliminate the need for selfish and unpatriotic competition and conflict.

The educational system bore the brunt of the conservative resurgence. In the 1870s, it imparted strictly utilitarian and materialistic knowledge; in the mid-1880s it focused more on Confucian ethics, Shinto mythology, and civic rituals. For the few who could afford to go beyond compulsory schooling, the Educational Code of 1872 had specified that a rigorous examination system would qualify students for middle schools, and the best would then take examinations for university. Founded in 1877, Tokyo University remained the only public institution at that level until 1897. Private universities such as Keiō and missionary schools provided lesser avenues for educational advancement. In 1886 the Ministry of Education established specialized higher schools above the middle schools. The First Higher School funneled students into Tokyo University for positions in the most prestigious ministries. Some higher schools offered degrees in liberal arts for students going to universities and then to careers in the bureaucracy or business world. Others consisted of vocational schools, military schools, teachers' colleges, and women's colleges. Each socialized the students by crafting character suitable to their station in life.

Education prepared citizens to serve the nation; it also provided the opportunity for personal advancement. The oligarchs opened the ranks of government service to men who had demonstrated talent and ability. The way they measured these qualifications was through academic achievement, but only men from families affluent enough to support them through years of schooling had any chance of success. Women were to serve the state as wives and mothers. Class and gender thus placed limits on equality, and the promise of social mobility concealed an economically stratified society.

Education trained citizens in the civic virtues personified by the emperor. In the 1870s and 1880s he toured Japan to unite the people under his gaze. Newspaper reports of his diligent work habits and concern for his subjects' welfare made him into a symbol of national unity and progress. He moved his headquarters to Hiroshima during the Sino-Japanese War (1894–1895), celebrated war victories, and appeared at imperial funerals, weddings, and wedding anniversaries. Hung in every school and public building, his portrait had to be treated with utmost respect. In 1890 he issued the Imperial Rescript on Education. It urged students to practice filial piety, harmony, sincerity, and benevolence; to respect the constitution; to obey the laws; and to be loyal to the *kokutai* (national polity).

The 1898 Civil Code adjusted the norms of western jurisprudence to the conservative concern for civic morality. Unless the primacy of the house and the patriarchal authority of the household head were maintained in law, the legal scholar Hozumi Yatsuka warned, reverence for the ancestors, loyalty, and filial piety would perish. The Civil Code affirmed legal equality, individual choice, and personal ownership of property for all men and single women, regardless of their former social status. Succession was to follow the male line, with all assets to go to the eldest son. A husband had authority to dispose of his wife's real property, though not her personal property (her trousseau); he decided when and whether to register a marriage and their children. Divorce by mutual consent freed both partners for remarriage in a continuation of Edo period practice. The Civil Code thus balanced a concern for social stability and modern, western norms with an understanding of customary mores.

IMPERIALISM AND MODERNITY

When Japan appropriated and adapted western industrial technology, juridical institutions, constitutional theory, and culture, it also imbibed western imperialism. Gaining colonies compensated for the humiliation suffered in accepting unequal treaties, put Japan on the side of the civilized world by exporting enlightenment to the backward peoples of Asia, and demonstrated Great Power status. A sense of national identity that could unite factory owners with factory workers demanded imperialist enterprises to divert attention from their differences. Social Darwinism taught that nations had to conquer or be conquered. Seeing what had happened to China and India, Fukuzawa Yukichi urged Japan to "escape from Asia" lest it too be conquered. (See **Documents: Fukuzawa Yukichi's "Escape from Asia."**)

The connection between modernity and colonization appeared early in the Meiji period. Japan's overtures to China in 1870 included an effort to extract an unequal treaty because having taken steps toward a modern centralized state made it the more civilized. A treaty negotiated in 1871 granted mutual extraterritoriality. In 1874, Japan used the murder of Ryukyuan fishermen by Taiwanese three years earlier as an excuse to send an expeditionary force to Taiwan. The ostensible purpose was to punish the Taiwanese; a covert aim was to bring civilization to the natives by establishing a colony. The war dragged on for five months before a settlement reached in Beijing acknowledged China's claims to Taiwan and Japan's claims to the Ryukyus. The expeditionary force withdrew, though not before Japanese newspapers had celebrated its victory over barbarism.

The Ryukyus and Hokkaido became internal colonies. In 1871 the Ryukyus were incorporated into Kagoshima prefecture. In 1879, the king was invited to reside in Tokyo and become a member of the new Japanese nobility while a Japanese governor took his place. Japanese

DOCUMENTS

Fukuzawa Yukichi's "Escape from Asia"

The most prominent intellectual and promoter of westernization of Meiji Japan, whose views on domestic policy were decidedly liberal, here Fukuzawa takes a hard-line approach to foreign affairs. His ruthless criticism of Korea and China, published on March 16, 1885, can be read as justifying colonialism, while at the same time he urges his readers to reject the civilization they had to offer. In 1895, ten years after writing this call to action, he rejoiced at Japan's victory over China.

Civilization is like an epidemic of measles. The current measles in Tokyo, which has advanced eastwards from Nagasaki in western Japan, seems to have begun to claim more victims with the arrival of springtime. Will we be able now to find a means of checking this epidemic? It is obvious that we have no way to do so. We cannot put up effective resistance, even against an epidemic that carries with it only harm; much less against civilization, which is always accompanied by both harm and good, but by more good than harm.

Though our land of Japan is situated on the Eastern edge of Asia, the spirit of its people has already shaken off the backwardness of Asia to accept the civilization of the West. Unfortunately, however, we have two neighboring countries, one being called China, the other called Korea. The people of these two countries are no different from us Japanese people in having been brought up since olden times in the Asian culture and customs, and yet, whether because they are of another racial origin, or because, while similar in culture and customs, differ from us in the main lines of their traditional education, a comparison of the three countries, Japan, China, and Korea, reveals that the latter two resemble each other more closely than they do Japan. The people of those two countries do not know how to go about reforming and making progress, whether individually or as a country. It is not that they have not seen or heard of civilized things in the present world of facile communication; yet what their eyes and ears perceive have failed to stimulate their minds, and their emotional attachment to ancient manners and customs has changed little for the past hundreds and thousands of years. In this lively theater of civilization, where things change daily, they still speak of education in terms of Confucianism, cite humanity, justice, civility, and wisdom as their principles of school education, are completely obsessed only with outward appearance, are in reality not only ignorant of truths and principles but so extreme in their cruelty and shamelessness that for them morality is completely non-existent, and yet are as arrogant as if they never gave a thought to self-examination.

In our view, these countries have no likelihood of maintaining their independence in the current tide of civilization's eastward advance. Let there not be the slightest doubt that, unless they are fortunate enough to have motivated men appear in their lands who, as a first step to improve the condition of their countries will plan such a great enterprise of overall reform of their governments as our Restoration was, and succeed in altering their people's minds through political reforms, those countries will meet their doom in but a few years, with their territories divided among the civilized countries of the world. The reason is that China and Korea, confronted by an epidemic of civilization comparable to measles, are impossibly trying to ward it off, despite its inevitability, by shutting themselves up in a room, with the result being that they are cutting off their supply of fresh air and asphyxiating themselves. Though mutual help between neighboring countries has been likened to the relationship between the lips and the teeth, China and Korea of today cannot be of any assistance at all to our country of Japan.

Civilized western man is not without a tendency to regard all three countries as identical because of their geographic proximity and to apply his evaluation of China and Korea to Japan also. For example, when he finds that the governments of China and Korea are old-fashioned autocracies without abiding laws, the western man will suppose Japan too to be a lawless country. When he finds that the gentlemen of China and Korea are too deeply infatuated to know what science is, the western scholar will think that Japan too is a land of Yin-Yang and the Five Elements. When the Chinese display their servility and shamelessness, they obscure the chivalrous spirit of the Japanese. When the Koreans employ cruel means of physical punishment, the Japanese too are surmised to be just as inhuman. Such examples are too numerous to count. This may be compared to the case in which most of those in a string of houses within a village or town are foolish, lawless, cruel, and inhuman; an occasional family that heeds what is just and right will be eclipsed by the other's evil and its virtue will never be noticed. It is indeed not infrequent that something similar happens in our foreign relations and indirectly interferes with them. This should be regarded a great misfortune for our country of Japan.

To plan our course now, therefore, our country cannot afford to wait for the enlightenment of our neighbors and to cooperate in building Asia up. Rather, we should leave their ranks to join the camp of the civilized countries of the West. Even when dealing with China and Korea, we need not have special scruples simply because they are our neighbors, but should behave toward them as the westerners do. One who befriends an evil person cannot avoid being involved in his notoriety. In spirit, then, we break with our evil friends of Eastern Asia.

Source: Centre for East Asian Cultural Studies, comp., *Meiji Japan through Contemporary Sources, Vol. 3, 1869–1894* (Tokyo: Centre for East Asian Cultural Studies, 1972), pp. 129–133, modified.

fishermen and settlers had already spread north as far as Sakhalin and the Kuril Islands, territory that Russia claimed. In 1874 Japan evacuated Sakhalin and negotiated a treaty ceding it to Russia in exchange for Japanese control of the Kurils. It turned Hokkaido into a Japanese prefecture and established a modern definition of property ownership under which it sold off land the Ainu had customarily used for hunting and fishing to Japanese developers. Without material support, Ainu culture lost its meaning.

Japan's relations with Korea illustrate the relationship between modernity and imperialism. The oligarchs sent a diplomatic mission to "open" Korea in 1875–1876 that mimicked Perry's tactics in 1853–1854. The treaty forced on Korea replicated the unequal treaties Japan had been forced to sign in the 1850s. The following years saw successive incidents as factions at the Korean court abetted by Japan and China collided over the country's future course. In Japanese eyes, Korea was a weak, backward nation, easy prey for aggressive western powers. A German military adviser warned that were Korea to be controlled by any other power, it would become a dagger pointing at the heart of Japan. In 1890 Yamagata Aritomo linked parliamentary political participation with a militant international stance by telling the first Diet that for Japan to maintain its independence, it had to protect its territorial boundary, the line of sovereignty, and an outer perimeter of neighboring territory, a line of interest. Korea fell within Japan's line of interest.

The pressure brought by domestic public opinion to revise the unequal treaties affected Japan's diplomatic relations with its Asian neighbors. When negotiations for revision stalled in the face of western intransigence, clamor intensified for an aggressive stance toward China and Korea on the part of patriotic Popular Rights advocates as much as conservatives. In 1886 Britain and Germany proposed the partial abolition of extraterritoriality in exchange for allowing unrestricted travel by for-

eigners. The strength of domestic opposition to this compromise was so strong that the foreign minister had to resign. Finally, in 1894, western powers promised to abolish extraterritoriality and give Japan tariff autonomy in 1899.

Treaty negotiations took place in the context of the first Sino-Japanese War of 1894–1895. Fought over Korea, it lasted nine months. Japanese troops expelled the Chinese army from Korea, defeated the north Chinese navy, captured Port Arthur and the Liaodong peninsula in south Manchuria, and seized a port on the Shandong peninsula. The Treaty of Shimonoseki in April 1895 gave Japan Taiwan and the Pescadores, Port Arthur and the Liaodong peninsula, an indemnity, and a promise by China to respect Korea's autonomy. Japan's victory took western powers by surprise. In their eyes, it threatened peace and stability in East Asia. A week after the treaty was signed, Russia (with its own designs on Manchuria), France (Russia's ally), and Germany (hoping to steer Russian expansion toward what was now referred to as the Far East) collectively advised Japan to surrender its claim to territories in China. Despite popular outcry at the "Triple Intervention," the government had no choice but to obey. Russia then grabbed control of Port Arthur and the Liaodong peninsula.

SUMMARY

By the end of the nineteenth century, Japan had been transformed from a decentralized, largely agrarian regime into a centralized industrializing nation. Molded by schools and the military, informed by newspapers and journals, the peoples of Japan had become citizens. They had learned to ride on trains, wear western-style clothes, work in factories, and be self-reliant in striving for success. In dealing with the outside world, they had discovered that economic development and national defense required expansion abroad.

SUGGESTED READING

The transformation of the Meiji state has attracted numerous scholars. Works include J. M. Ramseyer and F. M. Rosenbluth, *The Politics of Oligarchy: Institutional Change in Imperial Japan* (1995); C. Gluck, *Japan's Modern Myths: Ideology in the Late Meiji Period* (1985); and T. Fujitani, *Splendid Monarchy: Power and Pageantry in Modern Japan* (1996).

For contrasting perspectives on foreign affairs, see W. G. Beasley, *Japanese Imperialism, 1894–1945* (1991), and S. Tanaka, *Japan's Orient: Rendering Pasts as History* (1998).

For economic development, see S. J. Ericson, *The Sound of the Whistle: Railroads and the State in Meiji Japan* (1996), and E. D. Westney, *Imitation and Innovation: The Transfer of Western Organizational Patterns to Meiji Japan* (1987).

Two excellent books on education are D. T. Roden, *School Days in Imperial Japan: A Study in Adolescence and Student Culture* (1975), and B. Platt, *Burning and Building: Schooling and State Formation in Japan, 1750–1890* (2004).

For social history, see M. Hane, *Peasants, Rebels, Women and Outcastes: The Underside of Modern Japan* (2003), and H. Fuess, *Divorce in Japan: Family, Gender, and the State, 1600–2000* (2004). For the media, see J. L. Huffman, *Creating a Public: People and Press in Meiji Japan* (1997). For "Civilization and Enlightenment," see D. Irokawa, *The Culture of the Meiji Period* (1985). For disease, see W. Johnston, *The Modern Epidemic: A History of Tuberculosis in Japan* (1995). For religious change, see J. E. Ketelaar, *Of Heretics and Martyrs in Meiji Japan: Buddhism and Its Persecution* (1990), and H. Hardacre, *Shinto and the State, 1868–1988* (1989).

For views from the periphery, see N. L. Waters, *Japan's Local Pragmatists: The Transition from Bakumatsu to Meiji in the Kawasaki Region* (1983), and M. W. Steele, *Alternative Narratives in Modern Japanese History* (2003).

CHAPTER EIGHT

Rise of Modern Japan (1900–1931)

The early 1900s found Japan ever more deeply entangled in world affairs. Wars on the Asian continent brought it colonies and complicated notions of national identity. Contradictory impulses toward democracy and totalitarianism, modernity and atavism marked the home front. The state impinged more directly than before on the everyday lives of Japanese citizens. The same mechanisms that allowed it to do so—conscription, education, and mass media—provided channels for people to create new organizations at the community level, oppose state policies, and define individual goals. Changes in the economic structure heightened the importance of industrial labor and the fears of social unrest. A new middle class provided a ready market for popular culture. The most visible signs of modern life concentrated in the cities, to the disgust of people who located the preserve of Japanese values in pristine communities of the countryside.

The first decades of the twentieth century are often analyzed to explain what came after. To what extent was Japan's descent into fascism preordained? Why consider countervailing forces, given that they failed? What is this period's legacy for postwar Japan?

A FLUID INTERNATIONAL ORDER

In the 1900s, foreign relations resonated throughout Japan's economy, politics, society, and culture. The imperative to challenge white supremacy by achieving great power status and rising in the hierarchy of nations shaped Japan's national identity. Colonies came to be seen as an economic necessity, both to supply raw materials for Japan's emerging industries and to provide living space for Japan's teeming population.

Japan began the drive for great power status by signing an alliance with Britain in 1902 and going to war against Russia in 1904–1905.

The alliance committed each country to come to the defense of the other should a third party join the enemy in time of war. It functioned as planned against Russia. Russia's leasehold on the Liaodong peninsula and fortification of Port Arthur threatened Japan's interests in Korea. When Russia refused to make concessions, Japan's military launched a surprise attack on Port Arthur. It hoped to win a short war before Russia could mobilize its larger army and bring it to the scene of battle, but the siege dragged on longer than expected. By the time Port Arthur fell, Japan's army was exhausted. U.S. President Theodore Roosevelt offered to negotiate a peace settlement. The Treaty of Portsmouth gave Japan the southern half of Sakhalin, Russia's leasehold on the Liaodong peninsula, the South Manchurian Railway built by the Russians between Port Arthur and Mukden and its associated mining concessions, and Russian acknowledgment of Japan's paramountcy in Korea. In demonstrating that a "yellow race" could beat the "whites," Japan inspired Asians with hopes that they could throw off the colonial yoke.

Japan landed troops in Korea two days before it declared war on Russia. Two weeks later, it forced the Korean king to accept a limited protectorate that made Korea Japan's ally and subject to Japan's lead in administrative matters. The Japanese army then occupied the country. Six months later, Korea had to accept Japanese financial and diplomatic advisers. They reformed the currency and drew up a government budget. They took over the communications system for reasons of national security. The army imposed martial law to prevent sabotage. The Taft-Katsura agreement of 1905 acknowledged Japan's control of Korea in return for Japan's acquiescence in the U.S. colonization of the Philippines. In 1906, Korea became a Japanese protectorate with Itō Hirobumi as resident general. Government offices had to obey Japanese advisers, courts came under the jurisdiction of Japanese judges, the Korean army was disbanded, a Japanese police force maintained order, and Japan took

Cartoon of Amaterasu and Britannia. This cartoon of Amaterasu and Britannia celebrates the 1902 signing of the Anglo-Japanese alliance. The goddesses representing Japan and Great Britain cast their benevolent protection over Korea. (*Saitama Municipal Cartoon Art Museum/DNPArchives.com*)

over Korea's diplomatic relations. When the king complained to the Hague Peace Conference of 1907, Itō forced him to abdicate. In 1909 a Korean nationalist assassinated Itō. In 1910 Japan annexed Korea. At the same time, Japan formalized control over Taiwan. Both remained in the Japanese empire for the next thirty-five years, and Japan had joined the ranks of imperial powers. (See Map 8.1.)

Japan envisioned that its empire would bring not only prestige, but also coal and iron for its factories, food for its people, a market for the export of finished products, and space for its expanding population. Taiwan supplied sugar

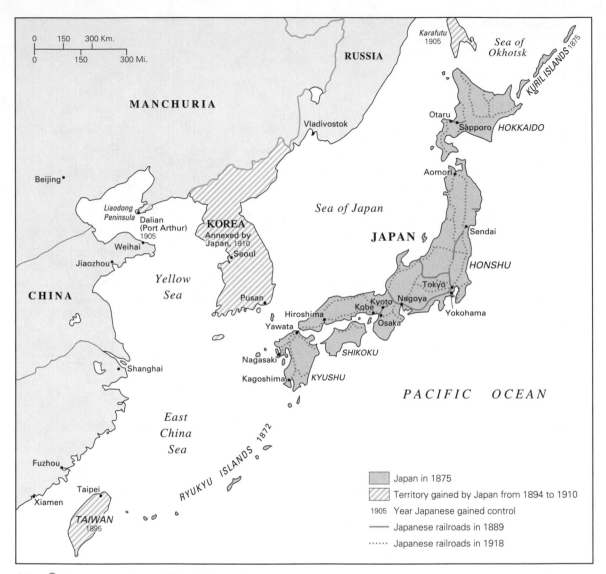

Map 8.1   Japanese Imperial Expansion, 1868–1910

financed by Japanese capital and, after 1920, rice produced on family farms that inadvertently promoted the island's economic development. The Oriental Development Company bought land in Korea to sell to Japanese settlers, channeled capital to Japanese-owned businesses, and participated in the development of Manchurian mines. The military government improved the infrastructure by building roads, railways, and opening schools. It ruthlessly suppressed all dissent.

Japanese who migrated to Korea enjoyed a higher standard of living than Koreans and special privileges in education and employment.

World War I proved advantageous for Japan both economically and diplomatically. Its alliance with Britain allowed it to absorb Germany's leasehold on China's Shandong province and acquire a mandate over German-held islands in the Pacific. In 1918, Japan invaded Siberia along with Allied forces. Japan also tried to impose the infamous Twenty-One Demands on China. Most of them ratified and prolonged Japan's existing privileges in Manchuria and along the China coast. The last set of "requests" would have turned China into a Japanese protectorate. A public outcry in China and abroad forced Japan to back down. The Chinese complained bitterly about the Twenty-One Demands at the Versailles Peace Conference, but to no avail. Despite the open door policy promoted by the United States, no western power was willing to challenge Japan's interests in China.

Following World War I, Japan collaborated with western powers. It joined the League of Nations. In 1921 it participated in the multilateral Washington Conference designed to preserve the status quo in the Pacific and China and prevent a new naval arms race. A delegation of Japanese businessmen sent abroad in 1921–1922 demonstrated Japan's commitment to participation in the developed world's economy. Japan had been unable to get a clause on racial equality in the Versailles Peace Treaty, and in 1924, the United States offended Japan by passing the Oriental Exclusion Act. Despite this insult, Japan signed the Kellogg-Briand Pact of 1928 that outlawed war in the settlement of international disputes. In 1930 civilian diplomats agreed to additional naval limitations in the London Naval Treaty over the navy's objections and without addressing the military's concerns regarding China. When the army acted on its own to take over Manchuria, it ended the era of cooperation with the West.

ECONOMIC DEVELOPMENT

In the early twentieth century, Japanese corporations took advantage of international technological and managerial innovations often called the "second industrial revolution." Japan's electrical technology became second to none. Electric streetcars appeared in Tokyo in 1904. Of Japanese households, 85 percent had electricity in 1935 compared to 68 percent in the United States. Techniques of mass production required both standardized equipment and scientific management or Taylorism, an American theory of rational labor practice that Japan adapted to make the work force more efficient. Localities hoping to attract businesses developed research centers to find foreign technology, channel it to the factory floor, and modify foreign products for domestic consumption. Large enterprises developed new metallurgical and chemical technologies, often at the prompting of the Japanese military, which promoted the automobile and the airplane.

A dual structure characterized Japan's modern economy. Conglomerates linked through holding and trading companies called *zaibatsu* (financial cliques) dominated the most modern sectors of the economy—mining, shipbuilding, machinery, steel, and chemicals—and produced standardized, high-volume products. Although each company within the *zaibatsu* pursued a single enterprise and remained legally distinct, access to the *zaibatsu's* capital through its bank, a central advisory committee that set policy and long-term goals, and interlocking boards of directors tied them together. In some cases *zaibatsu* cooperated in cartels that divided up raw materials and access to markets as in the textile industry and maritime shipping. *Zaibatsu* chairmen enjoyed access to bureaucrats and cabinet ministers, who steered public investment their way and smoothed the regulatory road. Small firms found niches as makers of specialty items and basic consumer goods such as processed food, housing, and clothing. They produced ceramics and toys for export by the *zaibatsu* and functioned as suppliers and subcontractors to the large enterprises.

Japan's industrial sector was well placed to take advantage of World War I. Coal fueled locomotives, factories, and generators. Steel works had capacity to spare. Mitsubishi both built ships and operated a worldwide shipping line in competition with the Sumitomo-backed OSK shipping company. These and other enterprises profited from the Allies' demand for munitions and war-related material. Japanese textiles and consumer goods filled the vacuum

Real National Income Produced, 1878–1936
(million yen at 1928–1932 prices)

Year	Total	Primary Industry	Secondary Industry	Tertiary Industry
1878	1,117	691	95	331
1890	2,308	1,429	224	655
1900	3,640	1,671	818	1,151
1914	5,665	2,127	1,354	2,184
1920	6,316	2,147	1,686	2,483
1925	9,268	2,779	2,216	4,273
1929	10,962	2,740	2,911	5,311
1930	12,715	2,477	3,550	6,688
1931	13,726	2,372	3,716	7,638
1932	13,843	2,594	3,987	7,262
1936	16,133	3,149	5,096	7,888

Primary industry = agriculture, forestry, fisheries. Secondary industry = mining, manufacturing, construction, transportation, communication, and utilities. Tertiary industry = commerce and services. Source: G. C. Allen, *A Short Economic History of Modern Japan* (New York: St. Martin's Press, 1981), p. 284.

left by the departure of British exports from Asia. Business profits soared, and Japan's gross national product jumped by 40 percent between 1914 and 1918. The percentage of real national income contributed by manufacturing passed that of agriculture.

Imbalances between different sectors of the economy and cycles of contraction and expansion characterized the 1920s. Japanese companies assumed that demand would continue after World War I. When Britain took back markets in China and South Asia and European manufacturing replaced Japanese exports, they found themselves overextended financially and forced to lay off workers. They had just pulled out of the postwar recession when the Great Kanto Earthquake of September 1, 1923, leveled factories and workshops between Tokyo and Yokohama: one hundred forty thousand people died, and five hundred seventy thousand structures (70 percent of Tokyo and 60 percent of Yokohama) were destroyed. Aftershocks ruptured gas and water pipes, snapped electrical lines, and halted transportation and communications. Most companies rebuilt using generous credit

provided through the government to banks, which led to a credit crisis in 1927. Trouble came to the domestic market when silk sales slipped and cotton mills in China cut into Japan's biggest Asian market. In contrast to stagnation and decline in the textile industry and agricultural sector, old *zaibatsu* grew by absorbing existing enterprises and diversifying into new areas. Founded in 1908, the Chisso chemical corporation became Japan's third largest manufacturer as a new *zaibatsu* and industrialized northern Korea. When the Great Depression hit at the end of 1929, Japan's economy was already depressed. Japan joined other industrialized nations in imposing steep tariffs on imports, secure in the knowledge that except for oil and scrap iron used in making steel, its colonies had given it the requirements for an autarchic economy.

CONSTITUTIONAL GOVERNMENT

In the public's eyes, the oligarchs' efforts to control the selection of cabinet ministers demonstrated the persistence of clique government dominated by men from Satsuma and Chōshū. To counter Itō Hirobumi's influence in the lower house, Yamagata Aritomo forged a faction of conservative bureaucrats, members of the Privy Council and the upper house, and prefectural governors. In 1907 he made it possible for the military to issue orders in the emperor's name independent of the prime minister. Itō's protégé among elected politicians, Hara Takashi, had experience in the Foreign Ministry and the business world that helped him to arrange compromises between the oligarchs and the Diet and showed him the way to manipulate the bureaucracy. During the Russo-Japanese War, Hara promised Seiyūkai support for the cabinet, and in return, he convinced Yamagata to trust him with the powerful position of home minister.

Hara used his control over the Home Ministry to make the Seiyūkai the dominant party in the Diet. The home ministry appointed prefectural governors and district chiefs. It ran the police, the health bureau, and the public works bureau. Hara worked with bureaucrats in the Tokyo office and built a following for Seiyūkai in prefectural offices. Since prefectural officials supervised elections and influenced the local economy, a prefecture with a bureaucracy that supported the Seiyūkai was likely to elect Seiyūkai politicians to the Diet. Hara also perfected pork barrel politics. Unlike the early parties that simply opposed government spending and tried to cut taxes, the Seiyūkai followed a "positive policy" of government spending for economic development. Railroad lines spidered across the country, linking cities, towns, and centers of Seiyūkai support in remote mountain villages. Roads, schools, bridges, irrigation works, and harbors blessed the districts that voted Seiyūkai.

Even before Hara became prime minister in 1918, Diet members had mastered manipulating the electorate. Businessmen provided political funds in return for favors. They also offered politicians and bureaucrats positions on their companies' boards of directors. In buying votes,

some Diet members relied on election brokers. Others used prefectural assembly members, tainting them as well with the stench of corruption. Playing on Yamagata's fears of a socialist revolution following the Bolshevik takeover in Russia and nationwide rice riots in Japan in 1918, Hara convinced him that party control of an expanded electorate was the safest way to channel popular unrest. The 1919 expansion of the electorate to 5 percent of the population benefited small landlords, not urban workers. In 1921 an unemployed railroad worker assassinated Hara because of what he saw as Hara's disdain for the military.

Between 1924 and 1932, selection of the cabinet shifted back and forth between the two major parties in the lower house. Former bureaucrats and prefectural governors became politicians and ran for the Diet. Although it was not in Seiyūkai's interest to widen the electorate, the pressure of public opinion, maneuvering by other political parties, and the Privy Council's fear of social upheaval led the Diet to pass a bill for universal suffrage for males over age twenty-five in 1925. In the next election three years later, eight proletarian candidates were elected out of four hundred fifty contested seats.

The politics of compromise developed by Hara continued after party cabinets became the rule. The Privy Council, House of Peers, much of the bureaucracy, and the military remained beyond the parties' control. Despite the efforts of the constitutional scholar Minobe Tatsukichi to devise a theoretical legitimization for party cabinets, they rested on neither law nor precedent but on a pragmatic balance of power.

The crises that bedeviled Japan in the late 1920s and early 1930s tested the limits of constitutionally sanctioned parliamentary democracy. Japan had to deal with the Great Depression and fears of Russian or Chinese threats to Manchuria. Right-wing ultranationalists inside the military and outside the government accused the parties of having traitorously weakened Japan by their corrupt pursuit of self-interest. In 1930, one of their number attacked Prime Minister Hamaguchi Osachi for having signed the controversial

London Naval Treaty. He died nine months later. Convinced that the party cabinet was about to sacrifice Japan's interests in Asia, colonels in the army acted unilaterally in taking over Manchuria. The early months of 1932 saw the assassinations of a former finance minister and an industrialist blamed for hardships brought by the depression. Prime Minister Inukai Tsuyoshi also died at the hands of a group of naval cadets, junior army officers, and civilians. The next prime minister was a military man, as were his successors to 1945 with two exceptions, both of whom supported the military. The parties still dominated the lower house, but they received only minor cabinet appointments. Even during the war, the Diet continued to function. The cabinet continued to decide policy, although the military's right of access to the emperor precluded debate over its actions. The constitution remained the law of the land.

Imperial Democracy

According to critics in Japan before World War II, liberalism's focus on the individual contradicted the notion that all Japanese were part of the same body politic, *kokutai,* also translated as "national essence." Democracy was a foreign import, antithetical to indigenous custom based on harmony, consensus, and service to the emperor. Many Japanese people proved them wrong by striving for a more open government and society. In the early twentieth century, the struggle for democracy engaged academic theorists, journalists, feminists, outcasts, and the working men and women who expressed themselves in riots and efforts to organize unions.

For Japanese intellectuals, liberalism meant representative government, constitutionalism, and rule by law. It meant individual rights and freedom from undue governmental interference in the individual's life. It distinguished between the naturalness of society and the artifice of the state. The problem for liberals was that imperial ideology defined the emperor as present at society's inception. The imperial institution was not to be analyzed as though it were an artificial construct

because it united state and society. Liberals were patriots. They approved of the government's efforts to promote industrialization and make Japan the equal of the West, and they never questioned the centrality of the emperor.

Intellectuals who professed liberal views jeopardized their careers. Yoshino Sakuzō had to resign his position at Tokyo University because he had argued that the people are the basis of the state and the aim of the state is to promote their well-being. The public interest, that of people as a whole, has to supersede the private, partial interests of oligarchs, bureaucrats, politicians, and businessmen. Minobe Tatsukichi argued that according to the constitution, the Diet, in particular the lower house, was the organ that represented the people. Sovereignty lay not in the emperor but in the state, and the emperor was one of its organs. In 1935 he was accused of disrespect for the emperor, his writings banned, and his membership in the upper house revoked.

Educated women promoted democracy through their organizations and deeds. Teachers, many of them Christian or influenced by missionaries, hoped to improve and reform society. The Woman's Christian Temperance Union found adherents in Japan because men's drinking wrecked the home. In 1886 the Tokyo Women's Reform Society opposed concubinage and prostitution, both deemed trafficking in women. Since the oligarchs kept concubines and the Meiji emperor fathered the crown prince on a concubine, the notion that civilized behavior included sexual fidelity was a hard sell. More acceptable was the Reform Society's work in aiding earthquake victims and providing financial support for former prostitutes. In 1901 members of the Reform Society joined the Greater Japan Women's Patriotic Association. Under its auspices they could speak in public to women, and they received government support for their activities.

The staging of Henrik Ibsen's *A Doll's House* in 1911 and inauguration of the journal *Bluestocking* marked the arrival of the "new woman" in Japan. The play offered a scandalous alternative to the government-sponsored ideology of "good wife and wise mother" when Nora walked out on husband and children. Matsui Sumako who played Nora gained fame as Japan's first western-style actress. Her tumultuous private life dramatized her rejection of domesticity. *Bluestocking* started as a literary magazine, but it soon became a forum for discussing women's roles and expectations. The feminist activist Hiratsuka Raichō and the poet, translator, and social critic Yosano Akiko debated state support for motherhood, Hiratsuka wanting government protection, Yosano arguing that state support would be degrading and would cost women their independence. They agreed that marriage is not sacrosanct, patriarchy need not go unchallenged, and women ought to have equal legal, educational, and social rights.

In the 1920s, feminists advocated family planning and women's suffrage. Katō Shidzue brought Margaret Sanger to Japan in 1924 to promote birth control as a way to deal with the threat to family budgets and women's health posed by too many children. The government refused Sanger permission to land until she promised to make no public speeches. The examples of Britain and the United States that granted women the vote after World War I and the growing numbers of women who followed politics in mass circulation newspapers and magazines convinced some politicians and bureaucrats that political rights for women marked advanced societies. In 1922 the Diet revoked the law that barred women from political meetings. In 1931 a bill for local women's suffrage passed the lower house but foundered on a conservative coalition in the House of Peers. Give women the right to vote, and they will stop having children, predicted one baron. The end to party cabinets stymied proposals for women's political rights.

Mass Movements

Modern mass movements emerged in the context of Japanese imperialism. In 1905, newspapers and speechmakers informed the public that the Russo-Japanese War had concluded without the indemnity that a great power deserved from a defeated foe and with slight territorial gain to justify the sacrifices made by Japanese troops. Riots began at Tokyo's Hibiya Park outside the palace and continued for three days, destroying over 70 percent of police boxes that provided shelter for policemen stationed across the city and fifteen trams. (See Map 8.2.) Smaller riots erupted in Kobe and Yokohama. All but two of the forty-four prefectures reported rallies in cities, towns, and villages. Between 1905 and the rice riots of 1918, Tokyo experienced nine serious riots, many part of larger movements that swept the nation. Although rioters attacked police stations and government offices, they did so in the name of the emperor. By conflating imperial and popular will, they differentiated between evil advisers behind the throne and the throne itself.

The rice riots of 1918 protested high prices, degrading work conditions, and governmental ineptitude. They began with fishermen's wives who organized demonstrations along the Toyama coast and grew to include urban rioters who castigated war profiteers and asserted a right to free speech, tenant farmers who demanded lower rents and decent treatment from landlords, and coal miners who demanded higher wages and respect as human beings. Out of them grew the mass movements of the 1920s for *burakumin* (outcast) liberation and labor organization.

Outcasts found that the Meiji transformation did not improve their lot. Losing the monopoly over leather work and other lucrative, if unpleasant, tasks brought poverty. The household registration system made it well nigh impossible for outcasts to escape their past. Schools refused to admit them, employers to hire them, landlords to rent to them, public baths and barbers to serve them, and other Japanese to marry them. When conscripted into the military, they were assigned menial tasks and never promoted. In the early twentieth century, the central government set up advisory committees to deal with the issue of poverty lest

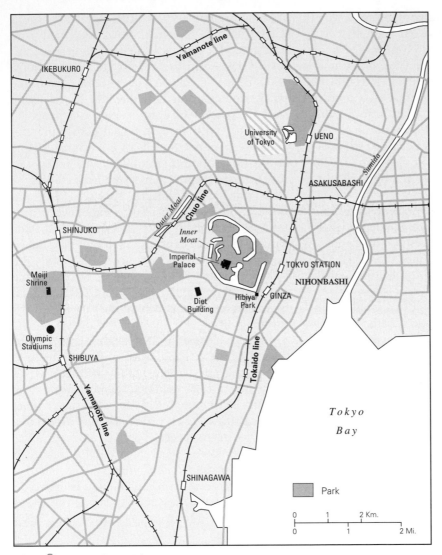

Map **8.2**   **Modern Tokyo**

socialism creep into Japan. Since *burakumin* were among the worst off, they became one focus. In 1908 the cabinet encouraged them to emigrate. In 1911 the Home Ministry started to distribute funds for the improvement of *burakumin* communities, and in 1920 it started the Harmony Movement to mobilize the *burakumin* to work for gradual reform. Private organizations lent support. Both assumed that the reason for discrimination lay in *burakumin* filth, ignorance, and immorality. In 1922, a group of

young *burakumin* organized the Leveller's Society (*Suiheisha*) to protest discrimination and promote the equality of all Japanese subjects before the emperor.

The *burakumin* liberation movement of the 1920s blamed the *burakumin*'s problems on prejudice and discrimination. The goal was to change social attitudes, but Leveller's Society members could not agree on tactics. Some believed in educational programs and nonviolent confrontations that aimed at greater democracy. Others wanted

Women Supporters of the Suiheisha. This nation-wide organization tried to end discrimination against burakumin in the 1920s. These women were from the Fukuoka branch in northern Kyushu. *(50* Years of History of Suiheisha *by Buraku Liberation Publishing House/DNP Archives.com)*

a social revolution to overthrow capitalism through challenging institutions and individuals known to oppose fair practices. Denunciation campaigns targeted primary schools that permitted students and staff to insult *burakumin* or public officials and individuals who had uttered derogatory remarks. The offenders would have to offer an apology, sometimes publicized in newspapers. In 1926, the first year of the Shōwa emperor's reign, antimilitarism plus anger at the treatment of conscript *burakumin* led to a movement promoting noncompliance with military organizations. Despite police repression, denunciation campaigns continued into the 1930s. Only after the outbreak of the China war in 1937 did the Leveller's Society agree to support national unity and the war effort.

Tenant farmers and industrial workers tried to gain acceptance for their organizations and legitimacy for their grievances. The 1898 Civil Code gave landlords the right to buy, sell, and lease land without any protection for tenants who might have farmed it for generations. Of Japan's farm families, 28 percent owned no land, while another 41 percent owned some and rented the rest. Tenants and tenant-owners organized unions in the 1910s to demand rent reductions and the right of cultivation, especially in the most economically advanced regions in central and western Japan, where landlords had previously been in the forefront of encouraging agricultural improvements. The tenants established a national federation in 1922 that grew to nearly seven hundred branches. In the 1920s, over eighteen thousand disputes between tenants and landlords filled police dockets.

Agricultural conditions in the 1930s began badly. The economic downturn in the 1920s when synthetic fabrics replaced silk and the government allowed the import of rice from Asia reduced the demand for agricultural products and unskilled labor. Real income for farm families declined by 30 percent. Unseasonably cold weather in the agriculturally backward northeast brought crop failures between 1931 and 1933. Landlords tried to repossess tenanted land, refused to reduce rents, or even tried to raise them. Debt-ridden farmers migrated to Japan's overseas colonies or sold their daughters into prostitution. Tenants petitioned the Agriculture Ministry for rural relief. The ministry responded by organizing cooperatives and providing funds for development. In central and western Japan, where absentee landlords no longer performed ceremonial and support functions, tenants lost their former deference. Their habit of looking on the land they cultivated as theirs led to rent refusals and conflict. By the mid-1930s, being a landlord was more trouble that it was worth. With the coming of war in 1937, agricultural conditions improved when the government moved to limit rice imports, and tenant unions disbanded in the drive for national unity.

Industrial development led to labor activism, though not labor solidarity. Heavy industry employed highly skilled and relatively well-paid male workers sufficiently educated to read newspapers and understand socialist theory. Textile mills continued to hire cheaper and, it was hoped, docile women and girls. Even in 1930, they constituted over 50 percent of the factory work force. Urban women found jobs as teachers, journalists, nurses, clerks, ticket sellers, bus conductors, telephone operators, actresses, and café hostesses. Small firms employed male and female workers at low wages to manufacture parts for other sectors of the economy. Below them were rickshaw pullers and delivery boys. At the bottom were the miners.

Worker grievances and the ability to organize varied across industries and within factories. The 1907 riot at the Ashio mine originated with ore diggers, the most highly paid workers, not copper refinery workers whose wages had recently dropped and who feared being laid off. The expansion in heavy industry and the need to raise productivity prompted factory owners to reduce worker autonomy and eliminate the bosses who contracted for specific jobs. Workers countered with demands that they be treated with respect. (See **Documents: Negotiations Between Strike Group Representatives and Company Directors.**) In 1912 they organized the Friendship Society (Yūaikai) to provide mutual aid, self-improvement classes, and improved relations with employers. If workers worked hard and deferred to foremen, then the factory owners ought to treat them with benevolence. To keep skilled workers, employers instituted a seniority system of raises and offered fringe benefits.

In many cases, implementation of paternalistic benefits came only after workers had launched work stoppages and strikes. Over one hundred labor disputes erupted between 1902 and 1917. In 1919 the Hara cabinet interpreted the Public Order and Police Act of 1900 to mean that workers might organize unions and go on strike so long as they remained nonviolent. In 1921 the Yūaikai became the Japan Federation of Labor. Union membership burgeoned in the 1920s, although it never included more than 8 percent of the industrial work force. Hundreds of strikes a year roiled both heavy and textile industries. Although owners resisted unionization, workers bargained collectively for higher wages, severance pay, a minimum wage, better working conditions, shorter workdays, an end to child labor, and improved housing.

Minorities

Although nationalist propaganda assured Japanese people that they were uniquely homogeneous, the pairing of colonialism and modernity created groups perceived as different. The government defined the Ainu as "formerly indigenous people" and demanded that they assimilate into the Japanese mainstream by renouncing their peripatetic lifestyle and settling in villages. Officials who supervised their transformation into tenant farmers, laborers, and welfare recipients in the course of selling off their lands and opening Hokkaido to development saw them as a dying race. Many Ainu accepted the necessity of assimilation despite discrimination at the hands of employers, teachers, and non-Ainu neighbors. Others objected to contradictory policies that made them use the Japanese language and forgo tattooing and earrings while setting them up as tourist attractions and anthropological exhibits. During the 1920s, Ainu scholars recorded Ainu songs, legends, and customs. Ainu activists created self-help programs to cope with alcoholism and violence. Social critics drew on radical thought to counter prejudice and discrimination. Fearful lest Hokkaido go red with the Soviet Union so close to its border, government officials and assimilationist Ainu founded the Ainu Society in 1930 to improve the individual lot through education and to remind Ainu of the gratitude they owed the emperor.

The government's attitude toward the Ryukyus was more complicated. The land tax was not imposed in the Ryukyus until 1903. Ryukyuans had a social hierarchy topped by a monarch and aristocracy that made sense in the eyes of Japanese accustomed to inherent social inequality. Ryukyuan nobles used their status to gain favors from the prefectural governor's office and insisted on their right to speak for the commoners. To be placed on a par with Ainu was, they felt, an insult to their superior culture.

Nearly three hundred thousand Koreans lived in Japan by 1930. The earliest arrivals in the late nineteenth century were students of Japan's resistance to western imperialism. Next came workers forced from their villages by colonial policies that expropriated land and put Japan's dietary needs first. Enticed by labor contractors who promised employment in factories, mines, and construction, workers ended up in low-paying jobs and substandard housing. Excluded from skilled labor except when used to break strikes, they performed dirty and dangerous jobs shunned by Japanese at wages half that of Japanese workers. Although the government made Koreans citizens of Japan and promoted an ideology of racial brotherhood under the emperor, Koreans in Japan were deemed inherently stupid, lazy, bellicose, and vicious. Accused of having set fires and poisoned wells following the Great Kanto Earthquake, thousands died at the hands of Japanese vigilantes.

Koreans who showed intellectual promise earned the mistrust of Japanese officials, who feared, with reason, that they harbored anti-Japanese sentiment. Korean students in Japan suffered arrest, imprisonment, and death for supporting national resistance movements and joining Japanese students who professed universal brotherhood, socialism, and communism. The Osaka Confederation of Korean Laborers earned official enmity when it called for an end to capitalism. Moderate Korean residents feared that opposition to colonialism would only invite repression. They organized mutual aid societies to help Koreans find work, adequate housing, and health care. Government officials promoted assimilation policies to bring Koreans gradually and peacefully into Japanese society, albeit with the proviso that ethnically they could never become Japanese.

Radicals

The government suppressed ideas it deemed dangerous in socialism and other western theories. In 1901 the Socialist Democratic Party enjoyed mere hours of existence before being outlawed. It advocated public ownership of land, capital, and communications; abolition of the military; education funded by the state; workers' rights to unionize; universal suffrage; and abolition of the House of Peers. It did not reject the emperor system, unlike the anarchosyndicalists Kōtoku Shūsui and Kanno Suga. He

DOCUMENTS

Negotiations Between Strike Group Representatives and Company Directors

This confrontation between strike group representatives Itō, Iwasa, and Shiga and company directors for the Yokohama Dock Company Tōjō and Miyanaga on September 28, 1921, exposes conflict between workers and management over work conditions and financial issues such as wages and severance pay. The hyperbole on both sides scarcely conceals fundamentally different attitudes regarding company goals, the value of work, and the treatment of workers.

Itō: Today the three of us have come as worker representatives with this petition.

Miyanaga: Does this demand for a 20 percent daily wage increase mean an average wage increase of 20 percent for all the workers?

Iwasa: Our wages average 1 yen 60 sen. Out of 1,000 people, if there is one getting 3 yen, the rest are getting around 1 yen 40 sen. With days off, one month is 25 days and, with a wife and children, we can't make ends meet. This is why we have asked for a pay raise. With the present severance pay, if one of us is fired, he is reduced to poverty.

Miyanaga: We want you to understand the company's situation. As you are well aware, the economy, especially the shipbuilding industry, is facing a severe depression. The question of how to support the workers in this situation is one that troubles us greatly. Because of the shipbuilding depression there have been many layoffs, and aware of your anxiety about this, the other day we announced that we would not carry out any large-scale layoffs. As for ship repairs, which this company has been engaged in since its founding, in good times we were able to charge the shipowners a good price, but today the situation is so bad that, even if we offer a price below cost, they won't take it.

Shipbuilding revived briefly after the war and we were able to make some profit, but now we are making no profit and are taking orders at a loss. In this depression, we are taking on such orders because we do not want to have to lay off you workers. We understand well your plight, but, even at present pay levels, the situation is as I have described, so we would hope to have your understanding regarding the pay raise. You also raised demands regarding severance and retirement pay. As I have already noted, our policy is to avoid layoffs at all costs in the hopes that this will reduce your anxiety, so we would like to gain your understanding on these points also. As for the fourth demand, you use the term "expel." Does that mean you want us to fire them?

All three: That's right.

Miyanaga: You want us to fire the three factory heads. However, the decision to take action against those who break company regulations does rest with these people. Although we hope to avoid such situations, every day two or three people are fired for breaking company rules, and there was nothing exceptional in the case of these three. Thus it would be difficult to take action [and fire the supervisors who had

opposed capitalists, militarists, aristocrats, and politicians on behalf of workers and farmers. She advocated overthrow of the government and assassination of the emperor. In what is

known as the Great Treason Trial of 1911, Kōtoku and Kanno were convicted and sentenced to death, although they were innocent of the charges brought against them. Ōsugi Sakae

fired three union members.] As for what the company will do in the future, we feel it would be best to work to harmonize your desires with those of the company and work from a position of mutual understanding. We are presently studying ways to promote your welfare. In due time, we are hoping to implement these plans. Thus we would like to gain your understanding regarding both the company's present position and future plans and have you pass this on to your fellow workers.

Itō: Are you saying you will absolutely not lay off any workers?

Miyanaga: I can't promise "absolutely" but . . .

Miyanaga and Itō (together): Insofar as possible.

Itō: In that case wouldn't it be better to decide on severance pay and relieve our anxieties in that way?

Miyanaga: Our thinking is that is would be even kinder to take the policy of avoiding layoffs rather than getting involved in the severance pay issue.

Itō: So you mean to say that there is no necessity to decide on severance pay? If your policy is not to lay off workers, well, this is a bit of an extreme example, but in that case wouldn't it be just as well to set severance pay at 10 to 20 thousand yen?

Miyanaga: I didn't say that there was no need. We are now considering the issue of severance pay.

Itō: You say "insofar as possible," but does that mean that in the eventuality of a layoff, you will handle it as in the past?

Miyanaga: We are now also considering the possibility of increasing the level in the future.

Iwasa: Isn't what you are saying merely that, if you accept our demands, your profit will be narrowed? For us this is a matter of life and death.

Miyanaga: You say "our profits are narrowed," but in fact, not only are we not expecting any profit, but the company is going so far as to operate at a loss.

Itō: We have already heard at length from Mr. Yamaguchi on this point and understand it well. In any case, we regard the fact that the company will not now announce its intention to change the present severance pay as an indication of the company's total lack of sincerity regarding this entire affair. Let's go back and report this to all the others.

Miyanaga: You say that we are insincere, but as I have already explained the company is striving to promote your welfare and guarantee your security, and we'd like you to report this to the others.

Iwasa: The other day a worker named Tsukui, who was working in one of your manufacturing shops, was fired for going to another shop and talking to a worker there. You said that this was a violation of company rules, so he was fired. But this is something which other workers are constantly doing. If you look for such little matters and fire someone everyday, pretty soon you'll have fired all the workers. Therefore, all your kind words are just the attitude of a man who stands laughing after having strangled seven people. We'll go and report this situation to all the other workers.

Source: Andrew Gordon, *The Evolution of Labor Relations in Japan: Heavy Industry, 1853–1955* (Cambridge, Mass.: Council on East Asian Studies, Harvard University, 1985), pp. 116–119, modified.

believed that society consists of two classes: the conquerors and the suppressed. It was up to workers to abolish the state and destroy capitalism. Following the Great Kanto Earthquake, he and his wife, the feminist and anarchist Itō Noe, were strangled by the police. The nihilist Kaneko Fumiko advocated Korean independence. She died in prison. In 1933, the proletarian writer Kobayashi Takiji, who had graphically depicted the brutal conditions of fishermen in *The Cannery Boat* (1929), died at the hands of the police.

During the 1920s, a few socialists enjoyed a brief opportunity to propagate their views. The Red Wave Society founded in 1921 urged women to join the fight against capitalist society that enslaved them inside and outside the home. Sakai Toshihiko organized a study group to discuss socialist ideas in the late 1890s. In 1922 he participated in the secret founding of the Japanese Communist Party. Inuta Shigeru launched a literary movement that advocated self-rule for farmers through land reform. Kawakami Hajime took a torturous path from religious movements and nationalism to Marxism, revolutionary communism, and the study of historical materialism. Between 1927 and 1937, socialists and Communists debated the nature of Japanese capitalism, seeking to find a balance between universal Marxist categories and the Japanese experience that determined the kinds of political action possible in the present. The Peace Preservation Law of 1925 promised punishment for attacks on the emperor system or capitalism. In the early 1930s, the police arrested over ten thousand people a year for propagating ideas disloyal to the emperor and dangerous to the *kokutai*. Their intent was to induce a repudiation of socialist thought and conversion to a belief in Japan's sacred mission. Men and women who refused to confess and convert remained in prison until after World War II.

MODERN URBAN CULTURE

Industrial growth and expansion of the government bureaucracy created a new middle class of salaried white-collar workers. (See **Material Culture: Houses for the Middle Class.**) In contrast to the old middle class of shopkeepers and landlords, these workers got their jobs through educational achievement and enjoyed the security of lifetime employment with fringe benefits such as subsidized housing and medical care. Income depended on seniority as much as proficiency or accomplishment. In his novels *Sanshirō* (1908) and *Kokoro* (1914), Natsume Sōseki depicted socially mobile young men from the countryside. Sanshirō found himself torn between an academic career, the glittering world of business, and a return to his village. *Kokoro* expressed the sense that the era of great expectations passed with the death of the Meiji emperor in 1912. His son, the Taishō emperor, was universally seen as a lesser figure. In the 1920s the opportunities for becoming extremely rich declined, but the new middle class continued to grow.

The Great Kanto Earthquake of 1923 that brought down brick buildings and wooden houses ushered in modern Japanese culture. The new Tokyo had more ferro-concrete. Even before the earthquake, the new middle class had started moving south and west of the city limits. Private railroads and the real estate developers who owned them intensified this trend. With the exception of the publishing industry, light industry moved east of the city; heavy industry moved south to Kawasaki. The space left behind filled with offices, retail shops, and entertainment arcades.

Modern culture incorporated a second wave of westernization driven not by national goals but individual inclinations. Dry goods stores had already transformed themselves into department stores at the turn of the century. After the earthquake, they added theaters, galleries, exhibition halls, and rooftop arcades. In 1926, vending machines started providing refreshment for travelers at Tokyo and Ueno stations. In 1927, the first subway in Asia connected corporate headquarters in Ginza with movie houses and cafés in Asakusa. Mass transit changed urban patterns of work, family life, leisure, and consumption. Unlike the old middle class that lived behind their business and shopped in the neighborhood, the white-collar worker commuted

MATERIAL CULTURE

Houses for the Middle Class

Houses built after the Great Kanto Earthquake for the new middle class were derived from western architectural styles. Rooms had fewer functions but greater privacy than before. They had walls and doors and were further separated from one another by corridors. Guests were received on the first floor at the front of the house in the parlor, decorated with sofa, chairs, antimacassars, and carpet on a hardwood floor beneath a small chandelier. In line with the changing social etiquette of the time, guests were discouraged from making unexpected calls, and the telephone gave them little excuse for doing so. The family living room overlooked the garden. Although located on the dark north side of the house, the kitchen had a floor. Bedrooms were on the second floor. A modern water supply made it possible for each house to have its own bath.

New middle-class furnishings were designed chiefly for entertainment and the convenience of the family, especially the wife, rather than being objects with which to impress guests. The living room ideally contained a phonograph and radio. Appliances included the gas range for cooking, a gas heater with ceramic grill, an electric fan, and an electric rice cooker. For reasons of etiquette and security, old-style houses had required that someone always be home to greet guests and guard the premises. Western-style front doors made it easy for the housewife to lock the door and go shopping, visit friends, or see a movie.

Modern Living Room. This modern living room was photographed for the journal *Homu raifu* (Home Life). Chairs, tables, potted plants, sofa, and cushions provide a western-style backdrop for the woman wearing kimono.

from his suburban home to his work downtown. The entertainment districts that grew up around train terminals enticed him to spend evenings at coffee shops and cafés.

The new middle class consumed a modern culture removed from politics. Mass literacy spurred the development of mass media. Self-help books and magazines taught the rudiments of popular science, how to be modern, how to succeed in business, and how to create the perfect home environment. (See Color Plate 9.) By 1920, eleven hundred newspapers found 6 to 7 million buyers. Registered magazines were ten times that number. Journals for men appealed to the highbrow, the middlebrow, and the vulgar. Women's journals, calibrated according to class, girls' journals, and boys' journals divided the market into ever more discrete segments. Retail bookstores jumped from three thousand in 1914 to over ten thousand in 1927. They sold complete editions of western authors in translation, serious works of idealist philosophy by the Kyoto School, novels by best-selling authors such as Tanizaki Junichirō (male) and Uno Chiyo (female), and illustrated books given to escapist sensationalism. Cinemas showed films from abroad alongside domestically produced animated cartoons and historical dramas. Movie stars became celebrities. Government-operated radio stations started broadcasting in the mid-1920s. Record companies churned out patriotic songs. Popular music celebrated romantic love and the delights of Tokyo, including hanging out in Ginza. A cheap escape from the workaday world was to watch small balls bounce down a pachinko board, the vertical version of the pinball machine.

Modern mass culture promoted a privatizing world of pleasure and self-expression. Women danced in chorus lines and performed in the Takarazuka Girl's Theater. (See **Biography: Kobayashi Ichizō**.) In the novel *Naomi* (1924–1925), Tanizaki depicted the transformation of a café waitress into a *modan gaaru* (modern girl; *moga* for short) who bobbed her hair, wore revealing dresses, and danced the Charleston. The *moga*'s less flamboyant companion was the *mobo* (modern boy). Together they scandalized onlookers by smoking cigarettes and holding hands in public. The late 1920s are often characterized by the words *ero, guro,* and *nansensu*—eroticism, grotesquerie, and nonsense, referring to both the flood of foreign words in urban vocabularies and the perceived decline in public morals. Materialism, individualism, and decadence had apparently replaced the beautiful Japanese virtues of diligence, decorum, and duty.

ALTERNATIVES TO MODERNITY

People repelled by modern culture found solace in folk traditions of rural Japan, high art of ancient Japan, and communities of the devout created by the new religions. Ethnographer Yanagita Kunio sought a cultural authenticity that had been lost in urban areas. He traveled from Tohoku to the Ryukyus, collecting folk tales and documenting what he viewed as pristine customs of the folk. Industrialist and builder of the Mitsui *zaibatsu* Masuda Takashi tried to preserve Japan's artistic patrimony and supported the government's system for designating cultural artifacts as national treasures. First established in 1897, the designation applied foremost to religious objects from the Kyoto area, declared Japan's sovereignty over its past, magnified differences between Japan and the outside world, and demonstrated that Japan possessed the trappings of world-class culture.

The new religions provided alternative visions of modernity that did not please the state. Deguchi Onisaburō, the organizer of Ōmoto-kyō, criticized government policies that disadvantaged the poor. In the 1920s, he proclaimed that as the Maitreya, he would establish a new order on earth, a message that found believers even among government officials and army officers. In the early 1930s, he founded a semimilitaristic youth group to restore the kingdom of God at the Ōmoto-kyō headquarters. Ōmoto-kyō was suppressed in 1921 and again in 1935. New religions

BIOGRAPHY Kobayashi Ichizō

Entrepreneur, politician, and diplomat, Kobayashi Ichizō (1873–1957) fostered consumer culture by founding a railroad, a department store, a baseball team, and the Takarazuka Girl's Theater. Kobayashi had wanted to become a writer, but after graduating from Keiō University, he joined the Mitsui Bank in 1893. In 1906 he left the bank to become executive director for a private electrical railroad near Osaka. Through hard work and creative planning in the building of new lines and improving service, he made his company dominant in train travel between Osaka and Kobe. In 1918 he became president of the newly named Hankyū electric railroad. To attract riders he expanded into real estate development by building suburban housing developments for the new middle class.

Kobayashi's interests tended toward popular culture. One of his train lines went to Takarazuka, a fading hot springs resort. To lure customers, he built a zoo and, in 1913, the Takarazuka Girl's Theater. In 1919 he founded the Takarazuka Music Academy to train young women for his productions. The first revue with chorus line and musical spectaculars was *Mon Paris,* staged in 1927. Having watched commuters surge through the Hankyū terminal in Osaka, he opened a market adjacent to the station in 1924. Five years later it became the Hankyū department store with restaurants, an art gallery, and a bookstore. Kobayashi also founded the Tōhō Cinema Company to make and distribute films. He built his movie empire with a mass audience in mind by scheduling show times and setting ticket prices for the benefit of workers. In 1936 he joined other railroad magnates and real estate developers to establish Japan's first professional baseball league to give people another reason to ride trains in search of entertainment. Loyal fans still cheer the Hankyū Braves. In 1940 Kobayashi reached the pinnacle of his career by becoming commerce and industry minister and special ambassador in charge of trade to the Netherlands.

Kobayashi insisted that the performers in the Takarazuka Girl's Theater be of unquestionable virtue; his aim was to provide entertainment for respectable women and to mold his actresses' character so that they could later perform as good wives and wise mothers on their most important stage, the home. The Music Academy provided training in etiquette, ethics, and homemaking as well as singing and dancing. On stage women played male roles; they also played Asians from countries incorporated into the Japanese empire. Lest actresses aspire to make the theater a profession, Kobayashi insisted that they retire at the peak of their popularity while they were still considered young enough to make a good match.

Source: Based on Jennifer E. Robertson, *Takarazuka: Sexual Politics and Popular Culture in Modern Japan* (Berkeley: University of California Press, 1998).

founded after 1905 more commonly based their teachings on Nichiren Buddhism and answered the needs of uprooted, underprivileged masses in the cities. Charismatic leaders preached a gospel of social equality and promised either a pure new world or salvation to come. They emphasized faith healing, deliverance from suffering, and a focus on this world's benefits. For recent urban migrants, the new religions provided self-help groups, a sense of identity, and a community that was neither self-righteously traditional nor alienating modern.

Twentieth-century agrarianism exhibited more virulent antimodernism. It identified agriculture as the ethical foundation of the state when agriculture was no longer the country's main source of wealth. Its adherents professed a farm *bushidō* (way of the warrior) that assimilated the farmers' virtues of diligence, frugality, fortitude, and harmony to loyalty and self-sacrifice on behalf of the state. This agrarianism criticized city life for making people selfish and ambitious; it detested capitalism for increasing the corrupting power of money, destroying the farm family economy, and eroding harmony between city and country. It demanded a spiritual alternative to materialism and a national alternative to universal socialism. Its nostalgic search for a return to a primitive rural society that manifested the *kokutai* frequently turned violent in the 1930s.

SUMMARY

By 1931, modern Japan had parliamentary democracy, an educated citizenry, and an industrialized economy. It also contained conflicting visions of what it meant to be Japanese, who should be incorporated into the nation and how, and what should be Japan's role in the world. The relatively peaceful world of the 1920s allowed space for controversy. When the Great Depression struck in 1930, plural and critical voices within Japan appeared as dangerous as threats from abroad to Japan's economic and national security.

SUGGESTED READING

This period is so well researched by scholars that only a sampling of recent works is listed here. For Japan in Asia, see P. Duus, *The Abacus and the Sword: The Japanese Penetration of Korea, 1895–1910* (1995); P. Duus, R. H. Myers, and M. R. Peattie, eds., *The Japanese Informal Empire in China, 1895–1937* (1989); T. Matsusaka, *The Making of Japanese Manchuria, 1904–1932* (2001); and M. R. Peattie, *Nan'yō: The Rise and Fall of the Japanese in Micronesia, 1885–1945* (1988).

For women, see G. L. Bernstein, ed., *Recreating Japanese Women, 1600–1945* (1991); B. Sato, *The New Japanese Women: Modernity, Media, and Women in Interwar Japan* (2003); and M. Hane, *Reflections on the Way to the Gallows: Rebel Women in Prewar Japan* (1988).

For labor, see A. Gordon, *Labor and Imperial Democracy in Japan* (1991); K. Nimura, *The Ashio Riot of 1907: A Social History of Mining in Japan* (1997); and W. M. Tsutsui, *Manufacturing Ideology: Scientific Management in Twentieth-Century Japan* (1998). For agriculture, see K. Smith, *A Time of Crisis: Japan, the Great Depression, and Rural Revitalization* (2001).

For minorities, see R. Siddle, *Race, Resistance and the Ainu of Japan* (1996); I. Neary, *Political Protest and Social Control in Prewar Japan: The Origins of Buraku Liberation* (1989); and M. Weiner, *Race and Migration in Imperial Japan* (1994). For riots, see M. L. Lewis, *Rioters and Citizens: Mass Protest in Imperial Japan* (1990).

For modern life, see S. A. Hastings, *Neighborhood and Nation in Tokyo, 1905–1937* (1995); S. Garon, *Molding Japanese Minds: The State in Everyday Life* (1997); J. Sand, *House and Home in Modern Japan: Architecture, Domestic Space and Bourgeois Culture, 1880–1930* (2003); and E. K. Tipton and J. Clark, eds., *Being Modern in Japan: Culture and Society from the 1910s to the 1930s* (2000).

World War II

In both the western and eastern theaters, World War II was characterized by indiscriminate bombing of civilian populations and death tolls in the millions. The aggressors were the Axis: Japan, Germany, and to a lesser extent, Italy. Allied against them were the British Commonwealth (including officially India and Australia), the United States, and the Soviet Union, along with the Chinese government under Chiang Kai-shek. What is known as the fifteen-year war began with Japan's takeover of Manchuria in 1931. In 1937 Japan launched all-out war against China. The war in Europe began in 1939 when Hitler provoked a declaration of war from Britain and France by invading Poland. The United States got involved when Japan bombed Pearl Harbor on December 7, 1941, and Hitler declared war on the United States.

Timeline: The Greater East Asia War

1931–1932	Japan's Kwantung army takes over Manchuria
1932	January 28: Japan bombs Shanghai
1933	May 27: Japan withdraws from the League of Nations
1935	November 24: Puppet government established in Beijing
1936	January 25: United Front against Japan
1937	July 7: Marco Polo Bridge Incident; Japan invades China
	November 20: Chinese capital established at Chongqing
	December 13: Rape of Nanjing begins
1938	United States embargoes war materiel to Japan
1939	May through August: Japanese and Soviet troops fight at Nomonhan
1940	Spring: U.S. Pacific Fleet moves to Pearl Harbor in Hawai'i
	September 26: Japan invades North Vietnam
	September 27: Japan, Italy, and Germany sign Tripartite Mutual Defense Pact
	October 15: United States embargoes scrap iron and steel to Japan
1941	April 13: Japan signs neutrality pact with Soviet Union
	July 26: Britain and United States cut off trade with Japan
	December 7: Japan attacks Pearl Harbor
	December 8: Japan attacks the Philippines, Wake, Guam, Hong Kong, and Malaya
	December 23: Japan bombs Rangoon, Burma
1942	January 23: Japan takes Rabaul north of New Guinea
	January 26: Japan lands on Solomon Islands
	February 15: Japan captures Singapore
	February 27–March 1: Battle of Java Sea
	March 9: Japan conquers Java

	April 9: U.S. Army on Bataan peninsula in the Philippines surrenders
	May 2: Japan captures Mandalay in Burma
	May 7: Battle of Coral Sea
	June 4–7: Battle of Midway
	June 12: Japan occupies Attu in Aleutian Islands
	July 9: Chinese Nationalist forces win a major battle in Jiangxi province
	July 21: Japan captures Buna, New Guinea; drives toward Port Moresby
1943	February 9: Japan retreats from Guadalcanal in Solomons
	July 1: Allied offensive in South Pacific
	July 29: United States drives Japan from Aleutian Islands
	November 22: U.S. troops land on Tarawa in Gilbert Islands
1944	February 2: Invasion of Marshall Islands
	February 17: Battle of Truk lagoon
	June 15–July 7: U.S. forces take Saipan
	August 11: U.S. forces take Guam
	August: Britain retakes Burma
	October 23–25: Battle of Leyte Gulf
1945	March 10: Firebombing of Tokyo
	March 17: United States captures Iwo Jima
	April 1: Invasion of Okinawa begins
	June 22: Okinawa falls
	July 26: Potsdam Declaration
	August 6: Atomic bomb dropped on Hiroshima
	August 8: Soviet Union declares war on Japan
	August 9: Plutonium bomb dropped on Nagasaki
	August 15: Japan surrenders

The belligerents each had reasons for fighting. Still angry at the punitive terms that included a loss of territory imposed on it by the armistice that ended World War I, Germany insisted that it needed living space for its growing population. Hitler's Nazi Party believed Aryans were superior to all other races and destined to rule the world. Many people in Japan believed it was superior to the rest of Asia. Junior officers agreed with the Nazis and the Fascists in Italy that social dislocations in the early twentieth century had resulted from individualistic liberalism expressed in hedonistic urban culture and the compromises and corruption of politicians. They opposed capitalism and the capitalist powers—England, France, and the United States—that dominated the world economically and militarily. They also feared universal socialism emanating from the Bolshevik revolution that threatened the national polity. Japan's government and many of its citizens believed that Japan needed colonies for its national security. Fear that Soviet expansion threatened Japan's interests in Asia led it to take over Manchuria. It fought in China to protect its interests in Manchuria; once in that quagmire, it was sucked inextricably into conflict with the Allied powers.

Officers in the Japanese army took control of Manchuria to protect Japanese railroads and mines built after victory in the Russo-Japanese War. The army installed a puppet government in what it called Manchukuo headed by Puyi, the last Qing emperor. Treating Manchukuo as a new frontier, it encouraged settlers to displace indigenous people in farming what then became wide-open spaces. By 1945, Manchuria had absorbed approximately two hundred seventy thousand Japanese immigrants.

Japan's conquest of Manchuria sparked a wave of anti-Japanese demonstrations and a boycott of Japanese goods in China's major cities. The Japanese navy retaliated by bombarding civilian quarters in Shanghai before the eyes of the largest international community in China. An explosion of outrage filled foreign newspapers, but foreign governments did little. The League of Nations sent a fact-finding team to China, and when the League Assembly accepted the team's report that castigated Japan's aggression in Manchuria, Japan withdrew from the League.

Japan's attempts to establish a buffer zone in north China fed the growing anti-Japanese nationalist sentiment among Chinese people. A national salvation movement led by student demonstrations demanding national unity and resistance to Japan erupted in Beijing and spread to other cities. The Communists in Yan'an issued a call for all to resist Japanese imperialism. Even warlords in southwest China joined the clamor, though their patriotic fervor was tinged with a self-interested desire to obstruct Chiang Kaishek's nationalist government in Nanjing. The United Front of 1936 allied Communists and Nationalists against Japan. The development of anti-Japanese organizations meant that when the Japanese army invaded north China in July 1937 to protect its interests in Manchuria and seize attractive resources, it met fierce opposition.

The war in China was marked by the first atrocities of World War II committed against civilian populations. Japan did not expect the level of resistance offered by Chinese troops that attacked Japanese forces in and around Shanghai in retaliation for Japan's capture of Beijing and Tianjin. Not until December did the Japanese army capture Nanjing. When the city surrendered, Japanese army spokesmen contended that Chinese troops had taken off their uniforms

Crying Baby. This photograph of a crying baby that appeared in *Life* magazine following the Nanjing Massacre garnered America's sympathy for China in its struggle against Japan. *(Getty Images)*

to mingle with the civilian population, thereby justifying the murder of thousands of Chinese civilians. Frustrated that five months of warfare had not resulted in decisive victory, Japanese officers encouraged their men to loot stores and rape women. The number killed is disputed even today. This horror was dubbed the "Rape of Nanking" by the foreign press. Although this was the worst, it was by no means the last of the atrocities committed by Japanese troops.

Shocked at the international outcry and disturbed by the troops' behavior that they had encouraged, Japanese officers decided that indiscriminate rape threatened Japan's international reputation and military discipline. To provide for what was deemed the soldiers' physical needs and to combat venereal disease, the army developed a system of "comfort stations," already inaugurated in Shanghai in 1932. Japanese prostitutes were primarily reserved for officers in the rear. To find women for soldiers on the front lines, the military turned to its colonies and then to territories conquered after 1940. Koreans composed 80 percent of the "comfort women" who serviced troops as far away as Burma and island Southeast Asia. In some areas they had to service up to fifty men a day for a modest fee per soldier. Only the end of the war brought release from sexual slavery.

The China war demonstrated the importance and limitations of air power. Having few planes of its own, the Chinese nationalist army had to use natural defenses to hold off Japanese troops and delay their advance. When Chiang moved his government to Chongqing in the mountains of Sichuan, nearly perpetual fog protected the city from Japanese bombers. The narrow Yangzi gorges precluded an overland attack. Instead, Japanese troops fanned out along the eastern seaboard and along railroad lines in the interior. By the end of 1938, they occupied cities and major towns from Manchuria to Guangdong. In the days before helicopters, their superior air power had less effect in the countryside.

Although Chinese living under Japanese occupation tried to remain inconspicuous, many had to make a choice between collaboration and resistance. Collaborators set up a provisional government in Beijing in 1937 to administer north China. In 1940, Japan created the Reorganized Government of the Republic of China under Wang Jingwei, a member of Chiang Kaishek's Nationalist Party who hoped to win peace with Japan in the name of Greater East Asianism. In 1943 Japan allowed him to declare war on the United States and Great Britain. In the countryside, persistent guerrilla warfare led Japanese army units to launch indiscriminate punitive missions against villages thought to be harboring Communists. These "rural pacification" campaigns proved ineffective. Although 1 million Japanese troops occupied China's richest regions for eight years, they could not subdue the people or find an exit strategy from a war neither side could win.

Japan expected more than collaboration from its Korean subjects in its war with China. It expanded cotton and wool production at the expense of cereals; it developed hydroelectric power in the north. In 1936, it declared a new policy of forced assimilation: all Korean were to be taught that they too were children of the emperor. Later it banned the use of the Korean language in classrooms and ordered Koreans to

adopt Japanese names. Japanese became the only language allowed in public offices and in record keeping by businesses and banks. Koreans had to worship at Shinto shrines and pray for the emperor's good health. Over six hundred thousand Korean men were drafted to work in Japanese and Manchurian mines, harbors, and factories. Although Japan taught that Korea and Japan were one, it did not trust the Koreans to fight its battles. By 1944 upwards of 4 million Koreans worked outside Korea, some as policemen and guards as far away as New Guinea, where they died in battles that made no distinction between combatants and noncombatants.

Japan's aggression in China provoked a response similar to what greeted Italy's conquest of Ethiopia in 1936. Both the League of Nations and the United States (which had not joined the League) officially deplored Japan's action. Neither tried to stop it, even though Japanese forces destroyed American property, sank an American warship, and killed American civilians. Fearful of Japan's intentions north of Manchuria, only the Soviet Union provided significant aid to China. It shipped munitions and airplanes to both Communist and Nationalist forces along with military advisers. Over two hundred Soviet pilots died in China's defense. In May 1939 the Japanese army in western Manchuria confronted Soviet forces at Nomonhan. The fight cost Japan eighteen thousand men and exposed critical weaknesses in the army's tactics and equipment. Japan sued for peace following the Russo-German Non-Aggression Pact signed in August. In 1941 Japan and the Soviet Union signed a neutrality pact. After Germany invaded the Soviet Union at the end of June, the Japanese army both kept alive the possibility of war with the Soviet Union and tried to honor the neutrality pact. Soviet aid to China came to an end with the outbreak of the war in Europe.

The United States relied on sanctions and threats to try to force Japan out of China and check Japan's expansion in Indochina. It placed a series of increasingly stringent embargos on goods to Japan and helped Chiang Kaishek by extending credit with which to buy American arms. When President Roosevelt had the Pacific Fleet move to Pearl Harbor to protect U.S. shipping lanes and intimidate Japan, Japan's navy took it as a threat to its interests in Micronesia and the South Pacific. In September 1940, Japan invaded North Vietnam to secure raw materials for its war machine and cut supply lines running to Chiang Kaishek. When the United States, Britain, and the Netherlands, which controlled the oil fields of Indonesia, cut off trade unless Japan pulled out of China and North Vietnam, Japan felt it had to fight or accept humiliation.

Neither the Allies nor Japan understood the other's motives, and they underestimated their opponents. Japan claimed to be liberating Asia from colonial powers. In 1940 it promoted, though it did not practice, the notion of a Greater East Asia Co-Prosperity Sphere, an economic regional power bloc similar to that envisioned in the western hemisphere under the Monroe Doctrine. In Japan's eyes, the United States and Soviet Union had everything they needed for an autonomous defense, but without colonies, Japan did not. Japanese soldiers saw themselves as spiritually superior to the materialistic West; they were hard and high-minded, whereas British and Americans were soft. Public opinion in the United States saw China as a victim of Japanese totalitarian aggression. Madame Chiang Kaishek gave an impassioned speech before the U.S. Congress in which she contrasted China striving for democracy and Japanese warmongers. Henry Luce, son of missionaries in China and owner of *Time-Life,* flooded his magazines with heart-rending pictures from war-torn China. Editorial cartoons drew on racial stereotypes to mock Japanese for their physical and mental inferiority and portrayed them as vermin to be exterminated.

Japan's desperation to find a solution to its war with China pushed it to open one battlefront after another, many over 3,000 miles from the home islands. To break through what it called the ABCD encirclement (American, British, Chinese, Dutch) and secure the oil crucial for its China campaign, it struck south. It bombed Pearl Harbor in hopes of forcing the United States to negotiate a settlement. Ten hours later, it launched an invasion of the Philippines, a U.S. colony. Britain had expected attack on Singapore to come from the sea; Japanese troops advanced through the jungle to capture the city. (The same month that saw the fall of Singapore also saw President Roosevelt sign Executive Order 9066 to place one hundred ten thousand Japanese Americans, over half of them U.S. citizens, behind the barbed wire of relocation camps in the western United States.) Within months Japan captured Indonesia, the Philippines, Guam, Wake, and the Solomon Islands. The Japanese army took over the rest of Vietnam, forced an alliance on Thailand, chased Britain out of Burma, closed the Burma Road that had carried to supplies to Chongqing, and threatened India and Australia. Combined with the islands taken from Germany in World War I, this gave the Japanese a vast empire, albeit mostly over water. (See Map C6.1.)

Beset with enemies from within and without, Japan's new empire lasted a scant two years. In some cases, men who were later to lead independence movements against western imperialism began by collaborating with Japan, as did General Aung San of Burma. When British soldiers beat a hasty retreat to India, units left behind formed the Indian National Army to fight for Indian independence. These instances serve as reminders that South and Southeast Asia welcomed Japan's message of liberation from colonial rule, but not the way it was delivered. Japan's arrogant sense of racial superiority soon made it enemies. Resistance to Japanese occupation from China to Indonesia to the Philippines contributed significantly to the Allies' counterattack. The British led Indian troops to reconquer Burma, Australians pushed Japan out of New Guinea, Chiang Kaishek's forces inflicted a major defeat on troops in China, the U.S. Army under General Douglas MacArthur advanced through the South Pacific before returning to the Philippines, and the U.S. Navy island-hopped across the Central Pacific.

Much of the fighting in the Pacific and Southeast Asia took place in jungles hated by both

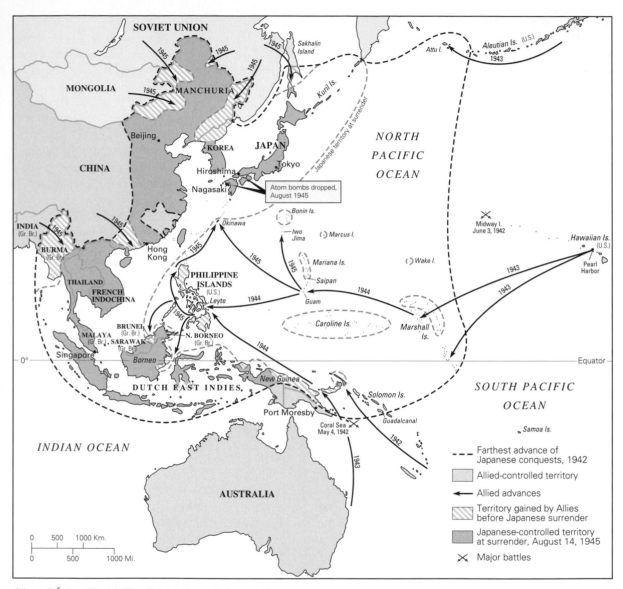

Map C6.1   **World War II in Asia and the Pacific**

sides. After four months on the Bataan peninsula in the Philippines, one-third of the U.S.
troops were in rain-dampened field hospitals
suffering from festering wounds, dysentery, and
malaria. Although the Japanese army used the
jungle to advantage in taking Singapore, its
troops too fell victim to disease in Burma and
Malaya. Japanese troops tried to cross the spine
of New Guinea from Buna to Port Moresby

over steep mountain passes covered with rain
forest. Thrown back by Australian forces, both
sides struggled through knee-deep mud to
engage an enemy seen only sporadically. Communications with headquarters broke down,
and fighting erupted haphazardly when individual units ran afoul the enemy.

Fighting on so many fronts meant that Japan
lacked the ability to provide its troops with

adequate supplies. Troops dispatched to far-flung islands and atolls were expected to live off the land. When U.S. submarines sank supply ships, they starved. Because the United States had signed a disarmament pact before the war that abjured submarine warfare as inhumane, Japan did not anticipate attacks on tankers and freighters sailing the western Pacific behind its defensive perimeter. In 1942, Japan received 40 percent of Indonesia's oil. Owing to the war of attrition, it received only 5 percent in 1944, and it received none in 1945. Taxis in Tokyo ran on wood-burning engines, and the air force adulterated scarce fuel with sap from pine roots.

Lacking adequate resources meant that the Japanese army and navy had to rely on men over machines. When Japan built runways on Pacific islands, it used human labor—natives, Koreans, Okinawans, prisoners of war. The Allies used bulldozers. At war's beginning, Japan had well-trained pilots flying the Zero, the most advanced fighter of its day. When those pilots were gone, their barely trained replacements had to fly against American pilots in planes constantly improved through new technology. Japan lost so many planes trying to defend Truk in Micronesia that American pilots called the battle "a turkey shoot." After the Japanese fleet lost six aircraft carriers at the battle of Leyte Gulf, the navy asked its pilots to crash their planes into enemy ships. Designated the Divine Wind Special Attack Corps to recall the typhoon credited with repelling Mongol invaders almost seven hundred years earlier, *kamikaze* pilots struck fear and loathing into Allied hearts. Nearly five thousand young men sacrificed their lives in a futile effort to stem the Allied tide sweeping toward Japan.

Air power made the decisive difference in the major battles on sea and land. From the battle of the Coral Sea, to Midway, to Leyte Gulf, although enemy ships saw each other's planes, the ships themselves never fought. Even before the attack on Pearl Harbor, the Allies had broken Japanese codes, and at the decisive battle of Midway, the United States used its knowledge of Japan's positions and intentions to sink three

of Japan's aircraft carriers and severely damage a fourth. The battle of the Coral Sea ended with Japan thinking it had lost, even though it sank more ships than the Allies. Throughout the war, Japan's admirals sought the decisive sea battle fought with battleships that would turn the tide of war just as Admiral Tōgō's stunning defeat of the Russian navy in 1905 had brought victory then. Little did they realize that aircraft carriers had made battleships irrelevant.

When Japan destroyed U.S. planes on the ground in the Philippines, it left U.S. troops defenseless against aerial attack. Later in the war, Japan's troops, and later cities, suffered the same experience once its air force had been decimated. The fall of Saipan in Micronesia after the navy lost over four hundred planes and every Japanese soldier had died in its defense put Japan's main islands within range of U.S. heavy bombers. The first raids, carried out at high altitudes, did little but psychological damage. Once General Curtis E. LeMay arrived from Europe, pilots in the Pacific perfected the art of carpet bombing, that is, dropping incendiary bombs at low attitudes that decimated Japan's wooden cities. In the largest air offensive in history, U.S. planes destroyed the remnants of the Japanese navy, shattered Japanese industry, and dropped forty thousand tons of bombs on population centers. Approximately ninety thousand civilians died in the firestorm that engulfed Tokyo. The plane that carried the atomic bomb to Hiroshima took off from Tinian, just north of Saipan. Its flight was virtually unimpeded.

Even before the fall of Okinawa that sacrificed one-quarter of the island's population to the defense of the homeland, cabinet members began to call for an end to the war. The army rebuffed them. With 5.5 million men relatively unscathed in China and Manchuria, it demanded that all Japanese prepare to make the ultimate sacrifice, to die like "shattered jewels" in protecting the emperor-centered national polity. Recalling President Theodore Roosevelt's mediation of an end to the Russo-Japanese War in 1905 and hoping to keep the Soviet Union neutral, the army finally agreed to let the

Suicide Bomber. A Japanese bomber makes a suicide dive on the *U.S.S. Hornet* on October 26, 1942, off Santa Cruz in the Solomon Islands. *(Bettmann/Corbis)*

Japanese ambassador to Moscow ask Foreign Minister Molotov for help. Busy with preparations for the Potsdam Conference, Molotov repeatedly put him off. On July 26, Churchill and Truman issued the Potsdam Declaration (Stalin did not sign it) demanding that Japan submit to unconditional surrender. Japan was to agree to allow occupation by foreign troops and to renounce all claims to territory on the Asian mainland and Taiwan. Its leaders and soldiers were to be tried for war crimes, and the Japanese people were to choose the form of government they wanted. The alternative was "prompt and utter destruction."

The Potsdam Declaration was both extremely specific and maddeningly vague. Japanese leaders had no way of knowing that destruction was to come via a bomb first tested ten days before.

To the distress of his loyal subjects, the declaration made no mention of the emperor. The cabinet decided to sit tight and hope for mediation by the Soviet Union. For three days in early August, the atomic bomb, the Soviet Union's declaration of war, and the plutonium bomb sent shock waves through the cabinet. At a climatic meeting on August 14, the emperor instructed the cabinet to surrender. Later, he made a recording to tell the Japanese people that they must bear the unbearable. Despite a plot by junior army officers to steal it, it was broadcast at noon on August 15. World War II was over.

After the war, Japanese military personnel were prosecuted for war crimes. In Indonesia, the Dutch convicted Japanese who had forced European women to service Japanese troops; they ignored cases involving Indonesian women. Other war crimes trials made no mention of comfort women. Nor did they include men from Unit 731 who had turned over their data on bestial experiments performed on Chinese in Manchuria to test bacteriological weapons. Instead the trials focused on crimes against humanity broadly defined as the decision to wage war; atrocities such as the Bataan death march in which thousands of American and Filipino soldiers died; the indiscriminate bayoneting of British doctors, nurses, and patients in Singapore; the machine-gunning, decapitation, and drowning of civilians in Southeast Asia; and the massacre of Filipinos in Manila at the end of the war. Japan's treatment of prisoners of war merited special condemnation; soldiers who survived surrender were starved, tortured, and forced to labor for the Japanese war machine in contravention of the Geneva Convention. The war crimes tribunals ignored atrocities committed by Allied forces.

Following World War II, the world split into two camps: the free world dominated by the United States and the Communist bloc led by the Soviet Union. An iron curtain came down in Europe. Forgetting that Japan's early victories had exposed their vulnerabilities, some western powers assumed that their former colonies in South and Southeast Asia would welcome them as liberators. The United States freed the Philippines in 1946. Britain pulled out of Burma and India in 1947. Two years later, the Dutch grudgingly granted independence to Indonesia. France refused to leave Vietnam until defeated in 1954. Civil war in China ended with the establishment of the People's Republic of China and the Nationalist Party's flight to Taiwan. Soviet troops began to enter Korea in August 1945. Hoping to prevent the whole country from falling into their hands, the United States got the Soviet Union to agree to a dividing line just north of Seoul at the 38th parallel. The two nations then sponsored the creation of two separate states on the Korean peninsula. Japan escaped that fate. Under U.S. occupation, it became a bulwark against communism.

SUGGESTED READING

There is a vast array of books on World War II. Some of the most recent include: E. Bergerud, *Touched with Fire: The Land War in the Pacific* (1996); N. Tarling, *A Sudden Rampage: The Japanese Occupation of Southeast Asia* (2001); and J. C. Hsiung and S. I. Levine, *China's Bitter Victory: The War with Japan, 1937–1945* (1992). The classic is J. W. Dower, *War Without Mercy: Race and Power in the Pacific War* (1986). On related topics, see K. Honda, *The Nanjing Massacre: A Japanese Journalist Confronts Japan's National Shame* (1999); Y. Tanaka, *Japan's Comfort Women: Sexual Slavery and Prostitution During World War II and the US Occupation* (2002); and S. H. Harris, *Factories of Death: Japanese Biological Warfare, 1932–1945 and the American Cover-up* (2002).

War and Aftermath (1931–1964)

Japan's war in Asia and the Pacific expanded in response to military imperatives and domestic problems. It spurred institutional and economic development; it caused devastation and loss of life. After surrender, the United States occupied Japan and instituted reforms designed to transform it into a demilitarized democracy. Those that had lasting impact built on trends apparent during the war; others, including Japan's diplomatic relations with the United States, sparked controversy. The despondency of defeat turned into a determination to rebuild. High-speed economic growth began in the 1950s. When the economy reached prewar levels of production in 1956, the government declared the postwar period to be officially over. In 1960 it announced the Income Doubling Plan. The 1964 Tokyo Olympics marked Japan's return to the world order and restored its self-confidence as a nation.

The further World War II recedes into the past, the more historians emphasize continuities across its divide. Although the impact of the war on individual lives is undeniable, its long-term consequences on the economy and society are more problematic. Other questions to consider are: Who was responsible for the war? What kind of impact did the Occupation have on Japan? What enabled the postwar recovery?

ROAD TO WAR

Military actions exacerbated by rural crises dominated politics in the 1930s. The army demanded support for its takeover of Manchuria in 1931; the navy criticized the limitations imposed by the London Naval Treaty. The armed forces transformed Japan into a militaristic state by forcing the Diet to curtail freedom of speech and approve its war budgets. Anger at capitalist *zaibatsu* for sucking the farmers' blood and at corrupt politicians who put their interests ahead of the nation erupted in abortive coups d'état that exposed factions within the military. Mass organizations drew the farmers' support to the military; farmers also participated in self-improvement drives sponsored by bureaucrats and civilian reformers. Only a few intellectuals dared criticize imperialist policies. For the majority of citizens, being Japanese meant taking pride in the slogan, "Asia for the Asiatics," which obfuscated Japan's colonizing project.

Junior Officers and the Citizenry

Radical junior officers drew inspiration from diverse sources. They heard their men's stories of sisters being sold into prostitution to save the family farm from moneylenders. They read in the newspapers of how the *zaibatsu* profited from currency speculation when Japan went off the gold standard in 1931. They studied Kita Ikki's *A Plan for the Reorganization of Japan*. Kita proposed that the "people's emperor" suspend the constitution and have the government confiscate surplus wealth, manage the economy, and provide social welfare and "world knowledge based on the Japanese spirit." When these goals had been accomplished, Japan would liberate Asia and "the Sun Flag of the Land of the Rising Sun will light the darkness of the entire world."[1] Officers modeled their plans for revolution on the Meiji Restoration. Like men of high purpose (*shishi*), they had to act to remove evil advisers who prevented the emperor from making his will known to the people. They credited violence with purifying the state and mistrusted old men who might tarnish their youthful idealism.

The junior officers responded to and exacerbated factions in the military. Their hero, General Araki Sadao, promoted spiritual training to inculcate devotion to the emperor and martial virtues of loyalty and self-sacrifice. The Japanese spirit (*Yamatodamashii*) sufficed to overcome mere material obstacles. His Imperial Way faction opposed the Control faction's arguments that battles could be won only by rational planning using the latest military technology and sophisticated weaponry. In 1935, an Araki supporter assassinated the Control faction's General Nagata Tetsuzan and electrified the nation with his diatribe against military men and their civilian toadies who had corrupted army and *kokutai*. On February 26, 1936, junior officers armed with the slogan, "Revere the Emperor, Destroy Traitors," led fourteen hundred troops to seize the Diet building and army headquarters, kill cabinet ministers, and call on the emperor to announce a Shōwa Restoration. Horrified at the threat of insurrection, the emperor summoned the army to suppress the rebellion. After a four-day standoff, the junior officers surrendered. They were executed along with their mentor Kita Ikki in a victory for the Control faction.

A symbiotic relationship developed between the military and the old middle class of shopkeepers and factory owners as well as teachers, low-ranking officials, and farmers. The army founded the Imperial Military Reserve Association in 1910, the Greater Japan Youth Association in 1915, and the Greater Japan National Defense Women's Association in 1932. Organized at the hamlet, not the amalgamated village level, the Reserve Association took over community functions such as firefighting, police, road and canal repairs, shrine and temple maintenance, emergency relief, and entertainment. It promoted drill practice, "nation-building" group calisthenics, and bayonet competitions. It hosted lectures by military-approved speakers, and it corresponded with battalion adjutants regarding the welfare and conduct of conscripts. The women's association sank roots in urban as well as rural areas. These associations identified the

---

1. George M. Wilson, *Radical Nationalist in Japan: Kita Ikki 1883–1937* (Cambridge, Mass.: Harvard University Press, 1969), pp. 75, 81.

individual with the community, the community with the army, and the army with the emperor.

Social Reform

In the 1930s, bureaucrats and social reformers focused on devastation resulting from crop failures in northeastern Japan. When students dispatched by Hani Motoko, journalist and founder of the magazine *Woman's Friend* (*Fujin no tomo*), reported that farmers knew nothing of modern hygiene and sanitation, spent money foolishly on ceremonies, lazed about, and drank, Hani established settlement houses that taught poor women sewing, cleanliness, etiquette, nutrition, and thrift. The Agriculture Ministry supported similar plans that promoted social education, agricultural cooperatives, economic planning, and moral betterment. The emphasis on thrift and frugality paralleled the nationwide effort by the Home Ministry, social reformers, educators, and women's leaders to increase Japan's savings rate, both to help individuals plan for emergencies and to fund national projects.

WARTIME MOBILIZATION

During eight years of war between 1937 and 1945 (see **Connections: World War II**), government ministries were often poorly informed, disorganized, and overextended. Faced with unexpected challenges, they cobbled together ad hoc measures and made mistakes in prosecuting the war overseas and on the home front. Just as the army and navy competed for resources, the former emphasizing the threat from the Soviet Union while the latter focused on the United States, so did civilian ministries duplicate each other's efforts and fight for control of domestic policy. Like the Germans, the Japanese at first refused to mobilize women, a policy that limited the war effort.

Civilian commitment to the war varied. Businessmen supported military goals so long as they did not threaten survival of their firms. Under pressure to conform, citizens greeted news of the first victories with exultation. Dwindling food supplies, higher taxes, and a black market led to forbearance and despair. Malnutrition increased the incidence of tuberculosis (one hundred sixty thousand deaths in 1942), rickets, and eye disease. First children and then adults fled cities for the countryside. When the flower of Japan's youth was called to make the supreme sacrifice in the Special Attack Forces (*kamikaze*), many did so gladly; others did not. (See **Documents: Excerpts from the Diary of Hayashi Toshimasa**.)

Unlike other belligerents in World War II, Japan's wartime leadership changed repeatedly. Seven prime ministers served between the outbreak of war with China on July 7, 1937, and surrender on August 15, 1945. Executed as a war criminal for having declared war against the United States, General Tōjō Hideki served concurrently as prime minister (1941–1944), army minister, home minister, and munitions minister and filled other posts as he perceived the need. He never directed naval operations nor did the navy inform him when it fought. Even the army general staff challenged his authority. Civilian bureaucrats, especially in the Justice Ministry, maintained their constitutional autonomy. Only the Shōwa emperor received complete information on military policy and operations, including plans for surprise attacks on American, Dutch, and British bases in 1941. For fear of jeopardizing the throne, he sanctioned military decisions as his ancestors had done for centuries.

Government planning of the economy began in 1931 when the Diet passed the Major Industries Control Law. It promoted cartels and required industries to tell the government their plans. In 1937 came the New Economic Order to make the Japanese Empire self-sufficient. Bureaucrats allocated funds to critical industries, nationalized electrical plants, supervised banks, and spun a web of regulation. The National Mobilization law of 1938 focused research on chemicals and machine technology. Large companies had to introduce on-the-job training for workers. Labor was rationed according to production needs. Military requirements prompted the rise of new industries in fields such as optics, determined techniques used in existing industries such as steel, and stimulated technological innovation. Wartime priorities transformed Japan's industrial structure. Textile industries declined; heavy and chemical industries expanded.

The Home Ministry bent social mores and popular culture to the war effort. Foreign words being considered symptomatic of foreign sympathies, "baseball" became *yakyū*. Martial music replaced jazz. Hair permanents were criticized because they were western and wasted resources. Women had to dress in baggy pants called *monpe*. The Communications Ministry founded the Dōmei News Agency in 1936 to channel national and international news to newspapers. It already controlled radio broadcasts through the national public radio station, NHK. To extend its reach, the ministry distributed free radios to rural villages.

The Education Ministry suppressed academic freedom and promoted patriotism. Professors critical of the war in China and military dominance over politics had to resign. School children performed physical exercises to build bodies for the emperor; after 1940 they volunteered for community service projects. Starting in 1941 they took paramilitary training to identify enemy aircraft and practiced charging with bamboo spears. Published in 1937, the textbook *Cardinal Principles of the National Polity* (*Kokutai no hongi*) taught students that the emperor was the divine head of state and benevolent father to the Japanese people. The Japanese were superior because of their racial homogeneity. They possessed a distinctive culture and history infused by the radiant presence of the imperial house. No sacrifice was too great to protect this unique heritage.

In the name of national unity, the government suppressed all pacifist new religions under the Religious Organizations Law of 1939. Social reformers and feminist activists joined the Greater Japan Women's Society that sent soldiers off to war and disseminated ways to practice frugality. Patriotic Associations united tenant farmers and landlords, workers and businessmen. The ideology of "dedicated work" valorized labor as a public activity in service to the nation. Neighborhood associations organized air raid drills and kept watch for dangerous thought. In 1944 the Home Ministry folded them all into the Imperial Rule Assistance Association.

A dedicated citizenry and long-range planning could not overcome growing shortages. The government struggled to shore up the collapsing economy. Lacking imported technology, companies developed new techniques that took military needs and scarce resources into account. The Zero fighter was crafted with extreme precision and used minimal amounts of steel regardless of the pilot's safety. In addition to the lack of fuel because of disruptions to shipping, the destruction of factories meant fewer manufactured goods such as fertilizer. Food production dropped.

Military conscription created labor shortages in industry and mining. The first to fill the gap were Koreans. In 1943, the government allowed women to volunteer for work in ordnance and aircraft industries. It drafted prisoners of war to work in steel plants and mines. The military ended educational deferments and drafted university students. In 1944 middle school boys started factory work.

The last months of the war brought widespread hardship. Evacuees to the countryside put an extra burden on scarce resources. Nutritional levels declined following the meager harvest of 1944. A few people criticized their leaders in anonymous graffiti and letters to the editor. Worker absenteeism rose, product quality slipped, and work stoppages spread. Although signs of disaffection were slight, they were enough to make politicians and bureaucrats worry about the threat of social revolution. By the time most factions in the government were willing to admit defeat, approximately 3 million Japanese had died. Despite the evidence of destruction, the emperor's announcement on August 15 that the war had been lost came as a shock.

DOCUMENTS

Excerpts from the Diary of Hayashi Toshimasa

Why do soldiers fight? What do they think about as they wait to die? This diary, written by Hayashi Toshimasa, a graduate of Keiō University who was killed in action on August 9, 1945, affords one answer to these questions and provides glimpses of the camaraderie and resentments that supported members of the Special Attack Forces in their final days.

April 13, 1945

First Lieutenant Kuniyasu was killed in action, as was Second Sub-lieutenant Tanigawa Takao. Everyone is dying away. The lives of plane pilots are short indeed. I just heard today that Second Sub-lieutenant Yatsunami also died the day before yesterday; he dove straight into the sea while participating in night-training, and his dead body was washed ashore yesterday onto the white beach of Kujūkuri-hama. Dear Yatsunami! I enjoyed getting together with him again here—the last time was in Mie. Dressed in his nightclothes, he came to my room rather late on the evening of the day before the accident, and we drank beer together. I wonder whether or not it was some kind of premonition. He was very gentle and quiet. When I said, "What a splendid nightwear," he just chuckled and said that it had been made by his wife, whom he just married in January. His wife too suffered the misfortune on this earth of a typical pilot's wife. How is she going to spend the long life that stretches ahead of her?

Tanigawa has a fiancée too, in Kobe. Those who were left behind may be unlucky, but their sacrifice is an offering for Japan's ultimate victory. So I would ask to please continue to live with strength and pride, and in such a way as not to bring shame to the brave men who courageously and willingly died for their country.

April 23

Nighttime flying began. After our flying operation we drank beer at a welcome party for Kamiōseko. I got a little high. Second Sub-lieutenant Kamiōseko and I were enraged at the current situation. It was all about our position as reserve officers in the Imperial Navy. Now I declare! I will not fight, at least not for the Imperial Navy. I live and die for my fatherland, and, I would go so far as to say that it is for my own pride. I have nothing but a strong antipathy for the Imperial Navy—absolutely no positive feelings at all. From now on I can say in and to my heart, "I can die for my own pride, but I would not die—absolutely not—for the Imperial Navy." How terribly we, the 13th class of pilots to come out of the "students mobilized for war" program, have been oppressed by the Imperial Navy! Who exactly is fighting this war now anyway? A full half of my classmates of the 13th class who were bomber pilots on carriers, and my friends, are now already dead.

I will live and die for my fatherland, my comrades of the 13th class, all those senior fighting men who are members of the "students mobilized for war" program, and, lastly, for my own pride. I shall do so cursing all the while the Imperial Navy, which to me merely means a certain group of officers who graduated from the Etajima Naval Academy.

June 30

It was raining when I woke up this morning, and I was so glad I could sleep some more that I pulled a blanket over me again. I got up a little after seven, took a late breakfast, and at a barracks I went over some slides designed to help us recognize the different types of enemy ships. Now I have finished with the slides. I returned to my own room, and am writing this and playing a record. Next door, on a blanket spread over the floor, Kamiōseko, Yamabe, Tejima, and Nasu are having fun playing bridge. No change outside—the steady rain continues.

I cannot begin to do anything about everything.

Simply because I shall have to leave this world in the very near future.

I should thank the Navy's traditional spirit, or rather their cliquishness, which drove Eguchi to say: "I want to go to the front soon—I want to die soon," and even drove me into that sort of psychological state. It even drove all the rest of us, university students transformed into pilots, into that same state of mind.

July 31

Today is a sortie day. It is the day for the eight planes of our Ryūsei (Falling Star) squad to carry out a special attack. The fog was extremely thick when I got up. It turned into water that dripped from the leaves and treetops on the mountain.

When I arrived at the airport, the items that were to be carried onto our planes were neatly set out in rows.

Last night, I completely changed everything that I was wearing. I also wound tightly around my waist the thousand-stitch cloth my mother sent me. Then there was the brand-new muffler my aunt in Yudate gave me.—In other words, I put on the very best things I had.

I am all alone and, expecting the sortie command to come along at any moment, I am writing this in an air-raid shelter.

Farewell dear Father, Mother, Brothers and Sisters, and other relatives and friends.

Please continue to live on enjoying very good health.

This time I am going right into Han Christian Andersen's fairyland, and I will become its prince.

And I shall be chatting with little birds, flowers, and trees.

I pray for the eternal prosperity of the great Japanese Empire.

August 9 A clear day

Once again the enemy's mechanized divisions are approaching the home islands.

In one hour and a half I shall leave here for the sortie, as a member of the special attack force. The skies are a breathtakingly deep blue, and there is a sharp touch of autumn.

August 9th!

Today I shall fly one of the very latest in war planes, a Ryūsei, and will slam it into an enemy carrier.

Source: *Listen to the Voices from the Sea: Writings of the Fallen Japanese Students*, comp. Nihon Senbotsu Gakusei Kinen-Kai, trans. Midori Yamanouchi and Joseph L. Quinn (Scranton, Pa.: University of Scranton Press, 2000), pp. 247–250, modified.

Japanese Women Working in an Ordnance Factory.
With able-bodied men drafted for the war effort,
women had to take their place in industry. *(AKG,
London)*

OCCUPATION

Defeat did not bring an end to hardship. The
suburban middle class was spared the fate of
poor and working-class urban residents who
lost everything in the firestorms, but everyone
was short of food. Farmers were better off,
although stunned by defeat that called into
question cherished ideals of loyalty, patriotism,
and service to the emperor. Occupation by a
military dictatorship under General Douglas
MacArthur began on August 30, 1945. At first
the mood was to punish Japan, perhaps by
returning it to an agrarian economy. After the

beginning of the Cold War with the Soviet
Union and the 1949 Communist takeover of
China, the emphasis shifted to making Japan a
bulwark against communism.

Despair and Liberation

The war left 6.6 million Japanese soldiers and
civilians stranded in enemy territory from
Manchuria to Southeast Asia. The Soviet Union
sent five hundred seventy-five thousand military
personnel and adult male civilians to Siberian
labor camps. Soviet soldiers raped and killed
women and children. Of Japanese settlers in
Manchuria, 50 percent died at the end of the
war, many at the hands of Chinese. Japanese settlers in Korea made their way across hostile territory to refugee camps and then on crowded
ships to Japan. Seventy thousand Japanese in
the Philippines had to wait until the end of 1946
before seeing Japan; the British and Dutch did
not return their prisoners of war until 1947. On
Pacific islands, pockets of Japanese soldiers resorted to cannibalism or starved. The last soldiers came home in the 1970s.

Repatriated soldiers and civilians met a cold
welcome in war-devastated Japan. War widows,
homeless orphans, and maimed veterans became
social rejects. Most shunned were the victims
from Hiroshima and Nagasaki, subject to radia-
tion sickness that turned them into pariahs.
With the economy at a standstill, there was little work even for the able-bodied. Competition
for jobs depressed already low wages. The winter of 1945–1946 was worse than the winters of
wartime. Rationed supplies of coal and food
were not enough to stave off freezing and starvation. Urban women traveled to the countryside to trade heirlooms for food and patronized
the black market.

For some, defeat meant liberation. If life had
no meaning, why not drink, take drugs, and
steal? In his 1947 novel *The Setting Sun*, Dazai
Osamu mourned the loss of prewar values and
presented the only choice left: to live for oneself
alone. People who celebrated the end to restrictions on freedom of thought and behavior had

an easier time coping with material shortages. Defeat vindicated the beliefs of prewar Marxists and socialists who hoped to build a just society out of the rubble of failed capitalist fortunes. The black market flourished at every train terminal, organized and patrolled by gangsters. Small factory owners made pots instead of helmets, and former soldiers became businessmen. Prostitutes called pan-pan girls who serviced GIs dressed in rayon dresses and nylon hose, curled their hair, and painted their faces in an orgy of self-expression not seen since the 1920s. The dominant themes in popular culture were titillation and sex; the carnal body replaced the *kokutai,* the body politic.

Occupation Goals

As Supreme Commander of the Allied Powers (SCAP—also shorthand for the Occupation bureaucracy), MacArthur intended to demilitarize Japan and work through existing governmental institutions to install democracy. The United States kept the Allies out of Japan by putting them on the Far East Commission (FEC) that oversaw SCAP policy. It met in Washington, D.C. The United States bought off the Soviet Union by handing over islands north of Hokkaido. Only judges for the Tokyo war crimes trials represented countries that had suffered under the Japanese war machine. One SCAP faction wanted to restrict Japan's international trade and dispatch the fruits of industrialization to Japan's victims as war reparations. The other consisted of economists and lawyers primed to practice social engineering. By instituting land reform, revising education, promoting labor unions, emancipating women, limiting police powers, and rewriting the constitution, they planned to make Japan fit to rejoin the community of nations.

What was to be done with the Shōwa emperor? He did not sign the instrument of surrender on September 2, 1945; that humiliation was left to a general and a diplomat. Instead, he, the cabinet, and his staff tried to distance him from responsibility for the war, taking a stance of plausible deniability on all decisions save the last that ended it. MacArthur dissuaded him from admitting even moral responsibility. Although the British wanted to try him as a war criminal, MacArthur believed that once the military was gone, the emperor was needed as a bulwark against communism. By refusing to accept responsibility for the war in which so many had died in his name, the emperor also alienated far right militarists. The issue of his responsibility for the war has continued to rankle at home and with Japan's neighbors. On January 1, 1946, the emperor announced that he was a human being, not a manifest god. Defined by the new constitution as symbol of the state, he continues to embody a national identity predicated on ethnic homogeneity.

Occupation Reforms

On October 13, 1945, the prime minister appointed a committee at SCAP's urging to consider constitutional revision. Political parties, progressive and socialist groups, scholars, and think tanks drafted constitutions ignored by the prime minister's committee. Its recommendations were so minor that in February 1946, MacArthur ordered his Government Section to take over the task lest a grass-roots movement for a constitutional convention lead to too much democracy and an attack on the emperor. His people hid their work from the United States and Japanese governments, the FEC, and other branches of SCAP. After conferences between SCAP officials and cabinet representatives to debate the draft, it was published in early March 1946. SCAP intervened repeatedly in Diet deliberations to limit discussion and prevent substantial revision. The new constitution replaced the Meiji constitution, to which it was offered as an amendment, when the Upper House approved it in October. The emperor promulgated it on November 3, 1946.

Articles in the constitution define the rights to life, liberty, and the pursuit of happiness as the rights to education, health care, police protection, work, and a minimum standard of living. Women received the right to vote. People detained by the police had the right to legal counsel. Freedoms included freedom from arbitrary arrest and unauthorized search and seizure plus freedom of assembly, speech, and religion. The judiciary became separate and independent. The Privy Council was dissolved in accordance with the principle of popular sovereignty. The Diet acquired the sole authority to make laws. Its vote of no confidence sufficed to dissolve the cabinet. Within the Diet, the Lower House of Representatives took precedence over the Upper House of Councilors, which became an elected body.

The new constitution had clauses that MacArthur would have deplored in the U.S. Constitution. Workers obtained the right to organize unions and bargain collectively, professors had the right to academic freedom, and women were guaranteed equal rights with men. Most controversial was Article 9: "The Japanese people forever renounce war as a sovereign right of the nation . . . land, sea, and air forces will never be maintained."[2] This wording was later interpreted to mean that armed forces could be created for self-defense. When the FEC insisted on a clause that limited the cabinet to civilians, this too was interpreted as implying the existence of a military. In 1950, SCAP wanted Japan to create an army to fight in Korea. Prime Minister Yoshida Shigeru refused. He created a Police Reserve, soon transformed into the Self-Defense Force.

Once the constitution had been promulgated, the Justice Ministry reformed the civil code. The new code emphasized the equality of the sexes and the dignity of the individual. It abolished patriarchal authority in the household, reiterated the freedom of marriage promised in the constitution, and required that all children share the family estate. This was not a burden for middle-class families whose assets consisted of their children's education. For shopkeepers, restauranteurs, or farmers, an equal division of property plus heavy inheritance taxes all too often meant selling off the patrimony.

SCAP quickly imposed additional reforms. The most radical forced landlords to sell their holdings to the government for resale to tenants, a measure met with approval by the Agriculture and Forestry Ministry that wanted a class of independent farmers even before the war. Absentee landlords had to relinquish all their land; resident landlords were allowed to keep only land they farmed themselves plus an additional five or so acres depending on the region. Although collecting tenant fees had already proved so onerous that many landlords welcomed the chance to sell out, they lamented the loss of their ancestral way of life. By 1950, farmer-owners cultivated 90 percent of Japan's agricultural land.

SCAP also intervened in educational reform. With American schools as the model, a new single-track system of primary school, middle school, and high school replaced the specialized higher schools. Compulsory education was extended to nine years. Teachers embraced the new curriculum that stressed the civic virtues of democracy and individual responsibility. Locally elected school boards selected texts, although in later years they did so from a list vetted by the Education Ministry. The Parent-Teacher Association involved mothers in school activities. New junior colleges, colleges, and universities made higher education available to a wider segment of the population than before. None rivaled Tokyo University, and all required that students pass entrance examinations.

SCAP kept itself above the law. Despite the separation of church and state, MacArthur allowed Christian missionaries to use U.S. government equipment and encouraged the emperor and empress to take instruction in Christianity. Censorship of printed materials and movies continued. Left-wing publications that criticized capitalism faced prepublication scrutiny. In movies, sword fighting and criticism of the emperor were out. Instead, SCAP encouraged movie makers to depict romance between men and women. The first mouth-to-mouth kiss made headlines.

2. Dale M. Hellegers, *We, the Japanese People: World War II and the Origins of the Japanese Constitution*, 2 vols. (Stanford: Stanford University Press, 2002), p. 576.

Economic Developments

Economic reform took many turns. Trustbusters took aim at the *zaibatsu* because they had contributed to Japan's war effort (Mitsubishi made the Zero fighter) and because their economic dominance appeared inherently undemocratic. SCAP ordered the holding companies for the ten largest *zaibatsu* dissolved, broke up the Mitsui and Mitsubishi trading companies, forced family members to sell their stock and resign from boards, and purged fifteen hundred executives accused of aiding the war machine. Japanese bureaucrats allowed government assets, including construction materials and machinery, to disappear into the black market or the hands of business cronies. To cover the deficit and the run on savings deposits at war's end, the Finance Ministry printed reams of money. Official prices soared 539 percent in the first year of the Occupation, with black market prices ranging from fourteen to thirty-four times higher. Fearing the destabilizing effects of inflation, at the end of 1948, Washington dispatched a banker from Detroit named Joseph Dodge. At Dodge's command, the government collected more in taxes than it paid out. It eliminated government subsidies to manufacturers. Public works, welfare, and education suffered cuts. Dodge curbed domestic consumption and promoted exports. He got the United States to agree to an exchange rate of 360 yen to the dollar. Deflation and economic contraction forced small businesses into bankruptcy.

The Korean War rescued Japan from the brink of depression and laid the foundation for future economic growth. The industrial sector gorged on procurement orders for vehicles, uniforms, sandbags, medicines, electrical goods, construction materials, liquor, paper, and food. Despite the prohibition on the manufacture of war materiel, Japanese companies made munitions. Their mechanics repaired tanks and aircraft. Businesses plowed profits into upgrading equipment and buying advanced technology from the United States through licensing agreements and the purchase of patent rights. Indus-tries that looked beyond the war for a way to compete in the expanding world economy incorporated the quality control method that the statistician W. Edwards Deming had introduced to Japan in 1949. By the end of the Korean War, the increase in wages and economic growth had brought food consumption back to pre–World War II levels. Consumers were able to buy household amenities and still put money into savings accounts.

Labor and the Reverse Course

To promote democracy, SCAP had the Trade Union Law issued in December 1945, and workers seized the opportunity to organize. Free to participate in politics, the Japanese Communist Party (JCP) and the Japanese Socialist Party (JSP) fostered trade unions. By the middle of 1948, unions enrolled over half of the nonagricultural work force, including white-collar workers, especially in the public sector. Other workers organized production control movements to take over businesses, factories, and mines that owners were accused of deliberately sabotaging in revenge for democratization. Like unionized workers, they wanted to get back to work and make a living wage.

Labor union activism led to the "reverse course." Workers united around issues including adequate food, support for working mothers, equal pay for equal work, and democratic elections. Before the postwar election of April 10, 1946, in which women voted for the first time, a rally in Tokyo brought together workers, farmers, Koreans, and ordinary citizens to listen to speeches by Communists, Socialists, and liberals demanding a people's constitution and criticizing the cabinet for obstructing democratic reform. On May 1, International Workers' Day, cities nationwide witnessed demonstrations in support of worker unity and democracy. On May 19, women joined demonstrations demanding that the emperor force the government to deliver food. Students held demonstrations a week later to demand self-government at their institutions. Socialist- and Communist-led labor unions formed in August organized strikes in October. In January 1947, the prime minister warned that striking government workers would be fired. A coalition of labor unions announced plans for a general strike on February 1. MacArthur called it off. In 1948 SCAP had the Japanese government issue regulations forbidding public employees to strike.

The reverse course had additional dimensions. The Cold War led the United States to view its erstwhile enemy as an ally against communism. SCAP compiled lists of "reds" to purge first the public sector and later, during the Korean War, the private sector. Approximately twenty-two thousand workers lost their jobs, and most of the JCP leadership went underground. Previously purged politicians, bureaucrats, and business leaders were rehabilitated. In 1948, plans to dismantle the *zaibatsu* came to a halt. The Diet gave the bureaucracy greater control over trade and investment than it had during the war. The Ministry of International Trade and Industry (MITI) had the Japan Development Bank lend money from the government's postal savings system to private companies. MITI also advised the Bank of Japan on its loans to private banks. It approved the transfer of foreign technology to industries it deemed worthy and provided them with administrative guidance. The Finance Ministry regulated currency transactions by restricting the amounts of money individuals and corporations could take or send out of the country.

Before ending the occupation, the U.S. Senate had Japan sign a peace treaty with the Nationalist Chinese on Taiwan that precluded recognition of and trade with the People's Republic of China. The peace treaty and security treaty signed with the United States plus associated agreements signed in 1951 continued the Occupation under a different name. After SCAP was dismantled in 1952, one hundred thousand American personnel plus dependents stayed on at military bases that dotted the islands. The right of extraterritoriality protected them from the Japanese judicial system and removed the bases from oversight by the Japanese government. Okinawa remained under U.S. military jurisdiction until 1972. Under the U.S. security umbrella, Japan was free to pursue economic development, although it had to follow the U.S. lead in international relations. On Bloody May Day 1952, four hundred thousand workers, students, and housewives denounced the Security Treaty, Japanese rearmament, the status of Okinawa, and government plans to pass an "antisubversive" bill that threatened academic freedom. Political positions divided between left-wing support for neutrality, democratization, and demilitarization and the conservative affirmation of alliance with the United States.

POLITICAL SETTLEMENT AND ECONOMIC RECOVERY

A host of political parties contended for Diet seats in the first postwar election of 1946. Yoshida Shigeru pulled together a coalition of conservative parties willing to make him prime minister, but he had to resign when elections the following year gave a significant share of the votes to the JSP. Taking advantage of the JSP's inability to deal with economic crises, Yoshida regained the prime ministership in 1948 and held it until 1954. He recruited former bureaucrats into his party whose administrative experience and skill at in-fighting gave them an edge in faction building. The JSP split over whether to support the U.S.-Japan Peace Treaty; it reunited in October 1955. The next month, the two conservative parties formed the Liberal Democratic Party (LDP). It dominated Diet and cabinet until 1993. During this period of one-party rule, heads of factions within the LDP selected the prime minister, who rewarded his supporters with powerful and lucrative ministerial appointments.

The LDP promoted economic growth as the nation's highest goal, less to enhance state power than to wean workers from socialism by offering them a better life. Starting in the late 1950s, the LDP spread the benefits of the growing economy across all sectors of society through higher wages and a higher standard of living. In 1958, it inaugurated national health insurance. It helped farmers increase productivity by mechanizing production and spreading chemical fertilizers and pesticides. The government paid villages to reorganize land holdings into fewer, bigger plots and individuals to diversify crops. It encouraged companies to locate factories in rural areas and hire farmers. It built roads and sewer systems. It restricted the import of rice and subsidized rice production. Through these programs and the outright purchase of votes, the LDP acquired a lock on rural electoral districts. The appeal of conservative policies to small businessmen and shopkeepers gave it urban votes as well.

The LDP also maintained power by aligning itself with bureaucrats and businessmen. Advisory groups composed of businessmen and bankers, consumers and union officials, consulted with cabinet ministers on policy and proposed legislation. Ex-bureaucrats either ran for office or joined corporations whose fortunes they had helped guide. Undergirding the web of personal connections was a flow of cash from businessmen to politicians to voters.

Political and Social Protest

Opposition parties in the Diet so little impeded the LDP juggernaut that citizens with grievances sought other forms of protest. Demonstrations against American bases and nuclear testing erupted periodically during the 1950s. The Japan Teachers' Union resisted the centralization of educational policy and personnel practices instituted by the Education Ministry in 1955. The General Council of Japanese Trade Unions (Sōhyō) opposed the Japan Productivity Center set up by Japanese businessmen with U.S. assistance because the unions feared it would exploit workers. When the government decided to switch Japan's chief energy source from coal to oil, the Mitsui Mining Company called for the voluntary early retirement of six thousand workers at its Miike mine in Kyushu. The union responded with a strike marked by violence and death that lasted 113 days. Workers learned that radical calls for class struggle undercut job security, and corporate managers learned that it was cheaper to transfer

redundant workers to other operations than to fire them.

The largest political demonstrations in Japanese history erupted from late 1959 to June 1960 over revision and extension of the U.S.-Japan Security Treaty. Negotiations removed the clause that permitted the use of U.S. troops to quell internal disturbances, but bases remained off-limits to Japanese scrutiny. Indicted as a war criminal and former minister in Manchuria, Prime Minister Kishi Nobusuke rammed the revised treaty through the lower house with the help of police who evicted the JCP and JSP opposition. Outraged at Kishi's high-handed tactics, masses of demonstrators gathered outside the Diet. Sōhyō had already coordinated strikes and mobilized workers against the treaty. The All Japan Federation of Student Self-government Associations (Zengakuren) organized weeks of agitation. Some 134 groups and organizations including farmers and housewives joined the protest. Kishi had planned to celebrate the revised security treaty by welcoming U.S. President Dwight D. Eisenhower to Japan, but Eisenhower canceled the trip. Daily demonstrations continued at the Diet and in cities across Japan. On June 18, several hundred thousand people surrounded the Diet, but they could not prevent the treaty's automatic ratification at midnight. Kishi resigned five days later. In 1965 Japan signed a peace treaty with South Korea, to the outrage of the left wing, which demonstrated against the exclusion of North Korea and the People's Republic of China. The ideological divide between conservatives and progressives sparked political unrest throughout the 1960s.

The constitution's guarantee of social equality and the Civil Code's emphasis on human dignity spurred the *burakumin* to renew their struggle for equal rights. Founded in 1955, the Buraku Liberation League (BLL) allied itself with the JCP and JSP to publicize unfair treatment by individuals and institutions. It participated in demonstrations against the renewal of the U.S.-Japan Security Treaty that gained it widespread support. Later protest marches focused nationwide attention on the *burakumin*'s plight. A government commission report in 1965 blamed

Demonstrations Opposing the U.S.–Japan Security Treaty. During demonstrations opposing the U.S.–Japan Security Treaty, men and women marched on the American Embassy demanding cancellation of President Eisenhower's visit, the prime minister's resignation, and dissolution of the Diet. *(Bettmann/Corbis)*

burakumin problems on unwarranted social and economic discrimination. The Diet responded in 1969 by passing the Special Measures Law for Assimilation Projects that decried discrimination without instituting measures to stop it. To ameliorate this defect, the BLL resorted to denunciation campaigns sometimes escalating to violence and threats that silenced public discussion of *burakumin* problems.

Women's organizations in the 1950s worked to protect children and encourage respect for mothers. Women joined movements to prohibit nuclear testing and to promote world peace for the sake of their children. They demanded clean elections. They elected women to the Diet who pushed for sexual equality and human rights. Women had campaigned for the abolition of state-sanctioned prostitution before the war; their goal became a reality in 1956 when the Diet passed the Prostitution Prevention Law

that took effect two years later. While it abolished legal protection for prostitutes, it did not eliminate sex work. Women justified political activism on two grounds: their responsibility for their families and their constitutional rights.

Post-Occupation Economic Development

International and domestic factors promoted economic growth. Under the Potsdam Declaration, Japan was guaranteed access to raw materials it had previously extracted from its colonies. Exchange rates remained stable until 1971. The world market was relatively open. Economic expansion across the free market world stimulated a growing demand for manufactured goods. Japan still had infrastructure developed before and during World War II. The most important prewar legacies were human resources—trained engineers, accountants, and workers—and the commitment to achievement through education. The first postwar generation of workers went into factories on graduation from high school, received on-the-job training, and worked long hours for the sake of their companies. Enterprise unions held demonstrations during the yearly spring offensive but interfered as little as possible in production. Management upped basic wages, promised lifetime employment, and distributed raises based on seniority. Workers came to live middle-class lives.

Heavy industries developed in wartime, and new companies that fashioned products for domestic consumption and export saw the greatest expansion. Steel producers, ship builders, manufacturers of synthetic fibers, and electronics and household appliance makers invested heavily in technologies imported from the United States and in labor-saving mass-production facilities. The government provided low-cost financing that made Japan the largest shipbuilder in the world in the 1950s. MITI protected car and truck manufacturers by forbidding foreign investment in the auto industry and imposing tariffs of up to 40 percent on imported cars. Companies that enjoyed less help from MITI were Matsushita, maker of household appliances, and the electronics innovator Sony. (See **Material Culture: The Transistor.**) Supporting corporate growth were subcontractors that produced quality components for finished products. Between 1947 and 1952, the economy grew at an average annual rate of 11.5 percent. From 1954 to 1971, it grew at over 10 percent a year, to rank second to the United States among free market economies.

Increases in domestic consumption stimulated high-speed economic growth. During the Occupation, SCAP broadcast images of American prosperity in the comic strip *Blondie* and other media to promote American values. Department store exhibitions and magazine advertisements illustrated the material life of the conqueror. Once the quality of food had improved, people wanted fashionable clothes. Every household wanted labor-saving devices such as a washing machine, refrigerator, and vacuum cleaner. Television broadcasts began in 1953 because the owner of the *Yomiuri* newspaper and key bureaucrats believed that national pride required Japan to have the latest technology. The wedding of Crown Prince Akihito to the industrialist's daughter Shōda Michiko in 1959 swept televisions from retailers' shelves as viewers reveled in the democratic dream of a love marriage. Beginning in 1955, a massive exodus from farms to cities fueled a housing boom of high density apartment buildings in suburbs. In these years, 90 percent of Japan's production went into the domestic market.

Postwar Culture

The consumption of mass culture stimulated growth in the entertainment industries, publishing, and film. Commercial television stations demanded an endless supply of programming. The government-owned NHK had two channels: one devoted to news analysis, dramas, and *sumo* wrestling, the other specializing in education. Magazine and book publishers continued prewar trends without the fear of censorship that had kept them from sensitive political topics. Kurosawa Akira directed *Ikiru* (To Live), which criticized bureaucratic arrogance. His 1951 film *Rashomon,* which questioned the possibility of knowing the truth, brought international recognition to Japanese cinema when it won the grand prize at the Venice Film Festival. A series with wider appeal was *Godzilla,* started in 1954, which drew on Japan's sense of victimhood by depicting a monster roused from the deep by nuclear explosion. Misora Hibari captured hearts with her songs of parting and loss. They spoke to the will to survive that had carried women through the hardships of war and Occupation. Public intellectuals and writers such as Maruyama Masao and Mishima Yukio questioned the ingredients of Japan's national identity. What did it mean to be Japanese if the nation's only goal was economic success? Wherein laid responsibility for wartime aggression?

MATERIAL CULTURE

The Transistor

Every electronic product today relies on transistors, symbol and product of the technological age. Invented by Bell Laboratories in 1948, the early transistors were too unreliable and delicate for consumer applications, and they could not handle high frequencies for the human voice. It took Sony researchers months of experimentation to find a useable combination of materials.

Sony introduced a transistor radio in January 1955, only to discover that it disintegrated in summer heat. The second version placed on the market in August had poor sound quality, but it sold domestically owing to its battery's long life. Sony could not compete with American transistor radios until 1957 when it started selling a tiny "pocketable" radio. More important than the radio's size was the technological breakthrough based on the high-performance alloy germanium. In 1960 transistor radios became Japan's second biggest earner on the export market after ships. Teenagers loved carrying them to parks, mountains, and beaches to listen to rock and roll.

Sony introduced the world's first all-transistor television in 1960 and successfully miniaturized it two years later. In 1964 Sony displayed a prototype of a transistorized calculator at New York's World Fair. Three years later it introduced a desktop calculator.

The transistors in the early radios, televisions, and calculators were huge compared to the silicon transistors in integrated circuits today that work liquid display calculators and watches. People typically buy electronic goods on impulse, indulging in a plethora of gadgetry that fills purses, pockets, and homes.

The TR-63. Sony's first successful transistor radio, the TR-63, could be called 'pocketable' only because Sony salesmen wore shirts with extra large breast pockets. *(Sony Corporation)*

New religions provided one answer to these questions. Founded in 1930 and suppressed during the war, Sōka Gakkai (value-creating society) was Japan's largest new religion in the 1960s. Its political arm, the Clean Government Party (Kōmeitō), founded in 1964, became Japan's third largest political party. Today its leaders serve as town councilors and school board offi-

BIOGRAPHY Daimatsu Hirobumi

Soldier, prisoner of war, women's volleyball coach, and Diet member, Daimatsu Hirobumi (1921–1978) gained worldwide fame for his draconian coaching methods when his team won the gold medal at the 1964 Tokyo Olympics.

Hirobumi's wartime experience marked him for life. Conscripted into the army after the attack on Pearl Harbor, he attended an officers' preparatory school in China and fought in China and Southeast Asia. The last months of the war found him in Burma with only raw bamboo shoots for food. Many soldiers died; sheer willpower kept him alive. He ended up at a prisoner of war camp run by the British in Rangoon. In revenge for the atrocities that the Japanese army had inflicted on British POWs and the humiliating surrender of Hong Kong and Singapore, British officers subjected Japanese POWs to shameful indignities. Hirobumi later recounted how he cleaned the latrines for British and Indian soldiers with his bare hands. Worse, he had to clean the female officers' rooms and wash the underwear that they removed before his eyes in a gesture calculated to be emasculating.

Repatriated to Japan after twenty-two months as a POW, Hirobumi found work coaching a women's volleyball team at the Nichibō textile factory in Kaizuka. At that time volleyball was a popular sport among factory workers because it could be played with just a ball in whatever space was available. In 1954 Nichibō organized a company team with Hirobumi in charge. In 1958, the team won all of Japan's major titles; in 1962 it won the world championship.

Hirobumi's training methods were brutal. He hurled balls at the players until they collapsed from pain and exhaustion. He insisted that they play regardless of injuries. He allowed them only three and one-half hours of sleep a night before the Olympics and had them practice for four hours the day of the final match. He also emphasized the incremental improvement of technique, relying on methods similar to quality control circles. His players once complained to the factory management that he was an enemy of women because he worked them unmercifully. He expected them to sacrifice everything for the chance to win, first for the company, then for Japan, just as he had sacrificed himself in wartime.

Eight-five percent of Japan's television sets were tuned to the Olympics the night the Japanese team defeated the Soviet Union in three sets. The women's unprecedented success made volleyball a national obsession. Hirobumi's fame swept him to a seat in the Diet's upper house in 1968. He lost his bid for a second term.

Source: Based on Yoshikuni Igarashi, *Bodies of Memory: Narratives of War in Postwar Japan* (Princeton, N.J.: Princeton University Press, 2000).

cers. It owns land, businesses, and shops. It provides a sense of family and community, help in finding marriage partners, jobs, loans, and higher education. The *zadankai*, a type of group therapy, helps followers solve personal problems and gain self-confidence. Sōka Gakkai teaches that the purpose of life is the pursuit of happiness; the three virtues of beauty, gain, and goodness bring happiness; following the teachings of Nichiren and having faith in the *Lotus Sutra* bring virtue. The constitutional guarantee of religious freedom and the population shift from country to town led to an explosion in the numbers of new religions and their membership.

Although they criticize the excesses of popular culture and consumerism, part of their appeal lies in their promise of material benefits.

The Tokyo Olympics of 1964 marked the climax of high-speed economic growth and a turning point in Japan's postwar history. (See **Biography: Daimatsu Hirobumi.**) The national and Tokyo metropolitan governments cleaned up and paved city streets; rebuilt stores, schools, and government offices; constructed stadiums at Yoyogi Park; dug new subway lines; laid new roads; and renovated Haneda Airport and connected it to the city by monorail. New hotels became Japan's first postwar high rises. The centerpiece of this vast public works project was the Shinkansen (bullet train), which covered the distance between Tokyo and Osaka in three hours and ten minutes. It was the fastest, most reliable, and safest train in the world.

Japan had been allowed to join the United Nations in 1956, and the Olympics marked the culmination of its reentry into the global community. Worldwide coverage of the games focused attention on Japan as a peaceful modern state. When Kawabata Yasunari received the Nobel Prize in Literature in 1968, the international accolade testified to Japan's acceptance by world opinion.

SUMMARY

Between 1931 and 1945, Japan passed through the dark valley of wartime aggression and deprivation. It recovered thanks to the changing international climate of the late 1940s and early 1950s, the reforms initiated by the U.S. Occupation, the protection provided by the security agreement with the United States, and the U.S. recognition that democracy required economic stability. It must not be forgotten that recovery also built on the educational and industrial foundation laid before the war.

SUGGESTED READING

For general coverage of this period, see H. P. Bix, *Hirohito and the Making of Modern Japan* (2000), and T. Nakamura, *A History of Shōwa Japan, 1926–1989* (1998). For prewar Japan, see M. Barnhart, *Japan Prepares for Total War: The Search for Economic Security, 1919–1941* (1987), and S. Vlastos, ed., *Mirror of Modernity: Invented Traditions of Modern Japan* (1998). For wartime, see S. Ienaga, *The Pacific War, 1931–1945* (1978); B. Shillony, *Politics and Culture in Wartime Japan* (1981); and L. Young, *Japan's Total Empire: Manchuria and the Culture of Wartime Imperialism* (1998). For the Occupation, see K. Hirano, *Mr. Smith Goes to Tokyo: Japanese Cinema Under the American Occupation, 1945–1952* (1992), and J. W. Dower, *Embracing Defeat: Japan in the Wake of World War II* (1999).

For the postwar era, see A. Gorden, ed., *Postwar Japan as History* (1993); A. Gordon, *The Wages of Affluence: Labor and Management in Postwar Japan* (1998); L. F. Hein, *Fueling Growth: The Energy Revolution and Economic Policy in Postwar Japan* (1990); J. V. Koschmann, *Revolution and Subjectivity in Postwar Japan* (1996); W. Sasaki-Uemura, *Organizing the Spontaneous: Citizen Protest in Postwar Japan* (2001); and B. Johnstone, *We Were Burning: Japanese Entrepreneurs and the Forging of the Electronics Age* (2000).

Contemporary Japan (1965 to the Present)

Japan's desire for peace with its neighbors was marked in 1965 by demonstrations against the Vietnam War. The storms of protest provoked by public policy decisions and industrial pollution were also signs that by the late 1960s, the consequences of Liberal Democratic Party (LDP) domination and high-speed economic growth could no longer be ignored. The 1970s brought political scandals, diplomatic crises, and economic opportunities in the midst of setbacks. Minorities and working women demanded political initiatives to ameliorate their condition. Economic adjustments positioned Japanese companies to expand in export markets. In the 1980s, Japan had the world's second largest economy, but the euphoria of seemingly unstoppable growth led to a bubble in overpriced investments. When it burst in 1990, the economy deflated. Although social problems increased, most Japanese people enjoyed low crime rates, clean cities, superb public transportation, and unprecedented prosperity.

Why did the Japanese economy rise so far and fall so fast? Are protest and demonstrations worth discussing given the power of the LDP and bureaucrats? Which social trends will prove enduring, and which will prove beneficial?

POLITICAL PROTEST AND ENVIRONMENTAL POLLUTION

The 1960s saw student movements worldwide, and Japan was no exception. Students joined citizen's movements to protest Japan's support for the American war in Vietnam under the U.S.-Japan Security Treaty at the same time that they attacked educational policies. At some universities, they criticized what they viewed as assembly-line style courses. At Tokyo University, medical students protested a top-down reorganization of the program that ignored their concerns. In January 1968 they went on strike. When the university administration refused to hear their grievances and expelled their leaders, students in other departments struck in sympathy. They wanted curriculum control, amnesty for students arrested in confrontations, and no riot police allowed on campus. To make their point, they barricaded the central building. The administration cancelled entrance examinations for 1969. On campuses across Tokyo, students launched sympathy strikes. On January 19, 1969, eighty-five hundred riot police retook the campus in a two-day battle broadcast live on TV. The Diet passed a University Control Bill giving the Education Ministry enhanced authority to punish students. Radical student groups went underground.

Japan's rise to prominence in world affairs and the increase in air travel led the LDP and the Transportation Ministry to decide on a new international airport for Tokyo in 1965. Farmers who owned land at the proposed site outside Narita protested because expropriating their land destroyed their livelihood, secrecy surrounding the decision demonstrated that popular opinion counted for naught, and the airport might be used to support the American war effort in Vietnam. Farmers petitioned prefectural and national ministries; they rallied support in the Diet among the opposition parties. When these measures failed, they built barricades and fortresses; they dug ditches to trap bulldozers; they chained themselves to fences. The radical student union Zengakuren helped with agricultural work and publicity. Citizens in peace, antinuclear, and environmental movements joined them because they were fighting against government indifference to the social costs of economic growth. Plans called for the airport to be built in six years; it took twelve. The government reduced the number of runways from three to one; a proposal in 1998 to add a second also faced opposition. Having learned its lesson, the government later built

Osaka International Airport on an artificial island in the bay.

At the end of the 1960s, the left and right wings attacked capitalism and materialism. Mishima Yukio created a paramilitary organization and received permission to join Self Defense Force military maneuvers. In 1970 he called on the soldiers at SDF headquarters to remember the sacrifices made in World War II and rally behind nationalist goals by overthrowing the government. When they laughed at him, he committed ritual suicide. Between 1970 and 1972 students in the Red Army robbed banks and post offices, hijacked a plane to North Korea, and machine-gunned travelers in Tel Aviv's Lod airport in support of Maoist revolution and Palestinian rights.

Less dramatic but longer lasting, citizens' movements arose in response to industrial pollution. In the 1950s, local and prefectural governments encouraged industrial development that spread pollution from cities to towns and made Japan the most polluted nation on earth. By the early 1970s about half the population complained of suffering from pollution (see Color Plate 10). Citizens' movements mobilized hundreds of thousands of ordinarily apolitical residents to sign petitions, visit industrial sites, display posters, and launch education drives to rally support in stopping potential polluters from building in their neighborhood. They warned against trusting promises by industry and local government that a proposed factory would not pollute, and they rejected charges that fighting to protect the individual's quality of life is egotistical.

Between 1932 and 1968 at Minamata in southern Kyushu, a Chisso factory produced acetaldehyde, a key ingredient in making plastics through a process that released methyl mercury as a by-product. Dumped into the water, mercury concentrated in shellfish and other marine life and then attacked brain cells in domestic animals and humans. Although mercury can kill in a few weeks, many victims suffered progressive debilitation leading to a vegetative state and death. In 1959, a Kumamoto University research

A Victim of Mercury Poisoning. Held by her mother, this sufferer has a malformed hand along with other physical deformities characteristic of the Minamata disease. *(AP/Wide World Photos)*

team traced the cause to the Chisso factory. The team lost its government funding. With support from the Ministry of International Trade and Industry, Chisso hired researchers that proved mercury was not at fault. Workers at the plant and community leaders blamed the victims' poor diet and unsanitary living conditions for their afflictions. In 1965 another outbreak of the disease in Niigata on the Japan Sea was traced to mercury discharged by a chemical factory. Despite efforts by company officials and government bureaucrats to undermine the investigators' credibility, the Niigata outbreak lent weight to the Minamata case. The victims launched petitions, demonstrations, and sit-ins. They attracted support from doctors, lawyers, filmmakers, journalists, and academics. In 1971 they sued Chisso. The verdict against the company in 1973 brought it to the verge of bankruptcy. The victims then sued the government. The Environmental Agency refused to comply with the court's recommendation to settle. In 1995 the cabinet accepted an out-of-court final settlement that denied governmental responsibility for either the disease or the delay in acknowledging the problem.

Diseases caused by pollution in Minamata and elsewhere exposed the costs of high-speed economic growth and the way politicians and bureaucrats insulated themselves from ordinary citizens. Despite free elections and a free press, pollution victims had to protest outside regular government channels. Owing to their demands, the government instituted stringent pollution controls in the 1970s and began spending a larger portion of the gross national product (GNP) on antipollution measures than any other developed nation. By 1978 air and water pollution had declined, and manufacturers had learned how to profit from measures to keep the environment clean.

STRAINS OF THE 1970S

Having enjoyed the economic benefits of supporting the United States during the Cold War, Japan was unprepared for the international crises that punctuated the 1970s. When President Richard Nixon announced in 1971 that the United States would no longer accept fixed exchange rates that overvalued the dollar, the yen rose 14 percent. Nixon intended to make Japanese exports to the United States more expensive and less competitive. Japanese companies survived by taking advantage of lower costs for imported raw materials. Nixon's second shock came in 1972 when he recognized the People's Republic of China without notifying Japan in advance. Prime Minister Tanaka Kakuei followed Nixon to China seven months later. In 1978 China and Japan signed a peace and friendship treaty. The first oil shock came when the Organization of Petroleum Exporting Countries (OPEC) embargoed oil to countries that had supported Israel in the 1973 war. Dependent on oil for 80 percent of its energy, Japan had to pay premium prices on the world market. Inflation rose, companies reduced energy use by cutting production, and consumers stopped spending. During the remainder of the decade, Japan built nuclear power plants. Companies so rationalized energy use that when

OPEC raised prices again in 1978–1980, they had a competitive advantage over less efficient firms in their prime export markets.

To retain dominance in the Diet and cabinet, the LDP catered to its core constituencies, sometimes to the point of scandal. Tanaka Kakuei had Japan National Railroad (JNR) build a bullet train line through the mountains to his constituents in Niigata, at the cost of $60 million a mile. It provided government contracts for his cronies in the construction business and fattened the purses of real estate developers. Although all Diet members collected money from businesses and individuals for whom they did favors, Tanaka's excesses were so blatant that public outcry drove him from office in 1974. In 1976 an investigation by the U.S. Senate disclosed that President Nixon had arranged for Lockheed Aircraft Corporation to pay Tanaka almost $2 million to have All Nippon Airways buy Lockheed planes. Despite the stench of corruption, LDP politicians held on to power because voters believed that the opposition parties were too ideologically driven and fragmented to be trusted with national policy.

Industry had to make traumatic adjustments. Some arose from increasing protectionist pressures, exemplified in a 1979 report to the European Economic Community Executive Committee that called the Japanese "work maniacs who live in houses little better than rabbit hutches."[1] Nixon demanded that Japan reduce its textile imports through voluntary restraints. The increase in oil prices hurt petrochemical and energy-intensive industries. Shipbuilders saw the market for tankers decline, which hurt steel. The shipbuilding industry survived by consolidating and moving into new fields such as ocean drilling platforms. The government helped workers with wage subsidies, retraining programs, and relocation expenses. To compete with low-labor-cost countries, the steel industry developed specialty high-value-added products. Automobile and electrical manufacturing grew. In 1980, Japan pro-duced more cars than any other country. Big electrical companies made generating plants and electric motors for trains; small firms made office equipment, household appliances, and entertainment items.

Although lifetime employment became a watchword, it covered less than half the work force. Toyota, for example, had permanent workers who received regular salary increases based on seniority and fringe benefits; during good times, it hired temporary workers, who were terminated when necessary. Over two hundred independent contractors made parts and components for cars in accordance with guidelines and timetables established by Toyota. Their workers enjoyed no job security. Women returning to the labor force after raising children typically worked at part-time or temporary jobs in small, often marginally profitable companies.

White-collar workers joined a firm straight after college and expected to stay with it for life. For indoctrination into company culture, first-year recruits lived in dormitories where they learned to maintain constant contact with their coworkers by working together and drinking together after work. Since only family men were deemed suitable for promotion, most workers soon married, perhaps to an "office lady" (OL) who understood that the company came first. Debuted in 1969, a popular movie series, *It's Tough Being a Man* (*Otoko wa tsurai yo*), commented on the conformity engineered by the straitjacket of company life through the eyes of an itinerant peddler who rejected job security for the byways of modern Japan.

Husbands and wives lived in separate worlds. Rural-based factory workers left farm work to parents, wives, and children. Only 2 to 5 percent farmed full time. For the urban middle class, a wife's job was to provide a stress-free environment for her husband. Since he had to devote full attention to his company, she managed the household, raised the children (preferably two), and did household repairs. The husband handed her his paycheck; she gave him an allowance, allocated money for food and other expenses, and saved the rest. Mothers devoted themselves

---

1. "Europe Toughens Stand Against Japan's Exports," *New York Times*, April 2, 1979, D:1, 5.

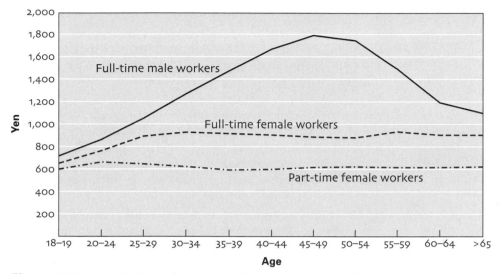

Figure 10.1   Hourly Wages for Japanese Workers, by Age, 1989
(*Mary C. Brinton,* Women and the Economic Miracle: Gender and Work in Postwar Japan
[Berkeley: University of California Press, 1992], p. 47.)

to their children's education, earning the opprobrium of being *kyōiku mama* (education mothers, implying an obsession with their children's educational success). When children needed extra help, mothers sent them to after-school schools. Mother consulted with teachers, attended Parent-Teacher Association meetings, volunteered at school, and supervised their children's nutrition, health, and homework. For the professional housewife, her child was her most important product. (See **Documents: Fujita Mariko, "'It's All Mother's Fault': Childcare and the Socialization of Working Mothers in Japan."**)

Continuing Social Issues

Women's career choices were limited. They typically worked after graduating from high school or junior college; to the mid-1980s almost 90 percent of companies rejected female graduates of four-year colleges because they had to be placed on a management track. Instead, women were hired as clerical or assembly line workers with the understanding they would retire at marriage or when

they turned thirty years old. In the late 1960s women got the courts to agree that this practice constituted sex discrimination. In the early 1970s the courts forbade mandatory retirement because of pregnancy or childbirth or at a younger age than men. Women objected to being kept from managerial positions and well-meaning restrictions on the hours they could work and the kinds of work they were allowed to do. In response, the Diet passed the Equal Employment Opportunity Act of 1985. Although it urged employers to put women on the same track as men, it made no provisions for sanctions if they did not. In 1976 women's earnings stood at 56 percent of men's; in 1988 they declined to 50 percent. Companies still refuse to promote women at the same rate as men. Rather than pay women equal wages, some companies do not hire women at all. Full responsibility for home and children makes it hard for women to work past childbirth. Once the children are in school, mothers take part-time jobs. Although the working woman in Japan is imagined to be single, most are married women over age thirty-five.

DOCUMENTS

Fujita Mariko, "'It's All Mother's Fault': Childcare and the Socialization of Working Mothers in Japan"

Various sectors in postwar society have made a fetish of conformity. This essay by a college professor provides a glimpse of how women enforce the standards for being a professional housewife. What are the conflicts between working and being a mother? How do women interact across the work divide? What is the role fathers are expected to play in child rearing?

A woman should recognize herself as the best educator of her child. An excellent race is born from excellent mothers. . . . Only women can bear children and raise them. Therefore mothers should be proud and confident in raising their children. It is also a fundamental right of children to be raised by their own mothers. . . . Employment opportunities should be given to those women who have finished raising their children and who still wish to resume working outside the home.

—1970 Family Charter by the Committee on Family Life Problems

I live in a small-scale *danchi* (apartment block) built for national governmental employees in the southeastern part of Nara City. The complex consists of three four-story buildings which house about 70 families. The occupants are mostly young and early middle-aged couples, though some are *tanshin-funinsha* (husbands who reside away from their families due to the relocation of their jobs). The ages of the children in this complex range from babies to junior-high-school students. There are only a handful of high school students. Therefore, the mothers' ages range roughly between 25 and 45.

Because the rent is substantially lower than in private housing, there is not much economic pressure for the wives to work. This explains the fact that the majority of wives are full-time housewives. The mothers of older children may engage in occasional part-time jobs. As far as I know, those women who work full-time are without children. If a couple has preschool children, the wives most certainly stay at home to raise them.

My contacts with my neighbors, especially the wives, are through the various activities of the *jichikai* (the voluntary association of the housing complex) such as a monthly clean-up of the common area. I also belong to one of the two Nara Citizens' Co-op groups available in the housing complex. Members of each group jointly order groceries, which the Co-op brings to the housing complex once a week. Members together divide the groceries according to each member's order.

As soon as my neighbors found out that I had a toddler, they assumed that I was a full-time housewife and mother. They never thought to ask whether I worked outside the home. Because I did have a job, they often found me walking alone without my son and they would always ask, "Where is

Despite decades of denunciation tactics, *burakumin* still faced economic hardship and discrimination. Under the Special Measures and Enterprise Law concerning Assimilation of

1969, national and local governments put sewage systems, paved streets, better housing, schools, hospitals, and fire stations in the ghettoes. In 1976, the Justice Ministry agreed to

Hosaki today?" indicating their expectation that I would always be with my child. The situation was complicated because at the time I was a part-time lecturer at a university and I did most of my work at home. My neighbors found this kind of work pattern very difficult to understand because to them work means regular employment between 8:00 AM and 5:00 PM. Telling them that my son was at day care was tricky because they would wonder what I was doing at home during the day instead of being at work. Only after I took a full-time teaching position, which keeps me away from home most of the time, were my neighbors convinced that I was actually working.

The fact that working mothers and non-working mothers do not belong to the same circle of friends became clear to me when I spent a day with my son instead of sending him to day care. I took him to the neighborhood playground where he played in the sand box by the other children. Since he did not have toys of his own (I did not know the children were supposed to bring their own toys), a mother told her son to let my son use his toys. Several mothers were present; they talked among themselves and politely ignored me. I said a few words to them and they replied, but that was the end of our conversation. I basically watched my son, and later played with him when he wanted to play ball. After half an hour, one of the mothers finally asked me whether I lived in the same apartment complex. The question astonished me because I had frequently seen them in the neighborhood. But, as far as they were concerned, I was a total stranger.

Our son frequently became ill his first year in Japan, perhaps due to lack of immu-

nity to the viruses he was exposed to at day care. He had hardly had even a mild cold while we were in the United States, and we were puzzled and distressed by his frequent fevers, respiratory problems, and even pneumonia. Soon after enrolling our son at Sakura Day Care, we asked the director if she had a list of baby-sitters, or if she would introduce us to people who would be willing, with pay, to take care of our son when he became sick. Her answer made us realize how unusual our request was in Japan: she was truly astonished by our question and replied that she had never heard of such people.

Our neighbors frequently offered the folk belief that "boys are more susceptible to all sorts of illness than girls when they are young" to explain my son's frequent sicknesses. But as soon as they found out that my work required me to spend two nights a week away from home, they started to use my absence to explain my son's illness. They thought Hosaki was lonely and thus became ill. No one openly criticized me for working until they found out about my absence. Then, they were quick to criticize the mother, making her absence the cause of illness, although the times of Hosaki's illness and my absence did not coincide and although his father was with him and took care of him. They sympathized with the father, who was, from their point of view, unduly burdened while the "selfish" mother was neglecting her duty of childcare.

Source: *Journal of Japanese Studies* 15:1 (Winter 1989): 70–71, 72–73, 80, 86, 87, 89, modified.

restrict access to family registers that could be used to trace individuals back to the "new commoners" category established in 1871. Private detective agencies then published lists giving

addresses for *burakumin* ghettoes. Their customers were companies, especially the largest and most prestigious, individuals, and colleges. In 1977, the overall unemployment rate was around 3 percent, but 28.5 percent of Osaka *burakumin* were unemployed. Those with jobs worked in small enterprises for low wages. Although most *burakumin* lived next to large factories, they never received more than temporary or part-time work.

Ainu and Okinawans launched movements in the 1970s to assert pride in their ethnic identities. Ainu protested that the 1968 celebration for the centenary of Hokkaido's colonization ignored them and their suffering. Kayano Shigeru opened an ethnographic museum in 1972 and wrote on Ainu language, folk tales, and practices of daily life. In 1994 he became the first Ainu elected to the Diet. He and other culturalists sought to restore seasonal ceremonies and protested plans to turn Hokkaido into an energy source for the rest of Japan with an oil-generated power station. The United States returned Okinawa to Japan in 1972, but left its bases on the islands. The local economy depended on servicing them and catering to Japanese tourists in search of a tropical experience at home. Okinawan music, dance, and crafts attracted aficionados on the mainland because they were seen as both a variant on primitive Japanese folk arts and exotic island culture. Although the national government spent lavishly on construction projects, it hired natives only in low-level jobs. *Burakumin*, Ainu, and Okinawan poverty rates and school dropout rates were higher than the national average. Negative stereotypes abounded, and outsiders tried to avoid marrying or hiring them.

Koreans resident in Japan (six hundred thirty-seven thousand in 1999) faced special disabilities in fighting discrimination. As long as Korea was part of the Japanese Empire, Koreans were Japanese citizens. The postwar constitution defined Japanese citizens as those born of Japanese fathers, and Koreans became permanent resident aliens. Although celebrities and spouses of diplomats found the naturalization process easy, working-class Koreans did not. They also suffered a division between supporters of North Korea, who followed a separatist path, and supporters of the South, who tried to preserve vestiges of Korean identity while sending their children to Japanese schools. Children and grandchildren of Korean residents who grew up in Japan and spoke only Japanese paid taxes, but they could not vote. They had to be fingerprinted for their alien registration cards. After years of protest, that requirement changed in 1991, and resident Koreans were allowed to vote in local elections. Still, Japanese refused to marry Koreans, employers to hire them, landlords to rent to them. Resident Koreans who protested were told they should go back to Korea.

Japanese nationalists ignored all evidence to the contrary in praising the virtues of their uniquely homogeneous race. The debate on Japaneseness (*Nihonjinron*) reacted to the protest movements of the late 1960s, universalizing social science theories that pigeonholed Japan solely in terms of economic development, and Japan bashing by foreigners. The more Japanese people ate, dressed, and lived like people across the developed world, the more they had to be reminded that they possessed a uniquely distinctive culture. According to *Nihonjinron*, "we Japanese" speak a language intrinsically incomprehensible to outsiders, think with both sides of the brain, and have intestines too short to digest Australian beef. "We Japanese" innately prefer consensus and harmony, and we put the interests of the group above the individual.

Despite social problems, by the mid-1970s, most Japanese people enjoyed unprecedented levels of prosperity. Income and salary disparities remained relatively narrow, and 90 percent of the population considered itself to be middle class. The proportion of total income spent on food declined while quantity, quality, and variety increased. The older generation ate rice, vegetables, and fish. Young people ate meat, dairy products, and spaghetti. Although Japan maintained the highest savings rate in the industrialized world, people had discretionary income to eat out, go to movies, and take vacations.

THE ROARING 1980S

Japan's recovery from the shocks of the 1970s put it on a collision course with its major trading partner, the United States. Japan adjusted to oil and pollution crises by building fuel-efficient, less-polluting cars. When stricter pollution emission requirements, consumer demand for higher quality, and increased gasoline prices caught Detroit by surprise, Japan's automobile makers seized the American market. To make Japanese goods less competitive, President Ronald Reagan devalued the dollar in 1985. Japan discovered that it was twice as rich as before. The yen bought twice as much oil, and since Japanese manufacturers had already streamlined production techniques, they needed half as much to make their products as their American competitors did. When Honda raised the price of the Accord by a thousand dollars, American manufacturers raised their prices as well.

American negotiators demanded that Japan import more foreign products. Japan had lower tariffs on manufactured goods than other industrialized countries, but it protected farmers by restricting food imports. It also had nontariff structural barriers to trade—regulations to ensure quality and safety, the requirement that car buyers show proof of an off-street parking space, a multilayered distribution system, and zoning that favored shops over supermarkets and discount stores. Despite reluctance to disturb a system that provided employment and political support, the LDP and the bureaucracy gradually reduced restrictions. Australian cheese appeared in supermarkets. Shakey's Pizza, McDonalds, Kentucky Fried Chicken, and family-style restaurants invaded Japan in the late 1970s. Seven-Eleven spawned a boom in convenience stores. In 1983, Disneyland opened its first international venue near Tokyo. In 2000 it welcomed 16.5 million visitors, the largest number for any theme park in the world.

Trade surpluses and a strong currency generated more capital than Japan could absorb domestically. With unemployment rates at about 3 percent and labor costs rising, companies built factories in low-wage countries on the Asian mainland. To get around protective tariffs, antidumping measures, and quotas, they built high-technology factories in developed countries, and Toyota became a multinational corporation. In 1982, industrial plants, equipment, and capital goods constituted 43 percent of Japan's exports. Japanese capital serviced the U.S. debt. Japan became the world's largest supplier of loans to developing countries and the chief donor of foreign aid, and it supplied 50 percent of lendable capital to the World Bank.

The electronics industry had two modes of expanding overseas. In setting up production facilities, first in Southeast Asia in the mid- to late 1970s and then in developed countries in the 1980s, parent companies retained complete control of local subsidiaries. The managerial staff was Japanese; the workers were local. The U.S. Semiconductor Industry Association accused Japan of dumping in 1985; in an agreement a year later, Japan agreed to voluntary quotas. Corporations then instituted cooperative ventures with partners in the United States and Europe to develop new technology or combine specialties. Automobile manufacturers followed suit: Toyota and General Motors, Nissan, Honda, and Ford operate joint ventures and exchange components at factories from Australia to Brazil to Europe and the United States.

Japanese capital investment deepened ties with Asian neighbors, while nationalist sentiment strained diplomatic relations. Japan dominated China's Special Economic Zones and invested heavily in Korea and the Pacific Rim, leading pundits to claim that it had succeeded in creating a Greater East Asia Co-Prosperity Sphere. In 1982, the Education Ministry approved a textbook for middle school and high school students that minimized Japanese aggression in China. This led the PRC, North and South Korea, and other Asian nations to denounce resurgent Japanese nationalism. Japan's aggression and its refusal to acknowledge the suffering it inflicted on Korean women were still issues in the textbooks prepared for 2005. Asians and some Japanese criticized visits by prime ministers to Yasukuni Shrine, where war criminals are enshrined. Textbook revision and Japan's refusal to apologize for waging war roiled popular opinion even as government leaders drew closer together. When the president of South Korea visited Japan for the first time in 1984, demonstrations erupted in Seoul.

The government faced domestic problems as well. The LDP did not want to raise taxes to cover deficit spending that started in 1973. Among the culprits were subsidies for farmers, public corporations—Japan National Railroad (JNR) and Nihon Telephone and Telegraph (NTT)—and national health insurance, which initiated free care for the elderly in 1972. Following the lead of Prime Minister Margaret Thatcher in Britain, a commission set up in 1981 promoted privatizing public corporations to relieve the government of drains on its resources and undermine the strength of the railroad workers' union. Although allowed to bargain collectively, unions in the public service sector did not have the right to strike nor did they have incentive to boost productivity. In 1975, railroad workers shut down the JNR for eight days in a strike to win the right to strike.

The conservative triumvirate of the free market world consisted of Margaret Thatcher, Ronald Reagan, and Nakasone Yasuhiro, Japan's prime minister from 1982 to 1987. Nakasone privatized JNR and NTT and took the government out of the business of selling tobacco and cigarettes. Beginning in 1982, the elderly had to contribute payments for health services. Nakasone urged a return to family values, especially the obligation of the younger generation to care for their elders. He attributed Japan's economic success to its ethnic homogeneity and funded research into the foundation of Japan's distinctive identity. He also called for internationalization so that government leaders would learn how to reduce trade friction and businessmen would feel comfortable with foreigners. His promotion of corporate capitalism made Japan a major player at the Group of 7 conferences of industrialized nations while he lectured the United States on its social and economic failings exemplified in racial diversity and the lack of a work ethic.

The Good Life

For many people, old and young, the good life meant material possessions. It meant automated bread-making machines, three-dimensional TV, and self-heating canned sake. It meant laughing at Itami Jūzō's movies about funeral practices, food, tax evasion, new religions, and gangsters. The good life made it easy to buy books and magazines (1.45 billion and 4.01 billion, respectively, in 1987). (See **Material Culture: *Manga*.**) Whether a meaning for life could be found in a late capitalist society divided Japanese writers. Murakami Haruki captured the absurdity of modernity in his novels *A Wild Sheep Chase, Hardboiled Wonderland,* and *Sputnik Sweetheart.* Yoshimoto Banana's *Kitchen,* a novella popular with college students, depicted a dysfunctional family and individuals alone in a postmodern world. Nostalgia for simpler times under the Occupation sold 4 million copies of *Totto-chan, The Little Girl at the Window* by the fast-talking television celebrity Kuroyanagi Tetsuko.

Rejecting the materialism of the present meant seeking the roots of Japanese identity. A self-styled Kyoto philosopher creatively interpreted the prehistoric Jōmon era as when Japanese lived in harmony with nature and each other in a community of man and gods. Mystically transmitted through the emperor system and buried deep within every Japanese, the national essence could be recapitulated by a visit to the *furusato* (home village). JNR's "Discover Japan" and "Exotic Japan" advertising campaigns promoted visits to thatched roof farmhouses foreign to urban residents. Villages striving to overcome depopulation revived agricultural festivals to attract tourists; castle towns put on daimyo processions. On Yaeyama in the Ryukyu Islands, a new tradition of sash weaving

MATERIAL CULTURE

Manga

Japanese comics called *manga* attained their present form in 1959 when they became a source of entertainment and information for all ages.

Early *manga* were printed on cheap paper and sold at a price that the working poor could afford. The first generation born after World War II grew up reading them and continued the habit through college and into their working lives. *Manga* gave them a chance to laugh at the restrictive conditions that enforced conformity while warning them that failing to work hard and toe the corporate line would lead to mockery. *Manga* and their close cousins, animated films, became the domain of Japan's most creative minds.

From the 1960s to the mid-1990s *manga* offered escapist fantasies, often violently pornographic, for white-collar workers on their daily commute. Science-fiction *manga* appealed to children and teenagers. *Manga* taught history to students studying for entrance exams. *Barefoot Gen* graphically illustrated the horrors of the atomic bomb explosion over Hiroshima. Cookbooks and biography could be found in *manga*. *Manga* explained energy policy, the value-added tax, investment strategies, and the principles of superconductors. *Japan Inc.: An Introduction to Japanese Economics in Manga* (1986) sold over 1 million copies in hardcover.

Manga reached their peak of sales in 1994. Publishing houses devoted one-third of their total output to *manga* and sold 553 million copies a year. Shibuya, the crossroads for youth culture in Tokyo, contained *manga* superstores where the clerks dressed as *manga* characters.

Manga. Manga provided education and entertainment. "The Manga Introduction to Superconductors" explained new technology in 1987 through the eyes of three young salaried workers who visit a research laboratory. *(The Manga Introduction to Supercomputers by Takashi Hashimoto and Fumio Hisamatsu)*

Manga and the Japanese publishing industry are in decline. Their former readers on trains and in coffee shops thumb cell phones with Internet connections or play handheld computer games.

for betrothal gifts became a way to assert a folk identity and sell souvenirs to tourists.

The search for origins scarcely concealed new and to conservative eyes troubling trends among Japanese youth. In 1978 the "bamboo shoot tribe" (*takenokozoku*) of middle and high school students dressed in outlandish and expensive costumes started appearing every Sunday near trendy Harajuku in Tokyo. (See Color Plate 11.) Late at night, gangs of motorcycle riders roared through residential neighborhoods, disrupting the sleep of salary men. In

Opponents of Narita Airport. Waving staves and wearing helmets, opponents of Narita Airport battled riot police protected by heavy shields, helmets, and padded armor. *(Corbis)*

1985 newspapers started reporting an increase in incidents of bullying, some leading to murder or suicide, in elementary through high schools. The "new breed of human beings" rejected the work ethic, harmony, and consensus of their elders. They took part-time jobs that did not require the commitment of a regular position. Since many of them lived with their parents, their income bought luxury items rather than necessities. They splurged on designer clothes, meals and entertainment, and trips abroad. Married couples demanded bigger living spaces and better plumbing. They wanted a shorter work week and longer vacations. Rather than put up with low initial salaries and long hours of after-work socializing, a few workers switched jobs, and some husbands went home to their wives.

Despite these problems, Japan's economy appeared unstoppable. In 1988, its per capita GNP surpassed that of the United States. The United States cited unfair trade practices and Japan's free ride under the American security umbrella. In 1989, Morita Akio, chairman of Sony, and Ishihara Shintarō, mayor of Tokyo in 2002, published *The Japan That Can Say No*. It criticized U.S. business practices and claimed that Japan bashing was the result of racial prejudice. It also castigated the Japanese government for fearing reform and Japanese people for being soft. Banks awash with yen urged capital on borrowers. Japanese art purchases led to an outcry that the cream of western heritage was being shipped to Asia. Mitsubishi bought Rockefeller Center in New York City. Sony bought Columbia Pictures. Real estate rose so high that land in Tokyo was valued at three times the entire United States. The tripling of the stock market inflated a speculative bubble.

MALAISE IN THE 1990S

For the LDP, political problems began in 1989. The Shōwa emperor died at the beginning of the year. For having remarked that the emperor bore some responsibility for the military's behavior during World War II, the mayor of Nagasaki was shot by a right-wing fanatic. The new emperor took Heisei, translatable as "achieving peace" or "maintaining equilibrium," for his era name. Prime Minister Takeshita Noboru inaugurated a value-added tax of 3 percent that infuriated consumers. Two months later he resigned because of publicity surrounding 150 million yen he had received from Recruit Cosmo, an employment information firm with investments in real estate and publishing. LDP faction bosses had difficulty identifying an untainted successor. Uno Sōsuke lasted barely six weeks before a palimony suit by his mistress brought him down. In the election that summer, the JSP under the female leadership of Doi Takako ran an unprecedented number of women candidates and gained control of the upper house. It also did well in the more powerful lower house in 1990.

The LDP faced challenges from members of its own party. Frustrated by elderly faction bosses who monopolized the prime ministership, younger politicians split the LDP. In 1993, Hosokawa Morihiro from the Japan New Party became prime minister when the LDP suffered defeat in elections for the lower house. The worst rice harvest in two hundred years forced him to allow rice imports from Asia for the first time since World War II. Farmers were outraged. He too was caught in a financial scandal. Two more non-LDP prime ministers followed him, neither capable of dealing with Japan's economic woes. The government's tardy response to the Kobe earthquake on January 17, 1995, which killed over five thousand two hundred people and left over three hundred thousand homeless, received much criticism. In 1996, a chastened LDP returned to power, and faction bosses picked the next prime minister. In 2001, they chose a third-generation Diet member, Koizumi Jun'ichirō, who promised liberals he would make structural reforms needed to bolster the economy and pleased conservatives by his call to revise the pacifist constitution.

Koizumi inherited a stagnant economy. The speculative bubble of the late 1980s collapsed when a recession in the developed world sent sales tumbling and competition from low-labor-cost countries eroded corporations' market share. The stock market lost nearly 40 percent of its peak value in 1990 and 65 percent by August 1992. When the inflated real estate market vanished, Mitsubishi had to sell Rockefeller Center at a loss. Corporations that had borrowed billions of yen to buy land or expand their businesses discovered that their debts exceeded their rapidly depreciating assets. Banks were reluctant to lend money. The Asian economic turmoil of 1997 caused by speculators dumping Asian currencies caused another recession in Japan. Two brokerage houses and a bank went bankrupt, leading to fears of depression. Economic growth, which had limped along at barely 1 percent per annum between 1992 and 1995, went negative in 1997. In 2002, bad loans ballooned to $1.3 trillion, and government debt climbed to 150 percent of the GDP. Except for an occasional quarter of slight expansion, deflation stalked Japan.

The LDP scrambled to stimulate the economy. In the 1980s it tried to revitalize rural communities by building culture halls and art museums and encouraging production of traditional handicrafts as souvenirs. In the 1990s it poured money into dams, roads, and postmodern public buildings. In 1991 the Tokyo Metropolitan Government moved into massive new headquarters that soared above office buildings and hotels, many half empty. Koizumi halted a project to turn a saltwater swamp into farmland while the government paid farmers not to plant rice. His proposal to privatize the postal savings system threatened the Finance Ministry's control over the $3 trillion in personal savings kept outside government budgets that it used to finance public works projects, prime the stock market, and buy government bonds. Proposals to streamline the bureaucracy, reduce regulatory oversight, and eliminate positions foundered on bureaucratic inertia. Near-zero interest rates and government support for nonperforming loans failed to stimulate business investment. The Education Ministry tried to make universities more responsive to the interests of industry and eliminate irrelevant fields in the humanities and social sciences. In 2004 national universities became independent entities.

Japan faced international criticism regarding its role in world affairs. The United States grumbled when Japan refused to commit troops to the Gulf War in 1991 even though Japan's military spending ranked third below the United States and Russia. Six months after the war, Japan sent six minesweepers to the Persian Gulf amid debate fueled by antiwar sentiment in the postwar generation over whether their dispatch violated constitutional restrictions. Japan also paid $10 billion toward the cost of the war and permitted its troops to participate in peacekeeping missions in Cambodia and East Timor. After the terrorist attacks in the United States on September 11, 2001, the Diet passed an antiterrorism law that allowed Japanese troops to provide rear-echelon support for the war in Iraq in 2004.

Social Problems for the Twenty-First Century

Japan's social problems also defied easy solution. In the 1980s, American social scientists praised Japan's educational system for producing literate students who scored far higher on mathematics tests than Americans. Japanese critics feared that schools were turning out soulless automatons with weak characters and no sense of national identity, unable to think for themselves, and lacking the creativity to put Japan in the lead of technological innovation. Preteenage rebels disrupted classrooms and terrorized teachers. In a series of high-profile crimes, youths killed classmates, tortured the homeless, and murdered elderly neighbors. Labor shortages in the 1980s in the sex trade and the dangerous, dirty, and low-paying work of construction and stevedoring brought men and women from Taiwan, the Philippines, Iran, and other countries to work as prostitutes and day laborers. About half entered illegally because the Labor and Justice ministries refused to acknowledge the need for their services. Immigration of Latin Americans of Japanese ancestry was encouraged because it was thought they would assimilate to the dominant culture. In 1999, 1.56 million foreigners lived legally in Japan out of a total population of 126.6 million. Tokyo became a more cosmopolitan city, but mainstream Japanese were quick to accuse foreigners of robbery, rape, and drug trafficking.

Economic stagnation and rising unemployment had social consequences. Corporations stopped competing to hire college graduates, and unemployment rose to an official rate of 5 percent in 2001. This figure excluded part-time workers who had lost their jobs, most of them women. The government reduced the duration and value of unemployment benefits. Job security guarantees covered just over 15 percent of workers in 2002. "Pay for performance" started to replace the seniority system of merit raises. Tokyo, Yokohama, and Osaka had long had a floating population of farm men from the north who spent the winter working as day laborers and congregated in flophouses. In the late 1980s permanent dropouts started to swell their numbers. Osaka laborers caused the worst rioting in nearly twenty years in 1990 in reaction to police harassment. Homeless people appeared as well. They built cardboard cities in parks and pedestrian tunnels that surrounded train terminals except when police periodically chased them away.

The search for meaning in a materialistic world took new paths. Right-wing militants who rode sound trucks blaring martial music and decorated with posters calling for the return of the northern territories held by Russia attacked the offices of the Asahi publishing company for articles showing disrespect for the emperor. Adherents of new religions such as the Unification Church and Mahikarikyō sought a sense of community and a merging of the individual ego in a larger entity. Aum Shinrikyō attracted students from Japan's elite universities, lawyers, and businessmen. Feeling persecuted by the Justice Ministry, in March 1995 its followers released Sarin, a poison gas, in the Tokyo subway system adjacent to National Police headquarters. It killed twelve people and incapacitated thousands. The LDP tried to revise the 1951 Religious Corporations Law to bring governmental oversight to the fund-raising, educational activities, and business-related income of the 183,970 registered religious organizations. Opposition by Sōka Gakkai's political arm and other religious organizations kept the 1951 law intact.

Starting in the late 1960s, LDP politicians urged women to have more children; thereafter they lamented the selfishness of young women who put consumerism ahead of maternal responsibilities. National health insurance, a 99 percent literacy rate, sanitary housing, and nutritious diets contributed to one of the lowest infant mortality rates in the world at 5 per thousand in 1989 and longevity rates for men reaching into the mid-seventies and for women into the eighties. Women had 1.57 children apiece, well below the 2.2 necessary to maintain the population. Couples who wanted a higher standard of living or worried about the costs of their children's education limited their family size regardless of political propaganda.

In 2000, 16 percent of the population was age sixty-five or older, and Japan had the oldest population in the industrialized world. In 2015 it is projected to be 25 percent, and 25 percent of the national budget will have to be spent on social welfare. Through the 1990s, corporations had plentiful sources of investment capital at low interest rates because Japan had the highest rates of personal savings in the world. With more people retired, the savings rate will drop.

The government wants to limit its costs for hospitals and nursing homes by having children care for parents. Elder sons with the traditional responsibility for parental care have trouble finding marriage partners because women increasingly prefer to take care of their own parents. Some farmers have even sought brides in the Philippines.

Although marriage is still the norm, it too has changed. The average age of marriage for women crept from twenty-two in 1950 to over twenty-six in 2000. Crown Princess Masako delayed marriage for a career in the Foreign Ministry until she was twenty-nine. Her only child is a girl. Since the constitution defines the ruler as male, allowing this child to succeed her father will require a constitutional change, devoutly desired by Japanese feminists. So many women opt for four years of higher education that the former junior colleges have become universities even though the decline in the college age population means that more are having trouble meeting their enrollment targets. In hopes of better futures than they perceive possible in Japan, some women seek academic degrees and employment abroad. Women want careers, and they have become increasingly choosy about whom they will marry and under what conditions. Older women have been known to divorce their retired husbands because they cannot stand having "that oversized garbage" underfoot every day.

SUMMARY

Japan is a mature industrial society. Its cities are among the world's cleanest and safest, and most of its citizens enjoy a comfortable life. Japanese foods are eaten in Europe and the United States; Japanese fashions and popular music are followed in Asia. Introduced in 1980, karaoke is performed around the world. Ōe Kenzaburō won the Nobel Prize in literature in 1994 for his writings that express universal truths regarding the human condition. Japanese politicians infuriate their Asian neighbors by calling the emperor a living god and Japan a divine nation while participating in Asian economic conferences. Lingering memories of the war and Japan's wariness of China's growing economic and military strength has not prevented Japan from trading more with China than with the United States, even as it offers support for the global war on terrorism.

SUGGESTED READING

For protest against Tokyo International Airport, see D. E. Apter and N. Sawa, *Against the State: Politics and Protest in Japan* (1984).

For recent books on pollution, see J. Broadbent, *Environmental Politics in Japan: Networks of Power and Protest* (1998), and T. S. George, *Minamata: Pollution and the Struggle for Democracy in Postwar Japan* (2001).

For politics, see R. J. Hrebenar, *Japan's New Party System* (2000). For legal issues, see F. K. Upham, *Law and Social Change in Postwar Japan* (1987).

For economic issues, see R. M. Uriu, *Troubled Industries: Confronting Economic Change in Japan* (1996). For minorities, see M. Weiner, *Japan's Minorities: The Illusion of Homogeneity* (1997).

For popular culture, see S. Kinsella, *Adult Manga: Culture and Power in Contemporary Japanese Society* (2000).

For recent books on women. see Y. Ogasawara, *Office Ladies and Salaried Men: Power, Gender, and Work in Japanese Companies* (1998); R. M. LeBlanc, *Bicycle Citizens: The Political World of the Japanese Housewife* (1999); and K. Kelsky, *Women on the Verge: Japanese Women, Western Dreams* (2001).

CREDITS

INDEX